Latin American Economic Development

D0949282

Latin America is one of the most interesting parts of the world. The region's illustrious history, culture, and geography are famous internationally, but in terms of economics, Latin America has been generally associated with problems. For many, the combination of a resource-rich region and poor economic conditions has been a puzzle. *Latin American Economic Development* provides the most up-to-date exploration of how this happened with a focus on why the continent can be considered to have underperformed, how the various Latin American economies function, and the future prospects for the region.

This textbook addresses the economic problems of Latin America theme by theme. The first four centuries of Latin American economic development are explained with reference to historical and institutional factors; the role of commodities; import substitution industrialization; and the resultant slow growth of the region. The development of Latin America during the twentieth century is examined through the policies of governments toward international trade and the management of the exchange rate. These policies lead to the accumulation of significant debt in the region that resulted in substantial economic instability. The final section of the book explains how all of these themes have contributed to two dominant problems for the region: poverty and inequality.

The purpose of this book is to provide a comprehensive text for increasingly popular undergraduate economics courses on Latin America. However, the book has been carefully designed for use by both students majoring in economics and for those in other disciplines looking for a wide-ranging guide to the region. This book should be an invaluable resource for undergraduates looking at Latin American economics, growth, and development.

Javier A. Reyes is an Associate Professor of Economics in the Economics Department of the Sam M. Walton College of Business at the University of Arkansas, USA.

W. Charles Sawyer is the Hal Wright Professor of Latin American Economics at Texas Christian University, USA.

Latin American Economic Development

Javier A. Reyes and W. Charles Sawyer

Routledge
Taylor & Francis Group

LONDON AND NEW YORK

First published 2011
by Routledge
2 Park Square, Milton Park, Abingdon, Oxon OX14 4RN

Simultaneously published in the USA and Canada
by Routledge
711 Third Avenue, New York, NY 10017

*Routledge is an imprint of the Taylor & Francis Group,
an informa business*

© 2011 Javier A. Reyes and W. Charles Sawyer

The right of Javier A. Reyes and W. Charles Sawyer to be identified
as authors of this work has been asserted by them in accordance
with the Copyright, Designs and Patents Act 1988.

Typeset in Times New Roman by Sunrise Setting Ltd, Torquay, UK

British Library Cataloguing in Publication Data
A catalogue record for this book is available
from the British Library

Library of Congress Cataloging in Publication Data
Reyes, Javier A.
Latin American economic development / by Javier A. Reyes and
W. Charles Sawyer.
p. cm.
Includes bibliographical references and index.
   1. Latin America—Economic conditions—1982
   2. Latin America—Economic policy.
      I. Sawyer, W. Charles.
      II. Title.
HC125.R4834 2010
338.98—dc22
2010037782

ISBN: 978-0-415-48613-2 (hbk)
ISBN: 978-0-415-49733-6 (pbk)
ISBN: 978-0-203-82932-5 (ebk)

Contents

Figures

Tables

Boxes

Preface

Trying to teach the economics of Latin America to undergraduate students can be a frustrating task. Attempting to cover 500 years of economic history inevitably involves a difficult set of tradeoffs. Spend too much time on history and the Lost Decade may end up being "lost." Allocate too much time to the late twentieth century and it is all too easy to neglect colonial Latin America and its lingering effects in the twenty-first century. There are countless other examples. A region that is large, diverse, and has a long history creates many such tradeoffs. At the start it has to be realized that one cannot cover *everything* in one semester. The problem then becomes one of deciding what is included in the course and what is not. While this solves the main problem, the question of how much emphasis to put on each topic is still on the table. The objective is to narrow the material to a manageable amount for the typical one-semester course. This is particularly the case in an area where there is no established "template."

In trying to narrow and balance the material in the book, we have consistently relied on a concrete decision rule which focuses on the students enrolled in the course. For the vast majority of students, this course will be their only exposure to the economics of Latin America. One can assume that for whatever reason they have an inherent interest in the area. It may be purely personal and/or involve their professional goals. Normally, this interest won't stop after the semester is over. Most of the students will continue to follow developments in the region throughout their careers. It is also safe to assume that very few will follow developments in Latin America by reading academic journals. Their main sources of information will probably be reading material in publications such as *The Economist*, the *Financial Times*, or the host of other sources of information that assume readers have a post-secondary degree. This situation sets up the primary decision rule for this book. Our objective is to equip students leaving this course with the minimum amount of information necessary for them to easily understand virtually anything about the economics of Latin America that they are likely to encounter in their careers. In modern parlance, we are attempting to help students become the proverbial "intelligent layman" with respect to the economics of the region. A simple thought exercise illustrates what the book is trying to accomplish. At the start of the course, most students might find reading an article on economics in the "The Americas" section of *The Economist* to be relatively difficult. In many cases, these articles are assuming that the reader has a certain background level of knowledge that most students don't have. The purpose of this book is to provide just this sort of information.

Major themes in Latin American economic development

In order to do this, the first task is to reduce the material to a manageable collection of common themes. The book is organized around the major themes listed below.

Growth

The most serious problem of modern Latin America has been that economic growth has been slow relative to much of the rest of the world.

History

One can rarely understand the current state of any economy or region without a basic understanding of economic history. This is particularly true with respect to Latin America.

Commodities

Many countries in Latin America are major producers and exporters of commodities and this has had a substantial influence on the economic development of the region.

Import Substitution Industrialization (ISI)

In the second half of the twentieth century, many countries in Latin America attempted to create industries designed to replace imports from developed countries. Import substitution industrialization has had very important implications for economic development in the region.

Trade policy

From the 1930s, Latin America has pursued trade policies that tended to make the markets of the region relatively closed from foreign competition. This overall policy had a tendency to make Latin America less integrated into the world economy.

Exchange rate policy

Countries have a choice of managing their exchange rate or allowing it to float. In Latin America, these choices at times have had serious implications in terms of economic growth.

Debt

A recurring theme in Latin American economic history has been the tendency for governments in the region to heavily borrow from banks and other financial institutions.

Macroeconomic instability

GDP growth, inflation, and unemployment have been somewhat unstable in many countries of Latin America. Unfortunately, this instability has been so pervasive that for many it is one of the defining characteristics of the region. Explaining this instability is one of the major tasks of this book.

Poverty and inequality

GDP per capita in Latin America is low relative to the high-income countries. In addition, Latin America has one of the most unequal distributions of income in the world.

Obviously, this is not an exhaustive list of all of the economic issues of the region. However, in keeping with the discussion above it represents a minimum list of subjects necessary for a student to be able to understand the current and future state of the region. Even with this minimum list of themes, covering this material in one semester could be difficult. In order to keep the amount of material manageable, the book has been written with an assumption about the students. The basic assumption is that students using this book will have had at least a one-semester survey of economics course or perhaps a two-semester principles sequence. Using this assumption, all of the tools of analysis used throughout the book are those used in principles of economics. We have found that this frees the instructor from attempting to teach *both* the materials and new tools of analysis. In turn, this frees up more time to spend on more material related to the region. However, we do not assume that students perfectly recall what they learned in principles. In most cases, the basic tools of analysis are briefly reviewed in order to ensure that students are prepared to use the tools to analyze economic issues in the region.

History and institutions

Historically, Latin American economics has been taught with an emphasis on history and institutions. Both of these are important approaches to the subject. Modern Latin America was born of an invasion from Europe and the subsequent 400 years are characterized by conditions that were not always conducive to economic growth. Further, in any economy or region institutions matter for economic development. As a result, the book includes a substantial amount of historical and institutional material. However, one cannot possibly cover all of this material. Again, in this regard there is a decision rule. Most of the historical and institutional information covered is that which still affects Latin America in the twenty-first century. This serves to make this material both more manageable and relevant to the lives of the students taking the course. An example of this approach is the box on "The War of the Pacific" in Chapter 4. While this conflict occurred over a hundred years ago, it still affects the relationship among the countries of a region of Latin America.

Analysis of economic policy in Latin America

To further narrow the scope of the course, we have avoided the some-times acrimonious debates over economic policy in the region. To a large extent, the countries of the region are operating under the general umbrella of "democratic capitalism." Policy in the region is now set by freely elected governments. No economist can perfectly predict the out-come of various policies nor perfectly prescribe policies for any particular country. However, economists have learned over the years that certain policies tend to have particular outcomes. For example, large govern-ment budget deficits financed by printing money tend to lead to inflation. Unfortunately, Latin America has been a proving ground for such major policy mistakes. Thus, the analysis of policy in the book focuses on what actually occurred in the past and the effects of recent changes in policy in much of the region. Our focus is on applying standard economic analy-sis to economic history and the current situation. We consciously avoid discussing what *should* have happened in the past or should occur in the future. The former is usually obvious and the latter is the prerogative of the citizens of the region. This allows the instructor to focus on analyzing the results of past policies and the potential outcome of current policies. Our focus is on equipping students with the tools of analysis to be able to analyze policy. Students with good tools of analysis can understand policy on a somewhat higher level than their more unfortunate contemporaries who can't.

In summary our hope is that this book will be of use to instructors attempting to teach an inherently difficult course. In this case, the difficulty is one of the sheer breadth of the material. What we have attempted to do is to reduce the amount of material down to an amount that balances student needs with the realities of the limited time available in a one-semester course. We've attempted to do this by using a limited number of important themes and by balancing history and institutions and standard economic analysis. Finally, for several reasons, we have tried to produce a book that to the greatest extent possible relies on economic analysis for guidance on questions of economic policy. As will be shown at many points in the book, ideology mixed with policy without economic analysis can lead to unfortunate outcomes.

Acknowledgements

Books don't appear out of a vacuum. Like coffee, this one has been brewing for a number of years. The frustrations of trying to teach the economics of Latin America led to many conversations over the years about just how to do this. As a result, the "contributors" to the process that culminated in this book are literally too numerous to mention. This is especially true for the main contributors to this process, our students. The years of reading exams and papers do a brutally efficient job of telling one what works and what doesn't, what's possible and what's not. More subtle, but just as revealing, is the excitement generated in a class when something works and the blank faces telling one what doesn't. An area study class such as Latin American Economics offers one further check on the material. This is the "now I understand why something happens in my country" look. Few things in a classroom are more rewarding and instructive. We would also like to thank a different class of students that have contributed to the approach used in the book. A class of good MBA students can really help one focus on what the point of a course is. Knowledge for the sake of knowledge is a valuable thing. However, knowledge that can be usefully applied can be of even greater value. In this regard, bright students with work experience can be very effective teachers.

A few more specific thanks are in order. We would like to thank Tom Fullerton for first planting the idea of writing this book. At the time, his suggestion was not taken seriously. A subsequent suggestion by Robert Langham was. His editorial work was absolutely critical in the development of this book. His support and especially his patience are deeply appreciated. Between this draft being written and the book you are reading is a morass of tedious detail that most readers, fortunately, will never experience. Thankfully, the authors didn't bear the brunt of it. If the authors are lucky, there is someone with an infinite reservoir of competence, patience, and good cheer that accomplishes this. For this book, we were lucky enough to have Louisa Earls turning the very rough draft into a "book." Finally, we would like to thank the University of Arkansas and Texas Christian University for providing the environment and resources for us to write this book.

1 Latin America and the world economy

For much of Latin America's history, the world economy has treated the region as a basket of natural resources that have been packaged and shipped to satisfy the consumption of richer foreign nations.

Shawn William Miller

Introduction

Since you are reading this book, it is safe to assume that you have an interest in Latin America. That's understandable. Latin America is a very interesting region of the world for any number of reasons. In terms of world history, language, literature, music, and more currently, sports, Latin America is a very influential part of the world. While this is common knowledge, the place of Latin America in the world economy usually is less well understood. If you were asked to write a paragraph about Latin America in the world economy, what would you write? For many, the answer would be "not much." The first objective of this chapter is to give you some useful background information on the region. The focus of the chapter is to provide basic economic data for Latin America and then to put this information into a global context. In this way, we can learn something about the economies of the region and also learn how Latin America fits into the larger mosaic of the world economy. A second objective of the chapter is to introduce a number of recurring themes concerning the economies of Latin America. All of the world's regions are distinctive in some ways. However, no region of the world such as Europe, Asia, Africa, or Latin America is completely homogeneous. Latin America is no different in this regard. There are several recurring themes that are common to most of the economies of Latin America. These major themes form a sort of roadmap for understanding both how the economies of Latin America are distinctive and why the economic performance of the region in the last century has been less than perhaps could have been possible. This introduction to these themes then allows us to consider some major economic policy debates that are common in the region. Economic growth in Latin America has spawned a healthy debate over various economic policy options for the region. Over the last century, several types of economic policies have been proposed and/or implemented. The relative merits of these policies have been vigorously debated for a long time. These policy debates are such an important part of the story of the economies of Latin America that the final part of the chapter provides a brief introduction to these different debates.

Latin America and the world

It's a reasonably safe assumption that any person in the world who has completed primary school could find Latin America on a map. Latin America comprises 14 percent of the world's land mass. In the Western Hemisphere, it accounts for 50 percent of the total area. However, the picture changes somewhat if one considers population. The population of Latin America is approximately 530 million or 7.9 percent of the population of the world. However, Latin America makes up 59 percent of the population of the Western Hemisphere. Relative to much of the world, Latin America is not a particularly crowded place. There are exceptions, such as El Salvador, but in general the view of much of Latin America outside of the major cities is more like the US or Australia than Europe or some parts of Asia. With nearly 10 percent of the population of the planet, Latin America is obviously an important place. However, this percentage perhaps paints too limited a picture of the importance of the population of Latin America. Part of this importance can be traced to the movements of people over the centuries. Countless millions have immigrated to Latin America in search of a better life. This immigration has created one of the most fascinatingly diverse regions of the world. The culture of Latin America is diversity in action. The indigenous culture of the area is overlaid with immigration from Europe, Africa, Asia, and the Middle East. Immigrants from Latin America to North America, Europe, and most recently Asia have in both small and large ways changed the character of these regions. The importance of Latin America in the world extends beyond its borders as millions of people living outside of the region have, in some measure, a connection to it.

There are also more general contributions of Latin America to the world at large. Four hundred million people in the world speak Spanish, making it the world's second most used language after Mandarin. Another 191 million people in Brazil speak Portuguese. This linguistic influence spreads beyond the borders of Latin America to the rest of the world. Spanish and Portuguese terms have crept into many of the world's languages through books, poetry, music, and films. Spanish words and phrases are now part of the language of the world. In the modern world, images from Buenos Aires, Rio de Janeiro, or Mexico City are as familiar as London, Paris, or Sydney. A similar story exists with respect to history. The preColombian civilizations of Mexico, Central America, and South America are well-known parts of the cultural heritage of the world. The literature of the region has been recognized by Nobel prizes. Many forms of music, dance, or art are immediately recognizable outside of the region as being "Latin American." It would take too long to discuss Latin America and sports. It is difficult to imagine football (the real one), tennis, boxing, American baseball, or track and field without teams and individual athletes from Latin America. All of this is just a way of expressing the importance of Latin America to the world at large. However, this book has a more specific purpose. In order to get a complete view of the importance of Latin America to the world, the study of the economics of Latin America is critical. In the next section we'll begin our study of the economy of Latin America.

The economic output of Latin America

In economics, it is usual to express the economic output of a country using the term Gross Domestic Product (GDP). GDP represents the output of all final goods and services produced in an economy during a year. Nominal GDP is GDP expressed in terms of current prices. In many of our discussions, we will focus on a related term, real GDP. Real GDP is GDP that has been adjusted for changes in the price level. This adjustment allows us to compare the output of the economy over time by factoring out price level changes. The basic data on GDP in Latin America is given in Table 1.1. The GDP of the countries of Latin America is shown in the table along with some global data for comparison. The columns of the table give data on population, total GDP, and GDP per capita. GDP per capita is simply total GDP divided by the population. In addition to information on Latin America, Table 1.1 contains information on the world economy and various subcomponents for comparison purposes. The World Bank divides the world into roughly three different types of economies. These are low-, middle-, and high-income economies.[1] Using the world and these three different types of economies provides the reference points necessary to give one a picture of Latin America's place in the world economy.

Notice from the bottom of Table 1.1 that the economic output of the planet is approximately $60 trillion. The output of Latin America is a bit over $4 trillion or over 6 percent of the economic output of the world. Among the countries of the region, GDP is highly concentrated. The GDP of Brazil and Mexico are over $1 trillion. From there a substantial drop occurs to GDP of over $300 billion for Argentina and Venezuela. Only three more countries in the region have a GDP of over $100 billion: Chile, Colombia, and Peru. The next largest economy (Ecuador) is roughly half the size of the smallest economy in the previous group. The other countries of the region are in a relatively tight cluster of GDP between $7 billion and $39 billion. As a result, there is a large variance in the absolute size of the economies of the region. Two of the countries are now in the trillion dollar club in the world economy. Argentina and Venezuela occupy a space between these two and the group of countries with a GDP of at least

Table 1.1 Population, GDP, and GDP per capita for Latin America, low-, middle-, and high-income countries, and the world, 2008

	Population (millions)	GDP[1] (billions)	GDP per capita[1]
Argentina	39.9	328.5	8,236
Bolivia	9.7	16.7	1,720
Brazil	192.0	1,575.2	8,205
Chile	16.8	169.5	10,084
Colombia	45.0	243.8	5,416
Costa Rica	4.5	29.7	6,564
Ecuador	13.5	54.7	4,056
El Salvador	6.1	22.1	3,605
Guatemala	13.7	39.0	2,848
Honduras	7.3	13.3	1,823
Mexico	106.4	1,088.1	10,232
Nicaragua	5.7	6.6	1,163
Panama	3.4	23.1	6,793
Paraguay	6.2	16.0	2,561
Peru	28.8	129.1	4,477
Uruguay	3.3	32.2	9,654
Venezuela	27.9	314.2	11,246
Latin America	530.3	4,101.5	7,735
High income	1,068.7	43,309.6	40,525
Middle income	4,652.3	16,722.1	3,594
Low income	976.2	564.6	578
World	6,697.3	60,557.0	9,042

Source: World Bank (2010).
[1] Data in current US dollars

$100 billion. In summary, the economies of the region run the gamut from four relatively large economies to a collection of medium to small countries in terms of GDP.

For some, the information on Latin America as a part of the world economy may be surprising. Obviously, Latin America is an important part of the world economy. However, its economic status does not quite seem to match what one would expect. This seeming disconnect is a theme that we will return to many times as we move through the book. Latin America's relatively small place in the world economy is not something that occurred overnight. This is the result of decades of economic growth in Latin America that was slow by international standards. In 1960, Latin America was 5.9 percent of the world economy. By 2009, it comprised 6.5 percent. This means that collectively the economies of Latin America have grown only slightly faster than the world economy overall. One of the primary purposes of this book is to shed some light on the relatively poor economic performance of the region. As we will see, there is no single explanation of this problem. The answers lie in many parts of economics and quite possibly some of the other social sciences. As we move through the book, we will try to cover the economic problems of the region that are "common knowledge." Ultimately, low growth of the economies of the region leads to another problem. Combining GDP with population yields GDP per capita. If the former is growing slowly, then the latter is as well. In the next section, we cover GDP per capita in Latin America.

GDP per capita in Latin America

Combining a population of 530 million and total GDP of $4 trillion, GDP per capita in Latin America is approximately $7,735. This simple statistic contains both good news and bad news. The good news is that most of Latin America is solidly middle income by global standards. Indeed, the average GDP per capita is in the upper realm of the world middle class. For the most part, modern Latin America is a far cry from the grinding poverty of the low-income countries of sub-Saharan Africa or parts of Asia. On the other hand, it is also still far from the easy affluence that characterizes North America or the high-income countries in general. Within the region there are substantial differences in GDP per capita. Six of the 17 countries of the region have GDP per capita in the vicinity of $10,000. The range for the rest of the region is from a low of $1,163 to $6,793. At the lower end of this range, life is not easy. Food, housing, health care, and some other basic amenities of life cannot be taken for granted. As we will see in Chapter 12, there is still a troublingly large percentage of the population of the region that is struggling to maintain the basics of life. Moreover, keep in mind that the average numbers for Latin American countries are masking a number of intra-country differences in standards of living. Incomes in rural areas are frequently far less than that of the urban middle class. These differences occur for a variety of reasons but this is a theme that we will return to on several occasions.

The situation we described in the previous section has an impact on the growth of GDP per capita in Latin America. Since the rate of growth of GDP has been slow relative to the world and other developing countries, GDP per capita growth has been relatively slow. In addition, population growth in Latin America during the latter part of the twentieth century was relatively fast by global standards. Putting the two factors together means that GDP per capita growth during the past century has not been particularly fast. It has been fast enough to put much of Latin America into the global middle class but not fast enough to put many of the residents of the region into a more comfortable standard of living. This problem is the primary focus of this book. Again there are no quick and easy answers to this problem. However, part of the problem has been a pattern of international trade that has been badly skewed by policy choices made by many governments in the region. Because of the importance of trade, the next section introduces the basic data on Latin America's trade with the rest of the world.

1.1 The Human Development Index

In the previous section the data for GDP per capita in Latin America was presented and discussed. Embedded in this discussion was an unstated assumption. This assumption is that human welfare is very highly correlated with GDP per capita. For the most part this is the case. Everything else equal, a higher GDP per capita is preferred to a lower one. However, there is obviously more to life than money. A large number of factors could cause a divergence between welfare and GDP per capita. To attempt to correct for this, the United Nations Development Programme publishes an annual ranking of countries by the Human Development Index. The index has three components with equal weights. The first is the usual GDP per capita. The second component is life expectancy at birth. Obviously, a longer life span is associated with greater or improved human welfare. A final component is education. A third of this component is adult literacy. The other two-thirds is the ratio of students enrolled in primary, secondary, and tertiary schools as a percentage of the school age population. The resulting index number varies from 0 to 1. Globally, the highest and lowest scores are 0.971 for Norway and 0.340 for Niger. The regional average for Latin America is 0.800. The index ranges from 0.699 for Nicaragua to 0.878 for Chile. All of the countries in the region fall into the high to medium categories for the index. Latin America performs better on this index than for GDP per capita. In no country of the region is life expectancy less than 70 years, and adult literacy rates are high. However, also notice that there is a gap between much of Latin America and the four high-income countries in the table. These differences are driven primarily by differences in GDP per capita and the gross enrollment ratio.

Table 1.2 The Human Development Index in Latin America, 2007

	Human Development Index
Argentina	0.866
Bolivia	0.729
Brazil	0.813
Chile	0.878
Colombia	0.807
Costa Rica	0.854
Ecuador	0.806
El Salvador	0.747
Guatemala	0.704
Honduras	0.732
Mexico	0.854
Nicaragua	0.699
Panama	0.840
Paraguay	0.761
Peru	0.806
Uruguay	0.865
Venezuela	0.844

(continued)

Table 1.2 The Human Development Index in Latin
America, 2007 *(continued)*

	Human Development Index
Latin America	0.800
Portugal	0.909
Spain	0.955
Canada	0.966
US	0.956

Source: United Nations Development Programme (2009).

Latin America and international trade

As we will see at a number of points in the book, international trade has
always been an important part of the economies of Latin America. Table 1.3
shows the basic data on Latin America's trade with the rest of the world.
Imports and exports of goods, services, and the total are shown in the table
for Latin America, the high-, middle-, and low-income economies, and the
world. Virtually everyone is used to thinking about trade in goods. However,
thinking about trade in services is not as common. International trade in
services comprises items such as transportation, tourism, business services,
and royalties and license fees. World trade in goods is nearly $16 trillion
while world trade in services is almost $4 trillion. The data for Latin America
is shown in the first row. Latin America's exports of goods and services to
the world are $872 and $101 billion, respectively. This yields total exports of
almost $1 trillion. This leaves the region accounting for less than 5 percent
of world exports. A similar story emerges on the import side. Latin American
imports of goods and services are $816 and $137 billion, respectively. Total
imports for the region are nearly $953 billion. Again, imports in Latin
America are less than 5 percent of world imports. In 2008, Latin America as
a whole imported slightly more than it exported. A substantial trade surplus
in goods was partially offset by a deficit in services. Notice from the data that
this is a normal pattern of trade for the middle-income countries as a whole.

At this point, recall that Latin America is 6 percent of the world
economy. However, in international trade it accounts for less than 5 percent.
Superficially, this doesn't seem to be a large difference. However, looking at
the data in a different way yields another way of thinking about international
trade and Latin America. The final column shows the importance of
international trade to Latin America. The degree to which an economy is open
to international trade can be measured by the ratio of exports plus imports
(X + M) to GDP (Y). The higher this ratio is, the more "open" an economy is
to the rest of the world. Conversely, the lower this ratio is, the more "closed"
the economy is. Looking at the data in this way shows how different Latin
America is from much of the rest of the world. The ratio for Latin America

Table 1.3 Latin America and international trade, 2008

	Exports (billions of current US dollars)			Imports (billions of current US dollars)			Trade openness
	Goods	Services	Total	Goods	Services	Total	(X+M)/ GDP
Latin America	872.4	101.2	965.8	816.2	136.6	952.8	0.47
HIC	10,703.1	3,072.4	13,775.4	11,104.3	2,689.0	13,740.9	0.61
MIC	4,967.0	766.7	5,667.8	4,395.2	829.9	5,223.9	0.65
LIC	170.7	36.4	196.1	237.7	44.8	282.5	0.85
World	15,755.3	3,875.6	19,863.2	15,665.8	3,556.9	19,164.7	0.64

Source: World Bank (2010).
Note: Data for Nicaragua in 2007 was used for the calculations. Data for Total Exports do not match those for exports of goods plus exports of services because these are computed with the Nicaragua data for 2007 while the total is as reported by the World Bank.

is 0.47. The global average is much higher at 0.64 and is very similar to the average for the high- and middle-income countries. The conclusion is that Latin America does not trade as much as most other high- and middle-income countries. Normally it is true that the more open an economy is to international trade, the faster the rate of economic growth.[2] This is one of the reasons that this measure of openness is considered important. In a Latin American context, we will see that a number of policies pursued by many countries in Latin America during the twentieth century had a tendency to reduce the degree of openness. It is a theme that we will return to on a number of occasions as we move through the book. However, international trade in goods and services is only part of inflows and outflows of money in an economy as it interacts with the rest of the world. Trade flows are critically important but they are only part of the picture. In the next section, we will consider other types of transactions that Latin America has with the rest of the world.

Capital flows and Latin America

As we will see in a later chapter, the mirror image of trade in goods and services (along with a few other items) has to be matched in some way by capital flows. In a simple sense, any imbalance in trade in goods and services must be offset by capital flows. Like trade flows, capital can flow either into a country (inflows) or out (outflows). To some extent most of us are vaguely familiar with capital flows but the general knowledge about these flows is usually sketchy. In the case of Latin America, these flows have been critically important. Since shortly after the wave of independence movements in the first part of the nineteenth century, capital flows into Latin America have been both a blessing and a curse. All developing countries need capital flows in order to attain the maximum amount of economic growth. As we will see in the next chapter, the amount of capital a country has relative to its labor force is a critical determinant of economic growth. Poorer countries normally are able to utilize a greater amount of capital than that which is provided by domestic savings. Developing countries frequently cannot generate enough domestic savings to produce an optimum amount of investment in new production facilities. However, these beneficial flows of capital do not always occur in a smooth or orderly fashion. Latin American economic history is marked by periods of rapid inflows of foreign capital coupled with sometimes disastrous outflows. In this section, we will provide a brief overview of these flows for Latin America.

Capital flows come in various types. With globalized financial markets, an important type of capital flows for developing countries are flows of portfolio capital. Portfolio capital is money that crosses borders in order to buy financial assets such as stocks or bonds. At times, this type of capital flow can be critically important because financial markets in developing countries are typically rather small. In such a case, large inflows or outflows of portfolio capital can cause significant volatility in these markets. As we will explain later in the book, large inflows and outflows also have large effects on trade flows and the exchange rate. Another important form of capital flow is foreign direct investment (FDI). FDI is the purchase of real assets, such as production facilities, in a foreign country. In this case, the augmentation of domestic investment by FDI is a critical part of the process of economic development.

Flows of portfolio capital can be extremely volatile. As a result, we will cover these flows in Chapter 9. At this point, our discussion will be restricted to FDI data given in Table 1.4. The first column contains data on FDI flows for Latin America, the high-, middle-, and low-income countries, and the world. The second column reports FDI as a percentage of the world total. In 2008, Latin America received nearly $121 billion in FDI. This amounts

Table 1.4 Capital flows in Latin America, 2008

	Foreign direct investment	
	Billions current US dollars	% of world
Latin America	120.7	6.62
HIC	1,225.3	67.20
MIC	571.6	31.35
LIC	26.4	1.45
World	1,823.3	

Source: World Bank (2010).
Note: Data for Paraguay was not available for calculations.

to 6.62 percent of world FDI. This percentage almost exactly matches the percentage of Latin American GDP in the world economy. This seems like a reasonable number. However, as a group the middle-income countries of the world have 28 percent of world output and 31 percent of world FDI. What this means is that the economies of Latin America do a bit worse than average in attracting FDI. As we will see in the next chapter, this tends to reduce the growth potential of the region somewhat. The next chapter also will provide some insight into why this might be the case.

Latin America and world resources

There are few areas in which Latin America is more important than in the area of the production of commodities. A commodity is the general term for products where one unit of the product is indistinguishable from another unit. For example, one bushel of wheat is indistinguishable from another. This leads to an interesting market structure for commodities. In general, the price of commodities is determined in a global market by the forces of supply and demand. Further, these markets usually are characterized by both inelastic supply and demand. In economics, inelastic pertains to the property of a supply or demand curve in which the quantity demanded or supplied does not change by much in response to changes in price in the short run (i.e. both are very steeply sloped). On the demand side this occurs because many commodities are necessary for the production of other goods (oil) or they are a basic product frequently used by consumers (rice). On the supply side, the production of most commodities cannot be easily changed in the short run in response to even a large change in price. The result of these technical conditions is that the prices of commodities are subject to a substantial amount of price volatility. For Latin America, large fluctuations in the price of oil, copper, and agricultural commodities are simply a part of the economic life of the region.

From the start of the colonial period in 1492, much of the interest in Latin America as a region stemmed from the relatively plentiful supply of some important commodities. The activities of the Spanish government in the extraction of gold and silver in Latin America from the sixteenth to the early nineteenth century is a part of world history that almost everyone is familiar with. Less well known is the importance of Latin America in the production of other important minerals such as oil, copper, tin, and, more recently, lithium. Latin America also is an important supplier of agricultural commodities. A short list of these commodities includes sugar, coffee, bananas, soybeans, wheat, and beef. What this means is that the production and export of commodities is even today an important part of the economic landscape of Latin America. It also makes land a critically important resource. Recall that when economists use the term land, they are not speaking of just some geometric area such as a hectare. They are also referring to any resources that the land contains or the potential use of the land to produce commodities. Thus, in Latin America, the ownership of land and the distribution of the ownership of land is an important public policy issue. Of course, this is true in any country, but it becomes even more critical in an area with a natural abundance of commodities.

Unfortunately, for a country or a region the possession or production of commodities can be both a blessing and a curse. In one sense, commodities are a lucky stroke for a country. The production of commodities may earn large amounts of money combined with low production costs. If used wisely, this windfall can be used to develop the country as a whole faster than would otherwise be the case. It might also allow for the development of downstream industries based on the use of these commodities. The downside of the possession of commodities is less obvious. However, start out with a simple thought question. Of the countries of the world that produce large amounts of primary commodities, how many of these countries have used this windfall to become high-income countries? The ratio of the countries that have managed to do this to the countries that have failed is depressingly low. New Zealand and Australia almost are exceptions that prove the rule. Unfortunately, Latin America falls into the denominator in this ratio. The region is very well endowed with commodities, but has failed to turn this into higher GDP growth. The reasons for this are numerous and Latin America is hardly alone in this regard. An egregious example is that Saudi Arabia is still a *middle-income* country. However, commodities and economic development is one of the major themes of the economics of Latin America that we will encounter as we move through the book. In the next section, we start to look at the overall economic problem of Latin America.

Latin America and the world: a summary

Two somewhat conflicting issues emerge from the material we've covered so far. First, in a broad sense Latin America is an important part of the world. Its vivid history, large geographic area, the relatively large population of the region, the effects of the region on the culture of the world at large, and its economic impact on the world make Latin America important. On the other hand, there is frequently a sense of something missing or something slightly wrong with this picture. This feeling isn't misplaced, there is something a bit amiss. Despite all of the above, Latin America is not what it *could* have been. Let's put this problem into more precise terms. One of the major, if not the most important, themes of this book is that economic growth in Latin America over the last century has been low relative to other parts of the world economy at a similar stage of economic development. Countries and sometimes regions grow at different rates: some faster, some slower. Unfortunately, Latin America tends to fall into the latter category. A commonplace comparison is the economic growth of Latin America relative to the rapid growth rates that have been common for decades in certain parts of Asia, particularly East Asia. In the second half of the twentieth century, many countries in East Asia transformed themselves from low-income countries to middle-income countries and in some cases high-income countries. These "growth miracles" are not accomplished overnight. A combination of the rule of 70 and relatively fast growth makes the difference. As you will recall, the rule of 70 is simply a way of roughly calculating the number of years it takes some variable to double in size. When applied to economic growth, the results can be startling. An economy growing at 10 percent per year doubles in size every seven years. If the growth rate drops to 4 percent, it now takes nearly 18 years for the economy to double in size. Economic growth in Latin America is much like the latter example. There has been economic growth in the region, but it has been relatively slow. The result of this is that Latin America today is a smaller part of the world economy than it could have been. To illustrate the problem, refer to Figure 1.1 below. In the figure, the lowest line is the average GDP per capita for Latin America from 1960 to 2008 measured in constant (2000) dollars. Measured this way, GDP per capita in the region has doubled over the last 50 years. However, two other lines are included in the figure. The next higher line shows what GDP per capita could have been if growth had been as fast as the fastest growing economy of the region, Chile. In the early 1980s, GDP per capita in Chile started to grow faster than the Latin American average. If Latin America as a whole could have achieved this growth rate, GDP per capita in the region would have been substantially higher than it is now. Unfortunately, while

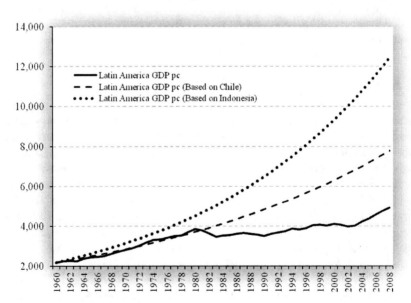

Source: World Bank (2010).
Authors' computations using 1960 as base year.

Figure 1.1 Actual vs. potential changes in GDP per capita in Latin America (constant 2000 US dollars)

Chile has been a fast-growing economy in Latin America, while it has not grown as fast as some of the economies of Asia. However, these economies have grown so fast over the last 50 years that this comparison may not be completely relevant. Many of these economies started this period as low-income economies, whose growth can naturally be much faster.[3] As a result, we show a final comparison with growth in Latin America with an Asian country with some characteristics similar to Latin America. Indonesia is a large country that is a major commodity exporter. Further, the country had a long history of authoritarian government coupled with some internal instability. As we move through the book, it will become clearer why using Indonesia as a comparison may be more useful than Hong Kong, Singapore, South Korea, or Taiwan. The highest line shows what GDP per capita in Latin America *could* have been if economic growth in the region had been as fast as it was in one of the more slowly growing economies of Asia with some of the same problems as Latin America. This line compared to the actual collective GDP of the region is the heart of the economic problem of Latin America. There has been decent economic growth. However, it could have been much better. It should have been possible for the region to do as well as Chile or Indonesia. Over time, such differences produce startling differences in GDP per capita. While the arithmetic exercise is interesting, one needs to keep in mind that this lost GDP would have made a tremendous difference in the standard of living of the average person in Latin America.[4]

A natural question at this point is: what has caused economic growth in Latin America to be relatively slow? This is especially puzzling for a region in the middle of the world economy that is endowed with a large number of valuable natural resources. Sadly, there is no simple or certain answer to that question. Economists have been studying the issue for a long time and it is fair to say that no definitive answer has emerged from this research. However, it is also true that we now understand a substantial part of what went wrong. In general terms, a mixture of the history of the region, its natural endowments, and poor economic policy have tended to lower the economic growth of the region. The answers to the questions are not yet complete, but there are a number of recurring themes in Latin American economics that form a sort of "standard list" of issues that help to understand the relative economic underperformance of the region.

1.2   Latin America and the United States

The focus of this book is the economic development of Latin America. As we saw in the chapter, Latin America is intertwined with the rest of the world and the development of the region is very much related to the world economy. However, the economies of Latin America are even more closely linked to the two high-income economies in the Western Hemisphere, the United States (US) and Canada. Here we will look more closely at the economic relationship between Latin America and the US. Much of the discussion can be extrapolated to Canada but the Canadian economy is about 10 percent of the size of the US economy, so for the sake of brevity, we will focus on the former. The economic relationship between Latin America and the US is summarized in Table 1.5.

Table 1.5 The economic relationship between Latin America and the US, 2007 (billions)

Imports	364.4
Goods	330.7
Services	33.8
Exports	279.9
Goods	222.4
Services	57.5
Capital Flows	
FDI	63.4
Portfolio Capital	116.5

Source: US Bureau of Economic Analysis (2009).

The first part of this relationship concerns GDP. The total GDP of the US is approximately $15 trillion. The GDP of Latin America is $4 trillion. At this point the economy of the US is almost four times the size of the economy of Latin America. This sort of disparity means that economic events in the US tend to have an outsized effect on Latin America. The reverse is not the case. None of the economies of Latin America are large enough for economic events there to have a large effect on the US economy. This disparity is exacerbated by trade and capital flows. Approximately a third of Latin America's exports are accounted for by the US Economic conditions in the US can have a substantial impact on Latin American exports. Also, Latin America is somewhat dependent on the US as nearly a third of imports originate there. The story is even more pronounced for capital flows. Half of Latin America's FDI comes from the US. In addition, portfolio capital flows into and out of the region can be large. In 2007, they amounted to nearly $117 billion. On the other hand, in some years there have been large flows out of the region. The above figures are conservative. They do not account for other flows such as the remittances of workers from Latin America or flows of public and private aid into the region. For better or worse, the US and Latin America are locked into an economic relationship that is important for the US but much more important to Latin America. If the relationship between the two seems strained at times, the numbers above explain at least a part of that strain.

Recurring themes in Latin American economic development

In the process of explaining economic growth in Latin America, a number of themes keep cropping up. They appear with such regularity that they are just part of the "conventional wisdom" about the economies of Latin America.

In this case the conventional wisdom has become so because it is essentially correct. An important aspect of the economies of Latin America is their relative homogeneity. Each country in the region has its own distinctive characteristics. However, to a surprising extent there are many important similarities. These common themes are sufficiently important that they will come up time and time again as we attempt to explain the economic characteristics and performance of the countries of Latin America. The following is a list of these themes and a short description of each one to help begin our study of the region.

Growth

The most serious problem of modern Latin America has been that economic growth has been slow relative to much of the rest of the world.

History

One can rarely understand the current state of any economy or region without a basic understanding of economic history. This is particularly true with respect to Latin America.

Commodities

As we have mentioned above, many countries in Latin America are major producers and exporters of commodities. As we will see, this can have a substantial influence on the economic development of a country.

Import substitution industrialization

In the second half of the twentieth century, many countries in Latin America attempted to create industries designed to replace imports from developed countries. Import substitution industrialization (ISI) has had very important implications for economic development in the region.

Trade policy

From the 1930s, Latin America has pursued trade policies that tended to make the markets of the region relatively closed from foreign competition. This overall policy had a tendency to make Latin America less integrated into the world economy. The results are reflected in the data in Table 1.3.

Exchange rate policy

Countries have a choice of managing their exchange rate or allowing it to float. In Latin America, these choices at times have had serious implications in terms of economic growth.

Debt

A recurring theme in Latin American economic history has been the tendency for governments in the region to heavily borrow from banks and other financial institutions. As we will see, this borrowing at times has been a source of economic instability.

Macroeconomic instability

GDP growth, inflation, and unemployment have been somewhat unstable in many countries of Latin America. Unfortunately, this instability has been so pervasive that for many it is one of the defining characteristics of the region. Explaining this instability is one of the major tasks of this book.

Poverty and inequality

As indicated earlier in the chapter, GDP per capita in Latin America is low relative to the high-income countries. In addition, this relative poverty is not a burden that is equally shared by all segments of the population of Latin America. In comparison to the rest of the world, Latin America has one of the most unequal distributions of income.

This list of major themes in Latin American economics is not exhaustive. However, they do cover much of what makes Latin America distinctive in an economic sense. To a large extent, the interplay of these themes will serve to explain both the economic history of the region and its current place in the world economy. Notice that the majority of these themes are related to government policy. The actions of governments are rarely perfect and in any country or region can be the subject of debate. In the case of Latin America, the debate over government policy has been active and this debate is now where we turn our attention.

Major economic policy debates in Latin America

> And, of course, to my left-wing friends, whose ideas I share, in the hope that we may also agree on ways to achieve them.
>
> Hernando de Soto

The relatively slow growth of the economies of the region naturally has led to the question of its causes. The debate has tended to center on a set of policy choices made by most of the governments of Latin America during the Great Depression or in the following decade. In general, governments can allow the development of the economy using some mix of market forces coupled with a variety of government policies. Latin America in the second half of the twentieth century is a classic example. With the notable exception of Cuba, most governments in Latin America developed by relying on the actions of individuals and private sector firms. However, there was heavy intervention by the state in the form of ISI. In reality, ISI is not a policy but a collection of policies that are designed to develop industries that, in many cases, may not have even existed in a free market. From the middle of the twentieth century, the use of ISI was extensively pursued in Latin America. Although this set of policies was gradually abandoned in the 1980s, its impact on economic growth in the region and its lingering effects are still the subject of debate.

The growing realization that ISI was not a sustainable policy for economic development in the region logically led to the search for an alternative set of policies. In determining economic policy, there is a common tradeoff between the amount of decision making that is left to the private sector and how much is done by the government. As we will see, ISI was heavily tilted toward government intervention in the economy. As the performance of this set of policies was not as successful as was hoped, there has been an inevitable tilt of policy in Latin America towards greater reliance on market forces. For better or worse, this general drift in the direction of market forces has come to be known as Neoliberalism. This movement from ISI to more market-based economic policies has been highly contentious. This is so much so that Neoliberalism is a term most frequently used by its critics. Indeed, the debate has come to the point where it is somewhat hard to define exactly what the term means.[5]

A somewhat more precise way of relating the policy changes that have occurred in Latin America since the 1980s is to refer to the Washington Consensus. The Washington Consensus refers to a loose collection of economic policies that have been promoted by multilateral institutions in Washington, DC such as the World Bank, the International Monetary Fund (IMF), and a number of think tanks. John Williamson has summarized the main points of the Washington Consensus into a short list of general economic policies.

- A fiscal policy appropriate for macroeconomic conditions.
- A focus on improving the welfare of the poor by improving basic services that promote economic growth such as education and infrastructure.
- A tax system featuring lower marginal tax rates levied on a larger base of taxation.
- Market-determined interest rates.
- Realistic exchange rates.
- Liberalization of trade barriers.
- Relatively free flows of FDI.
- Privatization of inefficient state enterprises.
- Government regulation that does not restrict competition.
- Protection of property rights.

The list above is a useful way to think about economic policy in Latin America. This list of economic policies is a loose description of economic policies that are commonplace in most high-income countries or faster-growth middle-income countries. They are the source of some controversy in Latin America partially because economic policy in many countries of the region prior to the 1980s was so far away from these sorts of policies. The controversy also is partially a result of the movement away from ISI and towards more market-based economies. As we will see, this movement has caused a substantial amount of economic dislocation and not a small amount of short- to medium-term economic discomfort. Not surprisingly, the failures of ISI coupled with the economic dislocations of changing economic policies have led to the consideration or in some cases the adoption of policies that do not neatly fit into either the older ISI or Neoliberal molds. At times these policies are referred to as being associated with heterodox economics. However, this term refers to a number of different schools of economic thought that are outside of the mainstream of modern economic thought. Part of the problem with policy debates in Latin America has to do with how one defines economics in the twenty-first century.

The Washington Consensus outlined above is just a set of statements representing the mainstream view of economic policy in a well-managed economy. To a certain extent, the same thing can be said of Neoliberalism. However, in the policy debates concerning Latin America there has been a tendency to define both the Washington Consensus and Neoliberalism as being extremely rigid and dogmatic extensions of free-market economics. While both are relatively free-market oriented, the Washington Consensus is hardly a "pure" free market list. Indeed, one could just as easily call the list above the Madrid or Lisbon Consensus, as the Washington Consensus could be used to characterize virtually any high-income country such as Spain or Portugal.[6] In the mainstream of economics, there is a substantial role for government. The real question is not the size of the government relative to the private sector but using government policy to create growth consistent with other sometimes noneconomic objectives. As a result, this book tries to consider Latin American economic history, current policy, and policy changes in a somewhat different way. Much of what this book is trying to accomplish is to help one understand what actually occurred in the economic history of Latin America rather than dwelling on what *should* have occurred. We consider the recent policy changes more in terms of changes that have actually been implemented. Our description of potential economic policy is thoroughly mainstream. As we will see, Latin America never was and most probably never will be as free market as Hong Kong. Centuries of policy distortions have left their mark. Our task is to help understand how the past influences the present and the future. ISI is a perfect example. The dismantling of ISI is ongoing. Again, our task is to describe the economic fallout. With respect to current economic policy or potential changes in policy, we will analyze those as they come up using cost/benefit analysis. Every potential policy change has potential costs and benefits. For many policy changes there may be no hard and fast answers. However, cost/

benefit analysis can always be a useful tool in thinking about both past, present, and future economic policies.

Thus, the focus of this book is on economic reality and not economic rhetoric. Latin America is an economically complex region with a long history. To understand the economics of Latin America, you'll need a number of tools of economic analysis. Learning these tools and then applying them in a Latin American context is the purpose of this book. It is not our purpose to criticize the intellectual authors of some economic policies in Latin America that perhaps did not work as well as was hoped. On the other hand, we see little point in debating the movement of Latin American governments towards more market-oriented policies or changes in the opposite direction. These changes in policy are occurring within a democratic framework both in Latin America and other parts of the world. Essentially, we'll be assuming that countries in Latin America are operating in the context of some form of democratic capitalism. Fortunately, both democratic and capitalism are very large tents that easily encompass most of the countries of the region. In short we are concerned with the realities of economic history and current and future economic policy. We purposefully chose to leave the sometimes heated rhetoric surrounding Latin American economic policy to others. We find that learning the tools of analysis and the serious study of policy provide more than enough work for a course.

Key terms and concepts

commodity – products where one unit of the product is indistinguishable from another unit.

exchange rate – the price of one currency in terms of another currency.

foreign direct investment (FDI) – the purchase of real assets, such as production facilities, in a foreign country.

Gross Domestic Product (GDP) – the market value of all final goods and services produced in an economy in a year.

heterodox economics – a term describing the collection of schools of thought in economics that are currently outside of the mainstream of the economics profession.

import substitution industrialization (ISI) – a set of policies designed to replace imports of industrial products with domestic production.

inelastic – the property of a demand or supply curve that changes in price have only a small impact on the quantity demanded or supplied.

International Monetary Fund (IMF) – a multilateral agency created in 1945 to promote international monetary stability and cooperation.

Neoliberalism – in a Latin American context, the tendency to shift government economic policy from a heavy reliance on government intervention in the economy to more market-based economic policies.

portfolio capital – the purchase of financial assets, such as stocks and bonds, in a foreign country.

Washington Consensus – a term referring to a loose collection of primarily market-based economic policies.

World Bank – a multilateral institution that makes loans to developing countries to enhance economic development.

Questions for review and discussion

1 Describe why Latin America is a relatively important region of the world. List some specific examples that were not given in the chapter.

2 In terms of GDP, how important is Latin America in the world economy?

3 Describe the economic position of Argentina, Brazil, and Mexico in relation to the rest of Latin America.

4 What is the average GDP per capita in Latin America and what is the range around this average? Describe how GDP per capita in Latin America compares with the same number in low- and middle-income countries around the world.

5 How important is Latin America in world trade in goods and services?

6 How does one measure how "open" or "closed" an economy is? Is Latin America on average more open or closed than the world economy at large?

7 What is the difference between movements of portfolio capital and FDI?

8 Describe the economic growth of Latin America relative to East Asia. Why does this difference matter?

9 List and describe some of the recurring themes in Latin American development.

10 Describe the Washington Consensus. How is it related to Neoliberalism?

References and recommended readings

Daude, Christian and Eduardo Fernandez-Arias. 2010. "Aggregate Productivity: The Key to Unlocking Latin America's Development Potential," pp. 23–43 in Carmen Pages (ed.), *The Age of Productivity: Transforming Economies from the Bottom Up*. New York: Palgrave Macmillan.

Edwards, Sebastian. 1993. "Openness, Trade Liberalizations, and Growth in Developing Countries," *Journal of Economic Literature*, 31(September): 1358–93.

King, John (ed.). 2004. *The Cambridge Companion to Modern Latin American Culture*. New York: Cambridge University Press.

Reid, Michael. 2007. *Forgotten Continent: The Battle for Latin America's Soul*. New Haven, CT: Yale University Press.

Skidmore, Thomas E. and Peter H. Smith. 2005. *Modern Latin America*, 6th ed. New York: Oxford University Press.

United Nations Development Programme. 2009. *Human Development Report 2009.* New York: Palgrave Macmillan.

US Bureau of Economic Analysis. 2009. *US Economic Accounts.* Washington, DC: US Bureau of Economic Analysis.

Weintraub, Sidney. 2010. *Unequal Partners: The United States and Mexico.* Pittsburgh: University of Pittsburgh Press.

Williamson, John. 2004. "The Strange History of the Washington Consensus," *Journal of Post Keynesian Economics,* 27(Winter): 195–206.

World Bank. 2010. *World Development Indicators,* Washington, DC: World Bank.

2 Economic growth and Latin America

It is a mistake to seek a single, overarching explanation for Latin America's relative failure.

Michael Reid

Introduction

In the previous chapter we introduced one of the central problems in the economies of Latin America. This problem concerns the rate of growth of GDP in the region. For much of the post-war era, economic growth in the region has been positive. However, the growth of the economies of Latin America has been slow relative to some other regions of the world at a similar stage of economic development. In this chapter we will begin to address this question in a more systematic way. In order to do this we must first learn a bit about how economists explain economic growth. The study of economic growth is both old and new. It is old in the sense that modern economics traces its roots to the publication in 1776 of Adam Smith's *The Wealth of Nations*. However, the full title of the book is instructive: *An Enquiry into the Nature and Causes of the Wealth of Nations*. In a broad sense, Smith was concerned with economic growth or what now is referred to as economic development.

Fortunately, the modern study of economic growth has been an active part of the economics literature in the same time frame that we are considering in the book: the last half of the twentieth century. During the 1950s, Robert Solow formulated the basic theory of economic growth that is still used to analyze changes in the rate of growth of GDP. This "classic" growth theory explains economic growth in terms of changes in the labor force and the stock of capital. In the first part of the chapter, our task is to explain this basic model and use it to analyze economic growth in Latin America. As is usually the case, the theory is both instructive and incomplete. The basic factors used in the theory are absolutely essential in understanding the economic growth process for virtually any country. However, it does not consider some important factors involved in the process of economic development. These deficiencies led to the development of "new" growth theory pioneered by Paul Romer and others. In the second part of the chapter, we will cover the more modern theory of economic growth which focuses on the accumulation of human capital and the role of technology in economic development. The development of the theory of economic growth will allow us to explain a substantial part of the story of economic growth in Latin America. The final part of the chapter concerns this growth accounting. Since this sort of analysis has been done for virtually all of the world's countries, at the end of the chapter we will be able to better understand why economic growth in Latin America has been relatively low.

Institutional basics

In many areas of economics, there is an implicit assumption concerning some preconditions that need to be in place within a single market (in the case of microeconomics) or the entire economy (in the case of macroeconomics). If these preconditions are not met, the usual theory we use in economics may not work as well. While there are a number of factors that can interfere with the workings of the market, there are two factors that are absolutely critical: property rights and the rule of law. The wretched conditions observed in the poorest countries of the world frequently are the result of the complete lack of either of these preconditions. Indeed, the very definition of a "failed state" is the almost complete lack of either property rights or the rule of law. Fortunately, this extreme lack of either precondition is not the case in modern Latin America. However, neither of these preconditions is a binary variable in the sense that a country either possesses them perfectly or does not. In the world, and in Latin America, there are variations in the degree of respect for property rights and the application of the rule of law. In the following two sections, we will discuss both preconditions in the context of Latin America.

Property rights

Property rights are essential to the workings of a market economy. For markets to work, it must be clear who owns what. If the buyer in a transaction cannot be certain that the seller actually owns the property, the transaction may not occur. Buyers need to be assured that the seller has the right to sell the property. If this is not the case, at some point another party might appear and claim that the seller had no right to sell the property in question. Further, the buyer needs to be confident that once some property is acquired, it cannot be arbitrarily taken away by another individual or the state. The enforcement of property rights has major implications for economic development. Everything else equal, the lack of enforcement of property rights makes market participants more reluctant to engage in many economic transactions. The optimum number of economic transactions would occur in an environment where property rights were perfectly enforced. Any reduction in the enforcement of property rights increases the risk of engaging in transactions. This increase in risk effectively increases the cost of normal economic activity. Of course, these increases in costs reduce the total number of transactions that occur in an economy. Fewer transactions translate into a lower level of overall economic activity and a lower GDP.

The utter lack of property rights one observes in a failed state has obvious consequences on economic activity. Transactions grind to a minimum and output per capita falls to barely subsistence levels. On the other hand, property rights in a high-income country usually are taken completely for granted. As will be the case in many different contexts, Latin America is in something of a middle ground with respect to property rights. The region did not start out well in this regard as the modern history of Latin America began with an enormous theft of property by the colonial powers from the indigenous population of the region. In any colonial system, and Latin America was no exception, protection of one's property from a monarchial colonial power was problematic. Protection of property rights was hampered in the post-colonial period by sometimes extreme political instability. In short, the region did not start out in a positive way in this regard. In more recent times, prevention of outright theft of property may be a social problem due to ineffective enforcement of common laws regarding the protection of property. In more complex cases, the settlement of property disputes may be slow and difficult due to the state of the legal system and the courts. Likewise, the existence of corruption makes the rule of law less effective.

Since the subject here is economics, economists like to quantify things. Over the last twenty years, economists have worked to come up with numerical systems that at least in some sense quantify factors that may affect the economy such as the rule of law. The first such set of numbers is given in Table 2.1. The table contains a measure of property rights obtained from the annual *Global Competitiveness Report* published by the World Economic Forum. This data is derived from surveys of business executives and runs from 1 to 7 with the former being the poorest protection of property rights to the latter being the best. In a number of places throughout the book we will be presenting measures of this type in an attempt to bring some level of quantification to various economic, legal, and social factors that influence the performance of the economies of Latin America.

The data above indicates that property rights in Latin America lie somewhere in between the total lack of property rights and the observance of property rights indicative of a high-income country. The average of this index for Latin America as a whole is 4.0. However, this masks a substantial amount of variation. The highest scores for Latin America in Chile and Panama are equivalent to scores for Portugal and Spain. While lower than the scores for Canada and the US, they are still quite respectable for middle-income countries. On the other side, scores of 2.2 for Venezuela or 3.2 for

Table 2.1 Property rights in Latin America

Argentina	3.2
Bolivia	2.6
Brazil	4.6
Chile	5.4
Colombia	4.4
Costa Rica	4.6
Ecuador	3.2
El Salvador	4.2
Guatemala	4.2
Honduras	4.3
Mexico	4.1
Nicaragua	3.5
Panama	5.2
Paraguay	3.1
Peru	3.8
Uruguay	4.9
Venezuela	2.2
Latin America	4.0
Portugal	5.6
Spain	5.4
Canada	5.8
US	6.4

Source: World Economic Forum (2008).

Argentina are somewhat puzzling. Some of the poorer countries of Central America such as Guatemala and Honduras have scores above the Latin American average. While research on the effect of property rights on economic growth in Latin America is limited, it is safe to assume that the greater the extent to which property rights are enforced, the more economic growth would be enhanced. However, on average there is sufficient enforcement of property rights in Latin America to be able to use the model of economic growth discussed later in the chapter with some degree of confidence.

2.1   Squatting in Latin America

In a definitional sense, squatting is the occupation of unoccupied space or buildings without the legal permission to do so. Essentially, squatters are using land that they have no legal right to occupy or use. The phenomenon is so common that it is arguably the largest property rights problem in the region. Squatting usually is more common in urban areas but not exclusively confined to it. In Latin America, squatting is a very common form of housing for the poor. Virtually any large city in Latin America is ringed by squatter settlements, as the value of land diminishes with the distance from the center of the city. Squatters move into unoccupied land and proceed to build housing with whatever is at hand. Because they are informal, a major problem with these developments is the lack of the usual infrastructure associated with human habitation. This means no water or sewage service, no electricity, no public education, and little if any police services. The phenomenon is so common that squatters or their settlements are part of the common culture in most countries. In Mexico, they are referred to as paracaidistas (paratroopers) who literally drop in on unoccupied land. The favelas of Brazil are so common that they are home to an estimated 25 million people.

The problem is hardly just a Latin American problem. The United Nations (UN) estimates that there are nearly a billion squatters in the world. They constitute nearly a third of the world's urban population. The numbers are similar for Latin America. There are an estimated nearly 130 million squatters in Latin America. This is nearly a third of the urban population of the region and nearly a quarter of the total population. Laws on squatting in the region vary from being a crime in itself to being a civil matter between the owner of the property and the squatter. The situation is complicated by the fact that many squatters are occupying public land. In some cases, such as Mexico, squatters can become the de facto owners of unoccupied land after five years of peaceful occupation. In other cases, the squatters have formed such large communities that evicting such a large number of people is not tenable. An example would be the favela of Rocinho outside of Rio de Janiero which is home to an estimated 500,000 people. A common public policy problem in Latin America is the formalization of squatter communities to provide some form of property rights, official recognition, and the provision of public services. Note that the problem originates with a lack of property rights and ends with the recognition of the ultimate necessity of such rights in order for people living in urban areas to have any chance of escaping poverty.[1]

The protection of intellectual property rights

One of the more widely reported issues in property rights is the protection of intellectual property rights. Intellectual property can be usefully divided into two main areas. The first is copyrights and rights related to copyright. This applies to the work of authors and musicians. Companies or individuals that helped produce this sort of work may also have rights related to the work. Another sort of intellectual property is industrial property. Again, this type of intellectual property has two components. Companies or individuals with a distinctive product may have a trademark that cannot be used by others. The second type of industrial property is patents for a particular product or process. Intellectual property has been a particular area of interest in international trade negotiations. In general, intellectual property is more protected in developed countries than in developing countries. As the data in Table 2.2 below indicates, Latin America clearly falls into this pattern. On the same scale of 1 to 7 that was used in Table 2.1, the Latin American average for the protection of intellectual property rights is 3.0. It varies from 2.0 in Venezuela to 4.0 in Panama. Almost universally, there is less protection for intellectual property in Latin America than there is for property rights in general. This discrepancy is understandable. The protection of intellectual

Table 2.2 Intellectual property protection in
Latin America

Argentina	2.7
Bolivia	1.9
Brazil	3.3
Chile	3.6
Colombia	3.4
Costa Rica	3.5
Ecuador	2.4
El Salvador	2.8
Guatemala	2.7
Honduras	3.4
Mexico	3.2
Nicaragua	2.7
Panama	4.0
Paraguay	2.2
Peru	2.5
Uruguay	3.9
Venezuela	2.0
Latin America	3.0
Portugal	4.9
Spain	4.7
Canada	5.6
US	5.6

Source: World Economic Forum (2008).

property rights involves the collection of royalties and fees for the use of the property and the legal suppression of illegal use. In many cases, the property is the property of individuals and companies outside of the region. As a result, the protection of intellectual property is a less important item on the agenda of the governments of developing countries and Latin America is no exception. Perhaps there is even a hemispheric effect as the protection of intellectual property in Canada and the US is not exactly perfect. The issue is likely to remain contentious as the protection of intellectual property is a main goal of the high-income countries in international trade negotiations and for the US when it negotiates trade agreements.

The rule of law

Weapons have given you independence. Laws will give you freedom.
Francisco Paula de Santander

The second precondition is the rule of law. Normal economic transactions involve legally binding contracts. Sometimes, contracts lead to disputes among the parties involved. When this occurs there needs to be a sufficiently developed legal system for the state to determine what the appropriate outcome is and which parties have what obligations under the contract.

If there is no effective referee to enforce business contracts, far fewer business contracts occur. Market participants become reluctant to engage in normal economic activities because they cannot be sure that contracts will be enforced. Once again, the outcome is a lower level of economic activity. As is the case with property rights, the rule of law is never perfectly enforced in any country. Some countries have more rigorous compliance with the law than others. In general terms, enforcement of the rule of law in Latin America is adequate to allow the theory of economic growth that we will describe later in the chapter to be used. However, it is also generally recognized that problems with enforcement of the rule of law is a hindrance to economic growth in the region.

A serious problem in this regard is that the rule of law is difficult to define in an extremely precise way. However, there are a number of factors that one could consider that would have an impact on the rule of law in any country and are recognizable problems in a Latin American context. Each of these factors listed below are those that have been defined and to some extent measured by researchers at the World Bank.[2] In all cases the data indicates that the following factors tend to be problems in enforcing the rule of law in Latin America.

Enforcement of contracts – In almost any country, a business contract can be drawn up. The question then becomes one of enforcement. If the process of enforcing a contract involves an inordinate number of procedures or an interminable amount of time to enforce, then the existence of a contract may not be of much use. A large number of procedures and slow enforcement may lead to a situation where the costs of protecting one's rights are prohibitive. The available data on enforcement of contracts in Latin America indicates that the enforcement of contracts in the region can be difficult.

Judicial independence – In order for the rule of law to be observed it is important for the judicial system to be at least partially insulated from short-run changes in government. In many Latin American countries, this insulation is weak or nonexistent.[3]

Favoritism in decisions of government officials – In order for the rule of law to work properly, it is important for the law to be administered impartially. To the extent that the law is not administered in an impartial way, then the overall rule of law in a country is diminished.

Efficiency of legal framework – The effectiveness of the rule of law is heavily influenced by the efficiency of the legal framework. In this sense, we mean the ability of the legal system to handle disputes in a reasonable period of time. Further, the system needs to be such that it can be accessed by most, if not all, citizens. Legal systems in Latin America can be extremely slow and difficult for the average person to navigate. In this type of situation, the rule of law is not universally accessible to all and thus the overall application of the rule of law is diminished.

In all of the factors that affect the overall application of the rule of law, the data available indicates that Latin America tends to rank relatively low.

This situation is summarized in Table 2.3 below. Researchers at the World Bank have developed a system of ranking countries from −2.5 to +2.5 on the extent to which the country has an overall tendency to comply with the rule of law. In this case, a +2.5 would indicate perfect compliance with the rule of law and a −2.5 would indicate a virtually failed state. The variance in Latin America is large, with the highest score being +1.17 and the lowest score is −1.47. The Latin American average is −0.40. To put this into perspective, Portugal and Spain are both close to +1.0. Canada and the US have scores between +1.5 and +2.0. The information in the second column puts the data in terms of a percentile rank for all countries. Viewed this way, the average for Latin America is in the bottom third of the global distribution. While the application of the rule of law is not such that economic growth isn't occurring in Latin America, it is a substantial problem that tends to slow down the rate of growth.

The material above indicates that Latin America has had a sufficient application of property rights and the rule of law to foster positive economic growth. The basic preconditions are being met and both are slowly improving in the region. This being the case, we now turn our attention to a more formal model of economic growth. The basic theory of economic growth

Table 2.3 The rule of law in Latin America

	Percentile rank 0–100	Governance score (−2.5 to +2.5)
Argentina	39.0	+0.33
Bolivia	17.6	−0.96
Brazil	43.3	−0.44
Chile	88.1	+1.17
Colombia	35.7	−0.57
Costa Rica	61.9	+0.44
Ecuador	14.8	−1.04
El Salvador	28.6	−0.68
Guatemala	11.4	−1.11
Honduras	20.5	−0.86
Mexico	34.3	−0.58
Nicaragua	22.4	−0.84
Panama	50.0	−0.20
Paraguay	16.2	−0.97
Peru	26.7	−0.71
Uruguay	63.3	+0.49
Venezuela	3.3	−1.47
Latin America	33.9	−0.40
Portugal	82.4	+0.95
Spain	84.8	+1.12
Canada	96.2	+1.86
US	91.9	+1.59

Source: World Bank (2008).

was formulated and refined in the middle of the twentieth century. While this model does not provide a complete explanation of economic growth, it does explain a substantial portion of it. Moreover, a more complete model of growth is not entirely novel but builds on this basic model. As for most countries, the basic theory of economic growth will explain much of the growth of the economies of Latin America.

2.2   Judicial independence in Latin America[4]

As indicated above, a critical part of applying the rule of law in any country is the degree of judicial independence. In practice, this means that there needs to be an adequate degree of separation between the executive, legislative, and judicial branches of government. An independent judiciary can play a number of roles in improving the rule of law. First, it can serve as a check on the government by vetoing unconstitutional laws. Similarly, an independent judiciary is essential to act as an impartial referee in the case of legal disputes. Without a referee, the rule of law in a country is about as meaningful as rules in an athletic contest with no officials present. In some countries the judiciary can play a more active role in the policy process by interpreting the law in a way that amounts to influencing public policy. Finally, the judiciary may play a critical role in the country by acting as a representative for traditionally underrepresented groups in society.

The ability of the judiciary to perform its functions depends critically on several factors. It is essential that the judiciary have sufficient resources to perform its functions and have some budgetary independence from the other two branches of government. Second, the system of appointments is critical. If judges, especially at the supreme-court level, can be appointed without sufficient oversight, then the entire legal system may become compromised by short-run political considerations. Past the appointment process, judges need a sufficient guarantee of tenure to further insulate their decisions from changes in the government. Finally, the scope of judicial review needs to be broad enough to ensure that all parts of the legal system are subject to judicial review.

There is a general consensus that judicial independence is an impediment to the application of both property rights and the rule of law in Latin America. As described above, judicial independence is a multifaceted phrase that is difficult to condense into simple terms. As was done before, we present data that attempts to do this in an albeit crude fashion. The World Economic Forum provides survey data on the overall concept of judicial independence for most of the countries of the world. The data for Latin America is given in Table 2.4 below. As before, the countries are ranked on a 1 to 7 scale, with the former having the least degree of judicial independence and the latter having the most. Notice that the range in the region runs from 5.2 to 1.4. Obviously, the region is hardly homogeneous in this regard, but there are a sufficient number of countries with low rankings to indicate that this problem is not insignificant. While such rankings are far from perfect, notice that there is a correlation between these rankings and those of Tables 2.1, 2.2, and especially 2.3.

Table 2.4 Judicial independence in Latin America

Argentina	2.2
Bolivia	2.2
Brazil	3.8
Chile	4.5
Colombia	4.1
Costa Rica	5.2
Ecuador	2.0
El Salvador	3.2
Guatemala	3.3
Honduras	3.2
Mexico	3.4
Nicaragua	1.8
Panama	2.7
Paraguay	1.5
Peru	2.7
Uruguay	5.0
Venezuela	1.4
Latin America	3.1
Portugal	5.2
Spain	4.3
Canada	6.3
US	5.5

Source: World Economic Forum (2008).

A basic model of economic growth

In this section we will build a simple but quite powerful model of economic growth. This model was developed by Robert Solow and refined by many others during the 1950s and 1960s. The model can be variously described and we still use it today quite simply because it works. As we will see, economic growth is an extremely complicated process. However, there are some basic factors involved in the process that are common to every country.

Resources

In order for an economy to grow, it needs resources, or what economists call the factors of production. In general terms, these resources are referred to as land, labor, capital, and technology. In the discussion that follows, we assume that land is a constant. The borders of Latin America are now stable, so this particular assumption seems reasonable. More importantly for Latin America, the term "land" in economics refers to not only the land but all resources associated with the land such as oil, copper, gold, etc. In the way economists define land, Latin America is extremely abundant in land. However, since we are concerned with economic growth, the discussion of natural resources and commodities will be covered in Chapter 5. The discussion below will focus on labor, capital, and technology.

The economic growth of a country can be enhanced by having a country's labor force (L) grow over time. This increase can occur either through an increase in its natural population growth or through immigration. An increase in the labor force will tend to increase GDP. However, there is a potential problem lurking here. In some countries of Latin America, the population is still growing at a fairly fast rate. The ultimate goal is to increase GDP per capita. In the face of positive population growth, GDP must increase more rapidly in order to improve living standards in the region. Data on the population and labor force in Latin America will be shown in more detail in the next section.

Economic growth also requires an increase in the stock of capital (K). In economic terms, capital is the amount of money invested in business structures and equipment. The latter terms refer not only to the type of equipment that goes into a manufacturing plant but also to the type of business equipment needed to process information, such as computers and software. In the models we use in the next section, economic growth can be enhanced by the ability of an economy to increase the stock of capital as fast as possible. For the developing countries of Latin America, the stock of capital outside of the private sector may be critical. In order for capital and labor to produce the maximum output, the economic infrastructure of the country needs to be appropriate to the level of economic development. This sort of infrastructure includes water and sewage systems, paved roads, reliable supplies of electricity, and so on. Since much of this type of capital is developed in the public sector, we will cover this type of investment later in the chapter.

The final factor of production is technology. In economics, technology carries a somewhat different meaning than it does in common usage. Economists define a change in technology as anything that causes resources to be used in a more efficient way. Much of the time this means a change in technology as we usually understand it, such as an improvement in computer technology. However, for economists the term is much broader. What we are interested in is the relationship between inputs and outputs. For our purposes, a change in technology means that a country can either produce more output with the same amount of resources, or alternatively, produce the same level of output with fewer resources. This might occur because of better machinery or equipment. However, in this sense a change in management practices or an improvement in the institutional environment such as better enforcement of property rights could have the same effect. In any case, keep in mind that we are discussing technology in a very broad way. A way to express this broadness is to use an alternative phrase to describe this process: total factor productivity (TPF). In much of the discussion of economic growth, the terms "technology" and "total factor productivity" are used interchangeably. In both cases, it refers to the ability of an economy to produce gains in output beyond what would be expected from increases in the labor force or the capital stock alone. In the literature on economic growth in Latin America TFP is the most commonly used term and we will follow that convention here. As we will see, this term also now is the focus of the literature on this subject. In the next section, we will build a simple model to illustrate the process of economic growth for a typical developing country with adequate preconditions for growth.

The production function

Given the factors of production that we described above, we can now illustrate how these factors interact to produce a higher level of GDP. This relationship is illustrated in Figure 2.1. The vertical axis measures the level of real GDP (Y), and the horizontal axis measures the size of the labor force (L). To graph the relationship between real GDP and the labor force, we have held the stock of capital (K) and the level of technology or TFP constant. For the moment, we want to look only at the relationship between real GDP and the labor force. This relationship is known as a production function. First, notice that the relationship between real GDP and the labor force is positive. Everything else equal, as the size of the labor force increases the amount of real GDP that an economy can produce increases. Notice that the relationship is not linear. This is because we have assumed that the capital stock and the level of technology are fixed. The changing slope of the production function reflects the phenomenon of diminishing returns. Diminishing returns occurs when an increasing amount of a variable factor of production is added to a fixed factor of production. As the amount of the variable factor increases, the resulting increase in output becomes smaller. In this case, the fixed factor of production is the capital stock and the variable factor of production is labor. When the first few units of labor begin working with a large stock of capital, initially output rises rapidly. This is shown in Figure 2.1. As the amount of labor used increases from

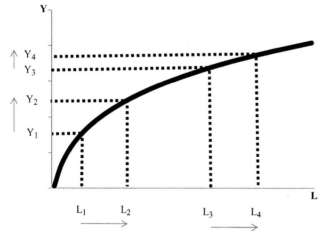

Figure 2.1 The production function and changes in labor

L_1 to L_2, real GDP increases sharply from Y_1 to Y_2. However, slope of the production function is not constant because of diminishing returns. Suppose that the same amount of labor is added shown by the increase in labor used from L_3 to L_4. In this case, real GDP still increases but by the smaller amount represented by the movement of real GDP from Y_3 to Y_4. The main concept to keep in mind is that changes in the size of the labor force are represented by a movement *along* the production function.

2.3 Population growth in colonial Latin America

The 500-year history of Latin America is littered with stories of tragedy. However, none is more tragic or important than the story of the change in population that occurred in the region in the sixteenth century. At the start it must be kept in mind that the historical record is not exact and there is considerable debate over the actual changes in population that occurred. For example, the population of Latin America in the year 1500 has been estimated to have been as low as 12 million and as high as 40 million. As a sort of average, we'll use the data estimated by the noted economic historian Angus Maddison as his estimates are somewhere in between these extremes. Maddison estimates that the population of Latin America in 1500 was 17.5 million. By the year 1600, the population was only 8.6 million. The population of the area declined by over 50 percent. Other estimates of the population decline range from a low of 14 percent to a high of 65 percent.[5] This situation is comparable to the Black Death in Europe that killed 45–50 percent of the population from 1347–1351. By any standard, the decline in population was an extreme event in the history of the region. Initially, the wars of conquest lowered the population. However, the major source of mortality was simply disease. In this case the killers were measles and smallpox. The arrival of Europeans introduced these diseases against which the population had no natural defenses. The epidemics, combined with the almost total absence of medical care, swiftly decimated the population. According to Maddison, the population recovered in the seventeenth century to a bit over 12 million. In 1820, on the eve of the wars of independence, the population had reached 21.2 million.

Such an extreme decline in the population has had permanent effects on the region. Thinking in terms of the production function, one can only imagine the decline in total economic activity engendered by such a severe decline in the population and thus the labor force. Such a staggering loss of life changed the position of Latin America relative to the rest of the world. In 1500, Latin America accounted for 4 percent of the world's population. It did not regain that relative importance until the dawn of the twentieth century. As one can see from the production function, population matters. A higher population means a higher potential labor force. When we present the statistics on the labor force later in the chapter, this demographic catastrophe should be kept in mind. The current labor force of Latin America is far smaller than it could have been under other circumstances.

Changes in the capital stock and technology

Fortunately, changing the size of the labor force is not the only way to increase real GDP. In the previous section, the stock of capital and the level of technology were held constant. Here, we examine what happens if one or both of these variables change. First, let us assume that the economy accumulates more capital. In the usual course of economic activity, all current income is not immediately spent. Usually, both consumers and businesses save part of their current income. Even if a country has only a rudimentary financial system, these savings may be loaned to a business. The business then may use the proceeds of the loan to invest in a new structure and/or plant and equipment. Notice that this new investment is a flow variable that adds to the country's stock of capital. This increase in the country's capital stock changes the production function shown in the previous section. Figure 2.2 illustrates the effect of an increase in a country's capital stock on its production function. The change in the capital stock shifts the production function upward. If the labor force is at L_1, then the level of real GDP given the initial production function is Y_1. An increase in the capital stock shifts the production function from F_1 to F_2. With no change in the labor force, the level of GDP increases from Y_1 to Y_2. The economy can now produce more goods and services for any given size of the labor force. This occurs because the capital-to-labor ratio (K/L) has increased. A worker with more capital can produce more goods or services than one with less. As the average capital-to-labor ratio rises, real GDP rises. The K/L ratio is one of the most important factors in economics. Everything else equal, a worker who has more capital to work with becomes more productive. In other words, the productivity of labor or output per hour is positively correlated with the K/L ratio. This is a critical part of the economic development process in Latin America. The more rapidly an economy can accumulate capital, the faster

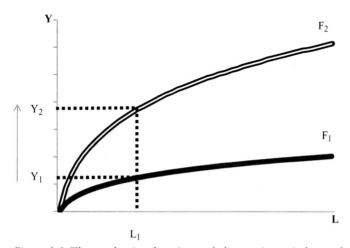

Figure 2.2 The production function and changes in capital or technology

it can grow. Further, increases in the K/L ratio increase the productivity of labor. This is important as changes in real wages are highly correlated with changes in labor productivity. Logically, this means that the higher the K/L ratio for a country is, the higher GDP per capita will be. In a later section of this chapter, data will be presented that illustrates this point.

A similar situation occurs when the level of technology or total factor productivity increases. Remember that technology in this case is the relationship between inputs and output. An improvement in technology should allow the economy to produce more goods and services with the same level of labor *and* capital. In other words, something is happening in the economy that increases the ability to mix labor and capital more efficiently. Graphically, the effect is the same as an increase in the capital stock. An improvement in technology shifts the production function upward from F_1 to F_2. The economy can now increase real GDP from Y_1 to Y_2 in Figure 2.2 with the same amount of labor. However, in this case the stock of capital has not changed. The increase in real GDP occurs solely as the result of being able to utilize the same amount of capital and labor to produce more goods and services.

This basic model explains a substantial part of the process of economic growth for virtually any country. Increases in the labor force, the capital stock, and technology will increase real GDP. Moreover, the model is an excellent place to ground one's thinking about economic growth in Latin America. As a developing region of the world, the population and labor force of Latin America is growing faster than in most developed countries. However, the theoretical concepts described above need to be given some measure of reality. In the next two sections, we will present the data on the labor force and the capital stock of Latin America.

The Latin American labor market

In this section, we will attempt to explain some of the basic data and characteristics of the labor force in Latin America. To understand the economic growth of the region, it is essential to have some idea of where along the production function Latin America lies and how fast the labor force is growing. However, the labor market in any country or region is nothing like a perfectly free market. While the labor market does have most of the characteristics of any other market, these markets are sufficiently special that there is a whole branch of economics dedicated to their study. For our purposes, they are special in two ways. First, labor markets work but they work slowly. Changes in labor markets are noticeably slower than in the market for a commodity such as coffee or soybeans. Second, and more importantly, labor markets are among the most heavily regulated markets in any country, and this is particularly true with respect to Latin America. The result of these factors is that one cannot simply infer the supply of labor from data on the population and the available labor force. Imperfections in the labor markets of the region influence the quantity of labor that is being supplied and what form it takes. In this section we will first present the basic data on population and the labor force in Latin America. From there, we will present a brief discussion of distortions in the labor market that are relatively common. Finally, there are a large number of workers from Latin America working in the US and other developed countries. This phenomenon is having important impacts on the region and needs to be kept in mind when analyzing the Latin American labor market.

The labor force

Table 2.5 shows the basic data on the labor force of Latin America. In 2008, the total number of workers was nearly 250 million. In other words, nearly half of the population of the region is in the work force. Brazil and Mexico alone account for almost 150 million workers. Argentina, Colombia, Peru, and Venezuela have labor forces between 10 and 20 million. In many cases, these statistics fail to capture the millions of workers in the informal sector of the economy. Also, missing from the labor force are the substantial number of workers working either legally or illegally in North America or

Table 2.5 The labor force in Latin America (millions of workers)

	1990	2008
Argentina	13.54	19.07
Bolivia	2.76	4.41
Brazil	62.63	99.95
Chile	5.00	7.68
Colombia	11.16	18.55
Costa Rica	1.16	2.11
Ecuador	3.48	5.74
El Salvador	1.92	2.50
Guatemala	3.09	5.30
Honduras	1.72	2.81
Mexico	29.93	46.71
Nicaragua	1.38	2.28
Panama	0.93	1.60
Paraguay	1.68	2.94
Peru	8.31	13.30
Uruguay	1.40	1.64
Venezuela	7.16	12.72
Latin America	157.25	249.30
HIC	443.50	501.52
MIC	1,622.16	2,159.84
LIC	276.90	441.42
World	2,342.57	3,102.77

Source: World Bank (2010).

Europe. Another way of putting this is that the labor force statistics shown in Table 2.5 can be considered as very conservative. Compared to the world, Latin America contains 8 percent of the global labor force. Officially, this is similar to Latin America's percentage of the world's population.

The total work force would allow one to define L in either Figure 2.1 or 2.2. Once one has established the size of the labor force and the production function, then real GDP becomes easier to ascertain. As shown in Figure 2.1, the labor force of a country or a region usually grows over time. This is especially true of Latin America. In 1990, the labor force of the region was 157 million workers. By 2008, it had grown to nearly 250 million. The region had added almost 100 million workers in 18 years. In percentage terms, the labor force of the region had grown by nearly 60 percent in 18 years. As is usual, this growth contains both benefits and costs. The benefits can be thought of using the production function. The rapid growth in the labor force means a rapid movement along a production function. This can potentially lead to faster economic growth. In this circumstance, such growth is essential. With the labor force growing so rapidly, the economy needs to grow at a fast pace in order to absorb the large number of workers entering the labor force. If GDP growth is slow, then problems of unemployment and underemployment become common. If employment is a problem in the face of a rapidly expanding labor force, then the problem may well be that the production function is not shifting upwards at a fast enough pace. Inadequate shifts in the production function would be a consequence of either a slow rate of growth of capital investment or slow technological change. As we will see later in the chapter, the growth of the capital stock in the region has been something of a problem. However, before considering that possibility we need to cover another problem with the labor markets of the region. As was stated earlier in the chapter, labor markets are among the most heavily regulated markets in any economy. Finding the socially optimal amount of labor market regulation is a difficult task in any economy. As we will see in the next section, this has been a noticeable problem in Latin America.

Labor market distortions

As mentioned above, the labor markets of Latin America do not work perfectly. In every country a variety of government rules and regulations exist that are designed to protect workers from some of the effects of the usual operation of labor markets. This area is so complex that it is impossible to cover the totality of policies that affect labor markets in the region.[6] However, we will attempt to provide some of the basic types of distortions that are common to the region and provide some information on how these distortions affect the performance of labor markets in Latin America relative to other parts of the world. As is usual, one must keep in mind that there is a large amount of variation within the region. For some of these factors mentioned below for some countries the distortions are so large that it is not an exaggeration to say that they may be one of the country's most important economic conditions. In other countries, the overall mix of policies may be troublesome in some regards as the regulations are not totally unrelated to one another.

The factors listed below are among the most important labor market distortions that are common in Latin America. While this list of factors is not exhaustive, it will give one a sense of what the most important issues are.

Job security regulations

In many parts of the world, countries try to enhance job stability by employing labor codes that make it more difficult for firms to adjust the level of their workforces. Specific examples of these codes may include a minimum advance notice for dismissal; the specification of the reasons for dismissal; mandated severance payments; limitations on temporary labor contracts; and consultations with the government prior to large-scale layoffs. While such regulations enhance the security of the existing workforce, they may hinder the creation of jobs in the formal sector of the economy. In this regard, Latin America has the most comprehensive set of job security provisions in the world.[7] In 9 out of 17 countries in the region, an employer must notify a third party before dismissing a redundant worker. Even if a worker can be dismissed, the employer must pay such workers. In Latin America, this "firing tax" is equal to 64 weeks of salary.[8] This hinders the development of more jobs in the formal sector of the economy. Despite more than two decades of economic reforms, these regulations have proven to be very difficult to alter.

Conditions of employment

The conditions of employment cover the various limitations on what employers may ask workers to do in terms of number of hours worked and other conditions of employment. These include the maximum number of hours in a work-week; overtime work; holidays; maternity leave; vacation days; and other conditions of employment. Relative to the rest of the world, Latin America has more restrictive conditions of employment than any region except for Central Asia and Eastern Europe. If such restrictions are the result of a democratic process, then they may not be suboptimal for society. However, they do have a cost. In Latin America, this cost is most clearly seen in the existence of a large, informal labor market. Regulations on conditions of employment have costs as well as benefits.

Social Security regulations

Social Security regulations refer to the payment by employers to designated funds for the retirement of workers, for unemployment compensation, medical payments, or other forms of social insurance. Quite obviously, these form a sort of tax on employers and potentially deter employment. The available evidence indicates that overall these payments in Latin America are not excessive by global standards. However, in a few countries such as Colombia, Panama, Argentina, and Venezuela they are as high as social security payments in developed countries.

The minimum wage

Virtually all countries have a minimum wage and the countries of Latin America are no exception. However, the minimum wage is one of the most contentious issues in economics. As we will see, it has varied effects that make the policy controversial. Relative poverty is a pervasive problem in Latin America and the minimum wage is one of the options that can be used to deal with it. However, the research on the effectiveness of the minimum wage in this regard is hardly conclusive even for developed countries. For developing countries, such as Latin America, the empirical evidence on this issue is relatively scarce. As a result, we will consider some of the larger issues in this debate and attempt to put them into a Latin American context.

A traditional discussion of the minimum wage misses two issues that are important in Latin America. First, the minimum wage has to be effective. In an inflationary environment, if the minimum wage is not indexed or regularly adjusted, then the mandated wage can become irrelevant because in real terms it is at or below the equilibrium wage. Inflation coupled with infrequent adjustments can also make the minimum wage volatile. In the case of Latin America there is evidence that the minimum wage frequently drops in real terms in many countries and is therefore volatile. Also, for the minimum wage to be effective, it must be enforced. In many countries in the region, enforcement is lax. This is often coupled with the existence of multiple minimum wages for various occupational categories that make enforcement more difficult than is the case in other institutional settings. The second issue to be considered is the existence of an informal labor market. In the region, a substantial portion of the labor force is employed in the informal labor market. This means that workers are either self-employed or working in firms that are operating outside of government regulation. Recent estimates indicate that 30 to 70 percent of Latin American workers are in the informal market and 1 to 45 percent earn less than the minimum wage.[9] As a result, the effects of the minimum wage have to consider the effects on the informal as well as the formal labor markets.

Generally, a minimum wage has two conflicting effects. Obviously, it can raise the wages of those who are covered. This enhances the welfare of some of the poor. However, a minimum wage that is above the equilibrium wage can have the effect of depressing the level of employment. Further, the minimum wage can affect wages and employment opportunities in the informal part of the labor market. Conclusions about the effects of the minimum wage in Latin America have to considered carefully as the empirical literature on this subject is not large. Also, a disproportionate number of studies have been done in Brazil. With these caveats, the effects of the minimum wage in the formal labor markets of Latin America are much as one would expect. An increase in the minimum wage tends to decrease employment for low-skilled workers in the formal sector of the economy. There is a demand curve for low-skilled labor and increases in wages for these workers tends to reduce the quantity demanded. However, it does increase the income of those that maintain employment. This is especially the case as in some Latin American countries the minimum wage is used as a benchmark for other occupational categories. As a result, the effects on the overall incomes of the poor are uncertain. It is with respect to the informal labor market that the effects become more interesting. The traditional view of the informal labor market is as a substitute market operating below the formal market. In this case, workers who lose their jobs in the formal labor market may not become unemployed but rather find alternative employment in the informal market. However, this may increase the supply of labor in this market and depress wages. The result is that income losses to low-skilled workers may not be as drastic as in a developed country where there are fewer employment alternatives outside of the formal sector. Also, the minimum wage may be used in some countries as a benchmark for occupational categories other than low-wage workers.[10] In summary, an increase in the minimum wage *may* have positive impacts on the distribution of income in Latin America.

Unions

A discussion of labor market distortions for any country is incomplete without a discussion of the role of labor unions. The main purpose of a labor union is to obtain wages and benefits for workers that are in excess of what would be provided in a free labor market. The conventional wisdom is that labor unions (sindicatos) constitute a significant labor market distortion in Latin America. As usual, the conventional wisdom isn't wrong but needs to be qualified. In the first place, labor unions are a much smaller percentage of the labor force in the area than was once the case. In every country of Latin America, the percentage of the work force that is unionized has declined over the last several decades. There are currently only two countries where slightly over 30 percent of the labor force is unionized (Brazil and Mexico) and only two other countries over 20 percent (Argentina and Nicaragua). For Latin America as a whole, only 14 percent of the labor force is unionized. While this is not trivial, the picture of the region as one where labor unions dominate the labor markets is not quite the case. While labor unions are undoubtedly a potent political force in some countries of the region, in most cases their impact on labor market conditions is not as strong as often imagined and their influence seems to be in long-run decline.

As the material above indicates, the labor markets of Latin America are large, diverse, and subject to substantial distortions. Summarizing this diversity is difficult at best. However, we will attempt to do this using an index developed by the World Bank that ranks the countries of the world according to a variety of conditions in the labor market. The index is constructed from five different variables measuring conditions in the labor market. These are: the difficulty of hiring workers; the rigidity of hours worked; the difficulty of firing workers; the rigidity of employment; and the cost of firing workers expressed in weeks of pay. The result allows one to rank the countries of the world based on the relative flexibility of their labor markets. The results are shown in Table 2.6. The data on labor market flexibility in Latin America summarizes how different the region is in this regard. The average global rank in the area is 126.2. The range runs from 66 to 180. In this regard, Latin America has relatively inflexible labor markets with respect to the world, much less the two high-income countries in the hemisphere. However, there is a noticeable difference here when comparing Latin America to Portugal and Spain. In terms of labor market flexibility, Latin America is very close to these countries. Despite being high-income countries, Portugal and Spain have noticeably inflexible labor markets. Whether or not this similarity is spurious is an intriguing question.

The data shown below helps to explain a number of stylized facts about labor markets in Latin America. First, in line with the purpose of this chapter

Table 2.6 Labor market flexibility in Latin America (world rank)

Argentina	130
Bolivia	180
Brazil	121
Chile	74
Colombia	80
Costa Rica	77
Ecuador	171
El Salvador	87
Guatemala	106
Honduras	156
Mexico	141
Nicaragua	66
Panama	172
Paraguay	177
Peru	149
Uruguay	79
Venezuela	180
Latin America	126
Portugal	164
Spain	160
Canada	18
US	1

Source: World Bank (2008).

there is at least a partial explanation of the relatively poor economic growth performance of the region. It is always hard to explain how a region full of hard-working and relatively well educated workers can produce relatively low economic growth. The mere possession of a quality labor force is not enough. If there are significant barriers to the effective utilization of these workers, then the potential productivity of the labor force is diminished. The negative effects on economic growth are obvious. Secondly, the size of the informal labor market becomes more understandable. If employment in the formal labor market involves a large amount of relatively inflexible rules, then there will be a tendency for employers to evade these regulations in the underground economy. While labor market regulations cannot form a complete explanation for the existence of the informal labor market, it is no doubt contributing to its existence.

As important as labor is to economic development, faster economic growth cannot be obtained without the use of capital. In the next section, we will present the basic data on the stock of capital in Latin America. The interaction between labor and capital can produce impressive rates of economic growth. However, if the growth of the capital stock is low, then economic growth may be low as well. In the next section, our task is to combine the information on the labor force above with information on the capital stock to give a more complete picture of economic growth in the region.

Capital and Latin America

As we indicated earlier in the chapter, an important component of the economic growth process is change in the stock of capital. As the capital stock increases, the production function increases, and GDP rises. As a result, rapid economic growth normally requires rapid increases in the stock of capital. This is especially true when combined with labor to form the aforementioned K/L ratio. As this ratio rises, the productivity of the labor force increases. This is critically important. Increases in labor productivity in the long run lead to increases in real wages. This makes sense as employers can only afford to pay higher wages in real terms if there is a concomitant increase in output per worker. A glimmer of this effect can be seen in Table 2.7. In this table the K/L ratio is given for each country in Latin America, the high-, middle-, and low-income countries, and the world. GDP per capita is shown in the final column. The K/L ratio for Latin America in 2007 was a bit over $2,000. It varies from nearly $4,000 in Argentina and Chile to a low of $516 in Nicaragua. The K/L ratio in Latin America is higher than for the middle-income countries. However, notice that it is substantially below average for the high-income countries. Now compare the K/L ratio to GDP per capita. The correlation between the K/L ratio and GDP per capita is not an illusion. As the K/L ratio rises, GDP per capita tends to rise. Notice that this is not just true for Latin America relative to the

Table 2.7 The capital—labor ratio and GDP per capita in Latin America

	1990		2007	
	Capital-to-labor ratio (K/L)	GDP per capita (constant 2000 US Dollars)	Capital-to-labor ratio (K/L)	GDP per capita (constant 2000 US Dollars)
Argentina	1,580	5,606.9	3,998	9,359.6
Bolivia	269	869.6	377	1,125.0
Brazil	1,397	3,354.8	1,416	4,274.0
Chile	1,490	3,067.0	3,750	6,082.0
Colombia	NA	2,210.3	NA	2,955.3
Costa Rica	1,486	3,111.5	2,191	5,123.7
Ecuador	898	1,296.9	1,053	1,656.5
El Salvador	524	1,571.0	1,117	2,621.7
Guatemala	486	1,446.4	819	1,877.8
Honduras	539	1,049.2	1,059	1,410.1
Mexico	2,413	4,966.3	3,408	6,542.6
Nicaragua	354	681.6	516	885.8
Panama	496	2,939.6	2,584	5,195.6
Paraguay	770	1,394.8	550	1,458.8
Peru	749	1,657.3	1,406	2,692.2
Uruguay	1,353	5,457.8	2,135	8,094.6
Venezuela	1,467	4,823.5	3,818	5,783.8
Latin America	1,389	3,520.7	2,029	4,776.6
HIC	9,446	21,358.9	12,714	28,715.6
MIC	588	1,077.3	1,146	1,900.9
LIC	120	261.2	227	361.2
World	2,208	4,587.0	2,887	5,975.7

Source: World Bank (2010) and computations by authors.

world but is also quite striking *within* Latin America. The relatively more prosperous countries have substantially higher K/L ratio than the poorer countries of the region. Again, this is not a total explanation of the differences in GDP per capita but it is important.

The data given above highlights the critical role of capital in the process of economic development. Everything else equal, the faster the capital stock grows, the faster GDP per capita will grow. The problem for Latin America can be seen from Table 2.7. From 1990 to 2007, the K/L ratio in Latin America increased from $1,389 to $2,029 or 46 percent. For the middle-income countries, the K/L ratio almost doubled. This difference shows up in GDP per capita. For Latin America, GDP per capita increased from $3,521 to $4,776 or 36 percent. For the middle-income countries, GDP per capita increased by 76 percent. To be fair, Latin America started out at a higher stage of development than many middle-income countries. However, on the other hand the K/L ratio of the high-income countries increased by 35 percent over the same time frame. Even accounting for different stages of development, the growth of the K/L ratio in Latin America has been slow. Our next task is to determine why this might be the case.

The data given above is informative, but it is also masking some important issues. If an economy is going to develop rapidly, then either the labor force must grow rapidly, the capital stock must grow rapidly, or the level of technology must improve. More often than not, rapid growth is a function of some combination of the growth of all three. Part of the problem with lagging growth in Latin America has been increases in the capital stock that have not been exceptionally high. This leads to the factors that can cause a large increase in the capital stock. In general terms there are two sources. First, a country could increase its capital stock by increasing the level of domestic savings. Savings generated by the public and the business community could then be funneled through the financial services sector to produce increases in the capital stock. However, in a low- or middle-income country it may be difficult to raise an optimal level of investment out of the available pool of domestic savings. Since savings is a function of income, lower levels of income tend to generate lower levels of savings. This is especially true in the case of Latin America. Relative to their level of income, Latin American countries do not produce the level of savings out of income that one would predict. While the reasons for this deficiency are not perfectly understood, the general sense is that lower levels of saving seem to be positively correlated with economic growth. As a result, it is not surprising that the relatively low levels of economic growth in the region have produced relatively low savings rates.[11] The problem is further exacerbated by somewhat inefficient capital markets. The purpose of capital markets is to efficiently transfer savings into productive investment. To the extent that capital markets are inefficient, then the savings being generated in an economy are not being invested as productively as they could be. Obviously, this produces economic growth that is lower than would occur if the savings were being invested in a more productive fashion. The general sense is that capital markets in Latin America are not as well developed as they could be given the income of the region and that this is a negative factor in terms of economic growth.[12]

The data on this problem can be seen in Table 2.8. The percentage of GDP that is being saved is given for all of the countries of Latin America. In 1990, FDI as a percentage of GDP was less than 1 percent.[13] For any country, this would be a relatively low figure. For most countries, the national savings rates were low by the standards of middle-income countries. The sum of FDI and savings for the region in 1990 was less than 20 percent. Under most circumstances, this percentage is unlikely to lead to a large increase in the production function or rapid economic growth. The data for 2007 is a perfect example of the positive changes that have occurred in the region over the last 20 years. FDI as a percentage of GDP has increased to nearly 3 percent. Savings as a percentage of GDP has increased by nearly 3 percent. Putting FDI and savings together, the amount of money being invested in the region has increased by nearly 5 percent. This sort of increase is the kind of trend that leads to more rapid economic growth.

New growth theory

The theory of economic growth described above is correct, as far as it goes. However, the theory is an incomplete explanation of the process of economic growth. Part of this incompleteness lies in the basic theory, reinforced by the empirical implementation of the theory. The primary problem is that the model does not explain technology or total factor productivity. This is assumed to be determined by factors outside the model. This is frequently referred to as the condition where technology is *exogenous*. As we will see later on in the chapter, this is an unsatisfactory state of affairs, especially with regard to Latin America. Empirically this meant that total factor productivity was being computed as a residual. Once one accounted for the amount of economic growth caused by changes in labor and the stock of capital, then any growth not accounted for was attributable to changes in total factor productivity. Determining something as important as total factor productivity by examining the residual of a regression equation creates more questions than it answers. Just what is determining what this variable is?

New growth theory has evolved since the 1980s in order to address this problem. In these newer models of the growth process, the level of technology is *endogenous*. That is, it is now explicitly in the model with other variables determining the level of technology. A key feature of these models is that the level of technology and by implication, the level of economic growth, can be enhanced by the accumulation of knowledge. More knowledge can increase the level of technology and become a driver of economic growth. Knowledge has another important characteristic. It can be accumulated without the constraint of diminishing returns. Indeed knowledge is usually subject to

Table 2.8 FDI and savings in Latin America

	1990			2008		
	FDI % of GDP	Savings % of GDP	Total as % of GDP	FDI % of GDP	Savings % of GDP	Total as % of GDP
Argentina	1.3	16.0	17.3	3.0	25.0	27.9
Bolivia	0.6	9.7	10.3	3.1	29.0	32.1
Brazil	0.2	18.9	19.1	2.9	17.2	20.0
Chile	2.1	23.7	25.8	9.9	22.2	32.1
Colombia	1.2	21.6	22.9	4.3	19.3	23.7
Costa Rica	2.2	11.6	13.8	6.8	15.5	22.4
Ecuador	1.2	11.2	12.5	1.8	30.8	32.6
El Salvador	0.0	12.2	12.2	3.5	7.7	11.3
Guatemala	0.6	10.7	11.3	2.1	14.2	16.3
Honduras	1.4	21.1	22.6	6.6	20.7	27.2
Mexico	1.0	20.3	21.2	2.1	24.9	27.0
Nicaragua[1]	0.1	15.7	15.8	6.7	14.3	21.0
Panama	2.6	24.2	26.7	10.4	26.2	36.6
Paraguay	1.5	19.7	21.1	2.0	15.9	17.9
Peru	0.2	16.5	16.6	3.2	22.5	25.6
Uruguay	0.4	14.1	14.5	6.9	17.9	24.8
Venezuela	1.0	27.2	28.2	0.1	34.7	34.8
Latin America	0.7	19.2	19.9	2.9	21.9	24.8

Source: World Bank (2010) and computations by authors.
[1] 2007 data used for Nicaragua

increasing returns rather than diminishing returns. If the accumulation of knowledge is important to economic growth, then obviously it is of some interest to understand what would enhance the accumulation of knowledge. In this regard, two factors are commonly thought to be important. First, the level of education in a society matters. The ability of the population to create and just as importantly understand and use new knowledge becomes extremely important. Another way of expressing this is the accumulation of human capital in an economy matters. Human capital is the education, training, and job skills embodied in labor which increases its productivity. Along with human capital, investments in research and development (R&D) also can enhance the level of knowledge. This is by no means an exhaustive list of factors that can change the level of technology and economic growth. Part of the reason these are important factors is that they can to some extent be quantified. In terms of Latin America, the former is more critical than the latter. Most of the world's research and development occurs in the developed countries where the conditions are most favorable for this kind of activity. To a certain extent this is a positive thing for developing regions such as Latin America. Potentially it gives them the opportunity to acquire knowledge inexpensively through trade or FDI.

While new growth theory is relatively easy to grasp as a concept, it is not quite so easy to quantify. Although a number of different measures have been proposed, the most usual way to look at the human capital of a country is to examine the educational attainment of the population.[14] The basic data on this is shown in Table 2.9 below. For a developing country, the first order of business is the reduction of illiteracy to as low a level as possible. One of the greatest success stories in Latin America is the low level of illiteracy. Literacy rates in the region are now approaching the standards prevalent in high-income countries. This is no mean feat as many developing countries remain mired in poverty as a result of the failure of the government to accomplish this basic function. Past primary education, the data for the region is less promising. For countries for which there is data for both the 1990s and the present decade, there has been some improvement in the number of students finishing secondary education and moving on to tertiary education. However, the situation is worse than the data in the table indicates. Even for those students that remain in school, the average quality or actual educational attainment of students that remain in school is low by international standards.[15] The problem is not necessarily the percentage of GDP being spent on education relative to other middle-income countries but the utilization of these resources. Making secondary and higher education more effective in Latin America is one of the most pressing problems in the region.[16]

For a middle-income country, research and development (R&D) is a less important factor in economic growth. R&D is a form of investment that societies make. With so many pressing investment needs in Latin America, both in the public and the private sector, it is not surprising that the level of R&D is low. For Latin America, the percentage of GDP accounted for

Table 2.9 Educational attainment in Latin America

	80s	90s				2000s			
	Literacy rate (% of people ages 15 and above)	Literacy rate (% of people ages 15 and above)	Labor force with (as % of total) — Primary education	Secondary education	Tertiary education	Literacy rate (% of people ages 15 and above)	Labor force with (as % of total) — Primary education	Secondary education	Tertiary education
Argentina	93.9	96.1	46.4	22.5	15.2	97.2	38.3	32.5	27.8
Bolivia	74.6	80.0	15.0	15.8	6.4	88.7	49.7	24.3	14.2
Brazil	91.1		34.5	49.4	12.6	88.7	42.9	28.9	8.6
Chile		94.3	25.1	49.9	22.9	95.7	24.6	48.8	25.2
Colombia		86.3	54.0	17.9	12.6	92.7			
Costa Rica	92.6					94.9	59.0	19.1	16.9
Ecuador	83.6	88.3				87.6	32.4	39.5	25.4
El Salvador		74.1	42.0	15.1	23.8	82.8			
Guatemala		64.2				69.1	58.3	12.2	5.4
Honduras						81.8			
Mexico	83.0	87.6	43.0	21.0	16.9	91.3	43.9	21.1	21.7
Nicaragua			58.6	8.8	6.0	77.3			
Panama	88.1	88.8	44.9	28.5	11.1	91.9	41.3	28.1	22.5
Paraguay	78.5	90.3	63.5	25.3	7.0	94.6	61.5	22.3	13.5
Peru	81.9	87.2	22.4	45.8	25.2	88.5	16.2	49.2	33.1
Uruguay	95.4	96.8				97.8	53.1	22.8	17.3
Venezuela	84.7	89.8				94.1			
Portugal	79.4	87.9	68.6	10.9	10.5	94.6	68.0	13.5	11.5
Spain	92.8	96.5	54.3	16.8	22.3	97.8	48.3	21.6	29.6
Canada			20.6	34.6	44.8		15.8	41.4	42.8
US			14.3	52.0	33.7		10.9	35.4	53.8

Source: World Bank (2010).

by R&D is approximately 0.5. Only Brazil and Venezuela have R&D spending approaching 1 percent of GDP. For the poorer countries of the region, this percentage is far less.[17] This should not be considered a large drag on economic growth in the region. With respect to R&D, the problem in Latin America has been the historically closed nature of the economies of the region. R&D normally is produced for the most part in high-income countries. The new technology that results from this is then transferred to the developing countries directly or indirectly through FDI or international trade. Interfering with the flows of FDI or restricting imports impairs this process. As we will see in later chapters, these impediments to FDI and imports have been substantial in the economic history of Latin America. The result is that technology transfers have not been as high as they could have been and may have slowed growth somewhat.[18] However, economic situations change over time and economic growth will make R&D a more important factor. There are already firms in Latin America which produce the sort of high-technology products for which R&D is a critical input. Indeed, you've probably already flown in one, i.e. an Embraer jet made in Brazil. At this point, such firms are not the average in the region but over time their number will grow.

At this point, we need to put some empirical content on the theory described in the earlier parts of the chapter. To review a bit, the basic theory of economic growth posits that economic growth is a function of increases in the size of land; the labor force; increases in the stock of capital; and improvements in total factor productivity. The new theory of economic growth adds two factors: increases in the amount of human capital and investment in research and development. While the basic theory and later modifications seem logical, it is always necessary to test theory against the data. This allows one to accomplish two things. First, it can tell you if the theory is correct or if it needs to be modified. Secondly, with respect to economic growth, empirical testing of the theory can be informative in a policy sense. Economic growth in Latin America is no different. In the next section, we will consider how the results of tests of economic growth in the region can be used to explain past policy problems and potential modifications in the future.

Growth accounting in Latin America

So far in this chapter we have considered the theory of economic growth and how it applies to Latin America. In considering each factor, we have discussed the data and some of implications of this data for economic growth in the region. What has been missing is some sense of "putting it all together" so to speak. As we will see, statisticians and economists have formulated a way of putting most of the factors together in a comprehensible way. In the jargon of the literature this is referred to as growth accounting. There are obviously a number of factors that influence economic growth. Each of them has a part to play in explaining why the growth of a country or a region has been what it was in the past. By explaining past periods of economic growth, one can perhaps see what went right or wrong over time. In the case of Latin America, such exercises are critical. The growth of the region is generally agreed to have been lower than it could have been. As a result, the results of a growth accounting exercise for Latin America are more than ordinarily important. What we will find is both illuminating and frustrating. Using growth accounting, we'll be able to narrow the scope of the problem of economic growth in Latin America. The bad news is that there is no magic bullet that will suddenly transform Latin America into East Asia. The good news is that the exercises indicate where the bulk of the problems are and that conceptually these problems can be remedied over time.

In accounting for growth in a country or region, economists usually put the theory we have described earlier in the chapter into a regression equation. With respect to economic growth, the equation usually takes the form of:

$$Y = F(K, L, H, A) \tag{2.1}$$

where:
Y = real GDP
K = the stock of capital
L = the labor force
H = human capital
A = total factor productivity

Equation 2.1 simply is expressing the relationship between economic growth and the factors that cause growth. In the equation, the growth of real GDP is expressed as a function of the growth of the labor force, the capital stock, human capital, and total factor productivity.[19] The use of statistics to analyze economic data is known as econometrics. The particular statistical tool being employed in this case is regression analysis. The data used in the analysis is available for the countries of Latin America for the last 50 years.[20] The exercise in growth accounting is straightforward. Economic growth (Y) becomes the dependent variable in a regression equation. Data on the labor force, the capital stock, and human capital is now readily obtainable. One can now "run" the regression through a large variety of statistical software packages. The results allow one to interpret the effects of changes in the labor force, the capital stock, and human capital on economic growth in a relatively straightforward way. The same cannot be said for total factor productivity. The effect of this factor is not measured directly, but indirectly. In a regression equation, there is a component known as the residual. The residual is where the effects of all factors not explicitly accounted for such as labor and capital are lumped together in one place. In growth accounting, the value of the residual is interpreted as a proxy for total factor productivity. This is a convenient convention, but for Latin America this residual turns out to be critically important.

Despite the explosion of econometric studies on economic growth, the number of specific studies on Latin America is rather small. Since these studies tend to produce rather consistent results, we will focus on a recent study by Fernandez-Arias *et al.* (2005).[21] The results of this particular study are shown in Table 2.10 below. The first column shows the average annual growth rate of real GDP per capita in Latin America from 1960 to 1999. While this growth of 1.25 percent is positive, it is a low number by international standards. The next four columns show the breakdown of this growth in terms of growth accounting. As one would expect, the growth of the labor force accounted for 0.43 percent of total growth. Slow population growth is not the source of the problem. The same is true of changes in the capital stock. This factor was contributing to 0.55 percent of total growth. At this point, notice that a very simple model of economic growth is accounting for a substantial amount of the total economic growth of the region. However, the importance of adding human capital can clearly be seen. Only by a small margin is human capital accumulation the second most important positive factor in economic growth in Latin America. While the educational system of the region leaves much to be desired, it is still contributing to economic growth. The final column shows the contribution of total factor productivity. The negative sign preceding 0.25 percent is not an error. In this study, total factor productivity growth in Latin America was negative for three decades. In terms of economic growth, this is an astonishing result. Unfortunately, for Latin America this is not uncommon. Virtually all studies of economic growth in the region report that TFP growth is, at best, relatively low. It is not the whole story of the relatively slow growth of the region but it is a substantial part of it.

To put together the entire picture of Latin American economic growth, comparisons with other parts of the world are useful. Table 2.11 shows the differences in the rate of growth of various factors in Latin America minus similar growth in the rest of the world, the developed countries, and East Asia. In these sorts of comparisons, two factors are critical. First, growth in Latin America is not constrained by growth in the labor force. The labor force of Latin America has been growing faster than most of the rest of the world. The accumulation of human capital does not seem to be the major problem. Human capital growth is only slightly behind the

Table 2.10 Growth accounting in Latin America, 1960–1999

GDP per capita	1.25
Labor	0.43
Skills	0.52
Capital	0.55
Total Factor Productivity	–0.25

Source: Fernandez-Arias *et al.* (2005).

Table 2.11 Differences in growth among world regions

	GDP per capita Growth	Labor	Skills	Capital	TFP
Rest of the World	−1.25	0.19	−0.01	−0.35	−1.07
Developed	−1.38	0.02	0.14	−0.38	−1.16
East Asia	−4.19	−0.33	−0.13	−1.62	−2.11

Source: Fernandez-Arias *et al.* (2005).

rest of the world and as one would expect has been high relative to the Developed Countries. Human capital is important for growth, but is not the most important factor.[22] Clearly, the accumulation of capital is a significant problem. Capital is contributing noticeably less to economic growth in Latin America than it is to growth in the rest of the world. In particular, the contribution of capital to growth in Latin America is one of main reasons it has not grown as fast as many other developing countries.[23] The bulk of the problem is total factor productivity. Compared to the rest of the world total factor productivity growth in Latin America is the largest contributor to the differences in growth. This is precisely what one would expect. Normally, total factor productivity growth is positive in an economy. Putting the usual positive growth for most of the rest of the world together with negative or slow growth of this factor in Latin America yields this result.[24]

A standard growth accounting framework has allowed us to do two things in this section. First, we were able to see what has caused economic growth in the region over the last three decades. A standard growth model augmented with some of the newer growth theory explains Latin American growth fairly well. In comparing Latin America to the rest of the world, the picture that emerges is not so encouraging. The accumulation of capital in the region lags behind what is occurring in the rest of the world. This is a problem that we will return to later in the book. The most serious problem of economic growth in Latin America is the growth of total factor productivity. In the next section, we will try to provide some understanding of why this problem exists.

Institutions and growth in Latin America

The information in the previous section allows us to narrow our discussion of relatively low economic growth in Latin America. Unfortunately, these results leave us in a somewhat unsatisfactory position. Much of the problem lies with the peculiar behavior of total factor productivity in Latin America. On this subject, the state of knowledge in economics is relatively poor. There are a host of factors that could account for this problem but the state of the theoretical literature is rather thin and the empirical literature even more so. This is a preface to what follows in this section. The problem has been identified but it is still poorly understood. The reader should be aware that the work on these issues is very preliminary and none of what follows should be considered anything like absolute knowledge. Rather, this material should be thought of as a list of promising leads in the search for an explanation of differences in total factor productivity among countries or regions. The discussion will proceed in three steps. First, we will explain the theoretical and empirical literature on institutions and growth and put them into a Latin American context. Second, we will review the limited empirical literature on institutional quality and economic growth in Latin America. Finally, we will review various commonly used measures of institutional quality and present the data for Latin America to illustrate the depth of the problem for the region.

Institutions and economic growth

> The Spanish colonies, therefore, from the moment of their first establishment, attracted very much the attention of their mother country; while those of the other European nations were for a long time in a great measure neglected.
>
> Adam Smith

In a sense, economists have known for a long time that the quality of institutions can affect economic growth. We alluded to this earlier in the chapter by pointing out that effective property rights and the rule of law were essential preconditions to economic growth. In this section, we are refining that basic idea. Institutional quality is far more complicated than just these two factors in general. Also, they are not binary variables. A country does not have the rule of law or property rights or not have them. As we saw earlier there are various degrees to which these factors apply. In addition, there are other measures of institutional quality that may be important for economic growth. What follows is a very condensed version of the state of knowledge on institutions and growth and how it may apply to Latin America. The modern study of institutions and growth can be traced back to the work of Ronald Coase, Douglass North, and others. Although this area of study has many variants, it usually is referred to as the "New Institutional Economics."[25] The basic idea of this literature is that economic growth is critically dependent on the quality of institutions in a country. There are startling differences in the level of economic development among countries or even regions that cannot be explained purely on the basis of growth in the labor force, the capital stock, or human capital. Much of the early work in this area was done by economic historians who focused on identifying institutional factors that tended to encourage economic growth or in their absence seemed to retard this process. In a Latin American context, the Peruvian economist Hernando de Soto pointed out the importance of institutional factors using Peru as a case study. Specifically, he demonstrated that the lack of well-defined property rights and extremely onerous business regulation was reducing the growth of the Peruvian economy.[26] The institutional approach to economic development has been an excellent point of departure for subsequent research. As de Soto's work has shown, it can provide critical insights to certain aspects of economic development. However, it left many questions unanswered and left economists in search of more general explanations concerning the relationship between institutional quality and economic growth.

Work on this problem progressed rapidly in the last two decades. As we will see, the newer research is not so much a departure from earlier work as an elaboration of previous findings. The research can be summarized in two complementary hypotheses.

The geography hypothesis

One of the most striking empirical regularities in economic development is the inverse correlation between proximity to the equator and GDP per capita. In its simplest form, the geography hypothesis uses geographic, climatic, and ecological differences to explain differences in GDP per capita. There are at least three different variants of this hypothesis. First, it is usually believed that a tropical climate may tend to lower labor productivity. Second, in a historical sense, the level of technology has been higher in temperate climates than in tropical climates. Third, Sachs (2001) has asserted that tropical climates carry a "disease burden" that is higher than that of temperate climates. As we will see, there is not much support for the geography hypothesis as a single explanation for relative economic performance. However, it is obvious that the second variant applies to Latin America. The technology available in precolonial Latin America was on average lower than that in Western Europe. Also, tropical diseases are prevalent in parts of Latin America closest to the equator. These diseases are capable of killing large numbers of people on an indiscriminate basis. At a minimum, the presence of such diseases is not a positive factor in terms of economic growth.

The institutions hypothesis

The institutions hypothesis simply is a summary of what we have already discussed. In this view a critical factor in economic development is the quality of a country's institutions that may enhance the probability of faster economic growth. Poor institutional quality is widely viewed as one of the most serious impediments to economic growth in Latin America.

The most recent research in this area is a fascinating combination of the two hypotheses.[27] Modern economic history starts around 1500, which is conveniently close to the intrusion of Europeans into Latin America.

The research starts with the assumption that the institutions hypothesis is critical. However, the institutions that European powers set up in the colonies were not uniform. It varied depending on the conditions the Europeans encountered. On the one hand, suppose the colonial powers encountered relatively low population density and the absence of tropical diseases. This situation would encourage the large-scale settlement of the area with migrants from Europe. In such a case, it would be logical to export as well the laws, customs, and institutions of the home country. This sort of situation could lead to subsequent economic growth. A combination of low population density coupled with a variant of the geography hypothesis can lead to a positive economic outcome.

A different set of conditions could lead to a less favorable outcome. If settler mortality was high per the geography hypothesis and the indigenous population was large enough to provide the necessary labor force, then the colonial power had an incentive to set up an *extractive state*. Since mass colonization was not possible, the income maximizing solution for the colonial power was to set up a system of government with little respect for property rights and no serious check on the power of the colonial government. This is a particularly poignant explanation for Latin America. The discovery of large quantities of gold and silver coupled with an initially large indigenous population made this outcome more probable. Past the initial wealth of precious metals, the list of valuable commodities available for exploitation in Latin America is long. Unlike the former example, the mechanisms of an extractive state are not favorable for long-run economic growth. Property rights and the rule of law were not a high priority for the colonial governments. How could they be when the initial conditions were the theft of property from the indigenous population and the forced use of workers to extract valuable minerals? As we will see in Chapters 4 and 5, the conditions in colonial Latin America were almost tailor made for the creation of an extractive state.

The argument presented above is compelling, but one must keep in mind that it is not conclusive. Much more research will need to be done before the logic and initial empirical work described above can be taken as "fact." With that said, an interesting extension of this research comes into play. Latin America gained its independence from the colonial powers in the 1820s. If the region was left at that point with a legacy of poor institutional quality, then why has this problem persisted for nearly 200 years? At this point, there is no clear answer to that question. Recent research into this question points to the ability of elites within a society to continue to dominate the political process. While the form of government may be important, what is more important is the possession of de facto power by the local elites. If income and wealth are dependent on the possession of land, broadly defined, then the local elites have a strong incentive to maintain a political system that may not be terribly different from that inherited from the former colonial powers.[28] The effect on economic policy would be predictable. It becomes very difficult to obtain the sort of economic policies that tend to foster rapid economic growth. As you move through the book, it is important to keep this argument in mind. In many areas, public policy in Latin America has been an impediment to growth. Also, in many cases, the existence of these policies may be familiar in terms of the reasoning discussed in this section. In the case of Latin America this has led to an active literature on the institutional factors that lead to public policy outcomes. As we will see in many of the chapters that follow, economic policy in Latin America has changed significantly over the last three decades. The institutional environment on average is becoming more like that observed in developed countries and the faster-growing middle-income countries. However, the process is nothing like smooth and continuous. The process has produced a lively literature on the institutional and political factors that influence economic policy.[29] The discussion above indicates the importance of institutional quality for economic growth. It was shown that this has been a persistent problem in Latin America for centuries. The next logical step is to think about the problem in more quantitative terms. In other words, can the problem be put into a statistical form that makes it easier to understand and aid in the design of policy. In the next section, we review the empirical literature on institutional quality and economic growth in Latin America.

Empirical evidence on institutional quality and growth

> The determinants of TFP are quite difficult to grasp.
>
> Andres Solimano and Raimundo Soto

As one might expect, the empirical literature on institutional quality and economic growth in Latin America is rather small. This is partially understandable. Economists spent much of the 1960s and 1970s refining the basic model of economic growth described earlier in the chapter. The 1980s saw the development and testing of newer models incorporating human capital and the role of R&D. The research on economic growth has only recently been focused on the critical role of total factor productivity. Once this was established, explaining what causes differences among countries is not an easy thing. As a result, it is not surprising that empirical research on total factor productivity in Latin America is rather thin. However, the few studies on this issue are yielding predictable results. Relatively low total factor productivity in Latin America has now been tentatively linked to factors that are not surprising given the history and nature of the region.

The earliest study to consider these issues in any systematic way is Taylor (1998). While this study focuses on low capital investment in Latin America, it contains an early attempt to quantify certain economic policies that adversely impact total factor productivity. The study isolates three policies in this regard: the existence of a black market for foreign exchange, the depth of the financial markets, and the relative price of capital. As we will see in subsequent chapters, all of these policies distort domestic economic activity and have the potential to lower economic activity. A more recent study by Cole *et al.* (2005) is in a similar vein. The study documents more carefully that the most important cause of lagging economic growth in Latin America is the poor performance of total factor productivity. They go on to show that a potential source of this problem is external and internal barriers to competition. These sorts of problems are well understood and will be covered in more detail in Chapters 6 and 7 of the book. In a similar vein, Chong and Zanforlin (2004) examine institutional factors that may influence growth in the region. Two of the major findings of this study are that openness to international trade enhances growth which is not surprising given that this is virtually conventional wisdom. However, as we will see, barriers to trade were extreme in Latin America during the twentieth century and so were a more important factor in suppressing growth than in other regions. Second, a measure of institutional quality used in this study was found to be an important factor in economic growth of the region.

At this point return to the same study that we used earlier to examine growth accounting in Latin America. Following on the previously reported results, the authors then attempted to isolate factors that governments can influence that were related in a statistically significant sense to low total factor productivity in Latin America. A similar set of factors was found to be important in a study by de Gregorio and Lee (2004). These factors were:

- *Institutional quality* – Institutional quality was measured using the International Country Risk Guide. This proxy includes risk of repudiation of contracts by government, risk of expropriation, corruption, rule of law, and bureaucratic quality.
- *Inflation* – As we will see in Chapter 10, inflation has been a chronic economic problem in Latin America. A high inflation rate coupled with large changes in the rate of inflation can seriously distort economic decisions. Everything else equal, countries with higher inflation tend to grow more slowly than countries with more stable prices.
- *Openness* – As mentioned above, one of the most established relationships in economic growth is that between a country's openness to foreign trade and growth. During much of the twentieth century, Latin American governments made a conscious policy choice to make their economies more closed to international trade.

Despite the rather small size of the existing literature, there is a strong consensus forming that institutional quality and government policies have lowered economic growth in Latin America relative to much of the rest of the world. The bad news is that decades of these policy choices cannot be retrieved. The good news is that faster economic growth in Latin America may be achievable with actions that the governments of the region can control. In the final section, we will examine where Latin America is in terms of institutional quality to see just how much ground the region needs to make up in this area.

Measures of institutional quality

One of the difficulties in quantifying the effects of institutional quality on economic growth in Latin America is the problem of defining just what constitutes institutional quality. Remember that the research in this area is relatively new, so no one at this point can answer that question with any real precision. Some of the factors that are important in this context were discussed earlier in the chapter: the rule of law, respect for property rights, an independent judiciary, etc. In this section, we will not attempt to come to any definitive answer to that question. Rather, we will present data for a number of different indexes of institutional quality and look for a common story. That story can be seen from the numbers presented in Table 2.12 below.

Table 2.12 contains four different measures of institutional quality that are widely available for most of the countries in the world. Each cell in the table represents a country's global rank on this measure. The first column

Table 2.12 Measures of institutional quality in Latin America

	Corruption (world rank)	Government effectiveness (world rank)	Doing business (world rank)	Competitiveness (world rank)
Argentina	109	102	113	88
Bolivia	102	170	150	118
Brazil	80	101	125	64
Chile	23	30	40	28
Colombia	70	90	53	74
Costa Rica	47	68	117	59
Ecuador	151	185	136	104
El Salvador	67	110	72	79
Guatemala	96	145	112	84
Honduras	126	142	133	82
Mexico	72	84	56	60
Nicaragua	134	180	107	120
Panama	85	75	81	58
Paraguay	138	174	115	124
Peru	72	132	62	83
Uruguay	23	60	109	75
Venezuela	158	177	174	105
Latin America	91.4	119.1	135	82.6
Portugal	32	43	48	43
Spain	28	41	49	29
Canada	9	8	8	10
US	18	18	3	1

Source: World Bank (2008), Transparency International (2008), World Economic Forum (2008).

contains the widely cited measure of corruption in a country produced by Transparency International. This is the first measure presented for a reason. Ask virtually anyone in a developed country what the most important problem is in Latin America and the answer is, invariably, corruption. Of course, corruption is a problem in the region. However, a glance at the table indicates that this is hardly peculiar to Latin America. Notice that the regional average shows that Latin America is rather average by global standards. Further, the region is nothing like uniform with respect to corruption. For some reason, the common perception of corruption in Latin America is not totally consistent with the data. The next column presents the rankings for Latin America reported by the World Bank on the ease of doing business in a country. It is a composite of factors involved in running a business such as employing workers, paying taxes, enforcing contracts, etc. It is here that one can visualize the difficulties of doing business in the region. The regional average is worse than the global average and there are many countries where doing business is obviously relatively difficult. This difficulty in doing business is compounded by relatively ineffective governments. Again the World Bank publishes data on government effectiveness around the world. On this measure, the governments of Latin America are relatively ineffective. Comparing these numbers to corruption, the latter is hardly the region's most serious problem. While none of these indexes are definitive, the overall picture is of a region with moderate problems with corruption, a poor business environment, and relatively ineffective governments. Under these circumstances, the econometric evidence presented in the previous section should not be surprising. Raising total factor productivity in this kind of environment would not be easy.

Despite the bleak data on institutional quality, there must be something about the region past these numbers. The final column presents data from executive surveys gathered by the World Economic Forum. This data is a ranking gathered from a composite of indicators on social and economic conditions in a country that make it more or less competitive in the world economy. Rather than being worse than the global average, the index of competitiveness is far better than the other reported measures. These numbers are representing something. It is obviously not honest government officials, a good business environment, or effective government. This data is derived from surveys of business executives. Executives are usually thinking not just about the present but the future. Perhaps the data is simply expressing expectations. If so, the economic future of Latin America looks brighter.

Key concepts and terms

capital-to-labor ratio (K/L) – the amount of capital per unit of labor used in the production of goods and services.

econometrics – the use of statistical techniques to analyze economic data.

geography hypothesis – the idea that geographic, climatic, and ecological factors can affect economic growth.

growth accounting – an examination of the factors that explain economic growth in a country or region.

human capital – the education, training, and job skills embodied in labor which increases its productivity.

institutions hypothesis – the idea that the quality of a country's institutions are a major determinant of its economic growth.

production function – a graph showing the relationship between real GDP and the factors of production.

total factor productivity – an increase in GDP not accounted for by changes in the labor force or the stock of capital.

Questions for review and discussion

1　List and describe some of the factors that influence the application of the rule of law in Latin America.

2　Explain why an independent judiciary is important in the application of the rule of law. What are the dimensions of this problem in Latin America?

3　Describe the changes in population in Latin America in the sixteenth century. Using the production function, show how this affected past and current economic growth.

4　Explain why an increase in the K/L ratio would tend to increase GDP per capita.

5　List and describe various labor market distortions that are common in Latin America. What does this mean in terms of economic growth? How could this lead to a large informal labor market?

6　Describe the effects of an increase in K on the production function. If Latin America had higher savings and FDI, what would this mean in terms of economic growth?

7　Using growth accounting, explain why Latin America tends to have relatively slow economic growth.

8　What is the link between institutional quality and economic growth? How has this affected economic growth in Latin America?

9　Describe how the geography hypothesis might apply to Latin America.

10　Corruption is the most pressing economic problem in Latin America. Explain why this statement is true or not.

References and recommended readings

Acemoglu, Daron, Simon Johnson, and James A. Robinson. 2001. "The Colonial Origins of Comparative Development: An Empirical Investigation." *American Economic Review* 91 (December): 1369–1401.

Acemoglu, Daron, Simon Johnson, and James A. Robinson. 2002. "Reversal of Fortune: Geography and Institutions in the Making of the Modern World Income Distribution." *Quarterly Journal of Economics* 117 (November): 1231–94.

Acemoglu, Daron and James A. Robinson. 2008. "The Persistence and Change of Institutions in the Americas," *Southern Economic Journal* 75 (October): 282–99.

Barro, Robert J. and Jong-Wha Lee. 2001a. "International Data on Educational Attainment: Updates and Implications," *Oxford Economic Papers*, 53 (July): 541–63.

Barro, Robert J. and Jong-Wha Lee. 2001b. "Schooling Quality in a Cross-Section of Countries," *Economica* 68 (November): 465–88.

Bils, Mark and Peter J. Klenow. 2000. "Does Schooling Cause Growth?" *American Economic Review* 90 (December): 1160–83.

Blyde, Juan. 2004. "Trade and Technology Diffusion in Latin America," *International Trade Journal* 18 (Fall): 177–97.

Chong, Alberto and Luisa Zanforlin. 2004. "Inward-looking Policies, Institutions, Autocrats, and Economic Growth in Latin America: An Empirical Exploration." *Public Choice* 121 (December): 335–61.

Cole, Harold L., Lee E. Ohanian, Alvaro Riascos, and James A. Schmitz, Jr. 2005. "Latin America in the Rearview Mirror." *Journal of Monetary Economics* 52 (January): 69–107.

de Gregorio, Jose and Jong-Wha Lee. 2004. "Growth and Adjustment in East Asia and Latin America." *Economia* 5 (Fall): 69–115.

de la Torre, Augusto, Juan Carlos Gozzi, and Sergio L. Schmukler. 2006. "Capital Market Adjustment: Whither Latin America?" *World Bank Policy Research Working Paper: 4156.* Washington, DC: World Bank.

de Soto, Hernando. 1989. *The Other Path.* New York: Basic Books.

di Gropello, Emanuela (ed.). 2006. *Meeting the Challenges of Secondary Education in Latin America and East Asia: Improving Efficiency and Resource Mobility.* Washington, DC: World Bank.

di Tella, Rafael, Sebastian Galiani, and Ernesto Schargrodsky. 2007. "The Formation of Beliefs: Evidence from the Allocation of Land Titles to Squatters," *Quarterly Journal of Economics* 122 (February): 209–41.

Djankov, J., R. La Porta, F. Lopez-de-Silanes, A. Shleifer, and J. Botero. 2003. *The Regulation of Labor.* NBER Working Paper 7892. Cambridge, MA: National Bureau of Economic Research.

Fernandez-Arias, Eduardo, Rodolfo Manuelli, and Juan S. Blyde. 2005. "Why Latin America is Falling Behind," pp. 3–54 in Eduardo Fernandez-Arias, Rodolfo Manuelli, and Juan Blyde (eds.), *Sources of Growth in Latin America: What is Missing?* Washington, DC: Interamerican Development Bank.

Field, Erica. 2007. "Entitled to Work: Urban Property Rights and Labor Supply in Peru," *Quarterly Journal of Economics* 122 (November): 1561–1602.

Gimenez, Gregorio. 2005. "The Human Capital Endowment of Latin America and the Caribbean," *CEPAL Review* 86 (August): 97–116.

Henisz, Witold. 2000. "The Institutional Environment for Economic Growth," *Economics and Politics* 12 (March): 1–31.

Hofman, Andre A. 2000. *The Economic Development of Latin America in the Twentieth Century*. Northampton, MA: Edward Elgar.

Interamerican Development Bank. 2004. *Good Jobs Wanted: Labor Markets in Latin America: 2004 Report*. Washington, DC: Interamerican Development Bank.

Interamerican Development Bank. 2006. *The Politics of Policies, Economic and Social Progress in Latin America: 2006 Report*. Washington, DC: Interamerican Development Bank.

Klein, Herbert S. and Ben Vinson, III. 2007. *African Slavery in Latin America and the Caribbean*. New York: Oxford University Press.

Kristensen, Nicolai and Wendy Cunningham. 2006. "Do Minimum Wages in Latin America and the Caribbean Matter? Evidence from 19 Countries." *World Bank Policy Research Working Paper Series: 3870*. Washington, DC: World Bank.

Lemos, Sara. 2007. "The Effects of the Minimum Wage in the Private and Public Sectors in Brazil." *Journal of Development Studies* 43 (December): 700–20.

Loayza, Norman, Pablo Fajnzylber, and Cesar Calderon. 2005. *Economic Growth in Latin America and the Caribbean: Stylized Facts, Explanations, and Forecasts*. Washington, DC: World Bank.

Maddison, Angus. 2001. *The World Economy: A Millennial Perspective*. Paris: OECD.

Maloney, William. 2004. "Informality Revisited," *World Development* 32 (July): 1159–78.

Maloney, William F., Jairo Nunez, Wendy Cunningham, Norbert Fiess, Claudio Montenegro, Edmundo Murrugarra, Mauricio Santamaria, and Claudia Sepulveda. 2001. "Measuring the Impact of Minimum Wages: Evidence from Latin America," *World Bank Policy Research Working Paper Series: 2597*. Washington, DC: World Bank.

Navarro, Juan Carlos, Juan Jose Llisterri, and Pluvia Zuniga. 2010. "The Importance of Ideas: Innovation and Productivity in Latin America," pp. 223–255 in Carmen Pages (ed.), *The Age of Productivity: Transforming Economies from the Bottom Up*. New York: Palgrave Macmillan.

Neuwirth, Robert. *Shadow Cities: A Billion Squatters: A New Urban World*. New York: Routledge.

Noble, David Cook. 1998. *Born to Die: Disease and the New World Conquest*. New York: Cambridge University Press.

North, Douglass C. and Robert P. Thomas. 1973. *The Rise of the Western World: A New Economic History*. Cambridge: Cambridge University Press.

Reinhart, Carmen M. and Ernesto Talvi. 1998. "Capital Flows and Saving in Latin America and Asia: A Reinterpretation," *Journal of Development Economics* 57 (October): 45–66.

Sachs, Jeffrey D. 2001. "*Tropical Underdevelopment*." NBER Working Paper 8119. Cambridge, MA: National Bureau of Economic Research.

Solimano, Andres and Raimundo Soto. 2006. "Economic Growth in Latin America in the late Twentieth Century: Evidence and Interpretation," pp. 11–45 in Andres Solimano (ed.), *Vanishing Growth in Latin America: The Late Twentieth Century Experience*. Northampton, MA: Edward Elgar.

Staats, Joseph L., Shaun Bowler, and Jonathan T. Hiskey. 2005. "Measuring Judicial Performance in Latin America," *Latin American Politics and Society* 47 (December): 77–106.

Taylor, Alan. 1998. "On the Costs of Inward-Looking Development: Price Distortions, Growth, and Divergence in Latin America." *Journal of Economic History* 58 (March): 1–28.

Taylor, Alan. 2003. *Foreign Capital in Latin America in the Nineteenth and Twentieth Centuries*. NBER Working Paper 9580. Cambridge, MA: National Bureau of Economic Research.

Tommasi, Mariano. 2006. "The Institutional Foundations of Public Policy." *Economia* 6 (Spring): 1–36.

Transparency International. 2008. *Corruption Perceptions Index, 2008*. Berlin: Transparency International.

United Nations Human Settlement Programme. 2003. *The Challenge of Slums: Global Report on Human Settlements 2003*. New York: United Nations Human Settlements Programme.

World Bank. 2008a. *Doing Business, 2009*. Washington, DC: World Bank.

World Bank. 2008b. *Governance Matters, 2008*. Washington, DC: World Bank.

World Bank. 2010. *World Development Indicators*, Washington, DC: World Bank.

World Economic Forum. 2008. *Global Competitiveness Report, 2008–2009*. Davos: World Economic Forum.

3 Growth and the environment in Latin America

> Without contradiction, this land is the best of all for the life of man: the air is exceptionally healthful, and the soil extremely fertile, all that is before you is delightful and pleasing to the human eye to a great degree.
>
> Pero de Magalhaes de Gandavo, 1576

Introduction

In the previous chapter, we focused on the sources of economic growth in Latin America. Until the 1980s, economists primarily were interested in the process of raising GDP per capita. This is understandable given the pressing economic needs of the majority of humanity residing in low- or middle-income countries. The study of economic growth in Latin America was no different in this regard. However, the rest of the world caught up with economics. The environmental movement born in the 1960s filtered into the discussions of economic growth in the 1970s and 1980s. The situation now is such that discussing economic growth without considering the environmental consequences would seem odd. Rapid economic growth in a low- or middle-income country can create extremely high levels of pollution and/or degradation of the environment. As countries move from low- to middle-income, levels of pollution can rise dramatically as the country industrializes and energy consumption both by producers and consumers rises rapidly. Globally, the focus of growth and the environment has been China. With less fanfare, Latin America is experiencing much of the same difficulties. In many parts of Latin America, drinking a glass of water or breathing can be hazardous to your health. When traveling in the region, this is just a nuisance. Unfortunately, for hundreds of millions of people living in Latin America environmental problems are a part of daily existence that is continually shortening lives and diminishing the quality of life. This is occurring even though economic growth in the region has been relatively slow. If the rate of economic growth picks up at some point, then the problems could quickly become more acute.

In this chapter, we will attempt to provide an overall picture of growth and environmental problems in Latin America. In order to do this, the beginning of the chapter will explain why pollution is a difficult economic problem to deal with and the interactions between economic growth and environmental quality. Next, we will consider the policy options available to governments in their attempts to deal with the difficult tradeoffs between economic growth and environmental quality. Since every region of the world is different, we will then focus on those environmental problems that are most serious in a Latin American context. The final section of the chapter deals with how economic growth and international trade are linked to environmental issues in Latin America.

Pollution as a negative externality

For the average person, pollution is a bad thing and should be gotten rid of, like the household trash. As we will see, pollution occurs for reasons that are plain to an economist. However, it cannot be gotten rid of completely. It is more a problem of a society generating the amount of pollution that is consistent with other societal goals. In order to understand the economic problem of pollution, we will first look at the supply and demand for some everyday good. Then we'll examine another good where the production of this good creates pollution and see how they differ. At that point, the problem of pollution and what to do about it will become clearer.

We will start out by looking at the demand and supply of a simple product like a book. The price of a book is determined by the supply and demand for books. This can be shown with a simple supply and demand graph such as Figure 3.1. In the figure, the demand for books is shown as usual as sloping downward and to the right. As the price of books changes,

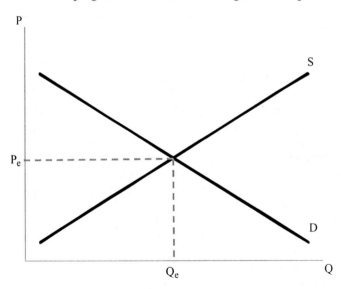

Figure 3.1 Equilibrium price and output with no externalities

the *quantity demanded* of books changes. The relationship is inverse, so if the price of books increases, the amount of books demanded decreases and vice versa. The usual supply curve is also shown in the figure. It slopes upwards and to the right indicating that as the price of books increases, the *quantity supplied* of books likewise increases. As you will probably have learned in a previous class, the intersection of the demand and supply curves shows the equilibrium in this market. The market price is shown in Figure 3.1 as P_e and the equilibrium quantity in the market is Q_e. This is an equilibrium price and quantity for the entire economy. Everything else equal, it will maximize social welfare. The economy is producing the correct number of books and the books are being sold at the correct price. What do we mean by the term "correct?" The price and quantity in this case is correct because all of the benefits and costs have been correctly accounted for. When you buy a book, all of the benefits of using the book accrue to you. You paid the price and you receive all the benefits. The same is true for the producer. The producer incurred all of the costs of producing the book and is paid the market price for incurring those costs. In other words, all of the benefits and costs have been *internalized* by the market. No third party has been affected by the production or consumption of the book. Free markets are very efficient at finding the correct equilibrium if all benefits and costs have been internalized or accounted for. If this is not the case, then the equilibrium price and quantity may not be correct. We now consider such a possibility.

In this case, suppose we are analyzing the market for paper. We use this example because of the technical characteristics of the production of paper. The production of paper is very energy-intensive. One way or another, the production of energy produces some pollution. Therefore, industries that are energy-intensive may be more pollution-intensive than they seem at first glance. This is a particular problem in Latin America, as the production of energy may well be more pollution-intensive than energy production in a high-income country. Secondly, a paper mill produces air pollution. Third, the production of paper produces a substantial amount of byproduct waste. The point of using paper as an example is that a simple and ubiquitous product produces a substantial amount of pollution that may not be immediately obvious. What is even less obvious is that all of the benefits and costs have not been internalized in the market. In other words, there are costs to society of the pollution caused by producing paper that are not being paid by the producer. In turn, this causes the supply of paper to be incorrect. If the amount of paper being produced is wrong, then both the quantity demanded of paper and the price is also incorrect.

If all of the benefits and costs of producing paper are not internalized in a market, then the resulting equilibrium is not socially optimal. A cost to society that has not been internalized in the market is referred to as a negative externality. This situation is shown in Figure 3.2 below. The demand curve looks much as before. All of the benefits of the consumption

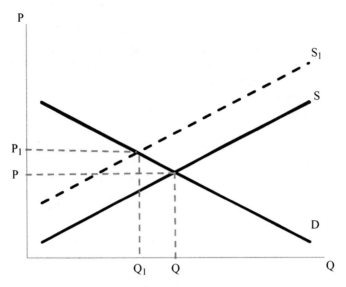

Figure 3.2 Equilibrium price and output in the presence of negative externalities

of paper have been internalized by the buyers of paper. The problem is not with the demand side of the market. The difficulty is on the supply side. The production of paper is producing costs to society that are not included in the costs of production for the paper-producing firm. There are negative externalities that produce costs being paid by society and not the firm. This means that the cost of production is too low. If the firm had to pay for all of the costs, the supply curve would not be at S. It would be further to the left at S_1. Notice that if the firm paid all of the costs there would be a decrease in supply. For any given quantity of production (Q), the production costs would be higher along S_1 than S. This makes sense because S_1 is including all of the relevant costs of producing paper. Now put this new supply curve with the demand curve for paper. If there are negative externalities and these are not being included in the costs of production, then the market price of paper is too low and the production of paper is too high. In this case the market is not producing the correct amount of paper and the price is wrong because the market cannot automatically internalize these negative externalities. Including all costs, the quantity produced should be at Q_1 and the price should be at P_1. To solve the problem, one would just need to calculate the value of the negative externalities associated with paper production, include them in the costs of production for the producer, and then the correct amount of paper will be produced at the right price.

Everything said about pollution and solving the pollution problem is conceptually correct. The problem of pollution in Latin America should be coming into focus. If an area is heavily polluted, then where are the supply curves for pollution-intensive products? They are closer to S than S_1. The difference between the two supply curves is some form of pollution control by the government. Market forces alone won't solve the problem. If there are negative externalities involved in the production of a product, then some regulation may be needed or the product will be overproduced and pollution levels will be too high.[1] This is a classic example of a market failure. Actually, the problem is even worse. If paper is too cheap, then per our first example, books will be too cheap. A misallocation of resources in one market can lead to misallocations in others. Distortions caused by a lack of regulating important negative externalities in one market can have

---

3.1 Natural disasters in Latin America

Desolating earthquakes and hurricanes overtake us unawares, and we live in perpetual ambush of inevitable geographic cataclysms.

Antonio S. Pedreira

No discussion of the environment in Latin America would be complete without mentioning natural disasters. Unfortunately, hardly a year goes by without some type of natural disaster occurring in some country of the region. Natural disasters are grouped into four broad categories:

- *Floods and related disasters* – floods, landslides and mudflows
- *Windstorms* – hurricanes, winter storms, tornadoes, and tropical storms
- *Geological disasters* – earthquakes, volcanic eruptions, and tidal waves
- *Droughts and related disasters* – droughts, extreme temperatures, and wildfires.

Using these definitions, Latin America has suffered 898 natural disasters between 1974 and 2003. Because of the disparity in location and size of the countries of the region, a comparable measure of the extent to which natural disasters are a problem is the number of people killed or affected by natural disasters per one hundred thousand of population. This data is shown is Table 3.1 below.

Notice that by global standards, Latin America as a whole looks rather tranquil. However, there is a significant variation among countries of the region from a low of 55 to a high of 2,767. Further, notice an unfortunate pattern in the data. The countries most likely to be affected by natural disaster are the poorer countries of Central America and Bolivia and the effects sometimes can be devastating in purely economic terms. Table 3.2 lists some of the major natural disasters that have occurred in these countries between 1974 and 2003 and the damage in terms of the previous year's GDP. In many countries of Latin America, natural disasters are a significant barrier to economic development.

Table 3.1 Natural disasters in Latin America

	Number of people killed or affected per 100,000 of population
Argentia	1,456
Bolivia	2,767
Brazil	1,196
Chile	778
Colombia	337
Costa Rica	1,390
Ecuador	638
El Salvador	1,773
Guatemala	2,774
Honduras	2,916
Mexico	173
Nicaragua	2,196
Panama	255
Paraguay	811
Peru	1,313
Uruguay	55
Venezuela	117
Latin America	1,232
World	3,135

Source: Guha-Sapir *et al.* (2004).

Table 3.2 Major natural disasters in Latin America, 1974–2003

Country	Year	Type of disaster	% of previous year GDP
Guatemala	1976	Earthquake	27
Bolivia	1982	Flood	14
El Salvador	1982	Flood	8
Bolivia	1983	Drought	31
Chile	1985	Earthquake	8
El Salvador	1986	Earthquake	27
Costa Rica	1991	Earthquake	9
Nicaragua	1991	Wildfires	8
Nicaragua	1991	Hurricane	51
Bolivia	1992	Landslide	7
Ecuador	1993	Landslide	4
Nicaragua	1994	Drought	9
Honduras	1998	Hurricane	42
El Salvador	2001	Earthquake	21

Source: Guha-Sapir *et al.* (2004).

important secondary effects. Since regulating the negative externalities associated with pollution is important, the next section of the chapter takes up that issue.

Pollution and environmental policy

> There are no solutions, only tradeoffs.
>
> Thomas Sowell

In the previous section, we considered the concept of pollution as a negative externality. We went on to show that if the production of a product was associated with a nontrivial amount of pollution, then the supply of the product would be too high. In turn, this would lead to prices for the product that are too low and production of the product that is too high. Conceptually, the solution to this problem was to shift the supply curve to the left far enough to generate a price and output solution that would be more appropriate in the presence of pollution. While this looks easy on a graph, in practice finding the right price and output combination is not an easy thing to accomplish. This section considers the difficulties associated with reducing the level of pollution in a country to a level that more closely approximates a social optimum. At the start, one needs to understand that these issues rarely have a "perfect" solution. The relatively pristine environment of Latin America that existed in 1491 is not going to return. However, the current state of the environment in the region clearly is not a desirable state. The first part of this section outlines a mental framework for thinking about environmental issues. In the next two sections, two widely used mechanisms for addressing pollution control are covered. Because environmental issues require government intervention, institutions and government effectiveness are critical factors in addressing environmental issues.

Cost/benefit analysis

Like most things in economics, decisions need to be based on the cost of something relative to the benefits. Pollution is no different in this regard. Pollution has obvious costs such as poor air quality, polluted water, or a scarred landscape. One must keep in mind that pollution is the cost that results from engaging in activities that provide benefits. Even in the simplest society, a person might tolerate breathing polluted air to obtain the benefit of consuming cooked meat rather than raw meat. In a modern economy, these problems multiply with the level of economic activity. Life without cars and trucks is hard to imagine yet the refining of oil can be a very pollutionintensive activity. Modern economies face the task of balancing the costs and benefits of pollution. As shown in the previous section, this is difficult because pollution is not internalized in the market price. In this case, to achieve a better social price and output one needs to calculate the costs of pollution that are passed on to society but not included in the market price. In reality, this is not an easy process. This is particularly true for a middle-income country where growth in GDP per capita is still a high priority. However, assuming that some estimate of the social cost can be computed, the total cost of production is higher than just the producers' cost of production. This is important in order to conduct a cost/benefit analysis. If this ratio is greater than one, then the total costs to society are in excess of the benefits and the activity needs to be curtailed to lower the ratio. This is frequently the case for pollution. Since all of the costs of production are not being included in the market price, then the market "overproduces." Notice that in a market without negative externalities, costs and benefits are likely to match. It is the presence of negative externalities, such as pollution, that can yield a ratio greater than one. In the case of Latin America, this is obviously occurring. Poor air quality, polluted water, deforestation, etc. are all manifestations of costs to society that are not being included in the market price.

A further complication is that economic decisions need to be made at the margin. In other words, pollution should be controlled up to the point where the marginal costs of more pollution control is equal to the marginal benefits. The marginal benefits of any activity tend to be highest for low levels of output and decline as more is consumed. The reverse is true of marginal cost. It usually starts out at a low level and rises with the amount produced. This is shown graphically for pollution in Figure 3 below. The marginal benefits to society start out high and gradually fall. This means that the initial benefits of any pollution are quite high but fall as the environment

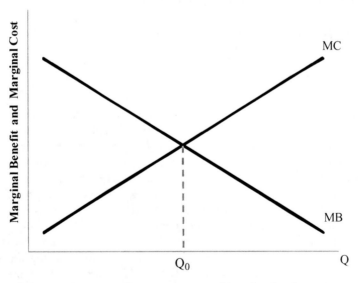

Figure 3.3 The marginal cost and marginal benefit of pollution

becomes more polluted. The reverse is true for the costs of pollution. It starts out being quite modest and rises. The optimal amount of pollution would occur where the two curves intersect at Q_0. Figure 3.3 is mostly a useful way to think about the right level of pollution control. Few, if any, countries are precisely at Q_0. However, it does give one a point of reference. How many countries, much less major urban areas, in Latin America, are at Q_0? Simple intuition would suggest that many areas of the region are to the right of Q_0. In this case, the marginal cost is far greater than the marginal benefit. Social welfare could clearly be improved by moving in the direction of Q_0. This would mean that the extra costs associated with pollution control are considerably less than the extra benefits. Finally, notice to the right of Q_0, the gap can be quite large. A thought exercise for Latin America might suffice to illustrate this. How far away from Q_0 is Mexico City?

Cost/benefit analysis conceptually can solve environmental problems. One just needs a calculation of the social costs that are not being included in the market price. In many cases, this is not an easy thing to calculate. For example, what is the social cost of air pollution in a large city in Latin America? One would at a minimum compare disease and mortality rates with the current situation versus a situation with less air pollution. Notice that the comparison is not with *zero* air pollution. The optimum level of pollution is not zero because recall that economic activities that produce pollution also create benefits. The situation becomes more complicated in that some of the costs are not borne by society immediately, but may be passed on to future generations. These costs also need to be included in the calculation of social costs. Even more difficult is the fact that some environmental problems impose costs on neighboring countries or in some cases, the planet. The point is that the calculation of environmental costs is very hard. As a result, a middle-income country is unlikely to achieve a perfect balance of costs and benefits. However, when pollution reaches very high levels then the costs of doing nothing become very high. In the next two sections, two common methods of dealing with pollution are outlined. Neither one can be perfectly implemented but they are indicative of the way governments deal with pollution, now or in the future. However, keep in mind that pollution control is a relatively new policy even in high-income countries.

A perfect template for pollution control has yet to be designed. As a result, the countries of Latin America are struggling with a social and economic problem that has not been perfectly solved even by two of the world's richest countries north of the region.

Command and control

Refer again to Figure 3.3. The optimal amount of pollution given the marginal costs and marginal benefits of pollution is Q_0. Assume for the moment that one knows the level of pollution associated with Q_0. If this is the case, then one solution to the problem is to force firms that pollute to cut their levels of pollution to Q_0. In the jargon of environmental economics this is known as the command and control (CAC) method of lowering the level of pollution. This would force the firm to do one of two things. First, they could cut their level of output to reduce the level of pollution they are discharging. Second, they could install pollution control equipment to reduce their levels of emissions to allowable levels. In either case, the level of pollution has been reduced. Notice that there is still pollution. Producing goods and services has benefits so the optimal solution is not zero pollution. Rather it is a level of pollution that to one extent or another is more consistent with a socially optimal level of output for a pollution-intensive good. The great virtue of the CAC method of controlling pollution is its relative simplicity. Government officials determine the level of pollution and firms must adjust their operations to that level. Since environmental regulations are relatively new in Latin America, CAC is commonly used as a means of pollution control. However, as the next section indicates, CAC is generally considered to be a second best method of pollution control.

Market-based initiatives

A strong market-based instrument decentralizes decisionmaking to a degree that the polluter or resource user has a maximum amount of flexibility to select the production or consumption option that minimizes the social cost of achieving a particular level of environmental quality.

Robert M. Huber, Jack Ruitenbeek, and
Ronaldo Seroa da Motta

While CAC is a frequently implemented means of controlling pollution, it is usually considered inferior to what is known as market-based initiatives (MBI).[2] Conceptually, it is possible to solve the pollution problem using a CAC policy. However, CAC has one major drawback. Once a producer has met the government-mandated pollution standard, there is no further incentive to reduce pollution. Producers are almost always in the best position to know how to reduce the level of pollution. With the right set of regulations, a government can give producers an incentive to utilize that knowledge in a way that both lowers pollution and reduces the production cost for the producer. The easiest market-based system is a pollution tax. The government first determines the social cost of pollution that is not included in the private cost of production. The producer is then charged a pollution tax equivalent to this cost. In terms of Figure 3.2, this would shift the supply curve for the pollution-intensive product to the left by the correct amount. In a purely static sense, a pollution tax would yield the same result as a CAC policy. In the long run, there would be a difference. The producer now has a clear incentive to determine how to lower the amount of pollution produced per unit of output. If she could do this, then the firm would become more profitable as the tax burden diminished. Also, this could be a source of competitive advantage *vis-à-vis* other firms in the industry. The use of MBIs seems to be increasing in Latin America. However, they should not be seen as a panacea. They can be difficult to administer and moving regulations from CACs to MBIs may not always be easy.

While pollution taxes are preferable to CAC, environmental policy can be improved further. Environmental policy should be concerned with the overall level of pollution in the country. A pollution tax sets the price of pollution but does not necessarily control the overall level of pollution in a country. The most commonly used method of controlling the overall level of pollution and providing the incentives of a pollution tax is to issue pollution permits. Permits issued to firms could then be traded to other firms and the market would set the price of the permits. Permits would then flow to industries where the marginal benefits of pollution are the highest. While such a system is theoretically appealing, the actual implementation of such a system is difficult. While it is unlikely that such a system would develop within Latin America in the near future, the policy is still of some relevance to the region. Global negotiations on controlling the total amount

---

3.2   Exporting environmentalism

In analyzing efforts to control pollution in Latin America, one tends to forget that environmental legislation is relatively new in *developed* countries. Using the US as an example, the Environmental Protection Agency (EPA) was not formed until 1970. Further, the US has been refining its regulations almost continuously since the formation of the EPA. Environmental issues are difficult and the US experience is not atypical. From the beginning, a focus of US environmental regulation has been the chemical industry. By its very nature the industry is pollution-intensive. The production of chemicals produces hazardous and nonhazardous waste; consumes energy heavily; relies on nonrenewable resources for its raw materials; and may release substances that enter the food chain or biological systems. Until the 1970s, the attitude of the US industry had been to fight regulation. This effort yielded limited success as the focus of US environmental policy shifted from pollution control to pollution prevention. The industry gradually came around to the notion that pollution prevention could be a source of competitive advantage and simultaneously put them less at odds with government and environmental groups. This led the US industry to adopt a policy known as Responsible Care. In general, the goal of the policy was to better align industry practices with the social environment it operates in and to stay ahead of the curve in terms of industry environmental policy. The development of Responsible Care coincided with the expansion of the industry into other markets, some of them in the more important developing countries such as Mexico and Brazil. In these markets, the companies took the concept of Responsible Care with them. In many senses, these countries are now on the same path as the US decades ago and the firms understand that operating in a socially responsible way can be a source of competitive advantage.

Mexico is a good case in point. The country passed its first comprehensive environmental legislation in 1987. The beginning of free trade in the 1990s offered the possibility of exports to the US but only under the condition that Mexican firms were in full compliance with Mexican law. US firms also started investment in chemical plants in Mexico as they were now facing a much more open FDI environment. As they increased operations in Mexico, the US firms took the Responsible Care program with them. In the US, the program had become just a normal part of doing business and it was obvious that it was perhaps even more important in the context of a US firm operating in a foreign country. Perhaps slightly more surprising is that the Mexican chemical industry decided that the same program was a good idea. Mexican firms now routinely work with government, environmental groups, and community groups to try to find environmental solutions to the problems that are inherent in the industry. In a sense, the US chemical industry is "exporting" a form of environmentalism. Limited data on this issue indicates that US firms operating in Mexico are more pressured by corporate headquarters and colleague pressure than by the Mexican government. The program has been less successful in Brazil in terms of participation by Brazilian firms. However, another study of Brazilian industry indicates that foreign firms or firms with significant foreign ownership spend more resources on reducing pollution than local firms.[3] Obviously, industry groups and FDI are not going to solve the problems of pollution control in Latin America. It remains to be seen if the nascent government agencies in the region can avoid the "regulatory capture" that can occur with government and industry cooperation. However, it does seem that FDI by firms from developed countries has the potential to create a positive externality for the region in terms of environmental quality.[4]

of greenhouse gases for the planet include an envisioned global system of tradable pollution permits. The implementation of such a system on a global basis would no doubt speed up any movement from CAC or pollution taxes to a tradable permit system. In the next section, some of the advantages of tradable permits are more closely examined.

The role of institutions

Legislation is really not the critical factor in environmental improvements. Legislation cannot guarantee that the intent of the legislator will be implemented in practice. The major problems result from the difficulty of establishing control and enforcement mechanisms to apply the legal provisions.

United Nations Environmental Programme

In the previous sections the theory of environmental protection has been presented as well as some of the common means of mitigating environmental problems. Attempts to address environmental problems in Latin America have focused on passing initial legislation to deal with these problems. This is a necessary first step as these problems will not be adequately dealt with in the absence of some form of government intervention. However, in the context of Latin America it is unrealistic to expect the level of environmental control that one typically observes in a high-income country. The purpose of this section is to raise some of the more common problems that have to be overcome in the process of getting the actual enforcement of the environmental regulation more congruent with the regulations themselves.

First, and foremost, is the issue of government funding of pollution control efforts. The government of any developing country faces an almost impossible task of allocating scarce resources among many pressing and competing needs. Sadly, pollution control is just one of many pressing needs. One is tempted to say that environmental concerns are absolutely fundamental. However, allocating resources among the environment, health care, education, etc. is no easy task. There is little formal study of this allocation but the general sense is that spending on environmental enforcement in Latin America is low and may be declining.[5] A related problem is that effective pollution control is not inexpensive. To be effective, the government agencies in charge of this must have well-trained personnel and expensive equipment. Both of these resources obviously are more scarce in Latin America than they are in high-income countries. This problem may be mitigated to some extent by the location of industry in Latin America. Most heavy industry tends to be heavily concentrated in a few areas.[6] Also, industries that are pollution-intensive are now well known. This may reduce the monitoring costs significantly and allow the government to reduce pollution significantly at a relatively low cost. This advantage is partially offset by the large informal sector. Producers in the informal sector may be pollution-intensive and controlling discharges in this environment may be difficult. On the other hand, the informal sector also may be producing a low percentage of output relative to the large firms in the formal sector.

The structure of government finance in Latin America may make MBIs an attractive proposition relative to CAC. CAC is a less flexible form of pollution control. However, the government is shouldering the costs of monitoring pollution and is receiving no revenue in the process. Pollution taxes now become doubly attractive. As mentioned above, they provide incentives for firms to find ways to produce output in a less pollution-intensive manner. They also produce revenue. Tax revenue in a developing country is always difficult to raise. In this case, revenue has been gathered in the process of obtaining another social goal. Offsetting this is the fact that many MBIs may be more difficult and expensive to monitor than CACs. There is some evidence of a movement toward pollution taxes in

Latin America as a means of raising revenue.[7] Also, governments in middle-income countries have to be aware that pollution control may constitute a regressive form of taxation. Spending by firms on pollution control may be passed on in the form of higher prices for consumer goods. This implicit pollution tax may be easily borne in a high-income country but may be much more burdensome in a country where GDP per capita is significantly lower. Tradable pollution permits would in theory solve many of these problems. They allow governments to control the overall level of pollution. Second, they solve the difficult problem involved with pollution taxes concerning what is the correct tax. Auctioned permits that are tradable force firms to reveal in a market what the right to pollute is worth. And they also raise revenue needed by the government. Given these advantages, one could assume that the global move to tradable permits will eventually reach Latin America.

Environmental issues in Latin America

In this section, we move from the general to the specific. In the first part of the chapter, the focus was on developing a framework for analyzing environmental problems in the context of Latin America. In this section, the focus will be on a short list of environmental problems that are especially acute in Latin America. This list is by no means exhaustive. Latin America has many of the same environmental problems as much of the rest of the developing world. However, each region of the world is different. For example, drought is a much less serious problem in Latin America than in Africa. Latin America is far from overpopulated by global standards, so some of the environmental issues in Latin America are different than in parts of Asia. These issues covered below are: water quality, air pollution, and deforestation.

Water pollution

Water quality has long been a serious environmental problem in Latin America. Polluted water is associated with a host of diseases such as amoebic dysentery, cholera, trachoma, and others. Such conditions can easily lead to death, especially in small children. Aside from this, frequent illnesses associated with polluted water lowers the productivity and earnings of the labor force. Less obviously, if clean water is scarce people may have to waste resources transporting water from a clean source or using part of a meager income to purchase clean water. In short, water pollution can carry a heavy economic and social cost. The statistics on access to clean water are given in Table 3.3. The first four columns indicate the access to improved (clean) water in rural and urban areas of Latin America. In 1990, less than two-thirds of the rural population had access to water from an improved source.

Table 3.3 Access to clean water and sanitation in Latin America

	Access to Improved Water Source (%)				Access to Improved Sanitation (%)			
	Rural		Urban		Rural		Urban	
	1990	2004	1990	2004	1990	2004	1990	2004
Argentina	72	80	97	98	45	83	86	92
Bolivia	49	68	91	95	14	22	49	60
Brazil	55	57	93	96	37	37	82	83
Chile	49	58	98	100	52	62	91	95
Colombia	78	71	98	99	52	54	95	96
Costa Rica		92	100	100	97	97		89
Ecuador	61	89	82	97	45	82	77	94
El Salvador	48	70	87	94	33	39	70	77
Guatemala	72	92	89	99	47	82	73	90
Honduras	79	81	92	95	31	54	77	87
Mexico	64	87	89	100	13	41	75	91
Nicaragua	46	63	91	90	24	34	64	56
Panama	79	79	99	99	51	51	89	89
Paraguay	44	68	81	99	45	61	72	94
Peru	41	65	89	89	15	32	69	74
Uruguay	100	100	100	100	99	99	100	100
Venezuela		70		85		48		71
Latin America	62.5	75.9	92.3	96.2	43.8	57.3	77.9	84.6

Source: World Resources Institute (2008).

By 2004, the percentage was over three quarters. For the urban population, the percentages went from 92.3 to 96.2. As in so many other areas of life in Latin America, conditions in the urban areas are considerably better than rural areas. The fifth through the eighth columns show access to improved sanitation in the two areas. In this case in 1990 only 43.8 percent of the rural population had such access. By 2004, nearly 60 percent had access to improved sanitation. In the urban areas, the percentages improved from nearly 78 percent to nearly 85 percent. The two are not unrelated. The lack of improved sanitation also frequently means water quality problems. More recently, water pollution has been caused by runoffs from agricultural land as well as from industry.

Solving the problem of clean water has been a vexing problem in Latin America for a long time. Water pollution from industrial sources can be dealt with using some mix of CAC and MBIs that have already been discussed. Since the number of polluters in the formal sector are frequently small in number and geographically concentrated, dealing with industrial water pollution should be a problem even a small and underfunded bureaucracy can deal with. Industrial pollution emanating from the informal sector is much more difficult to deal with, but once again while these producers are numerous, the amount of pollution coming from this sector should be small. Again, pollution coming from the informal sector is just another example of problems created by a policy mix that encourages economic activity to occur in this sector rather than in the formal sector of the economy. The largest problem affecting the average person in the region is the poor quality of water produced by the public sector in municipalities. In the first two chapters, the problem of institutional weakness in Latin America was covered at several points; this is just another specific example of this general problem. In this case, a potential solution to this problem is to privatize the public water system. In practice, this frequently means FDI in this critical sector. However, in Latin America this potential solution is not a panacea. The provision of water and sanitation services is a natural monopoly and private companies must be efficiently regulated if private provision is to work properly. The record in this regard is mixed. Privatization has led to riots in Cochabamba, Bolivia and a large-scale privatization in Argentina during the 1990s has been partially rolled back. Once again, government effectiveness is crucial. The private sector can potentially help solve this

Table 3.4 Industrial water pollution in Latin America

	Kilograms per day (in thousands)		Kilograms per day per worker	
	1990	2003	1990	2003
Argentina	186.7	149.5	0.20	0.23
Bolivia	8.4	12.8	0.24	0.25
Brazil	780.4		0.19	
Chile	66.8	72.9	0.22	0.24
Colombia	93.2	93.8	0.19	0.21
Costa Rica	27.3	31.2	0.20	0.22
Ecuador	25.6	41.2	0.23	0.28
El Salvador	7.7	22.8	0.22	0.18
Guatemala	16.1	19.3	0.27	0.28
Honduras	17.8		0.23	
Mexico	174.3	296.1	0.18	0.20
Nicaragua	10.5		0.27	
Panama	9.7	11.7	0.26	0.32
Paraguay	3.3		0.28	
Peru	56.1		0.20	
Uruguay	38.7	16.4	0.23	0.28
Venezuela	96.5	94.2	0.21	0.21
Portugal	147.9	133.6	0.15	0.14
Spain	320.3	374.6	0.17	0.15
Canada	321.5	313.4	0.17	0.16
US	2,565.2	1,897.5	0.15	0.13

Source: World Bank (2006).

long-standing problem in the region but only in conjunction with effective government regulation.

The other part of water pollution in Latin America is emissions by industry into the water supply. Table 3.4 presents data on the extent of the problem in the region. The first two columns show the absolute amount of water pollution by industry in 1990 and 2003. In general, the data is discouraging. The absolute amounts have increased in most countries and in some, substantially. The numbers in the first two columns are just a part of the environmental costs of economic growth in low- to middle-income countries. Also, notice that water pollution per worker is not increasing very much. As is evident from the data for the reference developed countries at the bottom of the table, the relationship between economic growth and pollution is not totally straightforward. With respect to environmental policy, industrial water pollution is one of the least difficult environmental problems to control. The largest sources of this pollution are normally quite visible and the number of firms engaging in the pollution is small. While industrial water pollution is not a trivial problem in the region, it is easier to make progress in this area than in others.

Air pollution

Much like water pollution, air pollution is a pressing environmental problem in almost any metropolitan area in Latin America. Many cities in the region are set in breathtakingly picturesque environments that can be glimpsed only through a screen of smog. This is annoying but the effects of air pollution on the health of the inhabitants of these cities is all too real.[8] Part of the problem is the location of industry in major urban areas. Industrialization usually is not a rural phenomenon. The other part of the problem is that the increasing affluence of the population of the region leads to a large increase in vehicles in use. In turn, this leads to a greater amount of air pollution generated by these vehicles.

The data can be seen in Table 3.5. Despite difficulties in the data, for most of the countries there has been a dramatic increase in the number of vehicles from 1990 to 2003. As the data for the four developed countries at the bottom of the table indicate, Latin America is in the process of "catching up" with the world's high-income countries in terms of the number of vehicles. Everything else equal, one might assume that air quality in the urban areas of the region must be deteriorating rapidly. However, the data in the first two columns tell a different story. In most of the countries of the region, air quality is improving. Of course, by developed country standards there is still a large amount of progress to be made. What seems clear from the data is that air quality is improving even as the number of vehicles is increasing. Since such regulation in the region is relatively new and is already having some effect, there are grounds for cautious optimism that air quality may well improve further.

Table 3.5 Urban air pollution in Latin America

	Particulate matter concentrations (micrograms per cubic meter)		Passenger vehicles (per 1,000 people)	
	1990	2003	1990	2003
Argentina	105	78	181	181
Bolivia	119	92	41	10
Brazil	41	35	88	170
Chile	85	56	81	136
Colombia	37	24	39	51
Costa Rica	50	40	87	185
Ecuador	37	28	35	53
El Salvador	46	40	33	
Guatemala	64	76	21	57
Honduras	44	46	22	61
Mexico	70	43	119	201
Nicaragua	49	32	19	39
Panama	58	58	75	107
Paraguay	109	103	27	88
Peru	98	68	128	46
Uruguay	235	154	138	
Venezuela	22	12	93	
Latin America	74.6	57.9	72.2	98.9
Portugal	53	41	222	463
Spain	42	40	360	558
Canada	25	21	605	577
US	30	24	758	808

Source: World Bank (2006).

3.3   Urbanization and the environment

In the previous two sections, we have covered problems with water and air pollution in Latin America. Part of what was being conveyed in those sections is that the thought of Latin America as an area where most of the population is living in an idyllic rural environment is not quite the case. Economic development in the region has drawn countless millions of people from rural villages and smaller cities into very large metropolitan areas. In 1975 only slightly more than half the population lived in urban areas. By 2000, it was 67 percent and it is projected to go higher. Notice the variation in the data. Urbanization tends to be lowest in the countries with the lowest GDP per capita. As these countries develop, urbanization rates are likely to rise and bring the regional average even higher. Latin America is already more urbanized than most regions of the world and seems poised to become as urbanized as the countries of North America.

Table 3.6 Urbanization in Latin America

	Percent of population in urban areas	
	1975	2000
Argentina	80.7	89.9
Bolivia	41.5	62.5
Brazil	61.2	81.3
Chile	78.4	85.7
Colombia	60.7	73.9
Costa Rica	41.3	47.8
Ecuador	42.4	65.3
El Salvador	40.4	46.6
Guatemala	36.7	39.7
Honduras	32.1	52.7
Mexico	62.8	74.4
Nicaragua	48.9	56.1
Panama	49.0	56.3
Paraguay	39.0	56.0
Peru	61.5	72.8
Uruguay	83.1	91.3
Venezuela	75.8	86.9
Latin America	55.0	67.0
Portugal	27.7	64.4
Spain	42.4	50.4
Canada	75.6	77.1
US	73.7	77.2

Source: World Resources Institute (2008).

The increasing urbanization of Latin America exacerbates environmental problems. High levels of discharges of pollution into the water supply and air combined with high population densities can contribute to the poor quality of life of the increasing number of people crowded into the large cities of Latin America. This makes progress on environmental issues more urgent, as ever more people can be expected to be impacted as the countries of the region become even more urbanized.

Deforestation

As we have alluded to earlier and will cover in more detail later in Chapter 5, Latin America is a region with a substantial amount of natural resources. One of the richest of these resources comes from the immense amount of natural forest. Forests cover over forty percent of the land area of Latin America. As a result, forest products have always been a major industry in the region and are currently the major source of income and employment for millions of people. The forest resources of Latin America are also a global resource. Twenty-four percent of the world's forest resources are in Latin America. The basic data on forest resources is shown in Table 3.7 below. When thinking about forest resources in Latin America, there is a natural tendency to think almost exclusively in terms of the rain forests of the Amazon basin in Brazil. Given the amount written about this area, this is perfectly understandable. Notice from the data that forty percent of Latin America's forests are outside of Brazil. The point is that forest resources are an important environmental issue in virtually every country in the region.

As we saw in an earlier section, pollution is a negative externality. In terms of air pollution, there are growing fears that the emission of carbon from industrial production and transportation equipment has the potential to change the climate of the entire planet. Carbon emissions now are seen as a global and not just local environmental issue. Forests play a key role in this. In essence, forests act as a natural way to reduce the amount of carbon in the atmosphere. It is for this reason that losing a significant part of the world's forests is an important environmental problem. Further, preventing

Table 3.7 Deforestation in Latin America

	Total forest area (thousands of hectares) 2000	Average annual percent change 1990–2000	Plantation forests	Average annual percentage change 1990–2000
Argentina	34,648	−0.8	926	
Bolivia	53,068	−0.3	46	3.7
Brazil	543,905	−0.4	4,982	3.2
Chile	15,536	−0.1	2,017	5.5
Colombia	49,601	−0.4	141	6.2
Costa Rica	1,968	−0.8	178	9.6
Ecuador	10,557	−1.2	167	2.4
El Salvador	121	−4.6	14	2.7
Guatemala	2,850	−1.7	133	
Honduras	5,383	−1.0	48	
Mexico	55,205	−1.1	267	
Nicaragua	3,278	−3.0	46	14.3
Panama	2,876	−1.6	40	17.3
Paraguay	23,372	−0.5	27	11.3
Peru	69,215	−0.4	640	15.2
Uruguay	1,292	5.0	622	15.3
Venezuela	49,506	−0.4	863	8.7
Portugal	3,666	1.7	834	
Spain	14,370	0.6	1,904	
Canada	244,571			
US	225,993	0.2	16,238	0.8

Source: World Resources Institute (2008).

deforestation is a far cheaper way to reduce carbon emissions than pursuing alternative strategies to reduce carbon emissions. In more technical terms, forests produce a positive externality. A positive externality exists when a product produces benefits to society that are not included in the market price. Forests obviously produce a positive externality. There is a benefit that the owner of forest products cannot charge the world for. In turn this implies that the indiscriminate cutting of forests yields a negative externality. In effect, trees are too cheap and since the market is not accounting for the externalities associated, the result is deforestation.[9] In effect, we are getting the same results that are shown in Figure 3.2. The supply is too large, prices are too low, and the equilibrium in the market is too high. This leaves owners of forest lands with the incentive to clear cut forests and then develop the cleared land for other uses such as agriculture or ranching. Unfortunately, high prices for commodities can encourage this trend. Since the owner of the forest is not being compensated for the positive externality, the incentives for deforestation remain in place. In any region this makes forest resources difficult to develop in an appropriate way. Forest products yield income in the current period but the resources can take many years to replace. In a sense, trees are a crop but a crop with a very long growing cycle. In Latin America and the rest of the world, the "farming" of trees is a growing part of the forest products industry. From Table 3.7, one can see that tree plantations are still a small part of the total forest resources of Latin America but the growth rate of this part of the industry is extremely fast. This cannot offset the deforestation occurring in most countries of the region shown in Table 3.7. While the annual rates of deforestation are small, the compound effects over decades lead to striking losses of a critical resource. Deforestation is an old story and many of the high-income countries went through a similar process at an earlier stage of development. For Latin America to break out of this historical pattern is not going to be an easy task as the incentives to use the resource to produce income and jobs in a middle-income country are high.

The problem is compounded in this case by the frequent absence of property rights. Much of Latin America's forest resources are on public land. In the Amazon Basin, less than a quarter of the land is privately held.[10] The rest is owned by the state. If this resource is not carefully policed, then the possibility of a tragedy of the commons exists. This occurs when there is a resource available and there are no clear property rights. In such a case, the resource may be depleted because of a lack of incentives for anyone to conserve the resource. If forest resources exist on public land and there is no effective control of the use of that resource, then deforestation can occur on land that is technically owned by the state. If government effectiveness is low, then the control of the destruction of forests on public land is a distinct possibility. This is especially true if the resource is geographically remote. In some countries the sheer enormity of the resource makes adequate policing of its use virtually impossible. The Amazon basin is one and a half times the size of India.

The material above shows that one of the most critical environmental problems for Latin America is deforestation. Forests form such a large percentage of land in the region that the effective use of this resource obviously is important. Effective utilization will not be easy. Forest resources are more likely to be used efficiently on private land but there is no guarantee of this. There are currently no tax or subsidy schemes in place that would adjust market prices to reflect the loss of a resource that produces a positive externality for the region and the world. A more pressing problem is that theoretically much of this resource in the region is on public land where the use is more easily controlled. Unfortunately, a mix of the vastness of forest resources and weak institutions for protecting it means that deforestation is occurring on land that should be protected. Even with more effective institutions, the incentive to develop the resource quickly in middle-income countries is strong. Government policy is caught in the middle of protecting a critical resource and economic growth. At a certain level of GDP per capita, stopping and reversing deforestation is possible as shown by the data for the high-income countries in Table 3.7. Applying this sort of situation to Latin America at this point in time is not realistic. No government in the region is going to stop the development of this resource for purely environmental concerns. In the meantime, the focus of policy in the region is slowing the rate of deforestation. While this is not a perfect outcome, governments in the region now are influenced by environmental concerns and are trying to balance this with economic growth. The task is not one that anyone would envy.

Biodiversity

An environmental issue frequently related to deforestation is biodiversity. Biodiversity refers to the number of different forms of life that occur in a local ecosystem or the earth as a whole. Biodiversity provides a number of benefits. As noted with forest resources, plant life can be an important component of pollution control. Second, a lack of diversity in agriculture may make the food supply more vulnerable to problems with a single crop. The Irish potato famine of the 1840s is a classic example of this risk. Currently about eighty percent of human food comes from just twenty types of plants. Biodiversity is a health industry issue as a large number of currently used and potential medications are derived from plant and animal life. A reduction in the number of species in the world potentially reduces the supply of medicines. Business and industry rely on a large number of plants and animal life for the production of countless goods and services. Finally, a diverse environment provides ascetic benefits to mankind. In economic terms, biodiversity is potentially very important. It also is a positive externality, a potentially very large one.

This implies that deforestation in Latin America is an even more important issue than indicated above. Deforestation involves a loss of habitat for many species. Even without deforestation, development in forests may reduce the number of species. The issue is especially important for Latin America. Five of the top ten countries of the world in terms of biodiversity are in Latin America: Brazil, Colombia, Ecuador, Mexico, and Peru. Ten percent of the plant and animal species in the *world* are found in Colombia. Preserving these resources is in some senses an even more formidable task than deforestation. The benefits of biodiversity are large, but what is the size of the externality? Even if that could be determined, what would be an optimal policy with respect to biodiversity? This area is difficult to deal with even in a high-income country. With respect to environmental policy in Latin America, it will be difficult to implement in a large-scale way. However, it is almost surely true that any estimates of the costs of deforestation are low because the positive externality of biodiversity hasn't been included. Because of biodiversity losses, the problem of deforestation is even more pressing than indicated above.

The environment and growth

A relationship that was mentioned at several points in the previous section was the tradeoff between environmental issues and economic growth. It is frequently the case that protection of the environment will involve either CAC policies or MBIs that will make economic activity more expensive. In turn, this expense may result in a slower rate of growth of real GDP. In a low- or middle-income country this is a difficult tradeoff. A polluted environment or the overuse of natural resources is not a desirable outcome. On the other hand, increasing GDP per capita is an important consideration. How to think about reconciling the two is the purpose of this final section of the chapter. In a sense, the earlier sections are the microeconomics of pollution problems in Latin America. This section covers some of more general issues involved in the process of balancing the environment and growth. The first part concerns obtaining a level of growth that is environmentally sustainable. In the next section, the results of a substantial amount of research about GDP per capita and pollution is summarized and put in a Latin American context. In the last section, the interactions among FDI, international trade, and pollution are covered.

Sustainable growth

Over the last two decades the concept of sustainable growth has become a more important part of the literature in economic development. Over the same time frame, sustainable growth has become an increasingly complicated term. At this point, sustainable growth can mean different things to different people. In other words, it is becoming hard to define the term. Sustainable growth originally applied solely to environmental issues. Over time, the concepts of economic and social sustainability came to be associated with the term. In this case, it is small wonder that the term is now difficult to define. For our purposes here, we will confine the discussion to sustainable growth in an environmental sense for two reasons. First, once one leaves the area of environmental sustainability, there is much less agreement about what sustainable growth means. Second, in this chapter the focus has been on environmental issues. Discussing sustainable growth in terms of the environment is a convenient way to summarize many of the environmental issues that have been covered so far.

Sustainable growth in the context of the environment begins with the concept of natural capital. Natural capital is the endowment of nature's resources possessed by a country or region. These resources such as fresh air and clean water can be used at various rates. In addition to natural capital there is also land as it was defined in the previous chapter. The question then becomes at what rate should these resources be consumed? There are three possibilities. If the consumption of natural capital is larger than nature's ability to replenish it, this leads to environmental degradation and is obviously an unsustainable situation. A second possibility is that the use of natural capital roughly matches nature's ability to replenish the resource. The final situation is where the economy is using natural capital at a lower rate than it is being replenished.

After reading the previous paragraph, it is fairly clear where Latin America is in terms of sustainability overall. The air pollution in the major cities is a classic example of unsustainable growth. The same situation holds for water pollution. The deforestation that is occurring in much of the region is just another form of unsustainable development. The vast forest resources of Latin America are being used at a faster rate than they can be replaced. In many cases in the past and in the present, natural resources such as precious metals or other minerals have been used at unsustainable rates. Most of the previous parts of this chapter have been specific examples of unsustainable growth. It is a chronic problem in the economies of Latin America. The problem is even worse than was initially described. Some of the problems outlined before are irreversible. The resources taken in the colonial era in many cases cannot be replaced. The loss of biodiversity in many cases cannot be reversed. Unsustainable growth can have long-run consequences that can be extremely large.

Making growth sustainable requires the use of the policies we described earlier in the chapter, but usually on a larger scale. Market prices cannot be expected to include costs imposed on future generations in the current market price. In calculating the negative externalities associated with certain types of production, it is now necessary to calculate not only the current effects but effects into an indefinite future. Of course, this makes the negative externalities even larger and the associated reduction in production larger. The cost/benefit analysis changes considerably when one starts accounting for costs and benefits well into the future as well as the current situation. Using either CACs or MBIs to control pollution becomes increasingly complicated as the analysis becomes much more complex.

What the above means is that in an environmental sense, sustainable development is a desirable social goal. However, implementing it in practice is very difficult. Done well, it would involve accounting for all the costs that the production of a good or service is imposing on the current and future generations that are not being included in the market price. In practice, even high-income countries would be hard pressed to accomplish this. In an area where governments may not be completely effective and the institutional environment is weak, an aggressive program aimed at sustainable development may not be possible. Even though sustainable growth may not be immediately achievable in Latin America, it is a useful benchmark. Like perfect competition or perfectly rational expectations, one may rarely observe perfect sustainable growth policies. This hardly makes the concept useless. It can serve as a guide to compare current policy to some optimum. While Latin America is certainly far away from perfectly sustainable growth, an important question is that of whether or not environmental policies in the region are moving towards that optimum or away from it? In the context of middle-income countries perhaps movements of policy and reductions in measurable levels of pollution should be seen as the progress they represent and a hope for a greener future. The next section presents a concept now common in economics indicating that such hope is not unrealistic.

The environmental Kuznets curve

For nearly twenty years, there has been a lively debate and a large amount of empirical research on the relationship between economic development and levels of pollution.[11] The debate was started by the results of a paper by Grossman and Krueger (1993). The paper introduced the concept of the environmental Kuznets curve. The curve is named after the relationship between GDP per capita and the distribution of income discovered by Simon Kuznets in the 1950s. In his research, Kuznets found an inverted U-shaped relationship between income distribution and GDP per capita. As the latter grew, the distribution of income would tend to worsen initially, peak, and then decline as GDP per capita increased. The environmental Kuznets curve is derived from the relationship that frequently is found in studying the interaction of GDP per capita and levels of pollution. A common relationship shows that as a country moves from low- to middle-income, levels of pollution tend to worsen. However, at some point the level of pollution peaks and then declines as a middle-income country moves to the high-income level. A typical Kuznets curve is shown in Figure 3.4.

The environmental Kuznets curve is now a common part of the lexicon of economic growth. Used simplistically, it carries a potentially important idea. This is that environmental concerns in developing countries will, in time, fix themselves. Pollution levels naturally rise as consumers in middle-income countries obtain goods such as cars and industry becomes a larger percentage of GDP. The curve indicates that eventually GDP per capita will become high enough that environmental conditions will improve. Among policy makers, this has become almost an unfortunate article of faith. In a middle-income country, growth in GDP per capita is usually the most important economic policy goal. With this constraint, environmental concerns are seen as *temporarily* being considered of secondary importance. Unfortunately, the empirical research on the environmental Kuznets curve indicates that this view of the relationship between economic growth and the environment is not quite so simple for a number of reasons. First, the peak of the curve is in an uncertain place. Various estimates have put it at around the middle of the world distribution of income ($3,000–$4,000) to as high as $15,000. The higher estimates would imply that much of Latin America has not reached that turning point and may not for a nontrivial amount of time. A second problem is that much of the empirical work on this subject uses data from developed countries. Extrapolating these results to the developing

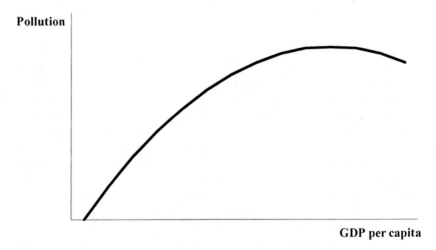

Figure 3.4 The environmental Kuznets curve

countries of Latin America runs the usual risk of transplanting results across countries with widely different institutional settings. What little research has been done using data from developing countries is yielding relationships that are not as neat as Figure 3.4 implies. Another drawback of the literature is that the empirical work to date covers a relatively small number of pollutants for which data is conveniently available. This is not reassuring given that the potential number of pollutants produced by consumption and production is large. Another difficulty is that environmental damage that occurs early in the process of economic development may in some cases be irreversible. Deforestation of virgin forests is a prime case in point in Latin America, although it also may apply to other forms of environmental degradation. Finally, the literature indicates that assuming that pollution simply is a function of GDP per capita is simplistic at best.

In a careful study of pollution in Mexico, Gallagher (2004) found little or no evidence of Mexico having reached the peak of the curve. Even less is known about the rest of the region. It is probably safe to assume that at some point environmental issues will become more important in the region, but few if any countries are now at that point. In the meantime, there may be decades of environmental damage, some of it irreversible, that is going to occur. With poverty and inequality still significant problems in the region, it will be difficult for policy makers to make environmental policy a higher priority. More study of these issues is badly needed to show that the current costs of pollution are quite high and the cost to future generations in the region may be extremely high.

Trade, FDI, and the environment

Over the last two decades, there has been an active literature in economics on the effects of international trade on the environment.[12] While there are endless variations of this literature, the basic idea can be expressed in a straightforward way. As an economy develops there are three effects occurring that can influence the overall level of pollution in an economy. First, there is the *scale effect*. Everything else equal, when real GDP increases then the overall level of pollution would tend to rise. On the other hand there is the *technique effect*. A higher real GDP increases incomes. This increase normally generates both the ability and the willingness of a society to reduce the level of pollution. Finally, there is the *composition effect*. Over time the industrial structure of any country changes. This is important in terms of the environment. As has been previously discussed, some industries are naturally more pollution-intensive than others. Everything else equal, a change in industrial structure in a country can change the overall level of pollution. For example, a decline in the steel industry coupled with an increase in the information technology industry might lower overall levels of pollution. With these three concepts in mind, we can now more easily think about the interactions among pollution, international trade, and FDI.

As you will see in Chapter 7, barriers to international trade have been falling since the 1950s. As trade barriers fall, the volume of international trade rises. In turn, as the amount of trade increases, the economic output of countries that trade more increases.[13] Thinking about the scale effect leads to the conclusion that international trade increases the overall level of pollution. On the other hand, trade leads to increases in real GDP per capita. In turn, these increases tend to reduce pollution via the technique effect. If nothing else changes, then the latter effect will frequently be larger than the former effect. However, there is still the composition effect to consider. International trade changes the industrial structure of a country. Export-oriented industries tend to become larger and industries competing with imports become smaller. The increased volume of trade leads to a reorganization of world production where some countries produce more goods in a particular industry and some less. This reorganization occurs as a result of differences in the costs of production among nations.[14] With the arrival of environmental regulations in the high-income countries, a new factor determining world production and trade was recognized. Countries have differential costs of production but they also have differences in the regulation of pollution. In general, low- and middle-income countries have fewer environmental regulations than high-income countries. This implies that countries with low levels of regulation could have lower costs of production in pollution-intensive industries. This could skew the world pattern of production towards these countries and lead to an overall higher level of pollution for the world. This might also lead firms to invest more heavily in pollution-intensive industries in these countries, exacerbating the basic problem. A convenient way to express this idea was to refer to these countries as potential pollution havens. The basic idea seems compelling but the research indicates that this is not happening to any great extent in the world economy. As we will see in later chapters, the FDI investment decision is influenced by a host of factors of which the level of environmental regulation is just one of many. In most cases, any savings realized by lower levels of environmental regulation pale in comparison to other factors involved in the decision. In other words, in most cases lax regulation occurs in countries where producing complicated products would at best be difficult. The small amount of research on Latin America is consistent with the overall results mentioned above. There is scant evidence of this phenomenon in the region.[15] A key finding has been little evidence of this occurring in Mexico which has less strict regulation than the US, is geographically close and barriers to trade are few. As was shown throughout the chapter, Latin America has significant environmental problems. Fortunately, the research on this subject for the region indicates that becoming a pollution haven in the world economy is not one of them.[16]

3.4 NAFTA and the environment

In 1994, Mexico joined the North American Free Trade Agreement (NAFTA) that previously included Canada and the US Critics of NAFTA in the US noisily predicted that a large number of US manufacturing firms would relocate to Mexico in order to obtain lower wages and escape environmental regulations in the US. With respect to the environment, the implication for the region was clear. Firms would close relatively clean plants in the US and open much dirtier plants in Mexico. This would damage both the environment in Mexico and potentially the environment in border areas of the US. With the passage of 15 years, there is now enough data to analyze the outcome of that forecast of NAFTA as the source of potentially large environmental problems. Fortunately, two careful studies of this issue have concluded that NAFTA has had little impact on the environment in Mexico. At first glance this may seem puzzling. Pollution is a serious problem in Mexico and it seems logical to conclude that NAFTA is part of the problem. Perhaps it is a part of the problem, but only a small one. The reason is that the reduction in trade barriers has two effects. First, it might change the composition of industry in Mexico by encouraging pollution-intensive industries. Gallagher (2004) and Gamper-Rabindran (2006) have found that this does not seem to be the case. Factors other than environmental regulation have influenced the composition of industry in the post-NAFTA era. On the contrary, over time, industry in Mexico is shifting to a mix of industries that is less pollution-intensive than in the past. What does influence the level of pollution in Mexico is economic growth. As the economy grows, overall industrial production in Mexico is rising and this in turn generates more pollution. Again, we are back at the tradeoff between growth and the environment. This is where trade and the environment has the potential to cross. It is widely accepted that increasing international trade in a country enhances economic growth. Since the point of reducing trade barriers is to enhance international trade, it is quite possible that these agreements increase growth and to some extent the level of pollution. Thus, trade agreements may lead to some increases in the level of pollution, just not in quite the same way many believe they do.

Key concepts and terms

command and control (CAC) – a policy to control pollution that sets an allowable level of pollution for producers.

cost/benefit analysis – an analysis using all relevant costs and benefits to determine the appropriate level of economic activity.

environmental Kuznets curve – a curve showing the relationship between GDP per capita and the level of pollution.

market-based initiatives (MBI) – the use of market signals to influence producer behavior with regard to pollution.

market failure – a situation where the production or use of a good or service does not occur where the marginal costs equals marginal benefits for society as a whole.

negative externality – a cost to society of producing a product that has not been included in the market price.

North American Free Trade Agreement (NAFTA) – an agreement to establish a free trade area consisting of Canada, Mexico, and the US.

pollution haven – the idea that a country with lower levels of environmental regulations may be able to produce and export pollution-intensive products more cheaply than countries with stricter regulations.

positive externality – a benefit to society of a good or service that is not included in the market price.

tragedy of the commons – a situation where individuals acting solely in their self interest may end up depleting a limited natural resource.

Questions for review and discussion

1 What is a negative externality? Describe an obvious example related to the environment in Latin America.

2 Using a supply and demand graph, show why gasoline in Latin America might be selling at too low a price if there were no regulations on air pollution by oil refineries.

3 Are natural disasters a significant economic development problem in Latin America?

4 Why would a country in Latin America use CAC to control pollution if there are better policies available?

5 Describe the problem of water pollution in Latin America.

6 How does urbanization contribute to environmental problems in Latin America?

7 Explain the factors that lead to deforestation in Latin America. How does this relate to biodiversity?

8 Describe the environmental Kuznets curve. How does it potentially apply to Latin America?

9 "Because of low levels of environmental regulation, Latin America is likely to become a pollution haven." Explain why this statement is false.

10 How could the reduction of trade barriers increase the level of pollution in the world? Has this happened in the case of NAFTA?

References and recommended readings

Birdsall, Nancy and David Wheeler. 1993. "Trade Policy and Industrial Pollution in Latin America: Where Are the Pollution Havens?" *Journal of Environment & Development* 2(Winter): 137–49.

Copeland, Brian R. and M. Scott Taylor. 2003. *Trade and the Environment: Theory and Empirical Evidence.* Princeton, NJ: Princeton University Press.

Edwards, Sebastian. 1993. "Openness, Trade Liberalization, and Growth in Developing Countries." Journal of Economic Literature 31(September): 1358–93.

Foster, Andrew, Emilio Gutierrez, and Naresh Kumar. 2009. "Voluntary Compliance, Pollution Levels, and Infant Mortality in Mexico." *American Economic Review* 99(May): 191–97.

Gallagher, Kevin. 2004. *Free Trade and the Environment: Mexico, NAFTA, and Beyond.* Palo Alto, CA: Stanford University Press.

Gamper-Rabindran, Shanti. 2006. "NAFTA and the Environment: What Can the Data Tell Us?" *Economic Development and Cultural Change* 54(April): 605–33.

Garcia-Johnson, Ronie. 2000. *Exporting Environmentalism: US Multinational Chemical Corporations in Brazil and Mexico.* Cambridge, MA: MIT Press.

Grossman, Gene M. and Alan B. Krueger. 1993. "Environmental Impacts of a North American Free Trade Agreement," pp. 13–56 in Peter M. Garber (ed.), *The Mexico–US Free Trade Agreement.* Cambridge, MA: MIT Press.

Guha-Sapir, D., D. Hargitt, and P. Hoyois. 2004. *Thirty Years of Natural Disasters 1974–2003: The Numbers.* Louvain: Presses Universitaires de Louvain.

Huber, Richard M., Jack Ruitenbeek, and Ronaldo Seroa da Motta. 1998. *Market-Based Instruments for Environmental Policymaking in Latin America and the Caribbean: Lessons from Eleven Countries.* World Bank Discussion Paper No. 381. Washington, DC: World Bank.

Jenkins, Rhys. 2003. "Has Trade Liberalization Created Pollution Havens in Latin America?" *CEPAL Review* 80(August): 81–95.

Lora, Eduardo, Andrew Powell, Bernard M.S. van Praag, and Pablo Sanguinetti (eds.). 2010. *The Quality of Life in Latin American Cities: Markets and Perception.* Washington, DC: Interamerican Development Bank and World Bank.

Miller, Shawn William. 2007. *An Environmental History of Latin America.* New York: Cambridge University Press.

Munasinghe, Mohan, Raul O'Ryan, Ronaldo Seroa da Motta, Carlos de Miguel, Carlos Young, Sebastian Miller, and Claudio Ferraz. 2006. *Macroeconomic Policies for Sustainable Growth: Analytical Framework and Policy Studies of Brazil and Chile.* Northampton, MA: Edward Elgar.

Romero, Aldemaro and Sarah E. West (eds). 2005. *Environmental Issues in Latin America and the Caribbean .* Dordrecht, The Netherlands: Springer.

Seroa da Matta, Ronaldo. 2003. *Determinants of Environmental Performance in the Brazilian Industrial Sector.* Rio de Janeiro: Research Institute of Applied Economics.

The Economist. 2009. "The Future of the Forest." pp. 27–29. June 13.

World Bank. 2006. *World Development Indicators.* Washington, DC: World Bank.

World Resources Institute. 2008. *World Resources Report 2008 Roots of Resilience: Growing the Wealth of the Poor.* Washington, DC: World Resources Institute.

4   Latin American economic history

> The weight of the past has sometimes been more present than the present itself. And a repetition of the past has sometimes seemed to be the only forseeable future.
>
> Enrique Krauze

Introduction

At the beginning of the book, a number of recurring themes in the economics of Latin America were introduced. Recall as well that the history of the region that is most relevant for our purposes begins at the end of the fifteenth century. Some of the economic themes that were introduced in the first chapter have their roots almost as far back as that. The discovery of the Americas was followed shortly by the discovery of gold and silver. In turn, this discovery set the region on a certain path of development. Gold and silver were just the first of many commodities that were and are important to the region. In a related vein, the exploitation of these commodities required enormous amounts of labor. Unfortunately, the labor market in colonial Latin America was not exactly the competitive market found in a labor economics text. In a similar way, the conquest of Latin America by the colonial powers produced a distribution of land that was in keeping with the way the land was acquired. The theft of the land from the indigenous population was followed by distribution of much of it to a small population of Europeans. The initial distribution of the land and the labor market conditions created a highly unequal distribution of income. In the economic history of Latin America, commodities, poverty, and inequality often share an uncomfortable relation to one another.

Other themes that were introduced earlier also have a long history in the region. Macroeconomic stability rarely has been a characteristic associated with Latin America. Although data limitations prevent much commentary on colonial economic performance, the data now available stretching back to the nineteenth century shows some of the same sort of instability that was associated with the region in the twentieth century. In short, macroeconomic stability seems to be a problem with historical roots. The same is true of debt. Many of the countries of Latin America became debtor nations upon independence. For some of the creditors, the loans were not a positive experience. Debt and its often painful aftermath are an integral part of the history of Latin America in the last 200 years. While the line between what is modern and what is history is indistinct, the origins of import substitution industrialization go back to the early part of the twentieth century. Enough time has passed that this era is becoming more and more a part of the economic history of the region.

Because of the long historical roots of some of the major themes associated with economic development in the region, the purpose of this chapter is to provide a brief economic history of Latin America. Of necessity, the coverage of this history can only be done in the most cursory fashion. The main purpose is to introduce some historical context and introduce some important events and concepts that are essential in understanding how the economy of Latin America came to be as it is. The chapter will proceed historically beginning with the colonial period, which covers nearly half of the relevant history. The period from independence until the latter part of the nineteenth century is covered in the third section of the chapter. The next sections of the chapter cover a brief golden age of economic growth from the late nineteenth to the early twentieth century, the interwar years, the period of ISI, and the recovery from these policies.

The colonial period

> I come for gold, not to till the land like a peasant.
>
> Hernan Cortes

The economic history of Latin America begins with the discovery of the Americas by Columbus in 1492. The immediate discovery of gold set off a flurry of activity by Spain to acquire whatever gold and silver were available in the hemisphere. The early sixteenth century was ushered in by the conquest of both Mexico and Peru and the beginning of three centuries of Spanish colonial rule in Latin America. During this period, there are three economic themes that developed that still influence the region. First, the goal of Spain was the plunder of gold and silver. This first commodity boom was just the first of many and new booms appear periodically and continue in the twenty-first century. The gold and silver boom was followed by widespread investment in agricultural commodities. The production and export of these products has always been, and still is, an important part of the economy of the region. Even today it is hard to imagine a Latin America that doesn't export commodities. As was true with all colonial powers, Spain imposed the policy of mercantilism on Latin America. The policy distorted trade and production patterns for hundreds of years and left a legacy everywhere it was imposed. Latin America is no different in this regard. Finally, the colonial history of Brazil is sufficiently different from the rest of Latin America that the section concludes with a consideration of these differences.

Gold and silver

Initially, the goal of the Spanish government was primarily the plunder of gold and silver. The sums involved were enormous. In the beginning of the conquest of the region gold and silver flowed naturally back to Spain as Spanish citizens wanted to repatriate their money home. After the initial plunder, it became necessary to begin working the original mines used by the indigenous people. The focus now shifted from simple theft to actually having to produce the minerals. Governments at the time were not inclined to do this on their own, so a means had to be found to develop the resource another way. In Latin America, this involved the development of the encomienda. An encomienda was a large tract of land granted to a Spanish citizen to develop. Technically, the *encomenderos* did not own the land but were simply holding it in trusteeship for the indigenous population and the land was to be eventually returned to the government. The indigenous workers were to be cared for by the *encomenderos* and given instruction in the Christian faith. Abuses of the system inevitably occurred through the use of debt or the simple reality that workers might not easily find employment elsewhere. While the workers were supposedly free, the labor market did not approximate what one would call a free labor market. The Spanish government also employed the mita system that was originally developed in the Inca Empire. Under this system, workers were obliged to provide free labor to the government for infrastructure projects. In effect, this was a tax paid by the population in kind (labor). While the system worked well under the Incas, it was frequently abused in the colonial period as workers were used in mining gold and silver. The interest of the Spanish government in the system was in the repartida. Land owners were granted land and access to cheap labor. In return, they owed the Spanish government a share of the output of the land. The repartida flowed back to Spain to be used for general government expenditures.

In a historical sense, the initial riches provided by gold were rather short lived. By the mid-sixteenth century the production of gold was in decline. At this point, silver came to dominate the mining sector in Latin America. This was enhanced by technological change. A technique known as mercury amalgamation was discovered. This allowed for the profitable extraction of silver from low-grade ore. This sort of silver mining required a much higher level of investment and commitment, and was a major reason for an increasing Spanish presence in Latin America. In turn, the encomienda system expanded. This production of silver occurred primarily in the Andes and Mexico. In the former, the center of production was Potosi. In Mexico most production occurred in the Zacatecas, Pachuca, and Sonora mines. The production of silver was so important to Spain that silver production affected the economic development of the whole region for nearly a century. Economic output in the rest of Latin America developed based on supplying the needs of the mining regions. Development in other parts of the region without gold and silver or resources necessary for their production languished. By the mid-seventeenth century the production of silver began to decline. The better grades of ore had been extracted and output inevitably fell. The repartida had to be adjusted downward to account for the lower production and some mines closed altogether. The closing of this era meant the economy of Latin America was about to undergo significant changes. However, as we move through other periods and look into the twenty-first century, the marks left by this initial part of colonial Latin American history are not hard to find.

Agriculture

With the decline in silver production that was occurring in the mid-sixteenth century, economic activity migrated toward the production of agricultural commodities. The age of exploration in the fifteenth century and subsequent discoveries by European explorers and later colonists had led to the introduction into Europe of commodities that quickly became goods for consumption that were in high demand. Some of these goods had trickled into Europe as early as the Roman Empire. However, distances and high transportation costs had kept prices for these products so high that they were prohibitively expensive for the merely well-off, much less the average consumer. The production of popular commodities in the Americas coupled with relatively cheap transportation costs lowered the prices of these commodities to the point where the number of European consumers who could afford some of this output was much larger.

The market was enhanced by the existence of *triangular trade*. The start of the process was the shipment of simple manufactured goods to the west coast of Africa. Goods were then exchanged for slaves. The slaves were then shipped to the Americas and sold at a major center of this activity such as Havana or Cartagena. The need for these slaves was twofold. Recall the devastating drop in population that occurred in Latin America during the sixteenth century. As the production of agricultural products increased, there were labor shortages in many parts of Latin America. In many cases, these shortages were difficult to fill with immigrants from Europe. While the indigenous population of Latin America had little protection against European diseases, the reverse was often the case: Europeans were susceptible to tropical diseases. The tragic solution was the importation of slaves from Africa who were better acclimated to both the climate and less vulnerable to tropical diseases. The proceeds from the sale of slaves were used to purchase commodities which were shipped to Europe and sold at a profit. The process could then be restarted.

The important commodities exported from Latin America during this period were sugar, cocoa, tobacco, hides, cotton, and indigo. Production of some of these commodities was associated with a succession of commodity booms centered in various parts of the region. The production of cocoa was originally centered in Venezuela in the early eighteenth century. The production of tobacco was centered in Cuba. Argentina prospered as a result of the production of hides needed for an expanding global leather market. European demand for sugar was especially high. Production was centered in the Caribbean but also in other parts of the region. Booms were also associated with lesser commodities such as indigo and cochineal. Mexico passed through this period in a somewhat different manner. Silver production in the country slackened but never fell as precipitously as it did in the Andes. The fading importance of gold and silver and the establishment of agricultural production was the high water mark of the interest of Spain in Latin America. Past the mid-seventeenth century, revenue from Latin America would never be as high as in the previous century and the country was distracted by events in Europe.

Land ownership patterns

The colonial economy of Latin America turned from mining gold and silver during the sixteenth and seventeenth centuries to the production of agricultural commodities. The mining of gold and silver had led to a particular type of land use in the region. As the economic structure of the region changed, the land use patterns did not. Recall that the Spanish government allocated large tracts of land to citizens for the mining of gold and silver. As the economy transferred to agriculture, the encomiendas discussed above continued. Several reforms of the system designed to lessen its abuses began occurring as in the early sixteenth century. However, no meaningful reforms were ever accomplished and the system was officially abolished in 1720.

What followed was hardly an improvement. The encomienda system was transformed into a collection of latifundia. Large tracts of land were formally held by a small group of landholders. Crops were grown primarily for export to Europe. Earnings from these exports frequently were repatriated. This meant that there were less of these earnings being reinvested in the region. Landowners had little interest in paying taxes for either schooling or the improvement of infrastructure. What investment there was in the latter was focused on transportation systems for getting crops to the ports and the ports themselves. With such poor infrastructure, many latifundia became *haciendas*.[1] These were almost feudal estates with little ties to even other parts of the country and were nearly self-sufficient. This had two effects that still can be seen in the twenty-first century. As we saw in Chapter 2, public education is an economic development problem in the region. This is not a new problem and its roots reach to this period. Second, the transportation infrastructure of Latin America is poor. Again, this is a problem with long historical roots. For the masses without extensive landholdings there was the prospect of some work on the latifundia. The more fortunate might hold a small plot of land for subsistence farming. These minifundias were a staple of the economy of colonial Latin America and are still a common form of land usage.

The extensive use of the encomienda system at the start of the colonial period put the region on an unfortunate path. Colonial Latin America was virtually born with an extremely unequal distribution of income. The transformation of the encomienda system into a collection of latifundias perpetuated the initial inequality. Further, large landowners had little interest in infrastructure beyond their holdings other than a minimal transportation system. Public education was unimportant as the mass of workers performed agricultural labor for which the human capital requirements were low. Because the possession of land would create income in future generations, the initial highly unequal distribution of land created a highly unequal distribution of income that tended to persist. Economic development became difficult as domestic markets were not well integrated due to poor transportation infrastructure. Human capital was not developed as no one in charge of the system saw any reason to develop it. To be clear, these historical legacies are not the only sources of income inequality in Latin America. However, it is an important factor in understanding the distribution of income in the region. Note too, that this situation is not one that existed because of market forces. Both the initial land distribution and the conditions under which much of the population labored were set by the state or landholders who had been given control of resources by the state.

4.1   Latifundia: a brief history

In the section above, the development of latifundia in Latin America was described. However, this pattern of land usage was not something that was used by the Spanish in Latin America for the first time. The use of the term can be traced back to ancient Greece. While large holdings of land were not common in Greece itself, the term was used to describe large land holdings in Egypt and Syria that produced agricultural products for export. As with many things, the Roman Empire borrowed the term to describe a pattern of land use that should have a familiar ring. In the early second century BC, large landholdings cropped up as the spoils of war with the expansion of the empire. Conveniently, conquest also provided slave labor to work the land. As the Roman Empire expanded to the Mediterranean, the pattern of land use followed. Most importantly in our context, latifundia were common in southern Spain. Smaller landholdings were granted to Roman soldiers as a reward for service in the legions. The owners of the latifundia frequently became spectacularly wealthy as productivity was very high and much of the output was exported. The owners of the land formed the backbone of the ruling class of the Roman Empire.

This pattern of land use reemerged with the retaking of Portugal and Spain from the Muslims. The *reconquista* provided the governments with large tracts of land for distribution. The government chose to allocate the land to the nobility, military allies, or the Catholic Church. In turn, the new owners established large agricultural operations producing commodities for both local consumption and export. It was a return to the Roman system minus the slavery. The concept was easily applied to Latin America because it already was common in Spain. Land gained by conquest was given by the government to nobility or others performing significant military or administrative duties. Formal slavery wasn't used in Spain or initially in Spanish Latin America. In Latin America there was an adequate supply of now landless indigenous people to work the land. The main point is that in Latin American latifundia was a concept with deep historical roots that unfortunately was replanted in a region where conditions were almost ideal for its use.

Mercantilism

The crown had forbidden the manufacture of luxury goods in the colony to eliminate competition with European imports, a stricture that stirred subversives to dream about separation.

John Ross

Like most governments of the time, the Spanish government used the policy of mercantilism in administering colonial holdings. At the beginning, there was little need for a formal policy. The acquisition of gold and silver by the Spanish naturally created a backflow of this wealth to Spain. Mercantilism was the predominant economic philosophy of the age. The focus of most governments was on maximizing the trade surplus using restrictive trade practices and attempting to lower the cost of exports. Spain was no different although there were some country specific variations on the general policy. First, all goods coming from Latin America and all goods going to the region had to pass through Spain. This had the effect of raising the prices colonists paid for goods and lowering the prices obtainable for exports. Neither of these effects are positive in terms of economic development. Those without large holdings were fortunate to be able to farm a minifundia for subsistence. Finally, Spain discouraged even the production of any goods in Latin America that would compete with production in Spain. This policy applied to both manufacturing and agriculture. In short, the mercantilist policies of the Spanish government were even more restrictive than was typical of the era.

The demise of Spanish mercantilist policy matched the decline of the country relative to the United Kingdom (UK) and to a lesser extent France.[2] The defeat of the Spanish Armada in 1588 was a highly visible sign of this demise. After this point, Spain found it increasingly difficult to enforce its mercantilist policies and illicit trade between Latin America and the rest of Europe became increasingly common. The Treaty of Utrecht in 1713 ceded control of the slave trade to the UK and gave British ships a legitimate reason to enter ports in Latin America. Spain formally granted the colonies the ability to trade among themselves in 1778. After this point, mercantilism was only a slight impediment to the economic development of the region.

As has been mentioned earlier and will be touched on many times in the book, Latin America historically has been somewhat isolated from the world economy. Further, trade within the region today is still somewhat less than one might expect. Nearly 300 years of Spanish mercantilist policy had something to do with this. The policies of the Spanish government were even more restrictive with respect to international trade than was typical of the era. The *annual* fleets of ships bringing goods from Spain and returning to Spain with commodities are a stark example of the mindset of the Spanish government. Trade was something done for the benefit of Spain with the economic welfare of Latin America a minor consideration. The suppression of any economic activity in Latin America in competition with Spanish production exacerbated the adverse effects of trade restrictions. Even worse, Spain regulated trade between ports in Latin America which increased the economic isolation of one part of the region from another. As with many economic policies, the direction of change is clear. These policies hindered the economic development of the region. The extent to which they did so is not clear. However, such a long history of relative isolation is not easily overcome.

Brazil: variations on a theme

The previous brief sketch of the economic history of colonial Latin America deliberately neglected the development of Brazil. The creation of what is now modern Brazil is an interesting example of accident and international diplomacy. Even before the Americas were discovered, the Pope of the Catholic Church had granted all lands south of the Canary Islands to Portugal. Following the discovery of the new world, a subsequent Spanish born Pope decreed in 1493 essentially that most of the land in Latin America belonged to Spain. Understandably, Portugal was unhappy with this decision and a solution was brokered between the two countries by the Vatican. The Treaty of Tordesillas signed in 1494 provided Portugal with more land in Latin America. In modern terms, Portugal was entitled to land in Latin America along a north-south line a bit east of modern Rio de Janeiro.[3] Spain never effectively interfered with Portuguese expansion into the interior of South America. This expansion was much more gradual than in the Spanish colonies. There were no obvious deposits of precious metal to exploit. The original export of the colony was brazilwood which was used to produce a popular dye in Europe. This success attracted the interests of the French in the colony and set something of a pattern different from the rest of the region. Portugal had continuous problems defending the colony from the incursions of other, more powerful, European powers. As a result of French interest, Portugal began encouraging greater colonization efforts in the early sixteenth century.

This effort was encouraged by the Portuguese government granting large tracts of land for development. These *fazenda* estates were very similar to the latifundia of the Spanish colonies. They very quickly were used to produce an important cash crop, sugar. By the mid-seventeenth century, Brazil was the world's leading producer. Since the production of sugar is labor-intensive, the development of the industry required a large labor force that the colony did not possess. The solution was an event that changed the face of Brazil. Large numbers of slaves were imported from Africa beginning in the late sixteenth century. The combination of sugar and the labor to expand the industry created yet another commodity boom in the region. As is usually the case, the boom ended with the Dutch starting their own plantations in the Caribbean after a failed attempt to wrest control of Brazil from the Portuguese. Another boom shortly followed on the heels of the decline in the sugar market. In the late seventeenth century, gold was discovered in the southeastern region of Brazil (Minas Gerais). This was followed by the discovery of diamond deposits in the early eighteenth century. Exploitation of these two resources created a spectacular boom in the colony that lasted well into the second half of the eighteenth century.

In general, the colonization and development of Brazil occurred more slowly than the rest of the region. This is logical as the colony did not initially yield the massive wealth of the Spanish colonies. While Portugal imposed many of the same mercantilist policies as Spain, the regulations were looser and not enforced as rigorously. After the discovery of gold and diamonds, Portuguese interest in and control of the colony intensified. However, the importation of slaves made it virtually impossible to restrict trade to Portuguese ships only; the demand was simply too great. Mercantilist policies were further weakened by a treaty between Portugal and the UK that formally gave British ships access to Brazilian ports. In summary, the colonial development of Brazil differed from the Spanish colonies in three important ways. Due to the absence of any initial discovery of mineral wealth, the early development of the colony was based on the production of agricultural commodities such as sugar and tobacco. Second, the mercantilist policies of the Portuguese government were never as thorough or rigorously enforced as was the case in the rest of Latin America. Finally, these policies ended much sooner because the natural trade relations of both the mother country and the colony were inextricably influenced by the world's rising economic power of the time, the UK.

4.2 Slavery in Latin America

In Chapter 1 we noted that Latin America is one of the most diverse regions of the world in many senses. Over the centuries, both larger and smaller migrations into the region have originated from all of the other regions of the world. One of the largest of these migrations was from Africa. Unfortunately, this migration was different. Unlike other migrations, this one involved forced migration, i.e. slavery. As one might expect, the origins of this migration are complex. Slavery had been known in Europe since the time of the Greek and Roman empires. During the Age of Discovery in the fifteenth century in Portugal there had been a small migration of African slaves to both Portugal and Spain. Portuguese ties with West Africa grew substantially during this period and provided the foundations for a steady supply of slaves that could be transported to the Western Hemisphere. This supply was awaiting a demand in the region which quickly materialized. Developments in mining and later agriculture grew into an enormous demand for labor. This demand could not be fully supplied from the indigenous population. Neither colonial power decided to extend a formal system of slavery to this population. Labor could be obtained without slavery in both Mexico and Peru as there were initially large concentrations of workers where they were needed. However, as noted earlier, disease took a huge toll on this population. In other areas, particularly Brazil, the indigenous population of hunter/gatherers was too small and difficult to control to provide satisfactory amounts of labor. Migration from Portugal and Spain was not an option. Portugal's small population at the time (1 million) made a large migration impossible. High wages in Spain coupled with military operations in Northern Europe reduced migration from Spain to a small amount.

The solution was large-scale importation of slaves from Africa. The numbers involved are truly staggering. Until the 1830s more Africans crossed the Atlantic than Europeans. The total migration from all regions of the world from 1492 to the 1830s is estimated to be 6.6 million. Of these, 4.5 million were African slaves. Within Latin America the major destination was Brazil. Other countries that received a substantial number of slaves were Colombia, Venezuela, Peru, and Mexico. This massive migration literally changed the face of Latin America. Today, somewhere between 100 and 150 million Latin Americans are descendants from this migration. The majority of this population is Brazilian. Nearly half of the population of Brazil is descended from African slaves. Data for other countries can be a problem as census procedures vary from country to country. However, there are substantial populations in Colombia, Venezuela, and Peru. This forced migration changed the face of many of the countries of the region. Imagining modern Latin America without this part of the population would be a difficult task.[4]

Independence and post-colonial turmoil

From the brief sketch of the economic history of colonial Latin America, one can already see the seeds of the decline of Portuguese and Spanish rule. Recall that the production of gold and silver in the Spanish colonies declined after the middle of the seventeenth century. While the production of agricultural commodities increased, revenue to Spain from the colonies was difficult to maintain. There were periodic commodity booms, but nothing like the flow of money from gold and silver would ever return. In addition, things were not going well in Spain itself. The defeat of the Spanish Armada in 1588 marked the beginning of a long decline. Spain could never match the industrial output of the UK and increasingly needed goods that the country could not produce. This led to the continual loosening of the commercial ties to Spain both formally by changes in law and treaties and informally (i.e. smuggling). In effect, over 300 years, the Spanish colonies of Latin America were slipping the bonds of control by Spain.

Three factors in particular led to the independence movements of the late eighteenth and early nineteenth centuries. First, there was the issue of taxation. Taxes were being collected locally and then shipped to Spain. There were also still residual restraints on trade. Increasingly these burdens were difficult to defend. Secondly, the top administrative positions in the colonies were always held by those born in Spain. After so long a time, much of the economic power of the region was held by those born and raised there. Invariably this led to tension as the people of the region did not have the usual rights granted to citizens of Spain. Then there was the question of land. The initial distribution of land left much of the population landless and impoverished. With little possibility of redress from the Spanish government, the idea of independence gave some hope for the future. However, the end of Spanish rule was determined as much in Europe as Latin America. French control of the Spanish government put the whole legitimacy of Spanish rule into question. It also put Spain in a situation where it could not hold on to the colonies as a result of political turmoil. In a decade of unrest between 1810 and 1825, most of Latin America had achieved independence from Spain. Under a somewhat different set of circumstances, Brazil became independent in 1822.[5] While independence brought constitutions promising liberal democracy, this did not last long. The various wars of independence had left many countries badly in need of reconstruction. Instead of reconstruction, independence brought boundary disputes among countries. This situation was compounded by groups seeking power not through voting but through violence. While Spanish rule (or misrule) had lowered economic growth in the region, what followed independence in many cases was worse in an economic sense.

Generally, economists don't have many positive things to say about wars and domestic violence. To understand why, we need to think back to the growth theory of Chapter 2. In terms of the traditional theory of economic growth, growth is a function of increases in the labor force and the capital stock. War and domestic violence diminish growth. The casualties of war translate into a lower labor force and a smaller GDP in the future. Similarly, war involves the destruction of a part of the capital stock. This is a particular problem in an area such as post-independence Latin America where the stock of capital was not large to begin with. The combination of these two factors can mean lower economic growth following the end of a military conflict. Newer versions of growth theory emphasize the positive effects on growth of the accumulation of human capital. Wars and domestic violence at a minimum can disrupt the educational process in a country. The loss of life also can mean a loss of human capital as well as just losing another worker. In an area where educational attainment was low to begin with, losing educated citizens to war can be particularly damaging. In short, the loss of labor, capital, and human capital that wars and domestic violence causes usually lowers economic growth. If the conflicts are severe, the negative effects may last for decades.

As we saw in Chapter 2, the most recent research on economic growth focuses on the role of institutions. To briefly review, it has been shown that two of the critical preconditions for economic growth are property rights and the rule of law. Without these two critical preconditions, economic growth is difficult at best. For all of its faults, the Spanish colonial government provided these two basic conditions. Property rights were established. They may have been initially arbitrary but at least they were clear. As time passed, the initial inequities in the distribution of land ossified into a highly unequal distribution of this critical resource. While this is not a desirable situation, the situation where property rights become uncertain is worse. If the government cannot protect land or other forms of property, then economic activity becomes difficult. During the wars of independence and subsequent conflicts, the protection of property rights in many parts of Latin America became problematical. The same is true for the rule of law. Colonial rule was far from perfect but for hundreds of years there was law and a government to enforce the law. Laws made in Madrid and Lisbon may have been inappropriate for the region, but at least there was law and a consistent means to enforce it. With independence this system of law broke down in many parts of the region.

In any economy, the consequences of a breakdown in property rights and the rule of law are dire. As was mentioned earlier, this virtually defines the modern concept of a failed state. For several decades in post-colonial Latin America, many of the countries of the regions would have qualified as failed states for substantial periods of time. Under these conditions, economic growth was minimal. While the promise of liberal democracy was not realized, the vacuum left by the exit of Spanish colonial rule was worse. The result was that some sort of stability was essential. Neither property rights nor the rule of law are binary variables. Stability in this sense means that the institutions of government are stable enough to provide enough day to day protection for the population that something like normal economic activity can occur. As a region, it took nearly three decades for this to occur in Latin America. The situation can be summarized by the frequent references to this period as the "lost decades."

By the 1850s, the worst of the wars and domestic violence in Latin America was over. Without strong democratic institutions, political power may accrue to whatever group or groups have the strength to exercise power. Thus, the enforcement of property rights or the rule of law becomes arbitrary. Who owns what or the application of law becomes arbitrary depending on who happens to be in power at the moment. In Latin America, this frequently meant rule by some combination of landed elites and the military. Such combinations of power frequently prove to be unstable. This instability in government would continue to plague the region for more than 150 years. Many of the institutional weaknesses described in Chapter 2 have their roots in this era. Further, the legacies of Spanish rule remained. The region was deeply divided in terms of the distribution of wealth and income. Educational levels were generally low. Except in major agricultural areas and ports, infrastructure in the region was poor. The legacy of mercantilism lingered in that the region was still isolated from the global economy. Economic activity was still dominated by the production of commodities and the manufacturing sector was small. With some exceptions in major cities, Latin America in the mid-nineteenth century could be characterized as isolated and poor. However, the instability of the first decades after independence had subsided and enough stability had been achieved that the region would be able to benefit greatly from the last part of the nineteenth century.

The Golden Age: 1870–1914

The decades following independence in Latin America eventually provided sufficient stability in much of the region for economic growth to commence along the lines developed in Chapter 2. Increases in the labor force coupled with the accumulation of physical and human capital began having their usual effects: GDP per capita began increasing. Indeed, the period from 1870 to 1914 marked something of a golden age of growth in the region.[6] As is usually the case, the rapid economic growth of the region during this period was a result of both favorable internal developments within the region coupled with a favorable external environment. To summarize in advance, Latin America had become sufficiently stable in terms of property rights and the rule of law. In addition, the world economy was experiencing an unusually rapid period of growth. In this section, we will cover both the internal and external factors that contributed to this period of rapid economic growth. Since Latin America did not fare nearly so well in much of the rest of the twentieth century it is important to understand what went right during this period to more fully appreciate what went wrong later.

In the first place, in the second half of the nineteenth century some measure of political stability had been achieved. For example, political turmoil ended in Argentina with the installation of the rule of an oligarchy in 1890. In Mexico, the *reforma* ended a period of political chaos and was followed by the *Porfiriato*. The liberal economic reforms and political stability created by the rule of Porfirio Diaz resulted in a golden age in Mexican economic history. Monarchial rule ended in Brazil and the country peacefully transitioned to a republic. The story varies from country to country but the common theme was that the turmoil that followed independence was dying down. Independence initially brought the promise of liberal democracy for the region. Unfortunately, that vision would not be fulfilled for another century and a half. Internal turmoil had been replaced by one version or another of authoritarian rule. As has been witnessed in more modern settings, authoritarian rule or rule by an oligarchy can be consistent with rapid economic growth. While political freedoms may have been suppressed, decades of turmoil in many countries make this outcome at least more comprehensible.

The return of something like internal stability to the region was matched by a relatively peaceful international environment. From the end of the Napoleonic Wars to the beginning of World War I, there were no major international conflicts. The influence of the former colonial powers, Portugal and Spain, had faded with uncharacteristic speed. Further, in 1823 the US declared the Western Hemisphere to be off limits to other potential colonial powers. With the notable exception of a French attempt to take over Mexico in the 1860s, the direct influence of colonial powers in Latin American affairs was negligible. Political influence was replaced by economic influence. The European country with the most active interest in the region was the UK This was logical as the UK during the nineteenth century was the world's most important economic power. During this period, economic ties between Latin America and the US strengthened. The end of post-independence turmoil helped usher in a wave of FDI from the UK and later from the US. Virtually nothing is more detrimental to FDI than domestic political instability or what is now referred to as "country risk." When the level of GDP per capita in a country is low, it is difficult for a country to grow rapidly. Since saving is a function of income, low GDP per capita usually translates into a low level of saving in a country. For a country in a state of autarky, it becomes difficult to generate enough savings to achieve a high level of investment. From our discussion in Chapter 2, this means that the production function for the economy does not increase as fast as it would if domestic investment is being augmented by FDI. The return of political stability to the region translated into an increase in FDI coupled with the increase in economic growth that one would expect.

4.3   The War of the Pacific

A major exception to the general tranquility of the region during the latter part of the nineteenth century was a major military conflict along the Pacific Coast of South America. A lingering problem following independence in this area was the borders among Bolivia, Peru, and Chile. Bolivia and Chile had attempted to settle their disputes by treaty in 1866 and 1874. However, distrust of Chile was such that Bolivia and Peru formed a defensive alliance in 1873. The tensions were exacerbated by economic interests. The province of Antofogasta (then in Bolivia) is a high mountain desert rich in nitrates. In this period, these nitrates in the form of salt peter used to produce explosives and guano used for fertilizer were extremely valuable. In addition, the region contains an incredible amount of copper. The resources were being exploited by British capital backing Chilean companies. Bolivia and Chile had reached agreement on the taxation of Chilean companies in 1874 but in 1878 Bolivia attempted to increase taxes beyond the previously agreed upon rates. A counterthreat by Bolivia to confiscate Chilean property led to an invasion of the country in 1879. The defensive alliance immediately brought Peru into the war. In order to hold Antofagasta, it was necessary for Chile to control naval access to the province. In a series of battles, the Chilean navy gained this control which led to a successful ground campaign. The military conflict ended in 1883. Chile had gained not only Antofagasta province, but two provinces in Peru. Under the treaty, the status of these two Peruvian provinces was supposed to be determined by a plebiscite to be held in ten years. Disagreement over the terms of the plebiscite resulted in the dispute continuing until 1929. At this point, US mediation led to one of the provinces being returned to Peru. Peru lost a war and a province. Bolivia lost a war, its access to the sea, and became a landlocked nation. Chile gained valuable territory at the expense of its two neighbors. For all of the countries of the area, the ill will generated by this war lingers into the twenty-first century partially because the region is still so important for its resources. While salt peter and guano are part of economic history, substantial revenues accrue to Chile from copper and more recently, lithium.

Growth in the region was assisted by rapid growth in the world economy. The period 1850 to 1913 has sometimes been referred to as the "first era of globalization." Rapid growth in the world economy was powered by changes in technology. The spread of railroads and steamships dramatically lowered transportation costs both domestically and internationally.[7] For Latin America this meant that commodities such as wheat could now be profitably exported. The refrigeration of meat allowed Argentina to begin large-scale exports of beef and mutton to Europe in the 1880s. The laying of transatlantic cable for the transmission of telegraph messages in the 1860s revolutionized communication in the world. This technology provided the basis for truly global financial markets to emerge. These developments changed the face of Latin America. For over 300 years, the region had been a relatively isolated backwater of the Spanish Empire. Fortunately, the return of political stability to the region occurred at about the same time the world economy was changing as a result of new technology. The decrease in isolation brought the ability to trade and increases in investment to the region. The result was that Latin America was much more a part of the world economy at the end of the nineteenth century than it was at the beginning.

These favorable developments in the world economy led to a large demand for commodities in the second half of the nineteenth century.[8] Improvements in transportation technology, the return of stability to the region, and the ability to produce large amounts of commodities at competitive prices created a very favorable environment for Latin American exports. Wool, wheat, hides, and meat poured out of Argentina in unprecedented volumes bound for Europe. Nitrates used in the production of explosives and fertilizers were exported in large quantities from Chile, Peru, and Bolivia.

Coffee and bananas were exported from the countries of Central America. Increasing amounts of coffee and then rubber were produced and exported from Brazil. Booms sometimes turn into busts, which is in the nature of commodities.[9] Despite the punctuations of periodic busts, the overall economy of the region enjoyed an unprecedented period of economic growth. Political stability made it possible for purely domestic economic activity to resume its normal course. Stability also made it possible for foreign investors to augment domestic savings and increase the overall rates of investment. Increases in exports of commodities further fueled growth. Government finances stabilized to the point that public sector investments could be made in ports and other parts of the transportation infrastructure. In modern terms, during this period much of Latin America was making the transition from low- to middle-income status. For some countries, the situation was even better. By the beginning of the twentieth century Argentina and Australia were roughly equal. Immigrants from Europe flowed into Argentina on the reasonable assumption that the country was a better bet than the US. Immigrants also arrived from China, Japan, and the Middle East.[10] To an economist, this is one of the main indicators of economic success. The decision to immigrate, especially in the nineteenth century, was a serious business. People making such important choices are unlikely to move to an area where future economic prospects are not considered to be good. Immigrants contribute not only labor but frequently they bring human capital as well. As we noted in Chapter 2, the potential effects on economic growth can be large.[11] The interaction of all of these positive factors created an environment of rapid growth that the region has never been able to replicate. As we will see below, the largest problem for the economy of the region in the twentieth century has been the inability to regain the levels of growth that was obtained in the late nineteenth and early twentieth centuries.

Wars and depression

One of the oldest economic myths is that war is good for the economy. While it may be beneficial for certain industries, military conflicts are a poor substitute for production and trade under peaceful conditions. The start of World War I brought both the boom in Latin America and the world at large to a halt. The next 30 years would include two world wars and a global depression. In this sort of environment, it would be difficult for any country or region to do well. Latin America was no different. The rapid growth of the Golden Age came to an end. However, the economic story for the region during these years is a complicated mix of change on many fronts. Along with slower growth, the region was grappling with changes in world commodity markets. To make matters worse, the collapse of the international monetary system made things more difficult both for the world and Latin America. The economic focus of the world and Latin America also shifted during this period. The major economic power of the nineteenth century, the

UK gave way to the new rising economic power, the US. For Latin America, this change was more important than for much of the rest of the world. This period also saw the beginnings of modern industrialization in the region. The development of this sector became one of the most important economic issues in the region in the post-war era. Like the rest of the world, the Great Depression was a devastating economic event for the region. Finally, World War II explicitly missed the region. However, the disruption of trade that it caused meant that neutral Latin America was not unaffected. As we will see, this period involves an important transition from the Golden Age to the next period of economic history in the region.

4.4   The world economy: a brief history

When the term "economic growth" is used, almost invariably what is being discussed is a country's GDP growth rate. However, no country or region is an economic island. Since all countries or regions are to a greater or lesser extent integrated into the world economy, it is reasonable to think about world economic growth. If the world economy is growing at a faster or slower rate, then it will be, accordingly, easier or harder for a national economy to grow.

To get some idea of the rate of growth of the world economy, economic historians have been constructing estimates of past GDP growth in various countries and aggregating these estimates over the past several decades. In general terms, they have identified distinct periods of growth in the world economy over the last 150 years.[12] From 1850 to 1914, the world economy experienced a prolonged period of rapid economic growth. Rapid advances in transportation and communication helped fuel the growth of trade both domestically and internationally in many countries. It is no accident that Latin America's Golden Age coincided almost exactly with this period. A period of slow growth began with the start of World War I and ended in 1945 with the end of World War II. In addition to two world wars, this period included a global economic depression. As we saw above, this was also a difficult period for Latin America.

A prolonged period of rapid world economic growth began in 1945. The period 1945 to 1973 was a golden age for the world economy, characterized by rapid increases in output and especially international trade. Growth in trade was partially a function of the dismantling of many of the trade barriers erected during the 1930s. Unfortunately, this period ended abruptly in 1973 with the rapid increase in oil prices. Latin America did not fare as well during this second boom in the world economy. This is partially true due to the set of policy choices discussed below. Unfortunately, for the region the end result of these policy choices occurred in the context of a world economy that was growing very slowly. The point is that economic outcomes for countries are not totally determined by internal factors. Good policy choices coupled with rapid world economic growth can produce sustained periods of rapid growth. As we will see, the reverse set of circumstances can produce very difficult economic conditions for a country or region.

During this period, commodity prices became unstable. The long period of rising commodity prices was followed by the instability in prices that in the twentieth century has become the norm. Further, declines in the demand for commodities can be doubly problematical. Not only does the volume of exports decline, but frequently there may be a concomitant decline in the prices of these commodities. The supply and demand conditions in commodity markets frequently make these price declines severe. These problems were not universal in the region. The outbreak of war led to increases in the demand for oil and other strategic raw materials. Countries such as Mexico and Venezuela benefited from this. Other countries that were more dependent on commodities used for personal consumption fared less well. Brazil and coffee is a relevant example. The periodic collapse in the prices of some commodities led to severe economic problems in some countries. Nitrate prices fell sharply causing serious economic problems in Chile. Coffee prices began a long fall with serious consequences for Brazil. By World War I, Latin America's integration into the world economy carried risks as well as rewards. On the one hand, if economists know anything about international trade it is that autarky doesn't work.[13] Everything else equal, trade enhances prosperity. Prior to the Golden Age, one of the region's economic problems was its isolation from the world economy. A part of the rapid growth of the region during this period can be traced to its increasing integration into the world economy. While such integration enhances growth, there is a cost. To the extent growth is dependent on exports, then that growth can be threatened by relatively slow growth in the world economy. This is what contributed to the end of the Golden Age in Latin America. Global growth slowed and with it the exports of commodities that were an important component of the overall rapid growth in the region.

The period before and after World War I also saw a major change in the relationships among Europe, Latin America, and the US. The war disrupted trade relationships as exports to the UK and France were encouraged and exports to Germany and its allies were discouraged. As the power of the UK in the world economy waned, so did its influence in Latin America. In many senses, World War I marked a change in the influence of the UK in the world economy. That influence was increasingly being replaced by the influence of the US. During the 1920s, the US had replaced the UK as the major source of trade and FDI for Latin America. Part of this was the normal pull of economic geography. Trade tends to be more intense between countries that are geographically closer. In this case, the relative health of the US economy both during the war and after, led to a closer trade and investment relationship between Latin America and the US.

This period also marked the beginnings of an increase in manufacturing in the region. While there had been some manufacturing output in Latin

America for hundreds of years, the sector remained relatively small. In the main, industry was of the craft or "cottage industry" variety. However, the boom of the Golden Age led to an increase in the amount of small-scale manufacturing. As the economies of the region became wealthier and more urbanized, the demand for consumer goods increased. In addition, investments in infrastructure helped to make industrialization possible. From 1913 to 1929, manufacturing in the region grew at a 3.0 percent annual rate. This rate increased to 3.9 percent from 1929 to 1945. While this may sound modest at first, one must consider that this period was not exactly a perfect environment for industrial development in any part of the world. The reasons for this growth are not entirely clear, but some factors no doubt contributed to the solid growth in manufacturing that occurred during this period that laid the groundwork for the much faster growth of industry that took place after World War II. One of the major factors involved was a breakdown in the international payments system. The war disrupted trade, FDI, and the flow of money in general to Latin America. The end of World War I brought some degree of stability to the international payments system. However, the advent of the Great Depression permanently shattered the old system. Instability in the payments system coupled with unstable prices for the exports of commodities meant that importing foreign goods was no longer a purely automatic process. In many countries, exchange controls were instituted. Exchange controls make the government or central bank the only legal buyer and seller of foreign exchange. In such a situation, one cannot just buy imports because one has enough domestic currency to do so. One must also obtain the requisite foreign exchange from the central bank. The effect was that imports were not as cheap or easy to obtain in all cases. As competition from imports fell, domestic manufacturing became relatively more attractive. Secondly, exchange rates became unstable. In most cases, the effect of the change was to make foreign goods more expensive.

Of course, such a change makes domestic production more attractive relative to foreign production. Finally, there was both an implicit and explicit increase in protection for domestic industry. Many tariffs in Latin America were *specific* tariffs.[14] As prices fell during the Great Depression, the level of protection with this sort of tariff rises. Tariffs were frequently raised as a matter of trade policy as the world economy experienced a trade war started by the US in 1930. In any case, an increased level of protectionism encourages domestic manufacturing. The effects on manufacturing were important but the region was starting from a very low base. By the end of the period manufacturing in most countries was still less than 20 percent of GDP.

Summarizing the economic changes that occurred in Latin America between the start of World War I and the end of World War II is not a simple matter. One way to view the period is in terms of the region dealing with a succession of economic shocks. First, the export-driven growth model of the Golden Age did not end in 1914. However, the disruptions of the wars coupled with the global slowdown in growth reduced the importance of commodity exports as a driver of economic growth for the region. Some commodities such as oil did well and countries such as Mexico prospered. But for most countries, booming commodity exports would never return as a reliable source of growth. The collapse of the global exchange rate system injected a new source of instability for the world and the region. It would be decades before Latin America fully adjusted to the new world of floating exchange rates. The two wars and the relative decline of the UK shifted the focus of Latin American trade and investment from the UK to the US. The establishment of new trade and investment relationships takes time for any country or region to adjust to. The Great Depression was a watershed event for Latin America and the world. The decline in demand and real GDP coupled with a global trade war made increases in economic activity for the region difficult. Perhaps one way to summarize the period is to think in terms of changes in restructuring. Latin America was being forced to change from a very successful model of economic growth based on exporting commodities to a booming world economy. The changes of this period meant that both the volume of these exports slowed and the prices received became much more unstable. As the parts of the economy connected to this export sector become relatively smaller, the resources need to move to another, faster growing, part of the economy. Both domestic changes and changes in the world economy were acting to favor the small manufacturing sector in the region. The combination of these factors led to a noticeable increase in manufacturing relative to GDP in the region. However, there were both internal and external constraints on the growth of manufacturing. The result was that manufacturing could not possibly grow fast enough in this period to make up for the slowdown in commodity exports. As we will see in the next section, the base was established for more rapid growth in this sector after World War II.

Import substitution

As we saw in the previous section, the manufacturing sector in Latin America began to grow somewhat faster in the early twentieth century than it did in the past. Initially, this was due to changes that were occurring outside the region. The changing nature of world commodity markets led to drops in export earnings for many of the countries of the region. These shortages prompted drops in imports of goods that could be replaced by local manufacturing. The collapse of the world economy in the late 1920s brought about the collapse of the global system of fixed exchange rates. For Latin American countries this frequently meant devaluations of the currency which made imports more expensive. As a result of the global trade war that occurred in the Great Depression, tariffs on imports rose across the region. Obviously, both devaluations and greater protectionism would tend to stimulate the development of local manufacturing. In summary, the changes that occurred in the world and the region from 1914 to 1945 tended to favor the growth of manufacturing. Since much of the growth in manufacturing was related to domestic consumption, it is easy to characterize this growth as import substitution. From sometime in the early 1930s to the early 1970s much of the growth of protected manufacturing in the region was geared toward production for the domestic market. However, in the early part of this process the increase was driven primarily by circumstances occurring outside the region and a collection of policies could best be described as being a reaction to a changing world economy.

After World War II, this *ad hoc* collection of policies began to coalesce into something more akin to a plan for economic development. As was mentioned in Chapter 1, import substitution industrialization (ISI) emerged as the dominant post-war policy for economic development in the region. There are a number of reasons for this. It seemed apparent at the time that the commodity driven boom of the Golden Age was unlikely to return. Second, in the post-war era the industrialization was more or less being taken as synonymous with economic development. Third, many economists in Latin America itself theorized that within the region industrialization designed to replace imports was a potentially attractive development strategy. In a sense, ISI was just a continuation of what was already occurring in the region. Industry had developed in the first half of the century primarily as a way to replace more expensive imports. Second, some of the tools of ISI such as high tariffs were already in place. Thus, in the post-war era ISI was more a continuation and formalization of what was already occurring than a set of policies designed from scratch. Since the formalization of ISI occurred in the late 1940s, we will date the start of that period from then.[15]

What followed was an almost three-decade period of the development of industry in the region primarily geared toward rapid industrialization based on the replacement of imports from the developed countries with production in the region. In one undeniable sense, the policy worked. During this period GDP per capita rose rapidly.[16] Industry grew and the agricultural sector shrank. This is not surprising as the overall policy was pursued in many countries rather aggressively. As we will see in Chapter 7, tariffs rose to astonishingly high levels. Frequently, these tariffs were supplemented by the use of import quotas. These industries were also supported by even more active policies. Private sector producers frequently were offered subsidized credit, tax relief, and other forms of government assistance. When possible, FDI was channeled into production for the domestic market. If no domestic or foreign firms could be induced to produce for the domestic market then the government might set up a state-owned enterprise (SOE) if the production was deemed to be critical to the overall success of ISI in a country.[17] Usually exchange rates were maintained at artificially low levels so that firms could purchase inputs at lower prices. As one would expect, this collection of policies led to a boom in the manufacturing sector in the region that lasted for several decades. In the beginning, ISI seemed superficially successful. GDP per capita was growing and agriculture was declining, both things that at the time were associated with successful development. Because industry was frequently geographically concentrated in a few urban areas, many of the major cities in the region were growing rapidly. Understandably, higher incomes, a larger industrial sector, and increasing urbanization created the sense that ISI was working.

Unfortunately, under this veneer of success all was not well. ISI began to lead to a number of distortions in the economies of the region that eventually led to its demise. The agricultural sector in the region usually was neglected. This was unfortunate as a substantial percentage of the population of Latin America resides in the countryside. Part of this neglect could be seen in the migration of workers to the industrial centers even in the face of high unemployment. These migrants were not being irrational. The wage gap between the rural and urban areas had become so large that a worker could still improve her standard of living through migration even if employment opportunities were limited. It is not accidental that the large "informal" sector in Latin America grew apace with the success of ISI. Second, in many countries government support of ISI led to ruinous macroeconomic policies. Government subsidies and support of SOEs meant that the national governments were running chronic budget deficits. With no private market for government debt, the alternative in many cases was simply printing money to cover the deficit. The effect on national inflation rates was what one would expect. ISI was contributing to macroeconomic instability. Inflation and the periodic attempts to reduce inflation were making the growth rate of real GDP for many countries in the region unstable. In addition, the policy was leading to chronic imbalances in international trade. Exchange rates were being held at too low a level to make imported inputs into manufacturing less expensive. Such a policy also encouraged other imports and perhaps more importantly discouraged exports. This was a particular burden for Latin America's traditional exports of commodities. These exports were diminished in importance, but they were still an important part of the economy of the region. As the period wore on, there was an increasing use of borrowing from foreign financial institutions to cover the imbalance in trade. This buildup of debt is an old story in Latin America that usually does not end well. Unfortunately, the final result of decades of ISI was almost predictable except for being more severe than would have been expected.

4.5 Latin American debt

Unfortunately, the terms debt and Latin America are closely connected. As with most such connections, this is not accidental. The history of Latin American debt stretches back to independence. As Latin America freed itself from Spanish colonial rule, the global business and finance communities understood that the region was potentially prosperous. Independence created high hopes of economic success not only within the region but among foreign investors. The new governments of Latin America needed foreign capital and at the time the money was readily available. Such borrowing is usually referred to as sovereign debt which is some form of debt guaranteed by a government. This form of borrowing was hardly new and had been routine in Europe for hundreds of years. What followed independence was a wave of borrowing by new and what turned out to be unstable governments of the region. The result was that much of this new borrowing was not repaid promptly and the resolution of investor claims took years to sort out. The relative stability of the 1850s ushered in a new wave of lending to the governments of the region. After some of the difficulties experienced by lenders after independence, the lending was more prudent and selective.[18] The success of this lending was given further impetus by the economic success of the region during the Golden Age. Unfortunately, this led to something of a bubble in lending. Sovereign debt is like most things, appropriate in moderation but potentially catastrophic in excess. Lending to the more successful economies such as Argentina in the late nineteenth century eventually became excessive. As we will see, like individuals, countries can find themselves in a position where they have taken on more debt than they can comfortably repay. In this as in other cases, defaults or suspension of debt payments occur. Debtors and creditors eventually resolve the issue over time. Creditors may not receive all the proceeds that are owed and defaulting countries lose some or all access to borrowing. The most recent debt crisis in the region in the 1980s was no different. Debtors borrowed too much and creditors loaned too much. The borrowing was driven by unsustainable polices and the lending proceeded on unrealistic assumptions about the ability of the countries of the region to repay debt. The oil shocks of the 1970s exposed both the problems of policy and the excessive optimism of the lenders. However, one should realize that the debt crisis of the 1980s was not something novel for the region; rather, an old story being repeated one more time.

The Lost Decade of the 1980s

By the early 1970s, ISI was putting a significant strain on the economies of the region. Most countries were still attempting to maintain fixed exchange rates that were the norm for the time. Unfortunately, the domestic inflation common in Latin America meant that the prices of imports and exports were becoming increasingly unrealistic. In the face of domestic inflation and a fixed exchange rate, imports were becoming ever cheaper. Countries pursued ever more restrictive policies designed to control the level of imports. Tariffs reached very high levels. Quotas on imports were commonplace. Exchange controls had to be used to ration the increasingly scarce foreign exchange. For many domestic producers, all was well. Imports of crude materials and intermediate products could always access sufficient foreign exchange. Others trying to import less "necessary" products might not be so fortunate. Likewise, exporters in the region were finding life increasingly difficult. With a fixed exchange rate, Latin American exports were becoming increasingly expensive in world markets. The region was still rather dependent on exports of commodities. In commodity markets, price may be the only relevant variable. As a result, Latin American commodity exports suffered. Exporting nontraditional products was difficult at best. Aside from the exchange rate, the industry that had developed in the region was designed to replace imports. It had developed behind a number of different forms of protectionism and thus was not internationally competitive.

The rapid growth of imports coupled with the difficulty of exporting meant chronic imbalances in international payments. Imports virtually always exceeded exports. In the absence of changes in the exchange rate, these imbalances were frequently resolved by countries borrowing in the international capital markets. As long as the amount of borrowing was relatively small, this solution was not a problem. However, the situation changed dramatically in 1973. The explosion in oil prices hit Latin America hard. While the region is abundant in resources, it is surprisingly poor in oil. Only three countries (Venezuela, Mexico, and Ecuador) are oil exporters. For the rest of Latin America, this meant a dramatic increase in the value of imports. The response to this increase in imports was ever larger borrowing. The difference was that the volume of borrowing had increased dramatically. Any hope of managing this situation ended with the second oil shock in 1979. As the 1970s ended and the 1980s began, it became increasingly difficult for the countries of the region to borrow more to service previously accumulated debt. In the end, countries were finally forced to devalue their currencies. It had become necessary to finally resolve the macroeconomic imbalances fostered by import substitution. The results were horrendous. As we will see in later chapters, a major change in the exchange rate can mean both higher inflation *and* lower real GDP. In Latin America, these effects were particularly harsh. The region was already suffering from inflation and this became even worse in many countries. The global recession of the late 1970s and early 1980s would have meant difficulties for the region anyway as exports of commodities and their prices typically fall. Further, the industrial base of the region had never been internationally competitive. Rising prices for imported inputs coupled with collapsing demand in domestic markets doomed many industries in Latin America. Further, governments could no longer afford to subsidize these industries in the face of the need to reinstitute some measure of fiscal responsibility and end the inflationary printing of money. Real GDP growth at first stagnated and then began a slow decline that persisted throughout the decade.

It is difficult to describe the wrenching changes that occurred in the region during the 1980s. The description above is simply an abbreviated introduction to what led to this decade. The causes of this Lost Decade are many and some stretch back decades. In many of the chapters that follow, parts of the explanation of this event are presented. One should be careful not to look for particular villains, plots, or conspiracies. Bad events of any type are usually caused by a multitude of factors that coalesce during a short period of time to produce some particularly bad outcome. The Lost Decade is no different in that regard. We will be able to put the explanation together in pieces as we move through the rest of the book. This is necessary because there is no one cause of the event. However, it is essential to understand what caused the Lost Decade as it was primarily the result of a number of poor policy choices that occurred over several decades. One has to understand what went wrong in order for the changes occurring in the region to make sense. The last 20 years has been a positive period for the region as a whole. This is understandable as better economic policy choices usually led to better economic outcomes.

Key concepts and terms

autarky – a situation where a country does not engage in economic relations with the rest of the world.

debt – borrowing by countries in the form of bonds or bank loans.

encomienda – the granting of land in the colonies for use by a Spanish citizen during the colonial period in Latin America.

exchange controls – a system where the government is the only legal buyer and seller of foreign exchange.

latifundia – large tracts of land held by individuals in Latin America for farming or mining.

Lost Decade – a period of low growth in Latin America during the 1980s.

mercantilism – a policy imposed on colonies requiring that all international trade be done through the colonial power.

minifundia – small landholdings owned by individuals in Latin America for subsistence farming.

quota – a government policy that limits imports of a product to a certain number of units.

repartida – the portion of the output earned by owners of encomiendas that was owed to the Spanish government in Latin America.

sovereign debt – a debt instrument guaranteed by a government.

state-owned enterprise (SOE) – a firm wholly or partially owned and managed by the government.

tariff – a tax on imported goods.

Questions for review and discussion

1 Describe the link between the discovery of gold and silver in Latin America and the beginning of the encomienda system.
2 Explain the repartida in terms of Latin America and Spain in the colonial era.
3 Describe the transition of Latin America from the production of gold and silver to the production of agricultural commodities during the colonial period.
4 Describe how the encomienda system tended to create persistent inequality in the distribution of income in Latin America.
5 How can the current problems of weak public education and poor infrastructure be traced to developments in colonial Latin America?
6 How did the mercantilist policies of the Spanish government hinder economic growth?
7 Explain the differences between the colonial experience in Brazil and the rest of Latin America. What accounts for this difference?
8 Using the theory of economic growth developed in Chapter 2, describe the effect of the wars of independence and postcolonial turmoil on economic growth in Latin America.
9 What factors led to the rapid economic growth of the Golden Age?
10 What changes occurred in the world economy from 1914 to 1945 which tended to increase the size of the manufacturing sector in Latin America?

References and recommended readings

Baer, Werner. 2008. *The Brazilian Economy*. 6th ed. Boulder, CO: Lynne Rienner.
Bulmer-Thomas, Victor. 2003. *The Economic History of Latin America Since Independence*. 2nd ed. New York: Cambridge University Press.
Cardoso, Eliana and Ann Helwege. 1992. *Latin America's Economy: Diversity, Trends, and Conflicts*. Cambridge, MA: MIT Press.
Drake, Paul W. 1989. *The Money Doctor in the Andes: The Kemmerer Missions, 1923–1933*. Durham, NC: Duke University Press.
Edwards, Sebastian, Gerardo Esquivel, and Graciela Marquez (eds). 2007. *The Decline of Latin American Economies: Growth, Institutions, and Crises*. Chicago: University of Chicago Press.
Klein, Herbert S. and Ben Vinson, III. 2007. *African Slavery in Latin America and the Caribbean*. 2nd ed. New York: Oxford University Press.
Mann, Charles C. 2006. *1491: New Revelations of the Americas Before Columbus*. New York: Vintage.
Nunn, Nathan and Nancy Qian. 2010. "The Colombian Exchange: A History of Disease, Food, and Ideas." *Journal of Economic Perspectives*, 24(Spring): 163–88.

Reynolds, Lloyd G. 1983. "The Spread of Economic Growth to the Third World: 1850–1980." *Journal of Economic Literature* 21 (September): 941–80.

Thorp, Rosemary. 1998. *Progress, Poverty and Exclusion: An Economic History of Latin America in the 20th Century.* Washington, DC: Interamerican Development Bank.

Williamson, Jeffrey G. 1999. *Globalization and History: The Evolution of a Nineteenth-Century Atlantic Economy.* Cambridge: MIT Press.

5   Latin America and primary commodities

I see where we are starting to pay some attention to our neighbors to the south. We could never understand why Mexico wasn't just crazy about us; for we have always had their good will, and oil and minerals, at heart.

Will Rogers

Introduction

Earlier in this book, we mentioned the importance of the production and export of commodities in Latin America. The first purpose of this chapter is to more carefully explain why commodities have been an important factor in the economic development of the region. Further, commodities are going to be an important part of the future of the region so an understanding of this part of the economy is important in the twenty-first century. In some regards, commodities are just another product to be analyzed using the familiar tools of supply and demand. However, commodities have their own peculiarities. Supply and demand still works, just somewhat differently in commodities markets. If commodities are a significant percentage of total exports and GDP, then changes in commodities markets can have ramifications for the entire economy. Since this is true for many of the economies of the region, we will introduce some of these issues.[1] Further, countries have policy choices concerning economic development. For a country that possesses commodities there may be noticeable differences in economic development policy. Finally, commodities potentially can distort the entire structure of an economy. This can happen even in a high-income country. For the middle-income countries of Latin America, commodities can be like dynamite: useful if handled with care but potentially dangerous. The brief history of commodities in Latin America in the next section begins to illustrate both the costs and benefits of commodities for a country or region.

Commodities in Latin America: a brief history

In previous chapters, we have touched on the importance of commodities in Latin American economic history. Commodities have not only been important in the past, but they continue to be an important part of the economic landscape of the region. The purpose of this section is to briefly review this importance and finish with the current data on commodities in the region. At the start, one needs to recognize two important characteristics of commodities. First, the production of commodities has a tendency to follow a boom and bust cycle. Commodity booms tend to have two sources. On the one hand, it is sometimes the case that a boom in a commodity follows its discovery and subsequent widespread use. Latin American examples of this would be coffee and tobacco. In another case, the boom may be caused by the discovery, not of the product itself, but a new source of supply. Newly discovered supplies of gold and silver in Latin America would be examples. As we will see in the next section, these booms usually contain the seeds of their own self destruction. If commodities are important in a country or a region, then this can make either economic development or more short-run economic management more difficult. This has been a significant economic problem in the region from the beginning. A somewhat less problematic, but still important problem with commodities is price volatility. Everyone is familiar with the gyrations in price in the world oil market over the last few decades. Oil is not a special case. In commodity markets, this price volatility is *normal*. If this seems a bit puzzling, the reasons behind this volatility are covered in the next section. At this point, one needs to understand that volatile commodity prices should be considered an economic fact of life. It's been this way for hundreds of years. Like commodity booms and busts, commodity price volatility makes economic management in many countries more difficult. Not only is the price of oil volatile but prices for other commodities produced and exported in the region also are volatile. Other than oil, some other important commodities are copper, soybeans, bananas, wheat, meat, hides, mutton, wool, coffee, sugar, and tobacco.

The history of commodity booms and busts is given in Table 5.1 below. As discussed previously, the early booms in the region were fueled by gold and silver. The data presents a story that is a bit less obvious. The major supplies of gold were quickly exhausted. Silver soon replaced gold as the primary source of commodity income for the region and had a considerably longer production run. Two other booms started in the mid-sixteenth century. Cochineal was a superior red dye to what was available in Europe and was wildly popular. Indigo had been used since antiquity, but Latin America provided a larger and cheaper source of supply. Tobacco, coffee, and sugar soon produced large demand in Europe. The first two were "new" products that were soon very popular consumer items. Of course, sugar was an old product. However, increasing supplies from the Western Hemisphere drove down the price. This decrease in price now allowed average consumers in Europe to purchase increasing amounts of sugar. The sugar-laden products that are now commonplace were new products in the eighteenth century made possible by cheap imported sugar. Notice from the table that Brazil was relatively late to participate in the commodity booms. Large-scale

Table 5.1 Commodity booms in Latin America

Commodity	Years	Countries
Gold	1492–1550	Mexico, Peru
Silver	1550–1650	Mexico, Peru
Cochineal	1550–1850	Mexico, Guatemala
Indigo	1560–1880	Brazil, Guatemala, Honduras
Tobacco	1600–1700	Cuba, Brazil
Sugar	1625–1750	Brazil
Gold	1700–1760	Brazil
Coffee	1720–1850	Brazil, Colombia
Diamonds	1725–1860	Brazil[1]
Guano	1840–1880	Bolivia, Chile, Peru
Henequen	1860–1910	Mexico
Rubber	1879–1912	Brazil
Oil	1910–1920	Mexico
Oil	1973–1982	Ecuador, Mexico, Venezuela

[1] A smaller boom occurred in the late nineteenth century with the discovery of secondary deposits in Venezuela.

production of sugar did not begin until the seventeenth century and the gold and diamond booms occurred about 100 years later. The nineteenth century saw smaller booms in guano, henequen, and rubber. All of these booms succumbed to the exhaustion of the resource (guano) or changes in technology (henequen and rubber). Like the global oil industry, the industry in Latin America was fueled by high prices for oil caused by World War I.[2] The end of this boom was followed by relatively low oil prices that persisted for over half a century. Historically, high oil prices are a relatively recent phenomenon. Since commodity booms have been a staple of the economy of Latin America for hundreds of years, it is unlikely that the phenomenon will ever completely disappear. Busts are sometimes caused by falling global demand for a product that re-emerges at a later date. The possibility of new booms cannot be discounted. A boom in the global demand for batteries is starting yet another commodity boom in western South America. Guano is economic history but lithium is beginning a boom. An old story is repeating itself in the same part of the region.

Along with the booms and busts in commodity markets there is the more usual issue of price volatility. Commodity prices naturally are more unstable than most prices because of the demand and supply conditions in these markets. For example, consider a product such as coffee. Coffee is a popular product but it is truly just another mundane agricultural crop. However, the price of coffee is subject to large fluctuations. If the problem were just coffee, then it would be a problem for Brazil and Colombia but not for the rest of the region. The difficulty is that this sort of thing affects *all* commodities. Commodity prices as a whole are subject to large fluctuations. Since Latin America exports many commodities, price volatility influences the regional economy. Table 5.2 shows the movements of an index of many

Table 5.2 World commodity prices, 2000–2005 (percentage change over previous year)

Commodity Group	2000	2001	2002	2003	2004	2005
All Commodities	1.7	−3.6	0.8	8.1	19.4	12.1
Food & Tropical Beverages	−0.1	0.4	0.4	2.3	13.2	8.8
Vegetable Oilseeds & Oils	−20.3	−6.4	24.9	17.4	13.2	−9.5
Agricultural Raw Materials	3.1	−3.9	−2.4	19.8	9.9	7.1
Minerals, Ores, and Metals	12.4	−10.8	−2.7	12.4	40.7	26.2
Crude Petroleum	56.6	−13.3	2.0	15.8	30.7	41.3

Source: United Nations Conference on Trade and Development (2006).

commodity prices in the first half of this decade. For commodities overall the price fluctuations can be extreme. This is particularly true for oil as shown in the last row. Most of us know about oil price fluctuations, but it is not an isolated case. Many other commodities exhibit price fluctuations that are just as extreme. The overall message being conveyed from the data is that the prices of individual commodities can fluctuate substantially. As we will see in more detail, the possession of commodities is a mixed blessing. The products contribute to the real GDP and exports of a country. However, they can be risky in terms of their contribution to the economy.

5.1 Cochineal

In Table 5.1, one can be excused for wondering what cochineal is. It is now an uncommon word, but it was once an important commodity in the world economy. Cochineal or carmine dye produces a red color. It was first cultivated by the Mayas and later the Aztecs in Mexico and Central America. Upon their arrival, the Spanish were immediately struck by the richness of the red color the dye produces which was far superior to anything available in Europe. The dye is derived from an insect that is a parasite of the cactus plant. A chemical the insect produces to protect it from predators is the source of the dye. As one can imagine, the production of the product is very labor-intensive. The dye was so popular that production in the Oaxaca province of Mexico grew rapidly. After silver, in the colonial period cochineal was Mexico's second largest export. Prices of cochineal were regularly quoted on the Amsterdam and London commodity exchanges.

Mexico's war of independence in the early nineteenth century disrupted the production of the product. Commercial production of cochineal then began in Guatemala. Unfortunately, in the mid-nineteenth century artificial red dyes were discovered in Europe. By the end of the century, cheaper dyes spelled the end of the industry in Latin America. Production of cochineal survived only as a small cottage industry. The story does not end there. In the late twentieth century, it was determined that artificial red dyes may be carcinogenic. As with many other products, the "natural" alternative is regaining popularity. The production of cochineal is now commercially viable again.

The microeconomics of commodities

In the previous section, it was shown that the production of commodities is subject to booms and busts. Even in the absence of these extremes, commodity prices are normally quite volatile. In this section, we will review the simple microeconomics of commodity markets. While the gyrations of these markets are a puzzle to most people, the reasons behind this volatility are not difficult to explain. As with most products the price of commodities and the amount produced and consumed are determined by supply and demand. A simple supply and demand model of a representative commodity is shown in Figure 5.1. To start, note that the demand curve has a negative slope. This indicates the usual inverse relationship between the price and the *quantity demanded*. If the only thing that changes is the price of the product, then there is a movement from one point to another along the same demand curve. If anything changes other than the price, then there is a shift of the entire demand curve. Such a shift is referred to as a *change in demand*. An increase in demand is shown by a rightward shift in the demand curve and a decrease in demand is shown by a leftward shift. Such changes could be caused by a change in the population or a change in income. Notice that in Figure 5.1, the demand curve has been drawn with a very steep slope. This was not accidental. It is portraying that the demand for this product is inelastic. In the context of a demand curve, this means that changes in price do not have a very large impact on the quantity demanded. Oil is a classic example of this effect. An increase in the price of oil reduces the quantity demanded. It just doesn't reduce it by a large amount. Inelastic demand curves are common for commodities. They also will help to explain why commodity prices are so volatile.

The supply curve for a commodity also is shown in Figure 5.1. Analogous to the demand curve, a change in the price is represented by a movement along the supply curve. This is referred to as a change in the *quantity supplied*. If the only change that occurs is a change in price, then there is a movement from one point to another along the same supply curve. A *change in supply* occurs when something other than the price changes. An increase in supply would be shown by a shift of the supply curve to the right. A decrease in supply is a shift of the curve to the left. Changes in supply can occur for reasons such as a change in the number of producers or a change in the costs of inputs into the production process. As with the demand curve, the supply curves for many commodities are relatively inelastic. Changes in price do not have a very large impact on the quantity supplied. For agricultural commodities, there may be only one growing season per year. A change in price after the crop has been planted may have only a minimal impact on the quantity supplied. For minerals such as oil or gold, it may be possible to increase the quantity supplied in the short run by a small amount. Larger increases in supply may take years as new supplies have to be developed with heavy capital investment.[3] The intersection of the demand and supply

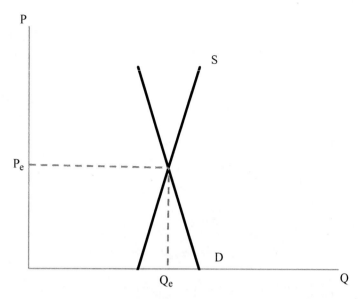

Figure 5.1 Equilibrium price and output for a commodity.

curves in Figure 5.1 determines the equilibrium price and quantity in this market. If there are no changes in either curve, then the price will be P_e and the equilibrium quantity is Q_e.

Commodity booms and busts

In commodity markets, both P_e and Q_e are subject to large fluctuations. We are now in a position to show more carefully why this is true. The demand for commodities can shift substantially to the left or right. This is shown in Figure 5.2. The discovery of new products in Latin America in the six-teenth century such as coffee, tobacco, or cochineal can lead to an enormous increase in demand. In the figure, this is shown as a shift of the demand curve from D to D_1. Because the supply curve is inelastic, any increase in demand translates primarily into an increase in price. The price moves from P_e to P_1. The increase in the quantity supplied is much smaller. This move-ment is only from Q_e to Q_1. Thus, a commodity boom is rather easy to touch off. Given market conditions, increases in the demand for a commodity can cause large changes in the price. A commodity bust is also easy to imagine. Cochineal is a good example. The appearance of a good substitute for the product caused a large decrease in the demand. In the figure, this is shown as a movement of the demand curve from D to D_2. A large drop in the demand causes the equilibrium price and quantity to fall to P_2 and Q_2, respectively. In this case, a large drop in the demand can cause a collapse in the price of the commodity. Cochineal is not an isolated example. Many of the booms

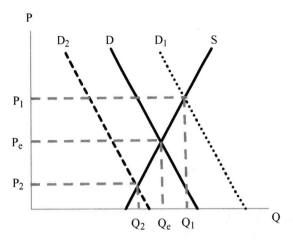

Figure 5.2 Equilibrium price and output with changes in demand.

presented in Table 5.1 ended the same way. Particular cases include indigo, henequen, and rubber. The effects on countries or regions of countries can be devastating. Latin America is dotted with once-prosperous areas that subsequently fell back into relative poverty after the end of a commodity boom.[4]

Like the demand curve, changes in the supply curve can cause a commodity boom. The demand for some commodities like gold, silver, or diamonds is so high that even a relatively large increase in supply may not lower prices by a substantial amount. This situation is shown in Figure 5.3. In this figure the initial demand and supply curves are D and S, respectively. The original equilibrium yields a price of P_e and quantity of Q_e. Notice that the initial price of gold is rather high because the demand is very large relative to the supply. The discovery of gold and silver in Latin America in the sixteenth century can be shown as an increase in the supply curve. This is represented by a shift of the supply curve from S to S_1. The new equilibrium price is lower at P_1. However, the lower price is not all that much lower. The world demand for gold is so large that the decrease in price is not that large.[5]

An increase in the supply of a valuable commodity has caused a boom. However, if the resource is exhaustible the boom can quickly turn into a bust. This has happened in Latin America. The large supply of gold was exhausted by the mid-sixteenth century. The production of silver began declining 100 years later. The story for diamonds in Brazil and Venezuela and guano in Bolivia, Chile, and Peru was essentially the same. In this case the supply curve might shift back to S. In such a case, a "new" equilibrium might occur at P_e and Q_e.

A commodity bust can happen even if the resource is not exhaustible like guano. The sugar boom in the seventeenth and eighteenth century is a good historical example. Increasing supplies of sugar coupled with rising

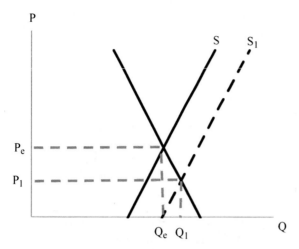

Figure 5.3 Equilibrium price and output with changes in supply.

incomes in Europe created a combination of both rising prices and output of sugar. However, unlike gold, the production of sugar could be expanded to new regions such as the Caribbean. Eventually, the demand for sugar ceased to rise as fast as the supply of sugar was increasing. This creates a situation much like that shown before in Figure 5.3. Increases in the supply of the commodity begin to drive down prices. If this persists for some time, the once expensive commodity can become quite cheap. With the use of supply and demand graphs, commodity booms and busts become more understandable. Changes in demand can both cause a commodity boom and also a subsequent bust if demand falls or simply does not grow at as fast a rate. Likewise, the exhaustion of a natural resource can cause a commodity bust as production falls. The reverse case can occur if production of a high-priced commodity can be extended to new areas and supply increases. One can take almost any of the cases in Table 5.1 and graph the trajectory of the boom and bust based on supply and demand conditions.

Price volatility

For many commodities, there may not be spectacular booms and busts. In some cases, an initial boom followed by a bust is then followed by market conditions that are typical for commodities: price volatility. This is exactly what was illustrated in Table 5.2. Commodity prices in the world economy are naturally volatile. Fortunately, we can adapt Figure 5.1 to show why this is true. We start with the effects of fluctuations in demand. This is shown in Figure 5.2. Because the supply of commodities is typically inelastic, small changes in demand can have noticeable impacts on prices. An increase or decrease in demand from D to D_1 or D to D_2 can have a noticeable impact on the price. A difference between P_e and P_1 or P_2 could easily be 10 percent. This means that the difference between the highest and lowest price for this commodity could be 20 percent in total. All of the determinants of the demand for a product could easily produce these sorts of fluctuations in price. In world commodity markets, an important determinant of world prices is the growth of the world economy. Commodity prices tend to be high when the world economy is growing rapidly and the demand for commodities is like D_1. A global slowdown tends to produce a demand for commodities more like D_2. Countries that produce and export commodities may well benefit greatly from a global boom but suffer disproportionately from a global downturn. Recall the Golden Age in Latin American economic history. It is not accidental that this period coincided with a global boom. Less favorably, the recent global economic downturn has seriously depressed the prices for some Latin American commodities such as copper. Notice also that changes in demand for commodities are normally *exogenous*. This means that demand is primarily determined outside of the country or the region. Thus, for Latin America the prices it receives for its commodities are determined by global supply and demand. The prices the region receives then becomes something like the weather: sometimes good and sometimes bad. As we will see, this compounds the problem of economic management for a country or a region. Fluctuations in world demand are particularly noticeable for commodities used in manufacturing. For Latin America, the most important of these products are oil, copper, and nickel.[6]

The supply of commodities can also shift. This was shown in Figure 5.3 above. An increase in supply is shown by a rightward shift of the supply curve from S to S_1. This has a large effect on the equilibrium price lowering it from P_e to P_1. The opposite effect occurs if the supply curve decreases from S_1 to S. Prices rise substantially from P_1 to P_e. In both cases, the movements in price are large because the demand curve is inelastic. In commodity markets, changes in supply are easy to imagine. For agricultural products, there are years of declines in production or crop failures due to weather. In other years, more favorable conditions produce a larger supply than is normal. Examples in Latin America are plentiful. Weather reports from Brazil are closely watched by soybean traders. Coffee traders watch crop conditions in Brazil, Colombia, and Central America. Chilean weather affects what Americans pay for certain fruits and vegetables. Inelastic demand for soybeans, coffee, and vegetables leads to the sometimes large fluctuations in the prices of these products. The supply curve for nonagricultural commodities can also change. The rate at which minerals can be extracted in the world economy can fluctuate. The rate at which new supplies of commodities are depleted in one area is not always perfectly matched by new finds elsewhere. This might lead to temporary reductions in supply and higher prices. At other points in time, the reverse can occur. New supplies may come on to the market at a fast rate. The fluctuations in supply may not be as large from year to year as is sometimes true in agricultural markets but they are still there.

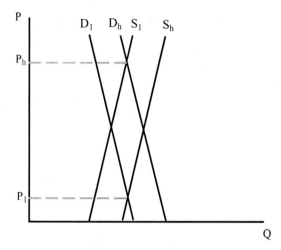

Figure 5.4 Changes in supply and demand in commodity markets.

Extremely large fluctuations in prices occur under the right set of circumstances. Figure 5.4 is a simple illustration of what can occur in commodity markets. In this figure there are two demand curves, D_l and D_h. They represent relatively low demand for a commodity and a corresponding high demand, respectively. There are two analogous supply curves labeled S_l and S_h. For convenience, the two most extreme price solutions are labeled P_l and P_h. A combination of relatively high demand and a low supply leads to a relatively high price, P_h. On the other hand, low demand coupled with high supply leads to a relatively low price, P_l. Notice that the difference between P_h and P_l is extremely large. These effects are what led to the large values observed in Table 5.2. It is also not difficult to see the cause of more minor volatility. As noted above, the demand for commodities in general is related to the state of the world economy. Global growth changes from year to year. As a result, the demand for commodities fluctuates somewhat each year. The supply of agricultural commodities literally can fluctuate with the weather. The supply of nonagricultural commodities also can fluctuate from year to year as new discoveries of supplies often don't match perfectly with the use of the resources. As we will see in the next section, this price instability of commodities has macroeconomic implications for many of the countries of the region.

5.2 OPEC

As indicated in the previous section, fluctuations in commodity prices can be a serious problem for countries where commodities are an important part of the economy. A theoretically attractive option is for countries producing these products to form a cartel. A cartel is an organization of producers that attempts to stabilize the price of a commodity by changing market conditions. In a technical sense this is easy to accomplish, as the supply is adjusted by the cartel to achieve the desired price. However, in practice this is not easily accomplished.

The most well-known cartel in the world economy is the Organization of Petroleum Exporting Countries (OPEC). OPEC was formed at a meeting on September 14, 1960. The original purpose of OPEC was to attempt to limit supply to combat low oil prices. The current members of OPEC are Algeria, Angola, Ecuador, Indonesia, Iran, Iraq, Kuwait, Libya, Nigeria, Qatar, Saudi Arabia, the United Arab Emirates (UAE), and Venezuela. The purpose of OPEC is to provide stable prices for both producers and consumers of oil in the world market. In order to do this, it must attempt to adjust the supply of oil in response to changing market conditions. It does this by establishing a quota or a maximum amount of oil each member country can produce. As recent fluctuations in oil prices demonstrate, OPEC has not been overwhelmingly successful as a cartel. In OPEC's defense, the task is virtually impossible. First, since the supply of oil cannot be changed quickly OPEC is inevitably in the business of forecasting demand. Any forecasting mistake increases the probability of a "wrong" price. Second, OPEC controls less than half of the world oil production. Since OPEC cannot control the output of nonmembers, it can't really control world oil prices. The reason Mexico and other countries are not members is related to how a cartel works. OPEC assigns each of its member countries a quota for exports in an attempt to control the world supply of oil. The result is that OPEC members must surrender an important economic decision to OPEC. Further, because of this problem, members of OPEC have been known to "cheat" on their quotas. The end result is that OPEC doesn't really control world oil prices. Influence might be a better description of the activities of the cartel. The experience of OPEC is one of the reasons other commodity cartels never developed. If a cartel cannot truly stabilize prices and interferes with national sovereignty on an important issue, then the possible benefits to a country may not outweigh the costs. Obviously, the three current Latin American oil producers have come to different conclusions about OPEC. As a potential oil exporter, it is not surprising that at this point Brazil is carefully considering whether or not to join OPEC.

The macroeconomics of commodities

The periodic booms and busts in commodities and the perpetual price instability are more than a nuisance to producers and consumers. In the case of Latin America, commodities are sufficiently important that changes in commodity prices can affect the entire economy. To see why this is true, we need to review the concept of real GDP that we introduced in Chapter 1. Specifically we need to consider the components of GDP. The components of GDP are given in Equation 5.1 below.

$$Y = C + I + G + (X - M) \tag{5.1}$$

The components of the equation are:
Y   Real GDP
C   Consumption by the public

I   Residential and Nonresidential Investment
G   Government spending on goods and services
X   Exports of Goods and Services
M   Imports of Goods and Services

From the equation the effect of exporting a new commodity or changes in
the price of exported commodities becomes clear. If commodity exports are
a high percentage of total exports, then changes in commodity prices can
significantly affect the total value of exports. In turn, this would change the
trade balance (X–M). Now, if exports are a high percentage of GDP then
the chain of logic would lead one to the conclusion that changes in commodity prices can affect the entire economy. A boom in commodity prices
could either lead to a trade surplus or reduce the size of the trade deficit.
Everything else equal, this would tend to increase real GDP. The reverse
would be true. A large decline in commodity prices would either reduce the
trade surplus or make it negative. This could have the effect of reducing real
GDP. The link from commodity prices to the entire economy is relatively
simple. A boom in commodity prices can cause rapid growth in GDP and
falling commodity prices may constitute a drag on the entire economy.[7]
    The critical part of the analysis is what percentage of exports are
commodities and what is the ratio of exports to GDP? In the case of Latin
America, these numbers are rather high. The data is given in Table 5.3 below.

Table 5.3 Commodities' share of exports and GDP in Latin America, 2008
          (millions of current dollars)

	Commodity Exports	Exports (Merchandise)	Commodity/ Exports	Commodity Exports/GDP
Argentina	46,346	70,023	66.2	14.1
Bolivia	5,966	6,448	92.5	35.8
Brazil	105,420	197,943	53.3	6.5
Chile	58,088	66,455	87.4	34.3
Colombia	24,740	37,626	65.8	10.2
Costa Rica	3,572	9,504	37.6	12.0
Ecuador	17,020	18,511	92.0	32.4
El Salvador	1,158	4,549	25.5	5.2
Guatemala	4,106	7,737	53.1	10.5
Honduras	1,864	6,458	28.9	13.2
Mexico	75,378	291,265	25.9	6.9
Nicaragua	1,252	1,489	84.1	19.0
Panama	1,023	1,247	82.0	4.4
Paraguay	4,042	4,390	92.1	25.3
Peru	21,510	31,529	68.2	16.9
Uruguay	4,343	5,942	73.1	13.5
Venezuela	89,594	95,138	94.2	28.6
Latin America			66.0	17.0

Source: World Trade Organization (2010).

Commodity exports as a percentage of total exports is exactly 66 percent. In virtually any year, commodity exports are a majority of the total exports of the region. Now we can take the logic one step further. The final column in the table shows commodity exports as a percentage of GDP. For the countries of Latin America, this averages 17 percent. In other words, nearly a fifth of the overall GDP of the region is accounted for by commodity exports. This information can be related to the data in Table 5.2. Commodity prices are very volatile. This price volatility naturally translates into volatility in overall exports. Since these exports are a relatively high percentage of GDP, the rate of growth of real GDP in many of the countries of the region can be substantially impacted by changes in commodity prices. This is an important point that we will return to again in Chapter 10. For now, one can see that commodity price volatility makes the management of GDP in Latin America more difficult than it would be if commodities were not such an important part of total exports and GDP.

Commodities and economic development

> The gratification of wealth is not found in mere possession or in lavish expenditure, but in its wise application.
>
> Miguel de Cervantes

The endowment of commodities is not evenly distributed around the world. Some countries have mineral resources and others do not. Some countries are able to produce certain agricultural commodities and others cannot. Latin America is a perfect case in point. Few of the world's regions are so richly endowed with *both* types of commodities. Commodities can be used as the basis for a more comprehensive development strategy. If managed wisely, commodities can be used to enhance the economic development of a country. If not, then the possession of commodities can be detrimental to economic development.

First, the production and export of commodities can be quite profitable. If the product is cheap to extract or easy to cultivate, production costs may be lower than the world market price. As a result, commodities can be a major source of tax revenue. In these cases, the government may be able to use this tax revenue to enhance economic development. Countries tend to move in stages from a dependence on agricultural production to a stage where manufacturing becomes more important. However, the development of manufacturing may require a substantial investment in the country's infrastructure. Revenues from the production of commodities may allow the country to finance this more easily than a country without such resources. The result is that the country may be able to grow faster. Second, the development of infrastructure may require imports such as capital equipment from the developed countries. In turn, these imports will require foreign exchange. The export of a commodity can allow the country to more easily afford these types of imports. This should be a familiar story from the Golden Age of Latin American economic history. Third, a country with commodities may find it easier to transition into manufacturing than a country without such resources. Many commodities are the start of the process of producing a final good. For example, sugar can be refined into a product that is sold to consumers essentially as is. It can also be used to produce more sophisticated products such as candy or rum. The obvious first step in this process for a country with commodities is to add value to the primary product. As a result, countries with commodities may be able to make the transition to manufacturing more easily than countries without commodities.

In practice, the scenario outlined above has been fraught with difficulties. In fact, these difficulties are so common in Latin America and elsewhere that they are sometimes referred to as the resource curse. Since Latin America is a large and heterogeneous region, not all of these problems apply to all countries. However, elements of the resource curse are, to a greater or lesser extent, part of the economic story of Latin America.[8] For example, the initial colonization of the region is the resource curse in an extreme form. The initial motivating factor in Spanish settlement of the region was the extraction of gold and silver for shipment back to Spain. Very little of this wealth was used for economic development. The indigenous population was decimated by European diseases and much of the labor force worked in mining and other activities in less than free market labor conditions. It is difficult to imagine that the possession of gold and silver was producing positive economic results for the region.

In the post-independence era, the possession of commodities has still been problematical for the region. Since the production of commodities can be quite profitable, the division of these profits between the private and public sectors can be troublesome. Understandably, private sector producers of commodities wish to hold on to their earnings. Governments on the other hand may see taxing commodities as a relatively easy way to raise revenue in a poor country. Under ideal circumstances, the government would find an optimal tax rate that maximizes revenue without discouraging production. This revenue would then be funneled into spending on infrastructure, education, etc. that would promote faster economic growth. However, even under the best of circumstances, using commodities to finance development can create tension between producers and the government.[9] Sadly, the production of commodities can also lead to corruption. Producers of commodities are vulnerable to the ability of the government to take part of the profits earned. Once the money has left the private sector, there is no guarantee that it will be wisely used. Aside from outright corruption, the problems may be more subtle. Revenues from commodities may be used to purchase support from the population that otherwise might not exist. Government employment may rise faster than would be the case if such revenues were not available. In short, the production and export of commodities may not lead to faster economic growth. Indeed, it is not difficult to imagine commodity earnings leading to relatively slow growth. There are at least some of these tendencies evident in Latin America. Despite being rich in commodities, the region is poor in infrastructure. Education and health care also suffer funding problems. This is always hard to reconcile. As we saw in Chapter 2, corruption is a problem in the region. One has to be careful not to blame this problem totally on commodities. However, a simple thought question might be helpful. Would there be less corruption in many Latin American countries if they had no significant commodities? The same sort of question applies to government employment and imports. Has income from commodities been used in some cases to finance a larger civil service and/or support higher levels of imports of consumer goods? The direction of these effects is probably clear. The magnitudes vary from country to country depending on the amount of money generated by commodities and the quality of government. Overall, it is difficult to say that the possession of commodities has been an unalloyed benefit to the region since independence.

Things become even more complicated with the existence of foreign firms in the production of commodities. The extraction of mineral wealth or certain agricultural commodities may require capital and technical expertise that the country may not possess. The production of commodities in a low- or middle-income country may require FDI. Negotiations between multinational corporations (MNCs) and the host country may be difficult in many circumstances. It is especially difficult if the commodity is an exhaustible resource. Conditions of entry, tax rates, and other variables can all influence the final outcome.[10] During the Golden Age the conditions were usually national treatment. Foreign firms faced taxes and regulations similar to domestic firms. However, with relatively weak governments in the region coupled with low taxes and light regulation, national treatment became an increasingly unacceptable form of regulation of MNCs especially for exhaustible natural resources. In other cases, export enclaves developed where MNCs were receiving preferential treatment rather than national treatment. In the twentieth century, the balance of power slowly shifted from the MNCs to the governments of the region. Taxes and regulations stiffened. In some cases, the local assets of the MNCs were expropriated with varying degrees of compensation.[11] In any event, the relationship between the governments of the region and MNCs involved in extracting natural resources has been difficult. In these cases, many countries have opted to produce their own resources using state-owned enterprises (SOEs). As we will see in the next chapter, SOEs have a checkered history. In theory, SOEs allow the country to extract all of the value from its commodities, but in practice this has proven to be difficult. The oil industry in Mexico and the copper industry in Chile are well known examples that have produced somewhat different results.

Finally, it has been difficult for Latin America and other regions to leverage their commodities into manufacturing based on these resources. The reasons for this are many, but a primary problem has been the level of tariffs and in some cases quotas in the developed countries. The structure of protection in developed countries is set up to encourage the processing of commodities there. This is done by escalating the tariffs by stage of processing. For example, raw commodities frequently have a low or zero tariff. If the product is processed into an intermediate commodity, the tariff rate rises. If the commodity is further processed into a finished good the tariff is still higher. The point of this policy is to import commodities as cheaply as possible. The tariff then encourages the processing of the commodity in the developed country rather than the developing country. This makes it very difficult for the developing countries of Latin America to develop manufacturing industries based on their plentiful commodities. This is not the only factor inhibiting industrial development in the region, but it has not helped. As we have seen in this section, the possession of commodities can theoretically aid economic development. For Latin America, the possession of commodities has no doubt made the region better off. It is hard to imagine Latin America without commodities. It is also difficult to say that the potential benefits of these commodities have been used to their fullest to enhance economic development. The resource curse has not afflicted the region as badly as has been the case in other parts of the world. On the other hand, traces of this effect are not difficult to find in the region.

Commodities and Dutch disease

In economics, industrial structure refers to the percentage of output that is accounted for by each industry within a country. If a country has significant production of commodities, this can affect the industrial structure of a country. Since Latin America definitely falls into this situation, the effects of commodities on the industrial structure of the region is worth considering. In a sense, these effects are obvious. A country with commodities will naturally have resources committed to their production. In the short run, more resources in the form of capital and labor in commodities means fewer resources elsewhere in the economy. The commodities and industries tied to them will be larger and other parts of the economy will be smaller. In the short run, this has to be true. However, there are other, less obvious effects at work when a country possesses commodities.

First, consider a commodity boom. Profits are extremely high in this sector of the economy. These high profits act as a magnet for resources in the other parts of the economy. Capital will naturally be invested as the rate of return will be relatively high. This is important in a low- or middle-income country because capital is a scarce resource. Other sectors of the economy may not be able to grow as fast as they are now competing for capital in a market where it was not plentiful to begin with. Marginal borrowers of capital get "crowded out" as the price of capital rises. The same thing happens with labor. Part of the high returns in the booming sector of the economy accrue to labor in the form of wages. In turn, wages may rise in other parts of the economy. This may make the production of goods outside the booming sector less competitive. The effect on the labor market is not just wages. The booming sector may also attract workers with the most human capital. In a country where human capital is a scarce resource, this may make growth more difficult in other parts of the economy. In total, an economy with a commodity boom may start becoming distorted not just in terms of industrial structure. Scarce resources such as capital and human capital are being diverted to one part of the economy. Wages may rise in the entire economy. While things are going well in the booming commodity sector, other parts of the economy are having a more difficult time growing.

As shown in Figure 5.2, commodity booms frequently end in a sometimes spectacular bust. In a frictionless model of economic activity, resources would be briskly transferred to other sectors of the economy with few transaction costs. Another way of putting this is that a bust would lead to a costless change in industrial structure as the commodity producing sector of the economy shrinks and the other parts of the economy now grow faster. In reality, the transitions are not always that smooth. The result of the bust is that resources are being released from the production of commodities. In the short run, which might be many years, the other parts of the economy cannot grow fast enough to absorb these resources. Even if they can, many of the physical and human resources may have become sector specific. Mining machinery may not be easy to adapt to other uses. Workers have built up useful skills in the commodity sector, but these skills may not be easily transferable to another sector. The inability of an economy to easily transfer resources from the former booming sector may lead to a prolonged slump in overall economic activity. A commodity boom may create an industrial structure in a country that is not easy to change once the boom ends. Similar, but smaller, effects of this type occur due to commodity price volatility. As the prices of a commodity rise, more resources may be temporarily pulled into the sector. Again, there are adverse effects for other parts of the economy. A dramatic fall in prices sets up a less severe version of the situation described above. How much these effects matter is related to how important a commodity is to the economy. A good example for Latin America would be the oil industry in Mexico and Venezuela. Oil is important to the Mexican economy. However, the Mexican economy is highly diversified and oil is just another important industry. Mexican goods and services are sold all over the world and oil is just another important export. High oil prices are good for the Mexican economy, but not critical. Venezuela is a different story. The oil industry dominates the economy of the country. The production of non-oil goods languishes for the reasons given above. High oil prices mean relative prosperity and low oil prices invariably means lower growth for the economy. The effects described in this section exist in both countries, just in different degrees.

On top of the description given above, in a floating exchange rate world a commodity boom can affect the exchange rate. Foreign buyers of the commodity must first purchase the domestic currency of the commodity producing country in order to purchase the commodity. This increase in demand for the commodity translates into an increase in the demand for the local currency. In turn, this can cause the exchange rate to appreciate. This appreciation has several effects. First, it makes imports cheaper.[12] This increases the relative price of domestically produced goods that compete with imports. Such industries are not only paying more for capital and labor, they may face downward pressure on prices. Second, exports of goods and services other than commodities become more expensive to foreign buyers. These price increases tend to lower the quantity demanded for a country's exports. In total, a commodity boom means a more difficult environment for the tradable goods sectors of the economy. The booming commodity sector leads to more imports and lower domestic production. It also can mean fewer exports and lower production in that part of the economy. This effect can be exacerbated if the booming sector is also pulling FDI into the country for its development. The effects on industrial structure caused by the exchange rate appreciation are in addition to what would be occurring even if exchange rates were unaffected.

The effects of commodities on industrial structure are in general referred to as Dutch disease. The term refers to the effects on the economy of the Netherlands that were noticed after the country began to export natural gas. It is now used to refer to a set of conditions that typically go along with a commodity boom. The boom in the commodity producing parts of the economy tend to cause hardship in other parts of the economy. In a small country with a large commodity boom, the ultimate effects can be a badly distorted domestic economy that is very vulnerable to a fall in commodity prices. The description of Dutch disease given above is a minimal outline of the effects. To a greater or lesser extent, the effects of Dutch disease are easy to find in Latin America. Commodity booms have pulled more resources in those parts of many economies with lasting effects on industrial structure. Adjusted for productivity, wages in Latin America tend to be high. This has worked to retard the development of other economic activities not related to commodities. Scarce investment capital has been attracted to commodities as they frequently offer higher returns. As we will see in Chapter 8, Latin America has had a history of overvalued exchange rates. This has encouraged imports and discouraged exports of products other than commodities. These effects have been felt most strongly in the manufacturing sector of the region. As we will see in the next chapter, Dutch disease cannot account for all of the problems of industry in Latin America. However, it is an important component of the overall picture.

Key concepts and terms

cartel – an organization of producers that attempts to stabilize the price of a commodity by changing market conditions.

Dutch disease – a term used to describe the effects of commodity exports on other parts of the economy.

industrial structure – the percentage of output that is accounted for by each industry within a country.

multinational corporations (MNCs) – corporations with operations in more than one country.

national treatment – the situation where a country's laws are blind with respect to nationality.

Organization of Petroleum Exporting Countries (OPEC) – a cartel that attempts to stabilize the price of petroleum in the world economy.

resource curse – the empirical regularity that countries rich in commodities frequently experience slow or low rates of economic growth.

structure of protection – an analysis of the variation in tariffs in a country.

Questions for review and discussion

1   Explain the two major problems that a country that produces primary commodities may face.

2   List the major commodity booms that have occurred in Latin America since 1500. Other than lithium, try to construct a scenario for another new commodity boom in the region.

3   Describe the rise, fall, and rise of the cochineal market in the world economy.

4   Graph a commodity boom for an exhaustible resource and the subsequent bust. How does the boom and bust cycle differ for a commodity where the supply can be increased?

5   What is OPEC? Show how a cartel could theoretically stabilize the price of a commodity.

6   Explain how changes in commodity prices affect real GDP.

7   How can the possession of commodities in a country enhance economic development?

8   Explain the resource curse. How has it affected Latin America?

9   How has the structure of protection in developed countries hindered the development of industry in Latin America?

10   What is Dutch disease? How does it apply to Latin America?

References and recommended readings

Gibbon, Peter. 2001. "Upgrading Primary Production: A Global Commodity Chain Approach." *World Development.* 29(February): 345–63.

Haber, Stephen, Noel Maurer, and Armando Razo. 2003. "When the Law Does Not Matter: The Rise and Decline of the Mexican Oil Industry." *Journal of Economic History*. 63(March): 1–31.

Lederman, Daniel and William F. Maloney. 2008. "In Search of the Missing Resource Curse." *Economia*. 9(Fall): 1–39.

Manzano, Osmel and Francisco Monaldi. 2008. "The Political Economy of Oil Production in Latin America." *Economia*. 9(Fall): 59–98.

Smith, Geri. 2007. "Beating the Oil Curse." *Business Week*. June 4. pp. 48–9.

Talbot, John. 1997. "The Struggle for Control of a Commodity Chain: Instant Coffee from Latin America." *Latin American Research Review*. 32(2): 117–35.

Topik, Steven, Carlos Marichal, and Zephyr Frank (eds). 2006. *Latin American Commodity Chains and the Building of the World Economy, 1500–2000*. Durham, NC: Duke University Press.

Topik, Steven and Allen Wells (eds). 1998. *The Second Conquest of Latin America: Coffee, Henequen, and Oil during the Export Boom, 1850–1930*. Austin: University of Texas Press.

United Nations Conference on Trade and Development. 2006. *Trade and Development Report*. Geneva: United Nations Conference on Trade and Development.

World Trade Organization. 2010. *Trade Profiles*. Geneva: World Trade Organization. www.wto.org

6 Import substitution in Latin America

The difficulty lies not so much in developing new ideas as in escaping from old ones.

John Maynard Keynes

Introduction

As we saw in Chapter 4, the Great Depression marked a turning point in the economic history of Latin America. The relative openness of the Golden Age ended in the protectionism of the 1930s. The ending of World War II also marked another turning point for Latin America. In the post-war era, much of the world began to slowly remove the protectionism developed during the 1930s. Latin America did not.[1] Moreover, Latin America went further than simply not reducing the level of protectionism. A large number of different policies were constructed to build up industry in the region. Not only trade policy, but industrial policy, exchange rate policy, and policies for the financial markets were harnessed together in support of the development of industry. As we will see in the last section of the chapter, this headlong rush to industrialize the region ended badly. That is why it is important to carefully outline in the next section of the chapter the original thought behind this movement.

Structuralism, dependency theory, and ISI

Latin American structuralism

To understand the origins of ISI in Latin America, one needs to briefly return to the Golden Age. Latin America prospered during this period by exporting commodities and importing products that it could not produce or could be produced more cheaply in other parts of the world. In more formal terms, the region exported products in which it had a comparative advantage and imported comparative disadvantage products. This sort of trade worked well for Latin America in the late nineteenth and early twentieth centuries. On average, commodity prices were high and export earnings were substantial. This allowed the region to easily import the manufactured goods that were needed for consumption and economic development. The onset of the Great Depression seriously dented the faith in this sort of trade not only in Latin America but much of the world. The export earnings of the region were falling but the prices of the manufactured goods being imported were not falling nearly as fast. This was creating serious strains in the balance of payments. As a result of this, a group of economists at the central bank of Argentina began researching this problem. By the late 1930s, Raul Prebisch and his colleagues had started to develop some economic reasoning on this issue. Part of the problem was introduced in the previous chapter. The supply of most commodities is inelastic. Thus, when the Great Depression hit, the prices of most commodities fell dramatically. On the other hand, it was posited that the supply of manufactured goods was much more elastic. This implies that if the demand for these goods falls then the price will not fall by a substantial amount. This is a reasonable explanation for some of the balance of payments problems Latin America was experiencing during the Great Depression. The prices of commodities fell much faster than the price of manufactured goods.

Following World War II, the United Nations (UN) set up the Economic Commission for Latin America (ECLA). As director of ECLA, Prebisch published an enormously influential book *The Economic Development of Latin America and its Principal Problems* (1950). This book was partially based on an earlier UN report, but the basic argument was expanded into a much more sweeping thesis. The start of the argument concerns the declining terms of trade that may face developing countries such as those in Latin America. Rather than being a short-run problem caused by a global downturn, it was asserted that the prices of commodities were falling relative to the price of manufactures over the long run. The declining terms of trade for developing countries would mean that over time more and more commodities would have to be exported to obtain any given amount of manufactured goods. Taken to another level, this argument contains an unusual conclusion: trade is making the developing countries of Latin America *worse off*. The reverse would be logically true. This trading relationship would be making the developed countries better off. For Latin American countries, a major problem was that the structure of the economy was oriented towards exporting commodities and importing manufactured goods. In order to break out of this, it would be necessary to change the structure of their economies. This came to be known as structuralist economics or the basic idea that the structure of an economy can have important effects on economic outcomes.[2] In the case of developing countries, an economic structure composed primarily of commodities was condemning these countries to poverty.

From structuralism to dependency theory

Prebisch's argument contained another idea that became enormously influential in the 1950s and 1960s. He argued that the world economy was divided into the developed countries which are the center of the world economy and the periphery countries that constitute the developing countries. The center countries produce technologically advanced manufactured goods that are sold both in the center and the periphery countries. However, the periphery countries being unable to produce these goods must purchase them from the center at ever-higher prices in terms of the commodities they produce. Under these circumstances, the countries of the center are gaining vastly more from international trade than the countries of the periphery. With its overwhelming amount of commodity exports and relatively little industry, the idea that Latin America was not benefiting from trade with the rest of the world was a compelling idea. It was so compelling that it was later extended to a whole school of thought in economic development known as dependency theory. In this view, the countries of the center were viewed as the *cause* of the relative poverty of the developing countries. The world economy was viewed as a system where the developing countries produced raw materials that the center countries needed for their prosperity. In return, the developing countries received as little as necessary from the center. The periphery was seen more as a hapless victim of the economic activities of the center. Further, the institutions of the world economy were arranged in a way that made progress in the periphery countries difficult at best. An important component of dependency theory was the thought that underdevelopment was something that was external to the developing countries. Dependency theory was extremely popular in much of the developing world, including Latin America. The idea that the world economy was a rigged game and that the destiny of the region was being set outside the region has some obvious appeal.[3]

Both structuralism and dependency theory contain ideas that are superficially plausible. Economic structure matters as can be found in any industrial organization textbook. Bolivia is not Belgium and differences in the economic structures of the two countries influence economic outcomes. Dependency theory springs from the obvious fact that the developed countries have more wealth and power than the developing countries. However, both types of analysis lead to a radical conclusion. This conclusion would not matter much if the theories were just the normal intellectual parlor games of academics. However, as Keynes pointed out long ago, the ideas of academics and scholars are sometimes extremely important. In the case of Latin America, these ideas turned out to have very serious consequences.

The argument for ISI

The basic ideas of Prebisch and others can be summarized in this way. The structure of developing countries led them to export commodities and import manufactures from the developed countries. Because of the declining terms of trade, in the long run this pattern of trade would not be beneficial for the developing countries. The implication of this is that the traditional theory of comparative advantage doesn't work for developing countries. This conclusion flies in the face of 200 years of economic theory. In retrospect, the acceptance of this thesis seems incredulous. However, one should keep in mind that in the early 1950s, there was virtually no *empirical* evidence on the benefits of trade based on comparative advantage. The declining terms of trade argument was at that point buttressed by data.[4] For the time, this was unusual. In any case, the argument that the traditional trade of the developed countries with the developing countries was injurious to the latter became something like a conventional wisdom. The solution implied that developing countries could only break out of this pattern of trade by developing domestic manufacturing industries. There were two possible options. The first option would involve developing low-wage manufacturing based on an abundance of cheap labor. This is in line with the traditional theory of comparative advantage where a country exports products it can produce cheaply and imports products that it has a comparative disadvantage in. However, if one believes that trade based on comparative advantage is not a welfare maximizing policy for developing countries, then this may not seem to be an optimal policy. The second option was to partially close off the economy to trade and develop industries not for export, but to replace imports from the developed countries. In this manner it was hoped to both change the structure of the domestic economy and reduce the imports of manufactures that were partially the source of the declining terms of trade.

In the early 1950s, this argument neatly fit much of the thinking on economic development. In a sense, economic development as a field of study was being born at this time. There were a large number of former colonies going through the transformation from colony to nation that Latin America had accomplished over 100 years earlier. The new countries were obviously poor relative to the developed countries. The common perception was that these countries were poor because the agricultural or commodity sectors of their economies were large. The perception was that the developed countries had become that way by a process of moving out of agriculture into industry. The influence of structuralist economics can be related to this perception. It was widely perceived that the developing countries would not be able to industrialize in a world economy where the developed countries already had a large amount of productive industry. The inevitable conclusion of this logic was that in order to industrialize the developing countries would need to heavily protect their domestic markets. In particular, they would need to pursue policies that substituted domestic production for imports. An adjunct to industrialization was increasing the rate of investment. At the time, the process of development was viewed as being heavily related to increasing the amount of investment in industry and raising the capital to labor ratio (K/L). As we saw in Chapter 2, this would tend to increase GDP per capita. This was being confirmed by the theoretical work done on growth theory at the time. With optimism that in retrospect seems unwarranted, the process of economic development seemed simple enough. Use protectionism to develop domestic industry, increase the rate of capital investment, and the developing countries would soon catch up with the developed countries.

This approach to economic development found widespread acceptance in Latin America. Latin American proponents of this approach also went somewhat further down this road. Embodied in much of the thinking of the period was a general feeling that market forces were a poor guide for the development process. This led to two other aspects of ISI in Latin America. First, the thinking was that wage rates were not very important and that wages could be raised to address poverty with no loss of employment. In a similar fashion, the exchange rate was controlled at a low rate. This made the importation of capital goods cheaper to aid in the process of industrialization. It was assumed that did not matter very much in terms of exporting commodities. Further, a low exchange rate could help dampen inflation.

As will be shown in this and later chapters, the policy did not work as planned. It was slowly abandoned in the 1980s but some of the policies adopted in the 1950s and 1960s are still in place. The above is not a justification for ISI. It is rather an attempt to explain the reasoning behind its implementation. Sixty years ago the process of economic development seemed simple. The developed countries were rich because they had industry that the developing countries of Latin America did not. It seemed totally obvious that the path to becoming a developed country involved moving from agriculture to industry. To accomplish this, it was necessary to engage in a program that involved developing domestic industry using a variety of government interventions. Heavy capital investment was assumed to be an important part of the process and once again government intervention of various types would be needed to do this. Given standard growth theory, this heavy capital investment would quickly raise GDP growth and GDP per capita. Government intervention in investment was necessary as it was felt market forces would not produce the intended results. The acceptance of ISI in Latin America was further enhanced by the fact that one of the most articulate proponents of it was the most famous economist in the region. Ultimately, these policies failed to accomplish their purpose. In retrospect, they were the cause of many of the difficulties that the region is still coping with in the twenty-first century. However, the policies were born out of a misplaced sense of optimism and a not well developed level of understanding of the process of economic development. As with virtually any failed economic policy, ISI was implemented in the 1950s as a simple solution to a complex problem and with the best of intentions. The initial implementation of these policies should perhaps be viewed as a series of honest mistakes. However, they continued long after the policy failures were becoming apparent. The reasons for that problem can be related to the details of how ISI was implemented given in the next section.

6.1 Raul Prebisch (1901–1986)

The name of Raul Prebisch is inextricably linked to ISI in Latin America and to dependency theory. In some quarters, his work is still considered seminal and important while in others it is considered in a somewhat less favorable light. In a common Latin American story, Prebisch was born in Argentina but his parents were German immigrants. He showed early promise, publishing six articles before finishing an MA in economics at the University of Buenos Aires. His early work mirrored the times, as the Argentina of the 1920s was an example of a country prospering based on the standard theory of comparative advantage. Like many others, the Great Depression changed his thinking. Working at the central bank of Argentina, he and his colleagues began research on why the country's terms of trade were deteriorating. This was the beginning of both the declining terms of trade argument and the concept of the world economy divided into a center and periphery. His move to Economic Commission for Latin America (ECLA) in the late 1940s was a natural extension of his earlier thinking on Latin America and the world economy. ECLA quickly became a center for heterodox economic thought both in Latin America and the world. His ideas proved influential in a policy sense as ISI became the dominant development policy of the region and to a lesser extent for many other countries outside of Latin America. His early work on the composition of the world economy became the basis for the later work on dependency theory. In the 1960s, Prebisch helped start the United Nations Conference on Trade and Development (UNCTAD). In broad terms, UNCTAD's agenda was to promote a "new world economic order" where the countries of the periphery would receive more equitable treatment in the world economy. While his term at UNCTAD and the organization itself were less than successful, his views on economic development had obviously changed. He had publicly given up on ISI as a development strategy. Instead he was an early proponent of the sort of internal reforms discussed in Chapter 2. He also worked for trade preferences for developing country exports and regional integration among developing countries.

The legacy of Raul Prebisch is hardly one of a radical. As President of the central bank of Argentina he was an inflation hawk and an advocate of fiscal responsibility. Revealingly, he was forced out of the central bank by Juan Peron. He was far ahead of his time in advocating the importance of central bank independence. In the 1930s, he worked on a multilateral plan to stabilize world commodity prices which has always been a problem for both producers and consumers. The plan failed but it reflected both his overriding interest in practical problems and the ability to recognize what works and what doesn't. For example, by the late 1950s, he was already becoming skeptical of ISI and worried about the neglect of exports from Latin America. His later work at UNCTAD reinforced this. ISI had failed and he had recognized the importance of outward-oriented trade strategies for developing countries. After leaving UNCTAD in the late 1960s, he was sounding the alarm about the growing debt burden of the region and the possible consequences. In hindsight, it is easy to criticize his work on ISI. While responsible for its creation, he cannot be held responsible for the subsequent thirty years of its heavy-handed application in Latin America. Aside from ISI, this other work during his career was surprisingly mainstream. The constant of his career was concern about economic development and policies to enhance growth in developing countries.[5]

How ISI worked

In the previous section, we outlined the theoretical justification for ISI. It may have been a flawed justification, but the policies were implemented nonetheless.[6] The basic idea was to develop domestic industry that would not otherwise have developed. In general terms, this was accomplished by protecting new industries from foreign competition through trade policy and enacting a wide-ranging set of programs to make industry more profitable than would otherwise be the case. In a developed country, this collection of policies to guide the development of industrial structure would be known as industrial policy. Among economists, industrial policy can create an uneasy feeling. On the one hand, all countries have an industrial policy of some sort. Changes in the regulation of business that are not universal inevitably favor one industry over another. Pollution-intensive industries are regulated more heavily than other industries. This is appropriate if there is some positive or negative externality associated with the industry. On the other hand, the unease over industrial policy occurs when the government chooses to favor an industry because it will enhance economic growth. For this to work, it must be the case that the government can pick which industries will grow faster than average in the future.[7] In a developed country, the industry is usually favored with a mix of tax breaks, government subsidies, or protectionism. In theory, the money spent now is an investment as faster growth in this industry will yield faster overall growth in the future. In a rich country, the social cost of a failed industrial policy would usually be some waste of resources and somewhat slower growth.

Industrial policy in a developed country is usually applied at the industry level. ISI in Latin America was industrial policy writ large. The subsidies were not the odd tax break or higher tariff for a particular industry. Rather it was an overall development strategy composed of a number of policies directed at industry *in general*. These policies were so important that they not only affected industry but the economy as a whole. This was as intended. Recall that the basic idea was to change the structure of the economy from agriculture and commodities to industry. The forecasted outcome was an acceleration of the rate of economic growth and an increase in GDP per capita. Unfortunately, policies can have unintended outcomes and this was the case for ISI. ISI worked in the sense that Latin America shifted more towards industry than might otherwise be the case. In order to understand ISI and its effects, this section presents the highlights of its major components.

Trade policy

Encouraging the development of industry in Latin America invariably meant wholly or partially excluding imports from competing with domestic firms. Almost always, this will mean higher tariffs. Recall that tariffs in Latin America were raised during the Great Depression. However, after World War II the paths of Latin America and the rest of the world diverged. By the mid-1930s it was recognized in the developed countries that the global trade war ignited by the US in 1930 had been a costly disaster for the world economy. After World War II, these countries quickly started trying to dismantle the protectionism of the 1930s. In particular, trade negotiations were started under the General Agreement on Tariffs on Trade (GATT) in 1947. To put it mildly, the countries of Latin America were not enthusiastic participants in GATT. Few countries joined at the beginning and many countries did not join until decades later.[8] However, this fits with the development of ISI. Under ISI, imports from the developed countries needed to be reduced. The whole point of GATT was to reduce protectionism. Given this incompatibility, many of the countries in Latin America did not bother to join GATT. As we will see in the next chapter, tariffs were not reduced from the levels of the 1930s. Instead the level of protectionism increased after World War II. In many cases tariffs were not sufficient to reduce the level of imports to desired levels. Frequently, tariff protection was supplemented by quotas. The combination of high tariffs and/or quotas led to astonishingly high levels of protection of industry in the region. In summary, trade policy was the most fundamental tool of ISI. Most of the other components of ISI would not have been very effective in promoting industry if similar goods could have been imported.

Exchange rate policy

As was mentioned earlier, a key component of ISI was an artificially low exchange rate. In terms of industrialization this had the advantage of making the importation of capital goods more inexpensive. The industries developed under ISI in Latin America tended to be oriented towards the production of consumer goods to replace imports. While these industries could produce goods for the domestic market, they were not capable of producing the capital equipment necessary for their production. These capital goods had to be imported from the developed countries. Since these goods are expensive, a low exchange rate (i.e. a strong domestic currency) could substantially reduce the initial cost of setting up an "industry" in a Latin American country. A hypothetical transaction may be useful in order to see this point. Assume that a firm in a country needed machinery to produce car batteries that cost $1 million. Further assume that the exchange rate is fixed at 10 pesos to the dollar. To the domestic producer, the cost of the machinery would be 10 million pesos. As will be shown in Chapter 8, this fixed exchange rate was commonly far below the equilibrium. For example, it may not have been difficult to imagine that the equilibrium exchange rate may well have been 20 pesos to the dollar. At this exchange rate, the identical piece of machinery would have cost 20 million pesos. In these situations, the lower exchange rate would constitute a very large subsidy to this industrial firm. This implicit subsidy did not end there. The imported capital equipment of course needed parts and sometimes foreign services. The same subsidy would apply to any subsequent imports associated with keeping the equipment running. In the three decades of ISI in Latin America, such transactions were commonplace. Whole industries were being developed from scratch in much of the region. Exchange rates were fixed at rates usually below market rates. Industrial activities were much cheaper to start up and keep running than would otherwise have been the case. This was intentional. Governments needed means to increase the profitability of new industries and exchange rate policy was one of them. Further, initially the policy was inexpensive. However, in later chapters maintaining a low exchange rate eventually became extremely expensive.

Targeted lending and financial repression

Usually, industries being developed under ISI were capital-intensive. Remember that this capital intensity was to some extent intentional. The larger the increase in the capital stock, the larger the increase in the production function for the country. This capital intensity also served to increase the country's capital-to-labor ratio. The hoped-for effect would be to increase wages in the capital-intensive industry and in an indirect way raise wages in the economy overall. The problem then became how to provide an adequate amount of capital for the initial investments required. Neither trade policy nor exchange rate policy would provide the start-up funds needed. Private sector banks might be understandably reluctant to loan large sums of money to finance the creation of new firms in industries with no historical track record in these countries. The problem was exacerbated by the small amount of capital available. Middle-income countries are usually abundant in labor but capital is scarce. The operation of an ISI development strategy required large amounts of capital in capital-scarce countries. The solution in many cases was the development of state-owned or state-subsidized development banks. Such financial institutions were set up all over the region to loan to industry in general or a particular industry. Capital could then be raised by the state, allocated to development banks and then loaned out to firms at relatively low interest rates. Thus the desired subsidy for investment in industry has been supplied by the state.

Financial subsidies sometimes came in a different form. Financial systems in some Latin American countries were subject to varying degrees of financial repression. Financial repression refers to government policies that influence the savings and investment decisions of individuals and financial institutions. These sorts of controls can consist of limits on interest charged or paid or government control over the flow of financial resources. For example, laws could limit the amount of interest paid to savers in order to provide less expensive financing for industry.

Financial repression can have several effects. First, it can reduce the amount of savings as individuals may either choose to save less or keep their savings in other less liquid forms such as land.[9] This can be a particularly serious problem if the interest rate paid to savers is low relative to the rate of inflation. As we will see in Chapter 10, inflation has been a persistent problem in the region. The amount of savings is partially dependent on the real interest rate. The real interest rate is the nominal interest rate minus the expected rate of inflation. This relationship raises the possibility that a seemingly reasonable nominal interest rate could leave savers losing money. For example, suppose that the rate paid by financial institutions to savers is fixed at five percent. This leaves savers with a positive rate of return only if the rate of inflation is less than five percent. Couple this interest rate with a 20 percent rate of inflation and the financial system is inflicting horrific losses on anyone trying to save for the future.[10]

Secondly, financial repression also can result in the misallocation of capital. At the start, it should be recognized that capital markets free of government intervention have been known to misallocate capital. The question becomes whether or not government allocation decisions are better. Among economists, the general thinking is that markets make fewer mistakes than governments. Prior to the 1980s, it was not uncommon for governments in Latin America to be involved in the allocation of over 50 percent of a country's investment funds.[11] This large-scale intervention by governments in the region in the allocation of capital led to widespread misallocations. This statement is not a value judgment. A country that is naturally capital scarce can ill afford to waste a scarce resource. Much of the capital directed by government intervention went into *capital-intensive* industries. The result was that much of the region's capital was being allocated into industries that were very unlikely to ever be internationally competitive due to the mismatch between the resources of Latin America and the type of industries being developed. The idea this was based on was superficially plausible: invest heavily and growth will follow. Unfortunately, investing heavily in the wrong industries may lead to results that are less than expected.

6.2 Capital flight and currency substitution

There are two phenomena that can be related to financial repression that anyone familiar with Latin America will recognize even if they don't know the exact economic terminology. The first is capital flight. Capital flight is the term used to describe the movement of money out of a country in response to adverse political or economic events. Usually the term is used in the context of a massive amount of capital moving in a short period of time. We will see this sort of capital flight again in Chapter 8. However, the movements often are more subtle as money may be moving more slowly over a longer period of time for exactly the same reasons. Financial repression can cause this sort of capital flight. With low interest rates and high inflation, the real rate of interest can easily be negative. With few alternative assets available in the capital markets of a middle-income country, then the temptation to move money to another country where financial assets that offer a positive real rate of return can be substantial. For example, a bank account in Miami or Panama is not exactly an uncommon thing in Latin America. This kind of capital flight does not make the headlines precisely because it is so "normal." This very normality is telling an economist that something is wrong.

For the less well-off a bank account in a foreign country may be an impossible dream. Even an account with a domestic bank may not be easy to obtain. However, a point many may miss is that the poor may lack education but this hardly means that they are not financially astute. Making ends meet in a middle-income country frequently requires the financial agility worthy of a modern financier. For this group, holding savings in a form that is not depreciating means holding on to any stable foreign currency that becomes available. In Latin America, this is usually US dollars. Hoarding savings in the form of dollars has been a common practice in the region. This holding of financial assets in foreign currency as a protection against losses is known as currency substitution. This phenomenon is not restricted to the poor. Wealthier investors may also engage in currency substitution. Notice that the definitions of capital flight and currency substitution are somewhat similar. In both cases, people are trying to protect themselves from financial loss. This hoarding behavior adversely affects long-run growth. A bank account in Miami or a hundred dollars hidden at home have the same effects. There is less money to be invested in the domestic economy.

State-owned enterprises (SOEs)

The drive to industrialize the countries of Latin America under ISI sometimes led to the development of SOEs. The protection of domestic industry through trade policy, the implicit subsidy of a low exchange rate, and the availability of cheap credit were sometimes not enough to create the sort of new industries governments were interested in. These sorts of industries usually fell into one of three categories. First, governments frequently desired the establishment of "heavy," i.e. capital-intensive industries present in high-income countries. Frequently, these industries were producing intermediate goods that were felt to be essential to the ultimate development of other upstream industries. In the mid-twentieth century, a prime example of this was the steel industry. The thinking was along the lines of "how can a country industrialize without steel?" Even under the conditions described above, there were no private investors available to start a steel company in a country without iron ore and coal. The solution in some cases was to set up an SOE to provide the desired industry. A later tendency was to develop "new" or "modern" industries that were human capital-intensive. Since Latin America was not well endowed in the 1960s and 1970s with human capital, enticing private sector firms into these industries was difficult.

Brazil attempted to set up computer and aerospace industries using SOEs in the absence of any private sector participation.[12] A final sort of investment in SOEs occurred for a different reason. Natural resources in many parts of the world are considered as a national patrimony that makes exploitation of these resources even by domestic private sector firms difficult. This is the case in Latin America as well. Following the model of the oil industry in Mexico, many countries chose to develop their natural resources using SOEs. In some cases, such as the copper industry in Chile and the oil industry in Brazil, SOEs have been successful. In other cases, the results have been disappointing.

6.3 Brazilian SOEs

As a general rule, the operation of SOEs in Latin America was not very successful. This is not a purely Latin American phenomenon. This organizational form has a poor track record in virtually every country of the world. In running an SOE, bureaucracy and inefficiency tend to be the norm. The usual profit motive is diluted by the state as whole or partial owner. If the entity runs at a loss, the usual penalties associated with that may not exist. Losses are the taxpayer's problem. Just breaking even is a success for an SOE. As a result of the financial crisis of the 1980s, many of the SOEs in Latin America were closed or privatized. The governments of the region entered the decade with government finances in poor condition. The crisis widened budget deficits and the losses being made by most SOEs became too large to continue to support. There were some exceptions such as Pemex in Mexico and Codelco in Chile but these two have control of important natural resources. SOEs not engaged in other areas are now a part of economic history.

In general, the same is true for Brazil. However, the country has produced two SOEs that have become internationally competitive companies. The most famous of the two is Petrobras which is engaged in the exploration and production of oil. The company began as a result of the controversial nationalization of all private oil reserves in the country. Unlike Pemex, Petrobras restricted its activities to the exploration and production of oil and left the wholesale and retail sides of the industry to the private sector. Brazil has historically been an oil importer so the company has had a high incentive to find and produce oil. In this process the company has been successful both in finding oil and developing the technology to produce oil offshore in deep water.[13] Its recent discoveries of two new fields in the Atlantic could turn Brazil into a major oil exporter. Part of the company's success may be its ownership structure. It is 55-percent owned by the government but private investors own the remainder.

An even more interesting company is Embraer (Brazilian Aeronautics Company). A Brazilian aircraft industry was conceived of by the government in the 1940s. This led to the creation of aerospace research institutes in the country. These institutes helped create the industry-specific human capital that is a prerequisite for any high-technology industry. In the 1960s the infant industry was able to design, successfully test, and build military transport planes. These planes were adapted for civilian use and Embraer was born as a joint venture between the government and private investors. Notice that like Petrobras, the company was started as a joint venture. Other types of planes were designed and produced in the 1970s and 1980s. The company was completely privatized in 1988 as the government was withdrawing from SOEs in general. The lack of new products in the late 1980s and 1990s led to the near death of the company. However, in the 1990s Embraer developed the regional jet which has become an enormously successful product. In 2008, the company delivered 204 planes and is now the third largest aircraft manufacturer in the world. Notice that the common thread here is the public/private character of both companies. These are not the only examples of Latin American companies that are successful in the world economy. They are unusual only in the sense that they began life as creations of the state and have been successful. As in most parts of the world, this is unusual.

ISI and MNCs

In the drive to industrialize the region, MNCs became part of the process. As we have seen, in some industries the subsidies being offered to the private sector were inadequate to produce the desired result, an industry. In other cases, even SOEs were not feasible due to the lack of industry-specific human capital necessary to begin production. In these cases, the participation of MNCs in the development of the local industry became essential. For a MNC there is frequently a choice to be made between exporting to a country and producing the product locally. This export versus FDI decision is dependent on a large number of variables. In the case of Latin America, the choice to engage in FDI frequently was not difficult. The high tariffs in the region coupled with the existence of quotas often made exporting to these markets unprofitable. If the domestic market was large enough, FDI became an attractive option. In general, the three largest markets in the region were Argentina, Brazil, and Mexico. These countries had large and growing populations that were profitable markets for firms selling consumer goods such as automobiles. Once established in these markets, MNCs had access to some of the same benefits as domestic firms. They were shielded from foreign competition and might have access to inexpensive foreign exchange. The plants set up needed inputs and parts produced outside of the region. To keep these plants running, governments had to provide access to foreign exchange for inputs and parts. MNCs could further enhance the profitability of these operations by using plant and equipment that was old or obsolete by developed country standards. New cars in Argentina were frequently models that had been out of production for years in the MNCs' home markets. Although the production volumes of these plants were relatively low, profits could still be reasonable due to high prices being charged for outdated products. While the country could obtain an "industry" in this manner, the consumers of a middle-income country were paying an implicit tax for this form of industrialization.

The relationship between the MNCs and the governments of the regions in this situation was complicated. The countries desired industry and reluctantly allowed FDI as a less than preferred means of accomplishing that end. FDI was virtually never on a national treatment basis but usually negotiated on a case by case basis. During this period, the activities of MNCs were viewed with some suspicion and governments strove to maximize the benefits of FDI and limit the perceived costs. This is not unreasonable as the source of profits in many cases was some sort of government policy that resulted in a relatively noncompetitive domestic market. For the MNCs, these investments were seen as the only feasible way to obtain access to growing markets. However, the production volumes were frequently small and the countries of the region are not easy places to do business. This is especially true for MNCs, who sometimes faced restrictions that the typical domestic firm did not. While there was a nexus of interests between governments of the region and MNCs, the relationship was uneasy. Governments obtained industry from the MNCs but often one that was a pale shadow of the industry in the source country. MNCs gained access to desirable markets but this access came in a form that was profitable only under a certain set of government policies. ISI created a certain type of FDI designed to "jump" over trade barriers and obtain certain kinds of subsidies. Not surprisingly, neither side of the bargain was ever entirely happy with the result.

The results of ISI

In theory, ISI was supposed to transform Latin America from a relatively poor region in the world economy to relative prosperity. The goal seemed achievable as parts of the region had been, at various times in history, relatively prosperous. In the 1940s it seemed obvious how to do this. The high-income countries had moved out of agriculture and into industry and gotten rich in the process. It seemed obvious that if Latin America could move out of commodities and agriculture and industrialize, the same result would follow. Further, the new development theory indicated that economic development was a relatively simple process. If a country could increase its capital stock and the K/L ratio, then GDP per capita would surely rise. In the previous section we indicated that things did not work out as planned. GDP per capita in the region increased from 1950 to 1980 but at a relatively slow rate. This was disappointing, but the collection of policies created numerous unintended consequences. In this section, we review a partial list of these problems.

Industrialization

The main purpose of ISI was to produce industry in a country as rapidly as possible. In the case of Latin America, the policies produced a dramatic increase in the ratio of manufacturing to GDP. If it were true that rapid industrialization automatically meant rising GDP per capita, then all would have gone to plan. However, one needs to go back and think about the phrase "import substitution" for a moment. Simple trade theory indicates what should be occurring in foreign trade and by extension what domestic production should look like. A country should be exporting products that it can produce more inexpensively than other countries. The earnings from these exports can then be used to buy imported products. The products that a country imports should be products that can be made in other countries more inexpensively than domestic producers can make them. This is how a country maximizes its welfare by trading. One of the main benefits of trade is that a country can improve its welfare by buying goods cheaply from foreigners as opposed to producing them domestically at a high cost. In the jargon of economics, a country exports goods in which it has a comparative advantage. It imports goods in which it has a comparative disadvantage. Now consider the likely results of ISI. By definition, a country imports products that it has a comparative disadvantage in production. By pursuing ISI, a country is deliberately building up industries in which it has already demonstrated that it has a comparative disadvantage. Imports will be replaced but at a cost that is guaranteed to be higher than the cost of imported goods. Industry will be developed but it will be industry that the country has a *comparative disadvantage* in production. Industry has been developed but it is an artificial and fragile sort of industry. It is a bit like growing a pine tree in a desert. It may be possible to do this, but only with a lot of care and feeding.

One of the main problems with ISI was the mismatch between the labor abundance of Latin America and the capital intensity of the industries being developed. A labor abundant region should have a comparative disadvantage in capital-intensive industries. In a region that is relatively capital scarce, what capital that was available was being poured into capital-intensive industries. Capital acquired through FDI also was funneled into these industries as a result of trade policy. By the 1960s industry in Latin America had developed along the following lines.

1   A typical industry that had developed was very capital-intensive. Although capital was scarce in the country as a whole, targeted lending meant an adequate supply of cheap capital.
2   If imported inputs were necessary for production, these could be imported inexpensively as the exchange rate was being held below equilibrium.
3   Troublesome foreign competitors could not profitably sell in markets with very high tariffs and quota protection.
4   The local firm may not have faced much domestic competition either. In a small market there may have been room for only one firm.
5   Even an inefficient firm in these circumstances could be quite profitable.

6 These profits made generous labor laws possible. High wages and higher administrative costs could be passed on in the form of higher prices. This was easier to accomplish considering the chronic inflation problems of the region.

By the 1970s many countries of the region had developed a sort of ISI enclave within the economy. The industrial sector was highly profitable and workers fortunate enough to have jobs in this part of the economy were relatively well-off by local standards. However, virtually the whole industrial sector was built not on the foundation of comparative advantage but on the existence of a certain set of government policies. Any combination of increases in interest rates, a depreciation of the currency, or changes in trade policy could severely damage industry. Since everyone was aware of this, the policy was difficult to change. Firms and workers (unions) both shared an interest in the continuation of ISI. Governments everywhere are not likely to change a policy supported by *both* business and labor. Government supported SOEs were going to be difficult to close. Too much capital had been invested and such firms had an especially close relationship with government. Many MNCs had invested heavily in the region on the basis of a certain set of policies. Their plants could not withstand a major change in policy. As we will see, it took a major *external* shock to cause a change in policy.

ISI and the informal sector

Industrialization had brought prosperity but not to the average citizen of the region. For firms and individuals outside of the ISI industries, things did not go as well. For consumers, goods frequently were expensive and quality was not up to world standards. An understandable reaction in many countries was smuggling to evade tariffs and quotas or small-scale production in the informal sector. For small and medium-sized firms or consumers, credit was difficult to obtain. Credit was first allocated to ISI industries and everyone else bid for what was left. Informal money lenders can fill the gap for some loans but many sectors of the economy found credit difficult to obtain. A similar situation applied to foreign exchange. Exchange controls favored industry both in terms of access and frequently with respect to price.[14] The usual black markets in foreign exchange were common. Government regulations could be dealt with by large firms with the resources to deal with the bureaucracy. Labor regulations that raised the price of labor above equilibrium meant that official unemployment and underemployment became high. Higher taxes that could be paid by firms in the ISI sector could not be paid by smaller firms. Tax evasion became normal in many countries. Under these circumstances, the development of a large informal sector of the economy is hardly surprising. However, the presence of large profitable firms made implementation of some regulations and taxes more reasonable. Many economies of the region became an odd mixture of the seemingly modern industrial sector and a large informal sector producing goods and services outside of the official regulations of the state. Every economy in the world has an informal sector, the only remaining question is how large it is. ISI did not create the informal sector in Latin America. The informal sector in Latin America has long historical roots tracing to excessive regulation in the colonial era. At least part of the abnormally large size of the informal sector in the region can be reasonably attributed to the unintended consequences of ISI.

ISI and agriculture

ISI inherently favored the industrial sector of the economy. As seen in the previous section, it implicitly made doing business in other sectors of the economy more difficult. Many of these effects were unintended consequences. The effects on the agricultural sector of the region were more ominous. The underpinnings of the whole development policy were built on the idea of reducing the importance of agriculture relative to industry. The policy worked in this regard as intended. ISI produced a brutally difficult climate for the agricultural sector. Targeted lending was designed to provide the bulk of the available investment funds to industry. Like other sectors of the economy, credit in the agricultural sector became more difficult to obtain. The exchange rate policy was a particular problem. Agricultural commodities sell in world markets and are usually priced in a major currency. The overvaluation of Latin American currencies was a severe handicap to exports of agricultural commodities from the region. The taxes, labor laws, and business regulations that firms in the ISI sector could withstand made business in agriculture extremely difficult. A farm is not a factory and government regulations that seem reasonable in the environment of the capital city can make farming in compliance with the law nearly impossible.

A further problem was infrastructure. The drive to industrialize meant that public sector investment in infrastructure tended to be in the large cities that were the location of much of the heavy industry. Infrastructure investment in rural areas languished. This was especially true of transportation systems. Roads are a crucial part of an efficient agricultural sector. With a poor network of roads, agricultural producers faced a cost disadvantage in exports on top of the frequent exchange rate problem. In summary, the policies necessary for ISI discriminated against the agricultural sector. As governments sometimes do, the policy favored comparative disadvantage industries and discriminated against a comparative advantage industry. Resources are being channeled to industries that may never grow fast and moved away from potentially faster growing industries. As we will see in the next section, this neglect had other consequences.

Urbanization and pollution

For a moment, consider the situation of a young person in a rural area of a Latin American country. The primary source of employment in the area is agriculture. However, production has not increased significantly in decades and wages are low. Education has been a difficult process. Primary schools are widely available and illiteracy is now rare. Secondary education is more difficult. Secondary schools don't exist in small villages and transportation on rural (dirt) roads makes obtaining further education difficult. The young person is facing a future of poorly paid agricultural labor with no real prospect of anything better in the future. Now let's assume that the annual wage for this young person is $500 per year. We will also assume that this young person potentially can earn $1,500 per year if employed full time in the *informal* sector in a large city. The migration of this young person from a rural village to a large city is hardly surprising. The income gap is easy to explain. Wages are higher in the large city partially because of the existence of high-paying jobs in ISI industries. These high wages tend to increase wages for all workers in the urban area and the policies of ISI make these wages possible. However, there is a complication. A large number of young people see this gap and decide to migrate. Not all of the new workers can find jobs in the formal sector. This drives the official unemployment rate up. There are still jobs available in the informal sector at high wages relative to the rural area. The work available may be sporadic and include periods of unemployment. However, the wage gap is so large that this young person could afford to be unemployed half the time and still be better off than remaining in the village.

The above is a simplified description of the Harris–Todaro model of rural to urban migration. Workers migrate in response to differences in income in rural and urban areas. If the income gap is large, workers may continue to migrate even in the face of high unemployment in the urban areas. Notice that the young person described above could be unemployed half the time and still have a higher income in the urban area. As long as these gaps exist, workers will continue to migrate. In much of Latin America, this gap can be traced to the existence of ISI. Even without this policy there would have existed an income gap that would have induced migration. The major cities of the region were going to become larger under any set of policies. However, policies that depress the agricultural sector and encourage industrialization are going to widen this gap. This encourages more migration than would otherwise be the case. These major cities are full of workers who migrated from the countryside and work and often live in the informal sector. A job in the informal sector and living as a squatter is a way of life for many of the poor in Latin America. These migrants may be poor and lack some formal education. Their continuing migration suggests that they are good at basic math, calculating probabilities, and forecasting. They migrate and stay in what appears to be difficult circumstances. Those circumstances can be seen and deplored. One needs to keep in mind that what they left was *worse*. To a certain extent, their situation is part of the collateral damage of ISI. Again, ISI did not *create* this situation but it no doubt exacerbated it.

Finally, consider the effects of all of this on the environment. Infrastructure in the country is scarce so heavy industries are locating in major cities where access to electricity and modern transportation systems are easiest. Also, these cities already have the largest pools of human capital necessary for modern industry. ISI industries were heavily tied to government policy so locating in the capital city of the country is an advantage. Mexico City would be a textbook case of these effects. The development of industry in the city begins attracting migrants from the rural areas. The initial migrants do very well and this encourages further migration. As long as the income gap persists, the population of the city continues to grow. An expanding ISI sector and a booming population in the city are not unrelated. The result can also be an environmental nightmare. As described in Chapter 3 many of these industries are inherently pollution-intensive. Environmental regulations are weak and enforcement may be lax. The booming population generates a larger demand for all forms of power from electricity to automobiles. Pollution standards in this sector also are low. The large informal sector and the large squatter population further aggravate the problem. As ISI encouraged rapid urbanization, it likewise contributed to environmental problems. The major cities of Latin America would not be pristine without the sort of industries that flourished under ISI, but they would be cleaner and less crowded.[15]

Fiscal and monetary policy

In much of Latin America, ISI put a persistent strain on government finances. In terms of fiscal policy, this usually meant a government budget deficit. In many countries, SOEs were a constant source of government spending. The correlation between SOEs and profits is not high in any part of the world. Latin American SOEs were no different. These entities tended to run persistent losses that had to covered by the government. Their existence was making government spending higher than would otherwise have been the case. Domestic private sector firms and MNCs were usually profitable and able to pay taxes. However, the rates they could afford to pay may not have been appropriate for other parts of the economy. This was leading to widespread tax evasion and the growth of the informal sector. The growth of the informal sector creates serious problems on the revenue side of the government budget. The net effect was that government budget deficits were virtually the norm in the region for decades in the mid to late twentieth century. A commodity boom might produce a temporary surplus on occasion, but a balanced budget or surplus was unusual.

In a developed country, fiscal policy can be separated from monetary policy. If the government runs a budget deficit, then the difference can be borrowed from either domestic or foreign lenders in the form of the sale of government bonds. Such a deficit may or may not be prudent, but it can be financed without affecting the money supply of the country. In a middle-income country, fiscal policy effectively becomes monetary policy. To understand this, consider the options of the government in the face of a fiscal deficit. The government cannot borrow by issuing bonds as in a developed country. No one would buy them. The ability to borrow by issuing bonds requires credibility that most governments of the region did not possess. The alternative became the printing of money and the expansion of the money supply. In this environment, a government budget deficit translates into a loose monetary policy. As we will see in Chapter 10, this usually leads to inflation. In many Latin American countries the inflation was catastrophic. By the 1980s, inflation and Latin America were two terms that were uncomfortably related to one another. As before, ISI was not the absolute cause of inflation in the region. However, it contributed to fiscal deficits that in the institutional environment of the times contributed to excessive rates of growth of the money supply.

The trade balance

Eventually the worst effect of ISI was the pressure it was putting on the trade balance. The ISI industries had a voracious appetite for foreign exchange. Equipment and intermediate goods had to be imported to keep the industries running. These imports were not inexpensive and as the industrial sector grew so did imports. The low exchange rate necessary to subsidize these imports encouraged other types of imports. Anyone who could get access to foreign exchange at the reduced price probably could make a profit. There was constant pressure on the demand for foreign exchange. In terms of exports, Latin America was still locked in the past. The region had been an exporter of commodities for centuries and remained so. The world economy was changing but the composition of exports had not. Aside from the occasional commodity boom, prices during this period were not high. Agricultural exports languished as government policy was not focused on growth in this sector. Exports of manufactured goods were limited. Manufacturers in the region were focused on serving the domestic market. Labor costs, taxes, and the burden of regulation made it difficult for firms in the region to successfully export manufactured goods. Difficulties in exporting translate into low foreign exchange earnings or more precisely, a limited supply of foreign exchange. Deficits in the trade balance likewise became normal in Latin America. Government rationing of foreign exchange became a common means of dealing with the outcome of a low exchange rate.

This situation was manageable until the 1970s. Two events occurred outside the region that eventually made continuing ISI untenable. First, the global system of fixed exchange rates collapsed in 1971. The developed countries simply converted to floating exchange rates and went on.

The countries of Latin America were reluctant to do this as the ISI industries were dependent on cheap imported imports. To a lesser extent other sectors of the economies of the region were operating under the assumption of a low and fixed exchange rate. The second event was the oil shock of 1973. Most of the countries of the region are oil importers. The increase in the price of oil caused large increases in trade deficits. Imports increased dramatically for most of Latin America and exports of commodities fell in tandem with the global recession. Trade deficits increased dramatically along with the need for foreign exchange. For some countries the solution was to borrow foreign exchange from commercial banks. This borrowing became large as the decade progressed. Depreciations of the exchange also accompanied these problems.

The second oil shock in 1979 was the beginning of the end of ISI. Governments in the region rapidly increased their borrowing. However, by 1982 this borrowing was dramatically reduced as lenders became increasingly concerned about the ability of countries in the region to repay their debt. The inability to borrow coupled with depreciations of the exchange rate threatened the entire industrial sector of the region and had a profound impact on consumption by the public.

The Lost Decade

> It is easy to turn an aquarium into fish soup. Reversing the process is much harder.
>
> Lech Walesa

As we will see in Chapter 11, an exchange rate shock is a traumatic event for any economy. The currency depreciates by a large amount in a very short period of time. In turn, this causes several other effects. First, the cost of all imports rises substantially. The ISI industries of the region that had been dependent on cheap imports for decades were unable to continue business as usual. The firms were frequently inefficient and simply could not cope with the increase in costs. The price of imports purchased by consumers also rises dramatically. In effect, there is an economy-wide cost of living increase. In a high-income country this would be annoying but manageable. In a middle-income country consumers at the low end of the income distribution are suffering real hardship.[16] For this part of the population of Latin America it was a problem of obtaining enough food to stave off malnutrition. There is also an effect on the output of the economy. Real GDP falls and as a result unemployment rises. Again this is more of a problem in a middle-income country. Social safety nets are weaker and government assistance to adversely affected workers is not as effective. The exchange rate shock has caused a very unpleasant combination of higher inflation and higher unemployment. While this situation is not unusual for a single country it is somewhat more unusual for an entire region to be affected. However, this is precisely what occurred in Latin America. The region as a whole adopted ISI in the 1940s and 1950s. As the policy developed problems in the 1970s, most of the region gradually abandoned fixed exchange rates in the face of two oil shocks. This was accompanied by a large amount of borrowing in foreign currency. Finally, the inability of countries of the region to continue this borrowing brought about a *regional* exchange rate shock.

Another way of viewing the problem is to consider what a trade deficit really is. Going back to our analysis in Chapter 2, consider the components of GDP.

$$Y = C + I + G + (X - M) \qquad (6.1)$$

To review, equation 6.1 shows that GDP (Y) is simply the summation of consumption by the public (C); nonresidential and residential investment (I); government spending on goods and services (G); and exports (X) minus imports (M). The final term is roughly equivalent to the trade balance.[17] Since this is an identity, we can rearrange the terms as follows:

$$Y - C - I - G = (X - M) \qquad (6.2)$$

Equation 6.2 allows us to consider what the trade balance is. Y represents the total production of the economy and C, I, and G represent the various forms of the consumption of this output.

Now if the sum of C + I + G is larger than Y this means that the economy is consuming more than it is producing. If this is the case, then (X − M) *must* be a negative number, i.e. a trade deficit. Fundamentally, a trade deficit is a statement that a country is consuming more than it is producing. This also means that the country is borrowing from the rest of the world. The imports must be paid for with foreign exchange. If the country does not have previously accumulated sources of foreign exchange, then it will need to borrow it. This is exactly what Latin America as a region did in the 1970s. Rising oil prices dramatically increased the cost of imports. The export of commodities could not rise fast enough to cover this increase. The governments of the region borrowed to cover the trade deficits. In essence, the region was living beyond its means. Domestic consumption was higher than production and the difference showed up as trade deficits covered with borrowed money. As with an individual, the day of reckoning came when the countries of the region were unable to make agreed payments on the debt. When this borrowing was no longer possible, the wrenching adjustments associated with an exchange rate shock hit virtually the entire region. The result was nearly a decade of inflation coupled with declines in real GDP and abnormally high unemployment.

In most cases, an exchange shock is the sort of unpleasant macroeconomic experience described above. The higher inflation and lower real GDP occur quickly after the depreciation and dissipate over one to three years. In the case of Latin America there were economic aftershocks that took nearly a decade to work out. In addition to the macroeconomic consequences, the economies of Latin America had to be fundamentally restructured. The decades of ISI had left the region with a large industrial sector that was uncompetitive in the world economy. ISI firms began to fail and the drain of SOEs on the public finances became unsustainable. Resources needed to flow out of the old ISI industries and into other parts of the economy that were more productive. Such a process is never easy. The labor and capital tied up in the ISI industries could not be costlessly transferred into other parts of the economy. To regain some degree of balance in international trade, the components of GDP given in equation 6.1 had to change. Both consumption and government spending had to be reduced. At the same time, investment had to increase to allow for the transition to a different kind of industrial structure. In the short run, these adjustments usually mean that the resources coming out of the declining sectors of the economy may be unemployed. In the jargon of economics, this causes a substantial amount of structural unemployment. This unemployment occurred on top of the unemployment that follows just such an exchange rate shock. In summary, the region was dealing with two problems at the same time. These were short-run macroeconomic difficulties and a fundamental restructuring of the economies of the region. In addition, the region was searching for a model of economic development with a more sound base than ISI.

The above is the briefest possible description of the Lost Decade. In order to completely understand the economic upheaval in the region requires more economic analysis than can possibly be covered in one chapter. Further, the region responded to this shock by making substantial changes in economic policy in a number of areas. In the next six chapters, this is precisely what we will try to accomplish. Much of the first six chapters concerned the economic history of the region and its effects on the current structure of the economies of Latin America. Going forward, more detailed chapters on trade policy, exchange rate policy, and macroeconomics will be necessary to obtain a more complete understanding both of what happened and the policy options facing governments of the region.

6.4   ISI and the American automobile industry

One of the more difficult things to understand is changes in industrial structure. Such changes are occurring continuously in a healthy economy. Consumer demand and costs of production are constantly changing. When we say GDP is growing at three percent this does not mean that all sectors of the economy are growing at that rate. Some are growing faster and becoming a relatively larger percentage of total economic activity. Some are growing more slowly and are in relative decline. Finally, some sectors may even be shrinking in absolute terms. Declining industries are just as important as expanding ones. For the expanding industries to grow to their potential, resources must be released from the declining industries. This is a process the economist Joseph Schumpeter referred to as "creative destruction." It is a normal part of economic growth. However, it is not unusual for the government to attempt to interfere with this process and direct resources into declining industries. These attempts can end badly if there is not a sufficient positive externality occurring. The result can be resources being tied up in industries that are no longer competitive and that are dependent on the government for support. Further, this support can serve to make the industry(ies) even less competitive over time. The government can find itself in a vicious circle where the initial support leads to less efficiency and the need for more support later. By the 1970s, much of the industry of Latin America had fallen into this pattern. The presumed externality of ISI was faster growth. In reality, this externality didn't exist and the industry and workers had become dependent on the government.

The same sort of thing can happen elsewhere. The US automobile industry was becoming less competitive in the 1970s. Years of dominance of the industry by three firms had led to companies that were more bureaucracies than private sector firms. As competition from Japan intensified, the firms and labor unions sought protection in the early 1980s and one of the three firms was rescued by the government. This protection allowed the industry to avoid the uncomfortable adjustments necessary to successfully compete. The recent economic crisis led to the failure of two of the three firms. Again, the government rescued both firms. Even with the protection and bailouts, the adjustments have been difficult. The owners of the firms have lost billions and tens of thousands of workers have lost their jobs with little hope of employment in the short run. In the case of the US this is a problem for a small portion of the population and the government finances. This is not a short-run problem and it will take years for the industry to return to normal. Now imagine this sort of problem occurring in a large number of industries at the same time in the same country. If you can imagine this situation, then you now have an inkling into the trauma of the Lost Decade for the people and governments of Latin America.

Key concepts and terms

balance of payments – a summary of all the international transactions of a country's residents with the rest of the world during a year.

capital flight – the movement of money out of a country in response to adverse political or economic events.

comparative advantage – the ability of a country to produce a good at a lower opportunity cost than another country.

comparative disadvantage – the situation where a country can produce a good only at a relatively high opportunity cost.

currency substitution – the holding of financial assets in foreign currency as a protection against losses.

dependency theory – the idea that the world economy is a system controlled by the developed countries (the center) to the detriment of the developing countries (the periphery).

exchange rate shock – a large depreciation of a country's currency that occurs in a short period of time.

financial repression – government policies that influence the savings and investment decisions of individuals and financial institutions.

fiscal policy – a macroeconomic policy that uses government spending and/ or taxation to affect a country's GDP.

General Agreement on Tariffs on Trade (GATT) – a trade agreement reached after World War II, designed to reduce the level of protectionism in the world economy.

Harris–Todaro model – the theory that rural to urban migration is caused by differences in the relative expected incomes obtainable in the two areas.

industrial policy – a policy or set of policies designed to stimulate the growth of an industry or affect the industrial structure of a country.

monetary policy – the policy of the central bank with respect to the growth rate of the money supply and interest rates.

real interest rate – the nominal interest rate minus the expected rate of inflation.

structural unemployment – unemployment that occurs as labor moves from one part of the economy to another.

structuralist economics – the idea that the structure of an economy can have important effects on economic outcomes.

terms of trade – the price of exports divided by the price of imports.

Questions for review and discussion

1 Explain how a global downturn could cause balance of payments problems in a country that exports commodities.
2 Describe the process that led many countries in Latin America to adopt ISI development policy in the 1950s.
3 What is industrial policy? How is it related to ISI?
4 What is financial repression? How is this related to capital flight and currency substitution?
5 Describe the relationship between ISI, FDI, and MNCs.
6 List and describe the characteristics of industrialization under ISI.
7 How did ISI damage the development of the agricultural sector?
8 How did ISI contribute to the urbanization and pollution problems in the region?
9 Describe the link between ISI and inflation in Latin America.
10 How did ISI lead to the Lost Decade of the 1980s?

References and recommended readings

Aizenman, Joshua. 2005. "Financial Liberalisations in Latin America in the 1990s: A Reassessment." *World Economy.* 28(July): 959–83.

Bruton, Henry J. 1998. "A Reconsideration of Import Substitution." *Journal of Economic Literature.* 36(June): 903–36.

Cypher, James M. and James L. Dietz. 2009. *The Process of Economic Development.* 3rd ed. London: Routledge.

Dosman, Edgar J. 2008. *The Life and Times of Raul Prebisch.* Montreal: McGill-Queen's University Press.

Edwards, Sebastian. 1995. *Crisis and Reform in Latin America: From Despair to Hope.* Washington, DC: World Bank.

Edwards, Sebastian. 2003. "Financial Instability in Latin America." *Journal of International Money and Finance.* 22(December): 1095–1106.

Furtado, Celso. 1963. *The Economic Growth of Brazil: A Survey from Colonial to Modern Times.* Los Angeles: University of California Press.

Kaminsky, Graciela L. and Carmen M. Reinhart. 1998. "Financial Crisis in Asia and Latin America: Then and Now." *American Economic Review.* 88(May): 444–48.

Mendoza, Plinio A., Carlos A. Montaner, and Alvaro V. Llosa. 2000. *Guide to the Perfect Latin American Idiot.* Lanham, MD: Madison Books.

Prebisch, Raul. 1950. *The Economic Development of Latin America and Its Principal Problems.* New York: United Nations.

Ross, John. 2009. *El Monstruo: Dread and Redemption in Mexico City.* New York: Nation Books.

United Nations Department of Economic and Social Affairs. 1949. *Relative prices of Exports and Imports of Underdeveloped Countries: A Study of Post-war terms of trade between Under-developed and Industrialized Countries.* New York: United Nations.

7 Latin American trade policy

However protection may affect special forms of industry it must necessarily diminish the total return to industry—first by the waste inseparable from encouragement by tariff, and second by the losses due to transfer of capital and labor from occupations which they would choose for themselves to less profitable occupations which they must be bribed to engage in. If we do not see this without reflection, it is because our attention is engaged with but a part of the effects of protection. We see the large smelting-works and the massive mill without realizing that the same taxes which we are told have built them up have made more costly every nail driven and every needle full of thread used throughout the whole country.

Henry George

Introduction

As we saw in the last chapter, one of the key features of ISI was the deliberate reduction of imports in the region. In parts of the discussion one probably picked up the impression that substituting domestic production for imports may not have improved the economic situation of Latin America. The purpose of this chapter is to show why the trade policy part of ISI led to such poor results. In order to do this it will be necessary to show why unrestricted international trade normally is an optimal trade policy. Sadly, this is rarely the policy that governments in Latin America or anywhere else pursue. Although there a number of government policies that interfere with trade, the most important for our purposes are tariffs and quotas. The second section of the chapter shows how these policies affect the domestic economy. The subsequent sections of the chapter cover the history of trade policy in Latin America before, during and after the implementation of ISI. This history is critical in understanding Latin America's relative isolation from the world economy, the Lost Decade, and the lingering effects of ISI in the region.

Comparative advantage

It is a truism in economics that trade enhances the welfare of a country.

Countries prosper by selling goods that can be produced cheaply to the rest of the world and buying goods from other countries that are expensive to produce domestically. As a result, ISI always was viewed with some suspicion, as one of its foundations was that trade was not enhancing the welfare of Latin America. In this section, we will slowly cover the standard theory of international trade that has been developed over the last 200 years. In the previous chapter we mentioned the concept of comparative advantage. Our purpose here is to explain comparative advantage in more depth. This explanation will more clearly show that a substantial part of ISI had questionable foundations. The next part of this section will cover what determines comparative advantage. The concepts of comparative advantage and disadvantage will allow us to more clearly understand how ISI distorted the economies of the region. These distortions impeded the economic integration of Latin America and has made the integration of the region into the world economy more difficult.

Trade based on absolute advantage

To start, we need to return to the previously introduced concept of mercantilism. As we explained in Chapter 4, mercantilism was the idea that countries could maximize their welfare by adding to their stocks of gold and silver. To accomplish this, countries tended to pursue policies designed to suppress imports and promote exports. While deeply flawed, the concept was the conventional wisdom concerning international trade for hundreds of years. The mercantilist policies imposed on the region during the colonial period were standard for the time. Writing in the late eighteenth century, Adam Smith was the first economist to question the validity of mercantilism. The device he used to do so employed the concept of *absolute advantage*. Absolute advantage is the ability of a country to produce a good using fewer resources than another country. A simple numerical illustration can be used to illustrate the concept. Table 7.1 shows the production of two sorts of goods: machines and commodities. Machines are simply shorthand for the sort of complex manufactured goods that Latin America has imported from more developed countries for the last 500 years. Analogously, commodities are shorthand for the minerals and agricultural products that have been the bulk of Latin America's exports to the rest of the world over the same time frame. For convenience, we are analyzing Latin America's (LA) trade with the rest of the world (ROW). The table shows that a worker in Latin America could produce either 2 machines per day or 15 units of a commodity.[1] A worker in ROW could produce 5 machines per day or 10 units of a commodity. If we compare workers in the two regions, Latin American workers are more productive at producing commodities. Workers in ROW are more productive at producing machines. Everything else equal, machines will be cheaper in ROW and commodities will be cheaper in Latin America. Notice that both regions gain from trade. Latin America can

Table 7.1 Trade based on absolute advantage

	Machines	Commodity
Latin America	2	15
Rest of the World	5	10

purchase machines much more cheaply than they can produce them domestically. ROW gets to purchase commodities at a lower price than they could produce them domestically. Smith was just showing that countries gain by selling products to the rest of the world and importing products that would be more expensive to produce domestically. The table also indicates that the *world* is better off trading. Notice that if Latin America specializes in the production of commodities, it will start moving labor out of machines and into the production of commodities. As one worker is shifted, the production of commodities rises by 15 units and the production of machines falls by 2. In ROW, the production of machines rises by 5 and the production of commodities falls by 10 units. As a result of shifting labor in both regions, world output of both machines and commodities rises by 3 and 5 units, respectively. Countries engage in trade to increase their welfare. However, in doing so the economic output of the world rises. This is a kind of positive externality for the world that frequently isn't mentioned. Trade is not a zero sum game where one country's gain is another country's loss. It is a positive sum game where all countries and thus the world benefit.

Trade based on comparative advantage

> Comparative advantage is the best example of an economic principle that is undeniably true yet not obvious to intelligent people.
>
> Paul Samuelson

Given the hundreds of years that mercantilist policy had been in place, proponents of the doctrine were not going to accept a different theory of trade based solely on Smith's work. This was aided by the fact that there was a potential flaw in his argument. To illustrate the problem, consider the data in Table 7.2. In this table, the numbers of machines and commodities produced for each region have been changed a bit. In this example, a worker in Latin America can produce 1 machine per day or 5 units of commodities.

Table 7.2 Trade based on comparative advantage

	Machines	Commodity	Relative Prices
Latin America	1	5	1/5 machine = 1 commodity
Rest of the World	5	15	1/3 machine = 1 commodity

A worker in ROW can produce 5 machines per day or 15 units of commodities. The difference here is that ROW has an absolute advantage in the production of both products. Using absolute advantage as a basis for trade, there is no reason for ROW to trade with Latin America. ROW has an absolute advantage in the production of both products.

The proponents of free trade initially had no answer for this criticism. In the eighteenth century the UK could produce most goods under conditions of absolute advantage. It wasn't obvious that free trade would enhance a country's welfare. From the publication of the *Wealth of Nations* until 1817, there was no explanation for the superiority of free trade over mercantilism. It was left to David Ricardo to show the gains from trade based on comparative advantage. In order to show this one needs to look at the fourth column of Table 7.2. This shows the relative price of the two goods in the two regions. In Latin America, the relative price of machines is 5 units of commodities. This represents the opportunity cost of producing an extra machine. To produce an extra machine, the region must sacrifice the production of 5 units of commodities. Another way of looking at the relative price is that a unit of commodities costs $\frac{1}{5}$ of a machine. In ROW, a worker can produce either 5 machines or 15 yards of cloth. This means that the relative price of 1 machine is 3 units of commodities. In ROW, the production of an extra machine means an opportunity cost of 3 units of commodities. As before, another way of expressing the relative price is that 1 unit of commodities costs $\frac{1}{3}$ of a machine. This particular bit of arithmetic is important. Looking only at absolute advantage, ROW can produce both goods more cheaply than Latin America. However, the prices of the two goods in the two regions are different. Commodities are cheaper in Latin America. They cost only $\frac{1}{5}$ of a machine while in ROW they cost $\frac{1}{3}$ of a machine. This is because the opportunity cost of producing commodities in Latin America is lower. The reverse is true for ROW. A machine costs only 3 units of commodities while in Latin America a machine costs 5 units of commodities. Latin America has a low opportunity cost of producing commodities and ROW has a low opportunity cost of producing machines. This gives Latin America a comparative advantage in commodities and ROW a comparative advantage in machines. Both countries can now benefit from trade even if ROW has an absolute advantage in both products.

We can now consider trade in a way that is very relevant to Latin America. In autarky, in order to produce a machine Latin America would have to sacrifice 5 units of commodities. ROW only has to sacrifice 3 units of commodities to produce a machine. By purchasing machines from ROW with commodities, Latin America can obtain a machine for 3 commodities rather than 5. By trading, the region can obtain either the same number of machines for fewer commodities or buy more machines. The problem with ISI should now be clear. In attempting to industrialize, Latin America substituted domestic production for imports. In the process, all of these domestically produced goods were more expensive than imports. Resources were being diverted from industries the region had a comparative advantage in to comparative *disadvantage* industries. While this is technically feasible, the economic argument for doing so isn't clear. Notice that the example applies to a single industry. Now consider the opportunity cost to a country of diverting production in this way across a large number of industries. If the policy is pursued vigorously enough, the losses to the economy can become quite large.

Comparative advantage and ISI

At this point we can now form a tentative link between the discussions of comparative advantage in this chapter and the ISI in the previous chapter. One of the underpinnings involved in the adoption of ISI was the idea that trade was harming the economic interests of Latin America. As we have shown above, to an economist this is a puzzling assertion. Raul Prebisch and others argued that because the region was experiencing a decline in the terms of trade, trade with the developed countries was not enhancing the economic development of the region. This view may be related to a common problem associated with analyzing the gains from trade. To understand the problem, it will be necessary to refer back to Table 7.2. In Latin America the relative price of a machine is $1M = 3C$. In ROW, the price is $1M = 5C$. These domestic prices determine the limits to trade. No one in Latin America would pay more than $5C$ for a machine. Likewise, no one in ROW would take less than $3C$ for a machine. The domestic prices have set the limits to mutually beneficial trade. No rational seller in either market would sell at a price lower than what could be charged in the domestic market. In this situation, both countries can benefit from trade at any price between $1M = 3C$ and $1M = 5C$. One of the limitations of our example is that the *exact* price that would prevail under free trade cannot be determined from the data. However, it is certain that no one in Latin America would pay more than $1M = 5C$. The only feasible prices for traders in the region is some price less than this.

However, there is a general principle that can be shown. For Latin America the closer the price is to the price in ROW ($1M = 3C$) the better off the region will be. This is because the region would be giving up fewer commodities to obtain a machine. The reverse is true. The closer the price is to $1M = 5C$, the worse off Latin America will be relative to ROW. While both regions gain from trade, free trade does not ensure that both regions will gain equally. As the price approaches the domestic price of your trading partner, your welfare will improve. As it approaches your own domestic price, your welfare diminishes.

It is here that perhaps the proponents of ISI came to an unfortunate conclusion. Unless traders in Latin America were irrational, it was virtually impossible for trade to be making the region worse off. No rational trader would have paid more for foreign goods than domestic goods. If domestic manufactured goods were not available, there was a reason for this. The opportunity cost of producing them was too high. It was cheaper for the region to trade commodities for goods that would have been too costly to produce. However, it may well have been true that the relative price of commodities was declining in relation to machines.[2] This would mean that Latin America was receiving fewer of the gains from trade. In our example this would mean that the relative price was moving toward 1M = 5C over time. While such a movement would reduce the benefits of trade for the region, it is *not* true that trade was making the region worse off. A declining terms of trade reduces the benefits of trade but it is not an argument for replacing imports with domestically produced goods that are more expensive than imported goods. That policy will make the region worse off. Spending ten pesos to produce a good domestically that can be purchased in the world market for five pesos is equivalent to buying machines at a price of 1M = 10C. Sadly, this situation that would virtually never occur in a free market became a normal set of affairs for many of the countries of the region.

7.1 The terms of trade in Latin America

In the previous chapter, we covered the role of the terms of trade (TOT) in the formation of ISI in Latin America. The argument was that the TOT was declining for Latin America and this implied that reducing international trade would improve economic performance in the region. While that argument was unfortunately not the case, this does not imply that the TOT is unimportant. Under normal circumstances, trade always will benefit a country. However, as we saw in the preceding section the gains from trade are not necessarily evenly distributed. In a crude way economists measure the distribution of the gains from trade by looking at the ratio of export prices (Px) to import prices (Pm). Px and Pm are measured as export and import price indexes, respectively. While the calculation of price indexes is always fraught with difficulties, they do convey some useful information about the gains from trade. If the TOT is trending upward for a long period of time, this would indicate that a country or region is obtaining more of the gains from trade and is experiencing an improvement in economic welfare. Less pleasantly, the reverse would be true. From independence to the late nineteenth century, the TOT for the region was on average rising. This is part of the story of the Golden Age of Latin American economic history. From that peak, the TOT declined almost continuously until the late 1940s.[3] The architects of ISI were right in one regard. During the period for which they had data the TOT for Latin America was in fact declining. Also this relates to the problems discussed in Chapter 5. If a region is a heavy exporter of commodities, the TOT will quite likely be subject to large swings. As a result the economic fortunes of the region may be strongly influenced by changes in the TOT. Unfortunately, this is not the end of the TOT story. Such changes still influence overall economic conditions in the region in the twenty-first century. One should keep this in mind for reference for some of our later discussion on macroeconomics, the exchange rate, and the balance of payments.

Comparative advantage, factor prices, and the distribution of income

While the analysis of the gains from trade given above is useful, it is also incomplete. The basic theory of comparative advantage does not really explain what *causes* comparative advantage. In this context, comparative advantage is a result of differences among countries in the opportunity cost of producing goods. That begs the question of what causes differences in opportunity costs. In the next section, we will present a basic theory concerning this issue and apply it to Latin America. Also, this theory is very useful in examining the influence of trade on the prices of the factors of production. Since trade influences factor prices it has a discernible effect of the distribution of income.

The Heckscher–Ohlin model

In the early twentieth century, Eli Hecksher and Bertil Ohlin produced a more complete theory of the causes of international trade. In the Heckscher–Ohlin model, the costs of production are determined by the relative abundance of the factors of production. In its most simple form, the model uses two factors of production: capital and labor. To start we will assume that Latin America is relatively labor abundant. On the other hand, we will consider ROW to be relatively capital abundant. Using a term we developed in Chapter 2, Latin America and ROW would have a low and high K/L ratio, respectively. This difference in the K/L ratio affects factor prices. In Latin America, labor would be relatively cheap and capital would be relatively expensive. In ROW, the reverse would be true. Labor would be relatively expensive and capital would be cheap. The model assumes that countries will naturally have different K/L ratios. These differences can be seen in Table 7.3. In this table the K/L ratios for the countries of Latin America and other country groupings are given. Notice that relative to these countries the K/L ratios for Latin America are low. In general, the region is abundant in labor.

To complete the model, we will make an assumption about the production process for machines and commodities. The production of machines always is capital-intensive. This means that the production process always uses a lot of capital relative to labor. The production of commodities always is labor-intensive. The production of commodities naturally uses a lot of labor relative to capital. From these assumptions, we can now determine the cause of comparative advantage. If the production of machines is everywhere capital-intensive, then it will be cheaper to produce machines in a capital-abundant country. In other words, ROW will have a comparative advantage in the production of machines because capital is cheap. Latin America would have a comparative advantage in commodities because commodities are labor-intensive and the region possesses cheap labor. Using a mix of factor abundance and factor intensities explains comparative advantage.

Table 7.3 Capital-to-labor ratio in Latin America

	1990	2007
Argentina	1,580	3,998
Bolivia	269	377
Brazil	1,397	1,416
Chile	490	3,750
Colombia	NA	NA
Costa Rica	1,486	2,191
Ecuador	898	1,053
El Salvador	524	1,117
Guatemala	486	819
Honduras	539	1,059
Mexico	2,413	3,408
Nicaragua	354	516
Panama	496	2,584
Paraguay	770	550
Peru	749	1,406
Uruguay	1,353	2,135
Venezuela	467	3,818
Latin America	1,389	2,029
HIC	9,446	12,714
MIC	588	1,146
LIC	20	227
World	2,208	2,887

Source: World Bank (2010).

The principle can be summarized as: A country will have a comparative advantage in goods whose production intensively uses its relatively abundant factor of production. This is one of the most powerful statements in economics. It goes a long way in explaining the pattern of trade for any country. In the context of Latin America, it is also important to keep in mind the other side of the coin: comparative disadvantage. A country will tend to have a comparative disadvantage in products that intensively utilize its scarce factor of production. For Latin America, capital would tend to be scarce and expensive. As a result, the region would have a comparative disadvantage in the production of capital-intensive products.

Other factors influencing comparative advantage

In its simplest form using two countries, two products, and two factors of production, the Heckscher–Ohlin model can logically explain comparative advantage. The results of the model can be generalized to many countries, many goods, and more factors of production. Fifty years of empirical research on the determinants of international trade have shown that there are factors other than just labor and capital that are important in explaining trade flows.

First, the assumption that labor is homogeneous can be an empirical problem. When we use the term labor abundant, we usually need to refine what we mean by the term labor. Aside from just the number of workers, there is the human capital embodied in the labor force. For some products, the key to comparative advantage is the abundance of human capital. As was shown in Chapter 2, the accumulation of human capital currently is a problem in Latin America. What this means is that Latin America on average would have a comparative disadvantage in human capital-intensive products. To an even larger extent, the same holds true for research and development (R&D). Some products are R&D-intensive. Their production relies on an abundance of R&D expenditures. Like most middle-income countries, the countries of Latin America spend a small percentage of GDP on R&D. As a result, the region tends to have a comparative disadvantage in R&D-intensive goods.

Trade, factor prices, and the distribution of income

One of the important insights that followed the development of the Heckscher–Ohlin model of trade was that international trade can affect the distribution of income in a country. To see this, consider what happens to industrial structure following a movement from autarky to trade. In our example there are two industries in Latin America: commodities and machines. The former is the comparative advantage industry and the latter is the comparative disadvantage industry. As trade opens up, the commodities industry will start to expand to satisfy both domestic consumption and the export market. On the other hand, the machine industry will begin to contract as some domestic production will be replaced by imports. However, these changes will influence the prices of labor and capital. Commodities are labor-intensive. As the industry expands, the demand for labor will increase substantially. There will be an increase in the demand for capital as well but it will be relatively small given production conditions for commodities. Where will the labor and capital for this expansion come from? The answer lies in the decline of the machine industry. As imports of machines increase, domestic production of machines will fall. This reduction will release labor and capital that is no longer needed in that industry. There is a mismatch at work here. The machine industry is capital intensive. As it shrinks, it is releasing a lot of capital and much less labor. The needs of the expanding commodity industry are the reverse. The industry needs a lot more labor and not much capital. This will affect the price of labor and capital. The demand for labor is rising faster than the increase in the supply of labor. As a result the price of labor rises. The reverse is true for the price of capital. The large increase in the supply of capital is occurring with only a small increase in the demand for capital. The result is that the price of capital falls.

The effects described above are known as factor-price equalization. Trade has a tendency to diminish the differences in factor prices between countries that trade. While trade does not usually lead to perfect factor price equalization, it will influence wages and the return to capital in a systematic way. We can now take this logic one more step. Specifically, trade increases the price of the *abundant* factor of production. It also decreases the price of the scarce factor of production. What this implies is that labor is now getting a larger share of national income. On the other hand, trade is diminishing the welfare of the owners of the scarce factor of production, capital. With trade, capital is receiving a lower percentage of national income. As one might expect, trade not only influences factor prices it also influences the distribution of income between labor and capital. The abundant factor tends to get a larger share of national income and the scarce factor loses. These effects of trade on the distribution of income are known as the Stolper–Samuelson theorem.

Now consider what this means in terms of Latin America. The region is clearly labor abundant. A movement from autarky to free trade would tend to change the industrial structure of the region. Labor-intensive industries would tend to become larger. In turn, this would increase the number of jobs in these industries. Because of factor-price equalization, wages would tend to increase. This increase in wages would increase the percentage of national income received by labor. Since Latin America is labor abundant, trade would tend to increase the welfare of workers in the region. The same is not true for the owners of capital. Trade would tend to reduce the return to capital and lower the percentage of national income going to the owners of capital. In developing countries, trade has the potential to improve the distribution of income. Labor is generally poor and trade tends to improve their welfare by raising wages. On the other side, trade tends to reduce the welfare of the owners of capital. In autarky they benefit from the ownership of a scarce factor of production. With trade, the return to the scarce factor falls. Since the owners of capital are usually well-off, their loss of income improves the distribution of income. As we will see, this has an unfortunate implication. To the extent that the owners of capital understand that trade is not in their best interest, they will have a tendency to resist it. This helps to make the high trade barriers in Latin America somewhat more understandable. To the extent that the owners of capital have any influence on government policy they are unlikely to be enthusiastic about international trade. This is an unfortunate result given the chronic income distribution problems of the region. As we will see, policies that reduce the amount of trade in Latin America tend to harm the interests of labor and improve the welfare of the owners of capital. Unfortunately, the story does not end there. Most countries do not allow free trade in goods and services. The world economy, and Latin America is no exception, is riddled with various barriers to trade. Although free trade maximizes the welfare of society as a whole, the benefits are not evenly distributed. Free trade produces losses for some industries and workers. To the extent that these groups can avoid these losses, they will attempt to do so. In the next section, we consider how barriers to trade tend to protect these groups and how the economy loses in the process.

The economic effects of tariffs and quotas

In the preceding chapters, we have implied that free trade will tend to maximize the welfare of society. In this section, we will show this in a more formal way. Once we have established the benefits of free trade, we will be in a better position to understand how trade barriers reduce welfare. This is a particularly important point in the context of Latin America. The region has a long history of high barriers to trade. This historical protectionism has lingered into the twenty-first century. In order to assess the damage this has done to the region, it is necessary to examine the effects of tariffs and quotas more carefully.

The effects of free trade

To analyze the effects of free trade, consider the supply and demand curves shown in Figure 7.1. Following our earlier example, we will look at these effects for the machine industry. Latin America has historically had a comparative disadvantage in the production of certain types of products. Again, we can think of machines as a generic example of the sort of products the region is likely to import. As is usually the case, the demand for machines slopes downwards and the supply curve slopes upwards. In a state of autarky, the price of machines would be P_d and the equilibrium quantity would be Q_d. We can now examine the welfare effects in this market. For consumers, the consumer surplus would be equal to the triangle A. This is the area below the demand curve and above the market price. It represents the improvement in welfare that is obtained by consumers because of the difference between what they would have been willing to pay and the market price of P_d. Analogously, area B represents producer surplus.

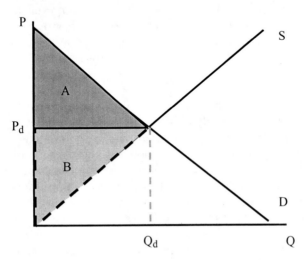

Figure 7.1 Equilibrium price and output in autarky

This is extra welfare that the producers receive as a result of being able to obtain a market price that is over their cost of production.[4]

Now suppose that there are other producers in the world economy that can produce machines at a price lower than P_d.[5] In this case, Latin America would start importing machines. Graphically, importing machines would be equivalent to adding domestic suppliers in the region. Imports would show up as an increase in supply. Foreign machine producers would keep shipping machines to Latin America as long as the price they can obtain there is higher than the price they can get elsewhere. In other words, they would increase exports to Latin America until the price in the region matched the world market price. In the end this process would yield a new equilibrium in the region of P_w and Q_2 shown in Figure 7.2. Domestic sales have increased because prices have fallen. However, domestic production has fallen from Q_d to Q_1. Domestic consumers are clearly better off and domestic producers of machines are worse off. Society is better off because the gains to consumers are larger than the losses to producers. To show why this is true, we need to examine the changes in consumer and producer surplus that are shown in Figure 7.2. As the price drops from P_d to P_w, consumer surplus grows from area A to area A + B + C + D. The domestic producers are not so fortunate. Producer surplus falls from area B + E to area E. The overall effects are clear. Consumer surplus increases by B + C + D. Producer surplus falls by B. The gains to consumers are far larger than the losses to producers. Society as a whole is far better off than was the case with autarky. Unfortunately, this optimal state is not the norm in

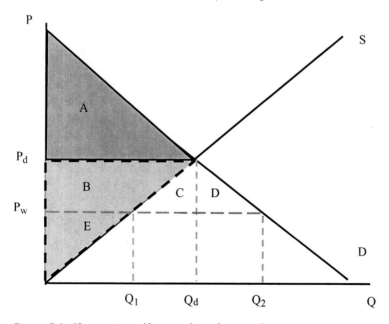

Figure 7.2 Changes in welfare resulting from trade

Latin America. Governments in the region have historically used barriers to trade to offset the effects on producers. The effects of these barriers are shown in the next section.

The effects of tariffs

We can now use the concepts of consumer and producer surplus to analyze the effects of restricting trade. Our analysis begins with the case of a country whose imports constitute a very small portion of world imports. The importing country is referred to as a price taker because it is so small that it cannot influence world market conditions. For Latin America this is not an unreasonable assumption.[6] In Figure 7.3, the domestic demand and supply of machines is illustrated. Before international trade, equilibrium price and output in the domestic market occurs at P and Q, respectively. Now, assume that the small country has a comparative disadvantage in the production of machines and decides to engage in international trade. In this case, the country will be able to import at the world price (P_w), which is below the domestic price, P. As we indicated earlier, this new equilibrium is clearly beneficial for the consumers of machines. It is as though a marketwide sale of cloth were occurring as the price of cloth declines from P without imports to P_w with imports. In addition, the quantity of cloth that consumers are willing and able to buy increases from Q to Q_2. However, with free trade the amount supplied by the domestic cloth industry contracts from Q to Q_1 as the price of cloth declines and imports increase.

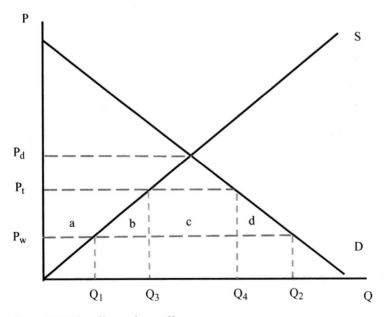

Figure 7.3 The effects of a tariff

Unfortunately, in Latin America this has been an historically unusual result. Either to raise revenue or to protect domestic industry, governments in the region typically have imposed tariffs on imports. Given that, let's assume that the domestic government imposes a tariff on machines of the amount T to restrict imports. Because we have assumed that the importing country is small, it cannot influence world market conditions. In this case, the world price of cloth will remain constant at Pw. The imposition of a tariff raises the price of cloth in the importing country by the full amount of the tariff, T. The result of this is the price of cloth in the importing country rises from P_w to P_t.

The higher price of imported machines has two effects First, the quantity imported falls from the horizontal difference Q_1 to Q_2 to the smaller amount Q_3 to Q_4. The decline in imports is a result of lower domestic consumption of cloth $-Q_2$ to Q_4 – and greater domestic production $-Q_1$ to Q_3. Second, consumers of cloth are clearly worse off. The price of cloth has increased and the quantity of cloth consumers buy has declined. As a result, consumer surplus in the country has declined. Specifically, the loss in consumer surplus is represented by the area $(a+b+c+d)$. As a result of the government imposing a tariff, consumers in the country lose. The remaining question is: who gains? The gainers in the case of a tariff are the domestic government and domestic producers.

The rectangular area c represents the tariff revenue that the domestic government collects. The quantity imported after the tariff is imposed is the horizontal difference between Q_3 and Q_4. The tariff (T) is the difference between the world price, P_w, and the price paid by domestic consumers, P_t. Multiplying the quantity imported by the amount of the tariff gives us the total tariff revenue collected by the government, area c. As a result, the government gains this area and the consumers lose it. If one assumes that the utility derived from government spending is the same as that derived from private consumption there is no net loss to society as a whole from the consumer losing area c and the government gaining it. Area a represents a transfer of consumer surplus to producer surplus. This transfer of welfare from consumers to domestic producers represents the domestic producers' gains from a tariff. From the standpoint of the domestic cloth producer, a tariff is not as good as autarky but it is preferable to free trade. The small triangle b represents the cost of resources transferred from their best use to the production of more machines $-Q_1$ to Q_3. This represents a loss to society, because in a free market these resources would have been used to produce a product in which the importing country has a comparative advantage.[7] Transferring resources to the tariff-ridden industry necessarily entails a loss of resources to some other, more productive industry. Finally, the area d represents a consumption effect caused by a tariff as consumers purchase less cloth $-Q_2$ to Q_4.

The areas a and c are redistributed from consumers to the producers and government, respectively. The net loss to society and the loss of consumer welfare are composed of area $(b + d)$. This loss to society is referred to as the *dead-weight loss* of a tariff. The dead-weight loss represents a real loss to the country. Since it is not transferred to another sector of the economy and it represents a waste of resources in economic terms.

Trade and transportation costs

The analysis we used to analyze tariffs can also be used to consider the effects of transportation costs. Positive transportation costs increase the cost of supplying foreign markets and shift the supply curve to the left. The result is that transportation costs both reduce the amount of trade and raise the price of imports. In effect, they act as a natural barrier to trade. The reverse holds true if transportation costs fall. A reduction in transportation costs would move the supply curve to the right. International trade would increase and prices of products in world markets would fall. These transportation costs affected the economic development of Latin America. In the sixteenth century transportation costs in international trade were extremely high. The sailing ships of the time were enormously expensive to operate as they were very labor intensive. In addition, unfavorable weather conditions and difficult maintenance could drastically increase the cost of a voyage from Europe to Latin America. The hurricane season in the Caribbean and the difficulties of navigating around the tip of South America made voyages at certain times of the year risky. All of these factors served to make a now routine voyage expensive. Under these circumstances it was only profitable to carry products that had a high value to weight ratio. The ships were incapable of carrying large volumes of cargo so international trade was mostly confined to very valuable goods. A look back at Table 5.1 confirms this. Prior to the mid-nineteenth century only expensive luxury goods were exported from Latin America. Notice that after 1850 more prosaic commodities started being exported. This was not an accident. The global boom in commodities trade that occurred in the second half of the nineteenth century was related to technological change. The widespread use of metal ships coupled with steam power dramatically changed international trade. These ships were capable of carrying large amounts of commodities at a very low price. Suddenly commodities such as guano, henequen, rubber, or oil could be profitably transported over long distances. The subsequent boom in exports contributed to the Golden Age of Latin American economic history. Further changes in technology made it possible to export commodities such as beef from Argentina to European markets. Finally, the widespread use of railroads made it possible to transport commodities from the more remote parts of the region to the ports for transportation to foreign markets. This revolution in transportation costs fundamentally changed the nature of international trade. Trade went from primarily goods to a much wider group of products. These changes fundamentally changed the nature of the world economy. The changes were even more pronounced for Latin America. The ability to sell a wider range of products to the world was the source of the globalization of Latin America in the late nineteenth century. The region we observe today is still to a large extent the product of technological change and the resultant drop in transportation costs. Transportation costs still affect Latin American trade. Recent research indicates that transportation costs for Latin American imports are nearly twice as high as those for the US. Even worse, transportation costs for *intra*-Latin American trade are just as high as trade with ROW. These higher transportation costs impose tariff-like losses on the region. Also, they may explain a part of the low amount of openness to trade for the region.[8]

7.2   Uniform tariffs in Chile

> Although there are no efficiency reasons for uniform import tariffs, there are practical political economy considerations for advocating a flat import structure.
>
> Sebastian Edwards

Most countries have a rather complicated tariff schedule with a different tariff for literally thousands of different product categories. An alternative to this is to have a *uniform* tariff or a single tariff for *all* imports. This neatly solves a number of problems with a complicated tariff structure. First, the tariff becomes easy to administer because customs officials would not have to worry about classifying a product into whatever category it might best fit. Second, a uniform tariff makes lobbying for protectionism much harder. If an import-competing industry wants an increase in the tariff, the tariff would have to increase on all imports. This is likely to create some resistance for several reasons.

- A general increase in the tariff is unlikely to pass by consumers completely unnoticed.
- Other industries capable of lobbying the government would likely do so.
- Firms purchasing imported intermediate products would see the increase in the tariff as a direct increase in their costs and would complain to the government. Under most supply and demand conditions, the firms could not pass all of this cost increase on to consumers and profits would fall.
- The same would be true of firms that are purchasing imports for final sale to the consumer.
- Firms that export may find tariff increases especially harmful as it may dilute their ability to compete in international markets. The net result is that more firms may lose from the tariff than the number of firms that might gain from it.
- Given the above, the optimal public choice strategy for a politician may well be *lower* tariffs.

What we have just described is much like what happened in Chile during the last 30 years. In the early 1970s, Chile had tariffs that were high and very complex. These tariffs were replaced by a 10 percent uniform tariff in 1979. In response to an economic crisis in the 1980s, the uniform tariff was raised to 35 percent. Since the mid-1980s the tariff has fallen to 7 percent.

The effects of quotas

As was shown above, tariffs are a very effective means of lowering the economic welfare of a country in any region of the world. Unfortunately, quotas are even more effective. In a later section of this chapter, we will discuss why quotas were extensively used as a trade policy instrument in Latin America. In a previous chapter we defined a quota as a quantitative restriction on the amount imported into a country. In this section, we will cover the economic effects of a quota and show that they are even more damaging to national welfare than tariffs.

Fortunately, the effects of a quota are very similar to the effects of a tariff. These effects are shown in Figure 7.4 below. In the graph the domestic demand and supply of machines is shown as before. Again we will assume that imports of machines lower the price in the domestic market from P_d to P_w. As before, the amount imported in this situation is the difference between the amount consumed (Q_2) and domestic production (Q_1). In this case instead of using a tariff to raise the price of machines, a quota on the amount imported is imposed. In the graph, the maximum amount that can be imported is reduced which effectively reduces the supply of imports. This reduction in supply reduces the quantity imported to the difference between Q_4 and Q_3. As before, the loss of consumer surplus is represented by the area a + b + c + d. The gain to domestic producers is the area a. The deadweight loss due to the quota is b + d. The difference with a quota is the area c. With a tariff this area represents government revenue. However, with a quota this revenue is lost. In this case area c is transferred to the foreign exporters.

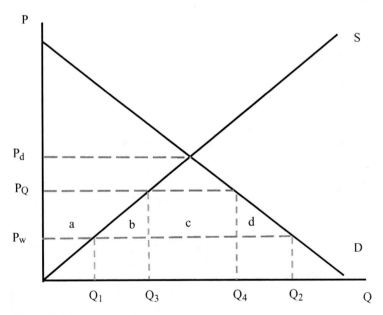

Figure 7.4 The effects of a quota

They can charge a higher price for their product and legally avoid paying a tariff. As a result, under almost any conceivable set of circumstances a quota is worse for the country than a tariff. Things can get even worse in the long run. If machines are at least a normal good, the demand for machines will tend to shift to the right as incomes increase. If the quota does not increase, then any change in demand is captured completely by the domestic producers. From their narrow point of view, a quota is better than a tariff. They only have to deal with a limited amount of foreign competition and if demand increases they capture all of this increase in demand. For domestic consumers and the government the situation is not as prosaic. Any increase in demand leads to further losses in consumer surplus and lost revenue for the government.

Notice that Figure 7.4 is suspiciously similar to Figure 7.3. The effects of a quota and a tariff are indeed similar. Under most circumstances they are equivalent. In this case the quota causes a gap between the world price (P_w) and the quota-constrained price (P_q). If one expresses this difference as a percentage of the latter price, one arrives at the *ad valorem* equivalent (AVE). AVE simply converts the degree of protectionism embodied in a quota and makes it comparable to an *ad valorem* tariff. In many cases in Latin America, imports faced both a tariff *and* a quota. Under these circumstances, the losses to consumers and the economy as a whole become even larger than would be the case if either instrument of trade policy were used in isolation. The AVE equivalent will become important in a later context. International trade rules prohibit the use of quotas as an instrument of trade policy. However, countries that begin the process of complying with these rules are not asked to simply eliminate quotas. They are allowed to convert quota protection into tariff protection. Under these circumstances, the resulting tariff would be the AVE.

7.3 Rent seeking

From the discussion of tariffs and quotas above, it would seem logical that most countries would pursue a policy of free trade. Trade barriers impose significant economic losses on a country. However, public policy in a democratic society is often more complicated than merely finding the optimal economic policy and implementing it. Trade policy is a good case in point. As we saw above, free trade maximizes the welfare of society. However, the gains from trade are not evenly distributed. The government loses tax revenue and producers lose some of their producers' surplus. In addition, workers in sectors of the economy that compete with imports have the same incentives as the firms they work for. A reduction in domestic production caused by imports may threaten jobs. As a result, both firms and workers have an incentive to lobby the government for restrictions on trade. While such restrictions may not benefit society as a whole, they do benefit certain groups. This lobbying for government policy that will aid particular groups but may harm society as a whole is known as *rent seeking*. Economic rents can occur when an individual or a group can earn money by manipulating policy as opposed to earning profits from production. In this case, the firms and workers are attempting to increase their income by obtaining economic rents rather than producing more goods and services. In their desire to maximize votes, government officials may conclude that the granting of rents may in some cases produce more votes.[9] This can occur because trade has the peculiar asymmetric quality that the gains from trade are widely diffused while the losses are very concentrated.

Rent seeking can be particularly damaging in the context of developing countries. In a small market, there may be only one or at most just a few firms in the industry. In this case, the costs of organizing the firms in the industry to lobby the government for protection can be relatively low. Such a situation is frequently the case in Latin America. In addition, manufacturing firms in the region frequently are unionized. Further, in many Latin American countries unions are a powerful political force. Adding to the pressure is that manufacturing centers in much of Latin America are either in or close to the capital city. Throw in even a modest amount of corruption into the mix and rent seeking can yield a rather high rate of protection for many of a country's industries. Unfortunately, rent-seeking is not confined to trade policy. Any form of government policy that can affect the economic interest of any group in society is susceptible to rent-seeking behavior. If one is ever prone to wonder why a country in Latin America is having a difficult time implementing a policy that would clearly improve the welfare of society, rent-seeking behavior may well be the answer.

Latin American trade policy

In economics, trade policy refers to government actions that influence the flow of goods and services to and from a country. In this section, we will briefly review the history of trade policy in Latin America. As is frequently the case in Latin America, there are relatively distinct historical periods where there were relatively uniform policy changes. In the next section, we will cover trade policy in the region from independence to the Great Depression. As we saw in the previous chapter, the 1930s were characterized by a substantial shift in overall economic policy in the region. These changes included changes in international trade that will be covered in the section on trade policy and ISI. The next two sections consider how ISI influenced the participation of countries in the region in international trade negotiations and movements towards other forms of economic integration.

Pre ISI trade policy

From the start there is a need to acknowledge an uncomfortable historical fact. For virtually all of its history, Latin America has had the world's most protectionist trade policy. As shown in the previous section, protectionism distorts domestic economic activity and lowers growth. Typically, it favors certain industries and workers at the expense of the welfare of society at large. Precisely why Latin America has been more prone to protectionism is not entirely clear.[10] Rather, the material that follows will focus on the known history of trade policy in Latin America and less on why this was the case.

In a sense, Latin America since 1492 has always been protectionist. As you will recall from Chapter 4, the new rulers of the region enforced the policy of mercantilism. Colonies were not free to sell to other markets and imports from anywhere other than Portugal or Spain were severely restricted. What is easy to forget is that this high level of protectionism lasted for over *300 years*. Given the historical precedent, it would have been very unusual for the region to have swiftly moved from mercantilism to a trade policy with low levels of protectionism. Given the historical legacy of mercantilism, what occurred was perhaps what one would have expected: high levels of protectionism. As we will see there were other factors involved in the determination of trade policy. However, the initial conditions were not conducive to free trade.

The end of Spanish colonial rule created another unfortunate effect. During the colonial era there was at least free trade among the various parts of the region. With the exception of trade between the Spanish colonies and Brazil, goods could move freely around Latin America. In modern terms, the region was a de facto customs union. Independence ended this situation. The wars of independence of the 1820s left Latin America balkanized into a large number of separate countries. Each country eventually erected its own barriers to trade and created their own currency. Both trade barriers and the lack of a common currency hinder growth. Many countries were too small to develop significant industry as there was no possibility of achieving economies of scale in many industries. The damage to growth in the region that this initial condition caused cannot be calculated. However, one way to think about the problem is to think in terms of the development of North America. Suppose that instead of two countries developing in the region, the region had fragmented into nearly 60 separate countries. Each of these "countries" would have its own barriers to trade and a separate currency. Intuitively, one can comprehend that this would have damaged the historical growth of the region. Just how heavy this damage would have been is not certain, but the direction of the effect is clear. Unfortunately, this is precisely where Latin America started. A part, by no means all, of the difference in the economic histories of North and South America can be traced to the unfortunate start of the latter region. This balkanization was exacerbated by small populations and low GDP per capita.[11]

The discussion above was focused on protective tariffs. The purpose of a protective tariff is to protect a domestic industry from foreign competition. Prior to the twentieth century tariffs often were levied primarily as a means of raising revenue. A revenue tariff is a tariff whose primary purpose is raising revenue for the government as opposed to protecting specific domestic industries. Under the circumstances, it was essential for governments to raise as much revenue as possible. The boundary disputes and internal violence created a large need for revenue by governments of the region. New countries frequently have limited options in terms of raising revenue. This was especially true for Latin America because independence destroyed the old colonial systems of raising revenue. The new countries of Latin America were left with a low ability to tax and few bureaucratic resources. In these circumstances, tariffs become an attractive means of generating revenue for the government that is both feasible and low cost. With violence and instability lasting for decades, tariffs were raised to extremely high levels to finance military expenditures. Finally, tariffs in this period were normally specific tariffs. A specific tariff is expressed as a certain amount of money per unit such as pesos per liter, etc. In more modern times, tariffs are usually expressed as *ad valorem* tariffs. An *ad valorem* tariff is expressed as a percentage of the value of the imported good.[12] In the situation faced by Latin American countries in the nineteenth century, specific tariffs had two advantages. First, they are easier to administer and are attractive in an environment where bureaucratic resources are scarce. Secondly, specific tariffs make it more difficult for dishonest customs officials to appropriate part of the tariff revenue. Aside from the details, tariffs before the Golden Age were quite high.

During the Golden Age of Latin American history, the region became much more integrated into the world economy. The end of Latin America's relative isolation was primarily on the export side of trade. As discussed in Chapter 4, lower transportation costs for commodities coupled with a boom in the world economy produced large gains in trade for much of the region. However, there was far less of an opening on the import side. Recent research on tariff rates in the region indicate that tariffs did not fall during the Golden Age but instead rose and peaked in the late nineteenth century.[13] Tariffs fell sharply after World War I but began a long climb beginning in the 1920s. As a result of the global trade war sparked by the passage of the Smoot–Hawley tariff in the US in 1930, tariffs in Latin America rose dramatically along with the general worldwide increase in protectionism.

The history of trade policy in Latin America before ISI can be summarized in this way. The mercantilist policies of Portugal and Spain left the region with a historical legacy of protectionism. The conditions surrounding independence exacerbated a pre-existing condition. Tariffs remained high as the governments of the region needed revenues for national defense and to maintain internal stability. While the region became more open to international trade during the Golden Age, the opening was more pronounced on the export side. Tariffs were high during this period. After a brief fall associated with World War I, tariffs in the region climbed during the 1920s and rose sharply during the global trade war of the 1930s. As we will see in the next section, ISI was less of a sharp break with the past than a continuation of a long historical record of protectionism. Latin America has virtually *always* had one of the highest levels of protectionism among the world's regions. The degree to which this reduced growth in the nineteenth and early twentieth centuries is unknown. However, the direction of the effect is clear.

7.4 The optimum tariff in Latin America

As we have seen in a previous section, tariffs can be used to raise revenue and to protect domestic industry. If one observes high tariffs then a reasonable question to ask is what are the forces driving this? In the case of Latin America in the nineteenth century the reasons for high tariffs seem reasonably clear. New and weak governments had few ways to collect revenue. Taxes on foreign trade were far easier to collect than other taxes so tariffs were a convenient solution to government revenue problems. However, governments setting tariffs to maximize revenue have to be cautious about imposing the *ad valorem* tariff that will maximize revenue. If the tariff is too low, then the government is not maximizing its revenues. On the other hand if the tariff is too high revenues likewise will not be maximized and smuggling will be encouraged. Although it was not known in the nineteenth century, there is a convenient formula for calculating the optimum tariff or the tariff that will maximize government revenue from the tariff. The formula is:

$$t^* = -1/(1 + e)$$

In the formula t^* is the optimum tariff and e is the price elasticity of the demand for imports. The critical variable is e. As the price elasticity varies, then the optimum tariff will vary. In the nineteenth century there is no way that governments in the region could have had explicit knowledge of these details. However, Coatsworth and Williamson (2002) have concluded that the observed tariffs in the region are consistent with available estimates of the price elasticity of import demand for the period. As in many other cases economic agents, in this case governments, may act as if they have more formal economic knowledge than one might guess.

Trade policy under ISI

As we learned in the previous chapter, the argument for protectionism as an economic development strategy gained ground in Latin America during the 1940s. This occurred as a result of the confluence of one old and one new factor in the region. Encouraged by the work of Raul Prebisch and others, protectionism as a means of industrialization and economic development seemed plausible. Secondly, the region has always been one of the most protectionist regions in the world.[14] Prior to and during the Great Depression tariffs in Latin America were high. The difficulty was that after World War II they were not reduced. As we will see in the next section, much of the rest of the world learned a hard lesson from the trade war of the 1930s.

This lesson was that trying to increase domestic production through protectionism doesn't work well. Unfortunately, thinking on this issue in the region did not follow these global trends. ISI provided a veneer of respectability for the idea that a country or a region might be better off trying to industrialize and more generally develop by reducing imports and thus stimulating domestic production. In the post-war era, tariffs in Latin America began a slow climb during the 1950s and 1960s. Tariffs peaked during the 1970s and have declined significantly since then. While most of the rest of the world was reducing tariffs, in Latin America they were *increasing*.[15]

Unfortunately, tariffs understate the actual amount of protectionism in the region. The high tariffs frequently were supplemented with protection by quotas that were covered earlier in the chapter. In this period, many countries in Latin America were still able to implement quotas with impunity. There were also other instruments of trade policy used for protectionism that are less well known but extremely protectionist in nature. An import license is a permission to import issued by the government. Under import licensing, a potential importer must not only be willing to pay the world market price plus the tariff but also obtain explicit permission from the government to engage in this transaction. At a minimum, the time involved in obtaining permission constitutes an additional implicit tariff. In addition, governments in the region sometimes required an import deposit before the product could be imported. Effectively, this would require the importer to prepay for the goods in order to begin the transaction. Because exchange rates were fixed during this period, governments in the region were free to set different exchange rates for different sorts of transactions. These multiple exchange rate systems frequently became an implicit means of protection as different classes of importers had access to foreign exchange at different exchange rates. Moreover, the system was frequently *ad hoc* in nature. Governments in the region during this period often were under extreme balance of payments pressure. Some of the measures described above were being implemented more to conserve scarce foreign exchange than provide explicit protection. However, the effects usually resulted in higher levels of protection, intended or not.

The effective rate of protection

While the tariffs in Latin America were high, the situation during the ISI period was actually a good bit worse than indicated. To understand why, we need to explain the concept of the effective rate of protection. The actual purpose of a tariff is to encourage domestic value added in an industry. If a product produced in a country incorporates any foreign components, then the structure of protection can affect the amount of protection afforded to a domestic industry. A simple example will suffice to illustrate the point. Suppose a producer of a consumer good in Latin America is importing 50 percent of the value of the product and the product sells for 100 pesos. The value added domestically is 50 pesos. If the tariff on the product is

20 percent, then the tariff inclusive price is 120 pesos. Because of the tariff the domestic value added is now 70 pesos. The effective rate of protection is the percentage increase in the domestic value added. In this case, it has risen by 40 percent. Thus the degree of protection afforded the domestic producer is not 20 percent but 40 percent. The general formula for determining the effective rate of protection (ERP) is:

$$ERP = (Tf - aTc)/(1 - a),$$

Where Tf is the tariff on the final product; Tc is the tariff on imported components; and a is the percentage of imported components. Although the number of outcomes of this calculation is infinite, it is very common for the effective rate of protection to be higher than the nominal tariff. This is because it is common for countries to have lower tariffs on inputs into domestic production than on final goods. Latin America was no different in this regard but ISI aggravated this situation. Many ISI industries were operating with a substantial amount of imported intermediate goods with final production occurring in the region. Under these circumstances, a nominal tariff of 35 percent could yield truly astonishing effective rates of protection. Effective rates of protection above 100 percent were not uncommon.[16] The important point is that any nominal tariff rate has to be considered in light of the effective rate of protection. In many cases, the actual level of protection is quite a bit higher than the posted tariff indicates.

The extremely high levels of protection profoundly distorted the economies of the region. As one can imagine, the losses for the consumers and the economies of Latin America were immense. On the other hand, domestic production rose and manufacturing for these protected domestic markets was being strongly encouraged. Moreover, these policies had two other effects. As the markets in Latin America closed to imports, firms wishing to sell in these markets began pursuing FDI. With the level of protection so high, FDI became a way to "jump over" the tariff wall and more profitably serve a protected domestic market. It also stimulated the use of SOEs when even high levels of protection could not entice the private sector into domestic production. Unfortunately, both domestic and foreign firms were almost completely focused on producing in the most profitable way for a very protected domestic market. Implicitly the protection was encouraging the development of industries that Latin America did not have a comparative advantage in. In many cases, the reverse was occurring. Firms were prospering in areas the region had a comparative disadvantage in. By the end of the ISI period in the 1980s, the industrial base of the region could not compete domestically without protection and was incapable of competing in international markets. As we will see in later chapters, ISI induced chronic balance of payments problems. The protected firms required imported inputs to continue to produce. This was coupled with an inability to obtain foreign exchange via exports. For a while, the way out of this dilemma was an increasing amount of debt. Once the amount of debt became unsustainable, then fundamental policy changes became unavoidable. An interesting question at this point is how was Latin America able to pursue protectionism for so long when the rest of the world was liberalizing trade? The answer is that much of the region simply avoided participating in the institutions that were fostering that process. In the next section, we detail the history of that nonparticipation.

Latin America and GATT/WTO

The trade war of the 1930s marked a new era for both the world economy and Latin America. Most of the world outside of Latin America quickly reached the conclusion that the trade war had been a catastrophic mistake. As early as 1934, the US had begun passing legislation that would eventually lay the groundwork for reducing the level of protectionism.[17] The latter half of the Great Depression and World War II prevented a major liberalization of world trade in the 1930s and 1940s. However, towards the end of the war the US and the UK had begun negotiations on the establishment of institutions that would turn out to be of critical importance for Latin America.

In 1944, the Allied countries met at a conference in Bretton Woods, New Hampshire to consider building institutions that would help to avoid a return of poor economic conditions after the end of the war. In Chapter 1 we mentioned the World Bank or more technically the International Bank for Reconstruction and Development. The initial purpose of the World Bank was to assist countries in rebuilding from the devastation of World War II. With that task largely accomplished the institution began loaning money in Latin America and other developing countries for specific economic development projects. The second institution proposed at the conference was the International Monetary Fund (IMF). Prior to the Great Depression, most of the countries of the world maintained a system of fixed exchange rates tied to gold (a gold standard). The economic stresses of the Great Depression led most countries to abandon the gold standard. In doing so, they effectively allowed their exchange rates to float. In the aftermath of these problems there was a general realization that a return to a classical gold standard was not possible. However, there was a consensus for a return to fixed exchange rates. Fixed exchange rates without a gold standard required an international body to oversee such a system. The IMF was the institution set up to oversee this new system of fixed exchange rates based on the US dollar rather than gold.

For our current purposes, the importance of the Bretton Woods conference was with respect to international trade. There was general agreement among countries that the trade war of the 1930s had contributed to the global economic contraction. As a result there was a general desire to find a mechanism to reduce tariffs to something like their prewar levels and construct a mechanism for preventing a reoccurrence of global protectionism. The result was a proposal to establish the International Trade Organization (ITO). The actual negotiations to create the ITO occurred from 1945 to 1948 and were concluded in Havana, Cuba. The refusal of the US Congress to ratify membership in the ITO meant that the organization never came into being. However, the backup position was not an organization but a treaty: the General Agreements on Tariffs and Trade (GATT). Under the auspices of GATT, the developed countries increasingly joined by the developing countries conducted international trade negotiations designed to slowly reduce the excessively high tariffs caused by the trade war of the 1930s. The purpose of GATT required contracting parties to agree to two basic principles.[18] First, tariffs were required to be on a most favored nation (MFN) basis. MFN embodies the principle of nondiscrimination. The lowest tariff for a product charged to any contracting party must be used for all contracting parties. More important for Latin America was the prohibition of the use of quotas as a means of protection. The mechanism for the liberalization was a series of multilateral trade negotiations (MTNs). These MTNs were usually referred to as "rounds" of trade negotiations. The first four smaller rounds were followed by larger MTNs known as the Dillion Round (1960–1961), the Kennedy Round (1962–1967), the Tokyo Round (1973–1979), and the Uruguay Round (1986–1994). The current Doha Round began in 2001 and the negotiations are still ongoing in 2011. Through the Kennedy Round, MTNs were completely focused on reducing tariffs. Beginning with the Tokyo Round the subsequent MTNs have been broadened to cover issues such as international trade in services, trade related intellectual property, and nontariff barriers to international trade. Among the countries that have been participating, trade barriers have fallen substantially over the last 50 years.

Until recently, the participation of the countries of Latin America in this process has been minimal. There are several reasons for this. From the start of the process the prevailing view in the region was that free trade was unlikely to enhance the economic development of the region. In the twenty-first century, this view seems almost bizarre but as discussed earlier it was the prevailing view of the times. A more important consideration was the issue of trade in agricultural products. Liberalizing trade in agricultural products was the most difficult problem facing the negotiations over GATT and the ITO. The failure of the ITO left the world with GATT. Unfortunately, in order to achieve an agreement trade in agricultural products was not covered. International trade in agricultural products thus became a free-fire zone in which countries could introduce forms of protectionism that were completely illegal for trade in other types of products. These products were precisely the sort of products that Latin America has a comparative advantage in. As a result the countries of the region perceived that GATT was almost irrelevant to their interests. This is illustrated in Table 7.4, which shows the dates on which the countries of the region joined either GATT or its successor, the World Trade Organization (WTO). Notice that the

Table 7.4 Dates of accession of Latin American
countries to GATT/WTO

Country	Date
Argentina	1967
Bolivia	1990
Brazil	1948
Chile	1949
Colombia	1981
Costa Rica	1990
Ecuador	1996
El Salvador	1991
Guatemala	1991
Honduras	1994
Mexico	1986
Nicaragua	1950
Panama	1997
Paraguay	1994
Peru	1951
Uruguay	1953
Venezuela	1990
Latin America	1978
Portugal	1962
Spain	1963
Canada	1948
US	1948

Source: World Trade Organization (2010a).

average date of accession for countries of the region was 1978. There were
a few countries that joined early but were never really serious participants in
MTNs. The majority of countries in the region did not join until the 1980s
and a number waited until the 1990s. Given the information above, this
means that Latin America missed the Kennedy Round, the Tokyo Round,
and the majority of the Uruguay Round. It was not until the 1980s that
Latin America became active in MTNs. To be fair, this lack of interest
in GATT was not confined to Latin America. In general, the developing
countries were late to begin participating in the process. As exports of
manufactured goods became more important, both the developing countries
and Latin America became more active participants in the process. In the
current Doha Round, Brazil has become an important voice for the interests
of Latin America and the developing countries in general. However, the
Doha Round is foundering on the rock of liberalizing trade in agricultural
products and limiting the subsidies to farmers in developed countries with
little comparative advantage in these products. These efforts have met with
limited success. As we will see in the next section, the liberalization of trade
in Latin America has followed a different path.

The most important factor illustrated by Table 7.4 is that being outside
of the official world trading system allowed Latin America to engage

in trade practices that would have been illegal under GATT. As already mentioned, the situation left Latin America free to impose quotas on any product. For the contracting parties to GATT, quotas could only be used to protect agricultural products. Second, under GATT tariffs were bound. What this meant is that tariffs for contracting parties could only be raised temporarily under certain circumstances.[19] For countries outside of GATT, there was nothing to prevent a country from raising tariffs on any product at any time. Through the mid-1970s, the countries of the region tended to increase tariffs because there was no restriction on this behavior. Thus while the rest of the world was reducing tariffs, the reverse was occurring in Latin America. The region was able to develop industries designed to replace imports by increasing tariffs and using quotas when that level of protection was not adequate. However, by definition industries designed to replace imports are industries that the country or region has a comparative disadvantage in. This was not an accident, but a deliberate policy choice. By the 1980s, the damage had been done. The region was left with industries that could not compete in domestic markets, let alone the world market. During this decade Latin America began the long painful switch to industries that the region has a comparative advantage in. Notice that the decline in tariffs that began in the 1970s coincides with the more active participation of the countries of the region in international trade negotiations. This participation is in the best interests of the region, but the decades of nonparticipation carried a heavy price. There was less pressure in the large MTNs for liberalizing trade in agricultural products that would have greatly benefited the region. More importantly, one can only imagine what might have been if Latin American trade policy had been in alignment with the rules of GATT.

RTAs in Latin America

In the post-World War II era Latin America was becoming more protectionist. However, in both the world economy and Latin America a new form of trade liberalization was being born. GATT obliged members to adhere to the principle of most favored nation or nondiscrimination in tariffs. However, the original agreement contained an exception. Article XXIV of GATT provided an exception to MFN for free-trade areas (FTA) and customs unions (CU). The former is an agreement between countries to eliminate tariffs on "substantially all" trade within a "reasonable period of time." In practice substantially all trade meant virtually all trade in nonagricultural products. Likewise, a reasonable period of time came to mean 15 years. A customs union goes one step further. This sort of agreement also requires the elimination of the various national tariff schedules and their harmonization into a single tariff schedule for all countries. From the beginning of GATT until the late 1950s, Article XXIV was not particularly important. What is now the European Union (EU) was created by the Treaty of Rome in 1957 but the number of other agreements was limited.

Article XXIV and the creation of the EU did have an impact on Latin America. The protectionist policies fostered by ISI had the effect of isolating the countries of the region from one another. Since many of these economies are small, the ability of industries to grow to an optimal size was severely limited by small domestic markets. The creation of the EU spurred a burst of interest in regional trade agreements (RTAs) in Latin America. Theoretically, such agreements would allow countries of the region to obtain some of the gains from trade and still protect their industries from competition from countries outside of the region. These thoughts led to the formation of the Latin American Free Trade Agreement (LAFTA) in 1960 which was composed of ten countries in South America plus Mexico. Twenty years of attempted trade liberalization came to an end with the collapse of LAFTA in 1980. Another RTA among the countries of the Andean Region was attempted. The Andean Pact was formed in 1969 as an ambitious project to form a CU in that part of South America. As in many cases of economic integration, the project proved too ambitious and foundered on the problem of forming a common external tariff (CXT) coupled with political instability in the region. Similar problems plagued the Central American Common Market (CACM). Launched in 1960, the CACM was initially more successful than other integration schemes in the region. However, war and political instability led to the eventual demise of the agreement. While the various economic integration schemes of the 1960s failed, they did set the stage for a renewal of RTAs in Latin America.

From the information given in the previous section, Latin America missed much of the liberalization of trade that occurred in the world economy fostered by GATT and later the WTO. However, tariffs in Latin America have been falling for over 20 years as a result of increased participation in MTNs and the spread of RTAs. If this seems to be a puzzle, then RTAs are the solution to the seeming contradiction. In this case, Latin America is no longer an outlier in the world economy but is now following a general trend. When the GATT was written, Article XXIV was conceived of as an exception to MFN that probably would apply primarily to what is now the EU. In the world economy, this seemed to be the case during the 1960s and 1970s. RTAs were formed in Latin America and elsewhere but they were more exceptions to the rule and their fate in other parts of the developing world were not dissimilar from the Latin American experience. Beginning in the 1980s, there was a noticeable increase in the number of RTAs in the world economy. By the 1990s and moving into the twenty-first century RTAs are now appearing to be the future of trade liberalization. The difficulty of negotiations during the Uruguay Round and the inability to conclude the Doha Round seem to be contributing to this trend. While liberalization under MTNs and RTAs are not mutually exclusive, countries that wish to move to freer trade can now do so more quickly by signing RTAs. This trend is evident in Table 7.5 below. The initial impetus seems

Table 7.5 RTAs in Latin America

Country	RTAs with
Argentina	CAN, Chile, MERCOSUR
Bolivia	CAN, Chile, MERCOSUR
Brazil	CAN, Chile, MERCOSUR
Chile	Australia, CAN, Canada, China, Colombia, Costa Rica, EU, EFTA, El Salvador, India, Japan, MERCOSUR, Mexico, Panama, South Korea, US
Colombia	CAN, Chile, MERCOSUR
Costa Rica	Canada, Chile, DR-CAFTA, Mexico, Panama
Ecuador	CAN, Chile, MERCOSUR
El Salvador	Chile, DR-CAFTA, Mexico, Panama
Guatemala	DR-CAFTA, Mexico
Honduras	DR-CAFTA, Mexico
Mexico	Chile, Costa Rica, EU, EFTA, El Salvador, Guatemala, Honduras, Israel, Japan, Nicaragua, NAFTA
Nicaragua	DR-CAFTA, Mexico, Taiwan
Panama	Chile, Costa Rica, El Salvador, Singapore, Taiwan
Paraguay	CAN, Chile, MERCOSUR,
Peru	CAN, Canada, MERCOSUR, Singapore, US
Uruguay	CAN, Chile, MERCOSUR, Venezuela

Source: World Trade Organization (2010b). Definitions: Comunidad Andino (CAN) – Bolivia, Colombia, Ecuador, and Peru; DR-CAFTA – Costa Rica, Dominican Republic, El Salvador, Guatemala, Honduras, Nicaragua, and the US; EU – European Union; EFTA – European Free Trade Association; MERCOSUR – Argentina, Brazil, Paraguay, and Uruguay

to have been the creation of the Mercado Comun del Sur (MERCOSUR) in 1991. MERCOSUR was formed as a customs union among Argentina, Brazil, Paraguay, and Uruguay. Tariffs among the countries were cut to zero by 2000 and a CXT was completed by 2006. Negotiations are now under way to produce a single market in the same sense that the phrase is used in the EU.[20] Less noticed but not unimportant is the Andean Community (CAN) composed of Bolivia, Colombia, Ecuador, and Peru. As is apparent from Table 7.2, there is an enormous amount of trade liberalization occurring in the region. CAN and MERCOSUR have freed up trade among eight countries in the region. Both Chile and Mexico have been actively signing trade agreements with a number of other countries in the region. Notice that every country in the region with the exception of Venezuela has signed at least one RTA. In addition, many of the listed RTAs involve free trade with countries outside of the region. NAFTA has effectively spread to include Central America and Chile. In addition, there are a number of ongoing negotiations to create further RTAs both within the region and with countries outside of the region.

As is always the case in economics, there are benefits and costs associated with the formation of RTAs. As shown earlier in the chapter, movements to freer trade are beneficial for the economy as a whole. On the other hand, firms and workers in comparative disadvantage industries normally experience a reduction in output and number of jobs available, respectively. The years of ISI meant the large-scale development of just these types of industries. Freer trade, either through MTNs or RTAs, has led to a substantial amount of change in the industrial structure of the region. The increase in trade caused by reducing trade barriers is technically known as trade creation. As tariffs and other trade barriers fall, prices fall and imports increase. If this is done on a multilateral basis then the increase in imports will come from the most efficient suppliers in the world economy. Unfortunately, the tariff cuts that occur under RTAs are not multilateral. Tariffs are cut for some countries, but not for others. RTAs involve explicit discrimination among exporters to a country. This can potentially cause a loss in welfare. To illustrate this, we will use a NAFTA example. Suppose that prior to NAFTA, Mexico was importing cars from both Japan and the US and imposing a 20 percent tariff. Further assume that cars from Japan and the US cost $18,000 and $20,000 before imposing the tariff and $21,600 and $24,000 with the tariff, respectively. Prior to NAFTA, Mexican importers would have a tendency to buy more cars from the more efficient Japanese producers. With the introduction of NAFTA, the arithmetic changes. Post NAFTA, American cars are now cheaper in the Mexican market than Japanese cars and Mexican imports would tend to shift from a more efficient to less efficient producer. While both Mexico and the US gain from NAFTA, the Japanese may lose. These losses to the Japanese are known as trade diversion. World welfare improves because of an RTA if the agreement causes more trade creation than trade diversion.[21] Economists generally have a dim view of trade diversion as it entails a loss of overall world welfare. For this reason, there is a strong preference of liberalization through MTNs. If tariffs are reduced for all countries then there is no trade diversion. One has to keep in mind that world welfare usually improves even with the existence of trade diversion so long as trade creation is larger.

Further, trade diversion is important in the context of Latin America. As countries lower tariffs, trade creation obviously occurs. However, who benefits from trade diversion? Recall that tariffs in Latin America have traditionally been high. Now consider the formation of MERCOSUR. Trade among the member countries will increase as tariff barriers fall. In addition, trade diversion may increase trade further for the member countries. While trade diversion detracts from world welfare it may improve the export prospects of the members of the RTA. The discriminatory reduction of tariffs may increase the ability of Brazil to compete with the developed countries in the markets of the other three members. Further trade diversion may have something to do with the spread of trade agreements in the region. Because of CAN and MERCOSUR, Chilean exporters may be losing exports to a very large combined market due to trade diversion. The optimum response for Chile is clear. By liberalizing trade with both RTAs they avoid the losses from trade diversion and gain economic welfare for themselves through trade creation. This logic is general. Any country in the region that is outside of any RTA in the region stands to lose exports. Under these circumstances, there will be pressure on countries in the region to effectively join RTAs to avoid losses of exports. This solution is not as elegant as the old LAFTA or the Free Trade Agreement of the Americas proposed by the US in the early 1990s. However, these RTAs appear to both more durable and more politically acceptable than some grand overall plan for the region. Countries can move in the direction of liberalization at whatever speed they deem to be either economically or politically acceptable to all parties. From Table 7.5 it is obvious that there are large regional differences in these preferences. This is exactly one of the main attractions of RTAs. Liberalization through MTNs can mean large reductions in overall trade barriers for every other member of the WTO. For the historically protectionist countries of Latin America, this may be too much change at too fast a rate with the rest of the world. RTAs allow for smaller liberalizations among countries with similar preferences. In some sense, the development of RTAs is reminiscent of the enlargement of the EU. It has taken 40 years for the EU to expand from the original 6 to 27 countries. Four of the countries of Europe have still not joined. Further, the enlargement was hardly smooth or continuous. It has occurred at a pace that the existing and new members find mutually agreeable. While far less formal, the expansion of trade agreements within Latin America is a work in progress that has been going on for only 20 years. Given the trade barriers that prevailed in the region as late as the 1970s, an amazing amount of liberalization in trade has already occurred.

7.5 Trade diversion in action: the EU–Mexico Free Trade Agreement

Any type of preferential trade agreement creates the potential for trade diversion. Lowering tariffs to zero for one or more of a country's trading partners creates potential losses for other countries that are not party to the agreement. Countries that are outside any preferential trade agreement are placed in an interesting position. If they do nothing they stand to lose exports to the countries within the agreement. Or, they can mitigate or eliminate these losses by joining the party, so to speak. The RTA between the EU and Mexico offers a textbook example of the latter reaction.

On November 24, 1999, the EU and Mexico concluded an RTA. The agreement allows for the bilateral phasing out of tariffs by 2010. The agreement also liberalizes trade in services and covers other issues such as public procurement, investment, competition and intellectual property rights, and a dispute settlement procedure. While this agreement is interesting, it is at least superficially a bit puzzling. When the agreement was signed,

EU exports to Mexico were a bit less than $10 billion and imports from Mexico are a bit more than $4 billion. In percentage terms, each of these numbers was less than 1 percent of EU trade. However, the share of EU imports had been on a downward trend since the mid-1990s. The EU had concluded that the most likely suspect was NAFTA. As tariffs fell for the US and Canada, exporters from the EU were losing business in Mexico due to trade diversion. Since Mexican tariffs are still high, the amount of trade diversion inflicted on outsiders such as the EU could be quite high. In order to prevent this trade diversion, the EU evidently decided that signing an RTA with Mexico was its best option. EU exports to Mexico are over twice the size of EU imports from Mexico. On the Mexican side, the motivation for the agreement is less clear. They may feel that the agreement is largely just replacing some imports from the US and Canada with competitive imports from the EU. In technical terms, the agreement produces little trade creation. This means little lost production in Mexico. The effects will mostly be felt by producers in Canada, the US, and the EU. This is not quite the end of the story. An RTA between Japan and Mexico went into force in 2005.

Key concepts and terms

absolute advantage – the ability of a country to produce a good using fewer resources than another country.

ad valorem **equivalent (AVE)** – the level of protection provided by a quota expressed as the percentage difference between the world market price and the domestic quota-constrained price.

ad valorem **tariff** – a tariff that is measured as a percentage of the value of the imported good.

capital-intensive – the condition that the production of a good requires a high K/L ratio.

effective rate of protection – a measure of the amount of protection provided to an industry by a country's tariff schedule.

factor-price equalization – the premise that international trade will reduce or equalize factor prices between countries.

Heckscher–Ohlin model – the theory that a country's comparative advantage is based on its endowment of the factors of production.

labor-intensive – the condition that the production of a good requires a low K/L ratio.

multilateral trade negotiations (MTNs) – a process of reducing tariff and nontariff barriers to trade among member countries of GATT or the WTO.

opportunity cost – the opportunity cost of a good is the amount of another good that must be given up to release enough resources to produce the first good.

protective tariff – a tariff designed to protect domestic industry from foreign competition.

regional trade agreements (RTAs) – a trade agreement between two or more countries that provides tariff reductions for only those countries that are members of the agreement.

revenue tariff – a tariff imposed by government whose primary purpose is raising revenue for the government.

specific tariff – a tariff that is measured as a fixed amount of money per unit imported.

Stolper–Samuelson theorem – the premise that international trade will reduce the income of the scarce factor of production and increase the income of the abundant factor of production in a country.

trade creation – the efficiency gain that results from a RTA because more efficient member countries displace less efficient member countries.

trade diversion – an efficiency loss that results from a RTA because less efficient member countries displace more efficient nonmember countries.

trade policy – government actions that influence the flow of goods and services to and from a country.

World Trade Organization (WTO) – the organization created in 1995 to replace GATT. The WTO administers multilateral trade agreements and settles trade disputes.

Questions for review and discussion

1. Briefly explain how trade based on comparative advantage improves the welfare of a country and the world.
2. Describe the changes in the terms of trade for Latin America from the middle of the nineteenth century. How did these changes lead to the conclusion that trade was making Latin America worse off? What is the flaw in that argument?
3. Describe how factor abundance leads to comparative advantage or disadvantage. What does this imply for Latin America's imports and exports?
4. How could trade based on comparative advantage improve the distribution of income in Latin America?
5. Show how tariffs and quotas affect the production and imports of a product. How would the trade barriers affect the distribution of income in Latin America if the goods being protected were capital intensive?
6. Explain the concept of rent seeking. How could this apply to trade policy in Latin America?
7. Describe trade policy before ISI in Latin America.
8. Explain how trade policy was a critical component of ISI.
9. What was the relationship between Latin America and the GATT/WTO?
10. Describe the evolution of RTAs in Latin America.

References and recommended readings

Bertola, Luis and Jeffrey G. Williamson. 2003. "Globalization in Latin America Before 1940," *NBER Working Paper No. 9687*, Cambridge, MA: National Bureau of Economic Research.

Blustein, Paul. 2009. *Misadventures of the Most Favored Nations: Clashing Egos, Inflated Ambitions, and the Great Shambles of the World Trade System*. New York: Public Affairs.

Blyde, Juan S. 2004. "Trade and Technology Diffusion in Latin America," *International Trade Journal*, 18(Fall): 177–97.

Cardoso, Eliana and Ann Helwege. 1992. *Latin America's Economy: Diversity, Trends, and Conflicts*. Cambridge, MA: MIT Press.

Clemens, Michael A. and Jeffrey G. Williamson. 2002. "Closed Jaguar, Open Dragon: Comparing Tariffs in Latin America and Asia before World War II," *NBER Working Paper No. 9401*, Cambridge, MA: National Bureau of Economic Research.

Coatsworth, John H. and Jeffrey G. Williamson. 2002. "The Roots of Latin American Protectionism: Looking Before the Great Depression," *NBER Working Paper No. 8999*, Cambridge, MA: National Bureau of Economic Research.

Coatsworth, John H. and Jeffrey G. Williamson. 2004. "Always Protectionist? Latin American Tariffs from Independence to Great Depression." *Journal of Latin American Studies*, 36(May): 205–32.

Cypher, James M. and James L. Dietz. 2009. *The Process of Economic Development*. 3rd ed. London: Routledge.

Eichengreen, Barry and Douglas A. Irwin. 2009. "The Slide to Protectionism in the Great Depression: Who Succumbed and Why?" *NBER Working Paper No. 15142*, Cambridge, MA: National Bureau of Economic Research.

Franko, Patrice. 2007. *The Puzzle of Latin American Development*, 3rd ed. New York: Rowman & Littlefield.

Haltiwanger, John, Adriana Kugler, Maurice Kugler, Alejandro Micco, and Carmen Pages. 2004. "Effects of Tariffs and Real Exchange Rates on Job Reallocation: Evidence from Latin America," *Policy Reform* 7(December): 191–208.

Krueger, Anne O. 1974. "The Political Economy of the Rent Seeking Society," *American Economic Review* 64(June): 291–303.

Marquez, Graciela. 1998. "Tariff Protection in Mexico, 1892–1909: Ad Valorem Tariff Rates and Sources of Variation," pp. 407–442 in John H. Coatsworth and Alan M. Taylor (eds), *Latin America and the World Economy Since 1800*. Cambridge, MA: Harvard University Press.

McKinney, Joseph A. and H. Stephen Gardner (eds). 2008. *Economic Integration in the Americas*. New York: Routledge.

Mesquita Moreira, Mauricio, Christian Volpe, and Juan S. Blyde. 2008. *Unclogging the Arteries: The Impact of Transport Costs on Latin American and Caribbean Trade*. Washington, DC: Interamerican Development Bank.

Nenci, Silvia and Carlo Pietrobelli. 2008. "Does Tariff Liberalization Promote Trade? Latin American Countries in the Long-Run (1900–2000)," *Global Economy Journal*, 8(October), Art. 2.

Sawyer, W. Charles and Richard L. Sprinkle. 2009. *International Economics*, 3rd ed. Upper Saddle River, NJ: Prentice Hall.

Williamson, Jeffrey G. 2003. "Was It Stolper–Samuelson, Infant Industry or Something Else? World Tariffs 1789–1938," *NBER Working Paper No. 9656*, Cambridge, MA: National Bureau of Economic Research.

World Trade Organization. 2010a. *Accessions* Geneva: WTO. www.wto.org.

World Trade Organization. 2010b. *Regional Trade Agreements*. Geneva: WTO. www.wto.org.

8 Exchange rate policy

> The produce of a country exchanges for the produce of other countries,
> at such values as are required in order that the whole of her exports may
> exactly pay for the whole of her imports.
>
> John Stuart Mill

Introduction

In this chapter, our focus changes essentially from microeconomics to
macroeconomics. In most of the previous chapters we have discussed
industries, exports, imports, industrial policy, and other government
policies that affected the economic development of Latin America. GDP was
mentioned in Chapters 2, 4, and 5, but the coverage concerned economic
growth and identifiable periods of economic history for the region. This
is different from macroeconomics. Macroeconomics is focused on the
movements of GDP, the level of unemployment, and the rate of inflation
over shorter periods of time. Typically, the focus of macroeconomics is one
to three years. The material in the rest of the book inevitably changes in
another way. In every country one is exposed to a steady stream of macroeconomic data concerning the output of the economy, measures of conditions in the labor markets, and various measures of inflation. Even if no
domestic data come out on a particular day, there is always information on
other parts of the region or the world economy. What one needs to understand is that prior to World War II, for the most part this data did not
exist. Over the last 50 years, economic historians have been painstakingly
reconstructing *annual* data for the years prior to 1945. This is still a work
in progress. As a result, short-run macroeconomic data on a monthly or
quarterly basis before this time hardly exists for the high-income countries
of the world. For the economies of Latin America, such data is virtually
nonexistent. The result is that our focus for much of the rest of the book
will be on the post-war era in the region. A substantial part of this choice
is related to the unavailability of data. The other part of this choice is that
macroeconomic policy as we now use the phrase was not really a part of the

economic history of the region prior to 1945. Why this is true will become clearer in the first section of this chapter.

The purpose of this chapter is to expand on our previous coverage of international trade. Our emphasis in earlier chapters was more on the microeconomics of international trade in the sense of how trade affects the industrial structure of a country. At several points, the overall balance of trade was touched on but not covered in depth. The first part of this chapter is a more complete description of a country's economic interactions with the rest of the world. For Latin America, this has always been important as the region began modern history as a supplier of important commodities to the rest of the world. As we will see, this trade creates inflows and outflows of money. In turn, these flows affect the price of the domestic currency relative to foreign currencies, i.e. the exchange rate. Each country in the world has to make a choice about how these flows are allowed to affect the domestic economy and/or the exchange rate. The countries of Latin America are no different in this regard. To understand both the history and the present situation of the economies of the region, it is crucial to gain a basic understanding of these choices and what each implies.

The balance of payments

Each country of the world maintains detailed data on imports and exports of goods. What is less commonly known is that each country to the greatest extent possible, records all inflows and outflows of money. Collectively, this data is referred to as the balance of payments. Within the balance of payments there are two major subcategories. The first is the current account. The current account is an accounting of international transactions that includes goods, services, investment income, and unilateral transfers. Notice that international trade in goods is included in the current account but other sorts of transactions are also included. However, the current account does not catch all of the flows of money into and out of a country. For example, notice that FDI is not included in the current account. FDI and financial transactions are part of the financial account. The financial account is a record of the difference between the holding of foreign assets by domestic residents and domestic assets by foreign residents. In this section, we will explain in some detail the different sorts of flows embodied in these two accounts. These details and the interactions of the current and capital accounts are essential to understanding the interaction of the countries of Latin America with the rest of the world.

The current account

To begin, we will present a set of data for a Representative Country in Latin America (RCILA). Each of the countries in the region is somewhat distinctive with regards to the balance of payments but also there are some common themes for the region. As a result, we do not present data for a particular country but a set of data designed to illustrate these common themes. This data is presented in Table 8.1 below. The data in the second column is designed to show a "normal" year for a country in the region that exports commodities but also exports other goods. Notice that there are both positive and negative numbers in the column. Inflows of money are shown as positive and outflows are shown as negative. The negative signs on outflows should not be interpreted as anything *wrong*. A country with no outflows would be far worse off as imports of goods, services, and capital are an essential part of a healthy economy. The negative signs simply are an accounting necessity in this case. The first two rows of the table contain data for exports and imports of goods. The difference between the two is the Balance on Trade. This is the most familiar representation of the interaction of a country with the rest of the world. It also can give a very distorted picture of these interactions. Countries also export and import services. These can be personal services such as tourism or business services such as financial services. The sum of all service flows forms the Balance on Goods. Added to trade in goods, this is the balance on goods and services. The next two items are a bit more complicated. Over time the citizens of countries may invest money in other countries. Eventually, some of the return on these investments (profits, interest, dividends, capital gains) may be repatriated to the home country. This appears as Income Receipts

Table 8.1 The balance of payments for RCILA (millions of pesos)

Current Account Transactions	
Exports of Goods	200
Imports of Goods	−180
Balance on Trade	20
Exports of Services	5
Imports of Services	−20
Balance on Services	−15
Balance on Goods and Services	5
Income Receipts from RCILA Assets Abroad	5
Income Payments of Foreign Assets in RCILA	−25
Balance on Investment Income	−20
Balance on Goods, Services, and Income	−15
Unilateral Transfers, Net	5
Balance on Current Account	−10
Financial Account Transactions	
Change in RCILA Assets Abroad	
Official Reserve Assets	−1
Private Assets	−2
Change in Foreign-Owned Assets in RCILA	
Official Reserve Assets	3
Foreign Private Assets	10
Balance on Financial Account	10

from Abroad. The reverse is true. Money invested in RCILA would probably create an outflow of money over time. In any given year, the difference between income from and payments to the rest of the world constitute the Balance on Investment Income. Adding this balance to overall trade in goods and services creates the Balance on Goods, Services, and Income. The next item is unilateral transfers. In general, a transfer payment is a payment made when there are no services rendered. The textbook case of a transfer payment is official development assistance. However, there are private unilateral transfers that are now equally or more important. Remittances are transfers of money from foreign workers to their home country. These are included in unilateral transfers along with the more familiar official development assistance. The addition of unilateral transfers leads to the Balance on Current Account.

With this short description of the Current Account we can now proceed to analyze the data in the table. This data is representative of inflows and outflows for RCILA in an average year. If the prices of commodities are favorable, then the country will export 200 million pesos a year. Imports are 180m pesos, so the trade balance is a positive 20m pesos. Exports of services are 5m pesos earned primarily from tourism and a small amount of business services provided to smaller countries in the region. Imports of services are larger reflecting domestic citizens traveling to foreign countries and the purchase of business services from high-income countries that have a comparative advantage in such services.[1] Given that capital is relatively scarce in Latin America, the outflows of capital from the region have been historically small. This is reflected in the current account as small earnings from investment income flowing into RCILA. On the other hand there has been a substantial amount of foreign capital invested in the region. This difference shows up as a deficit in the Balance on Investment Income. Again, this deficit should be viewed as perfectly normal for a middle-income country such as RCILA. In turn, this deficit makes the Balance on Goods, Services, and Income smaller than the previous Balance on Goods and Services. For a country like RCILA, unilateral transfers is positive. There may be more or less official development assistance for any given year. Recently, an increasingly important factor in Latin America has been remittances. The addition of unilateral transfers yields the Balance on Current account. Notice that for RCILA, this balance is a negative 10m pesos.

8.1 The current account in Latin America

One of the important facts that you should take away from the previous section is the importance of the current account. Despite its importance, data on the current account is not easily available. The same is not true of the balance on trade. This statistic is put out monthly with a time lag by most of the countries of the world. This is also the case for Latin America. On the other hand, the current account usually is published quarterly so the data is not as "fresh." Further, data for the current account frequently is released with the data on the rate of growth of GDP. Understandably, the information on the current account gets far less attention. As a result, there tends to be more focus on the balance of trade than on the current account. The problem is that the former can be a very misleading number. To illustrate some of these points, Table 8.2 presents data on the balance on trade and the current account for the larger economies of Latin America. This data is published every week in *The Economist*. Second, notice that every country in the table except Colombia and Mexico is reporting a surplus in the balance on trade. Finally, notice that only two countries are reporting a surplus on the current account. For three out of the six countries, the trade surplus turned into a current account deficit. In only one case was the current account "better" than the balance on trade. The lesson here is that the balance on trade is more readily available, but should be used with care.

Table 8.2 The balance on trade and the current account in Latin America

Country	Balance on trade	Current account balance
	(billions of $)	(billions of $)
Argentina	+15.9	+10.4
Brazil	+25.5	−18.9
Chile	+11.9	+0.8
Colombia	0	−6.0
Mexico	−9.3	−11.2
Venezuela	+6.7	−2.1

Source: *The Economist* (2009).

The financial account

While the current account gives a more extensive accounting of inflows and outflows for a country, it is not complete. Below the current account, other transactions are included in the financial account. The financial account records the difference between the holdings of foreign assets by domestic residents and domestic assets by foreign residents. As shown above, these transactions are done in either the public or the private sector. Changes in official reserve assets are given for both RCILA and the rest of the world. Every government of the world holds foreign exchange for a variety of purposes. Over a year, this stock of foreign exchange will become larger or smaller. If a government acquires foreign exchange, this will be recorded as an outflow of money as a foreign asset has been acquired. A more important factor is the purchase of foreign assets by domestic residents. These purchases take two forms. First, domestic residents may engage in FDI in foreign countries. Second, they may also purchase financial assets in other countries which are known as changes in portfolio capital. Both of these items represent outflows of money in the financial account. For Latin America these flows tend to be small as the economies of the region are capital scarce. The other side of the financial account is changes in reserve assets by the rest of the world and inflows of FDI and portfolio capital flows.

Governments in the rest of the world may acquire the currencies of countries in the region. These purchases show up as inflows of money into the domestic economies of the region. As before, these flows are typically small. The larger inflows are by the private sector in the rest of the world. In a well-managed middle-income country, there should be a substantial amount of incoming FDI and inflows of portfolio capital. The rate of return to capital frequently will be higher in Latin America than it would be in a high-income country. This makes sense as capital in the former is scarce relative to the latter. Similarly, the rate of return on financial assets such as stocks and bonds usually is higher in Latin America than it would be in the high-income countries. The result is that in most years the balance on the financial account would be positive: more capital is flowing into Latin America than is flowing out.[2]

Putting the current account together with the financial account yields an important relationship. The market continually is trying to balance the inflows and outflows of foreign exchange. Over a period of time such as a year, this means that the sum of the current account and the financial account must equal zero.[3] This means that if the current account is negative, then the financial account is positive. The reverse would be true. If the current account is positive, then the financial account is negative. Another way of putting this is that if one account is in deficit, then the other account is a surplus. The typical situation for a country in Latin America can be described in this way. It is common for the balance on trade to be positive. The country is exporting more goods than it is importing. It is also common for the balance on current account to be negative as a result of trade in services and net investment income. Unilateral transfers would normally be positive. There is nothing untoward about a deficit in the balance on current account. It will be offset by a surplus in the financial account. Money should be flowing into the country in the form of FDI and purchases of financial assets.

This discussion can leave one with the impression that this balancing of inflows and outflows always is a smooth and continuous process. Unfortunately, this is not the case. Both inflows and outflows can fluctuate substantially from one year to the next. A task for any country is to decide how to manage these flows. This decision is partly an internal choice by the government. However, the choices made by other countries also matters. No country in Latin America, or anywhere else, is an island. This management of inflows and outflows involves the choice of an exchange rate regime. Over the next several sections, we will describe the two major types of exchange rate regimes that were common in Latin America and the world during the twentieth century. The choices made by the majority of countries in the region turned out to be an important part of the story of the economic performance of Latin America.

Flexible exchange rates

We start our discussion of exchange rate systems in reverse chronological order for two reasons. First, most readers of this book have only lived in a world where exchange rates are allowed to fluctuate just like any other price. If trying to fix an exchange rate sounds a bit strange, don't feel alone. The idea is somewhat alien to an economist as well. Second, it is easier to explain exchange rates by first examining the normal situation where the exchange rate can move about in response to changes in market conditions. With these basics in mind, it becomes somewhat easier to show the effects of fixing the exchange rate. In this section, the basic analysis of exchange rates is explained. After developing the supply and demand model, the basic determinants of the exchange rate are presented and put into a Latin American context.

One of the first places that inflows and outflows show up is in the foreign exchange market. To see this, let's consider some common transactions. Suppose that a food company in RCILA wants to purchase wheat produced in the US. In order to accomplish this, the company must first exchange pesos for US dollars. This makes sense as it would be awkward to try to spend pesos in Kansas. This ordinary transaction illustrates the demand for foreign exchange, in this case dollars. It represents a typical transaction that ends up being an outflow of money from the country. Now consider an example of inflows. Suppose that a supplier to the building industry in the US needs to purchase water heaters. Considering all costs, it is determined that water heaters produced in RCILA are the best value available. In order to complete this transaction, the firm will need to end up purchasing pesos. This is accomplished by buying pesos and selling dollars in the foreign exchange market. This selling of dollars creates a supply in the foreign exchange market. Since these sorts of transactions are so commonplace, there is a lot of trading of pesos for US dollars in the foreign exchange market. Firms and individuals in RCILA are constantly buying dollars to purchase US goods and services. American firms and individuals are likewise selling dollars in order to obtain pesos. Just like any other market, this constant buying and selling creates the usual set of demand and supply curves. The natural result is a market price, the exchange rate.

Now let's put this information into a more formal framework. The demand for foreign exchange looks like any other demand curve: it slopes downwards and to the right. The only real difference is how we express the price. In this case, the price is the exchange rate. In addition, we will look at the foreign exchange market from RCILA's point of view. This means looking at the peso/dollar exchange rate or the number of pesos it takes to buy a US dollar. This demand for foreign exchange is shown in Figure 8.1. On the vertical axis is the exchange rate. The horizontal axis is the quantity of dollars which for RCILA is foreign exchange. To keep things simple, consider an exchange rate of 2P/$. This exchange rate falls roughly in the middle of the demand for foreign exchange. Now consider an exchange rate

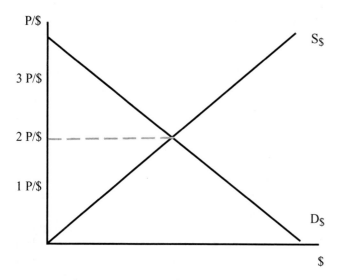

Figure 8.1 The demand and supply of foreign exchange

of 3P/$. In this case it now takes more pesos to buy a dollar. The peso has *depreciated* relative to the dollar. The reverse is true of an exchange rate of 1P/$. It now takes fewer pesos to buy a dollar, so the peso has appreciated relative to the dollar. In our prosaic example, at 1P/$ US wheat is a bargain. However, at 3P/$ US wheat has become very expensive. Again, if the only thing that happens is a movement in the exchange rate, then one is sliding up or down the existing demand curve for foreign exchange.

As is usually the case, the demand curve can also shift to the left or right. An increase (decrease) in the demand for foreign exchange is represented by a shift of the curve to the right (left). In general, two factors could cause such a shift. An important factor is a change in income in RCILA. If the economy is growing, then the demand for imports will grow and along with it the demand for dollars. This would show up as a shift of the demand for dollars to the right. On the other hand, a recession in RCILA would decrease the demand for imports and shift the demand for dollars to the left. The growth rate of the economy of RCILA will change over time and the demand for dollars will shift along with these changes. A second factor that will shift the demand for dollars is a change in relative prices. Assume that the rate of inflation in RCILA is 10 percent and that it is 5 percent in the US. If the exchange rate doesn't change then over time goods from the US are becoming relatively cheaper. In turn, this would increase the demand for dollars and shift the curve to the right. The reverse would be true. If inflation in RCILA is less than inflation in the US then over time imports would become more expensive. This would tend to shift the demand curve to the left. These factors set up a couple of important tendencies. First, a booming economy tends to lead to a depreciation of the currency. If everyone is trying to buy dollars then the number of pesos traders are willing to offer for dollars is going to rise. A booming economy may also mean a rising rate of inflation. Relatively high inflation would also tend to increase the demand for dollars and tend to lead to depreciation of the peso. By the same logic, a recession or low inflation would tend to lead to an appreciation of the currency.

In order to complete the analysis, a supply curve is necessary. In Figure 8.1, the supply of dollars in the foreign exchange market is shown sloping upwards and to the right. The logic behind this slope is straightforward. Suppose that the exchange rate is 1P/$. At this exchange rate the US demand for imports from RCILA would be low as a dollar would only buy 1P worth of goods. Following our example, water heaters from RCILA would be expensive. Traders would not be exchanging many dollars for pesos at this exchange rate. Now assume that the exchange rate is 3P/$. From the US point of view, water heaters from RCILA are a bargain. As a result, traders would be exchanging a lot of dollars to obtain pesos. In this case, the supply of dollars is directly related to the exchange rate. As the peso depreciates from 1P/$ to 3P/$, the quantity supplied of foreign exchange increases. The supply curve slopes upwards and to the right. This supply curve can also shift for similar reasons to the shifts in the demand curve. In this case, changes in income in the US can shift the demand for goods such as water heaters from RCILA. An increase in income in the US would shift the supply of dollars to the right as traders would need more pesos to buy goods in RCILA. A decrease in income in the US would shift the curve to the left. Relative prices also matter. If inflation in the US is higher than inflation in RCILA, then exports to the US will increase. This would shift the supply curve to the right. The reverse would occur if inflation in the US is lower than inflation in RCILA. US goods would become relatively less expensive and the supply of foreign exchange would fall as exports fell. Any shifts in the supply curve would affect the exchange rate. In Figure 8.1, the intersection of the demand and supply of dollars leads to an equilibrium exchange rate of 2P/$. Of course, a change in either the demand or supply of foreign exchange will change the exchange rate. This potential volatility has been an important factor in the economic development of Latin America.

Fixed exchange rates

Through much of its history, the countries of Latin America had maintained fixed exchange rates. In the twenty-first century, the idea of a fixed exchange rate seems peculiar. However, until 1971 it was the norm in the world economy. Prior to the Great Depression, many of the countries of the region were trying to fix their exchange rates under the gold standard or through other means. However, the onset of World War I weakened the system. The arrival of the Great Depression shattered it. Along with the rest of the world, the countries of Latin America slowly left the system.[4] The end of

World War II ushered in a new period of fixed exchange rates. Virtually all of the governments of the world wanted to return to fixed exchange rates after the chaotic period of the 1930s. However, it was also realized that a return to the gold standard was not possible. At a conference in Bretton Woods, New Hampshire in the US in 1944, an alternative system was formulated. The Bretton Woods system marked a return to fixed exchange rates. The link to the gold standard was retained with the US government committing itself to redeem dollars for gold at a fixed price of $35. All other currencies were then fixed to the dollar. The IMF was created to oversee the operation of the system. It maintained a pool of reserves of foreign exchange for countries to borrow to cover current account deficits. The system eventually broke down in 1971 as the US announced the suspension of the convertibility of the dollar for gold at the official price. As we will see the countries of Latin America were reluctant to abandon fixed exchange rates and slowly went to flexible exchange rates in the late 1970s and early 1980s.

Intervention in the foreign exchange market

Since we covered the basics of exchange rates in the previous section, we now turn our attention to the mechanics of a fixed exchange rate. Our discussion begins with Figure 8.2. As before, the equilibrium exchange rate is 2P/$. However, in this case the government has committed itself to fixing the exchange rate at this price. Unfortunately, this commitment does not reduce the propensity of the supply and demand curves to fluctuate. To start, we will consider how the system was supposed to work for a country like RCILA that exports a substantial amount of commodities. Assume that a commodity boom occurs and that the world price of this country's commodity is increasing. As the US has to pay more for the commodity, it will have to trade more dollars in the foreign exchange market to buy the requisite number of pesos. In turn this would cause an increase in the supply of foreign exchange. If the exchange rate was not fixed, it would just appreciate, i.e. a flexible price would take care of the situation. However, the government is committed to the fixed rate. In this case it would be necessary to purchase the excess supply of dollars to maintain the fixed exchange rate. The country's official reserve assets would rise as it acquired foreign exchange. In a well-managed country, the government would effectively "hoard" foreign exchange as a byproduct of fixing the exchange rate. As we saw in Chapter 5, commodity prices can also fall. A fall in commodity prices would lead to a decrease in the supply of foreign exchange. The US would need to exchange fewer dollars to obtain the same amount of commodities. In Figure 8.2, this is shown as a leftward shift in the supply of foreign exchange. With flexible exchange rates the exchange rate would simply depreciate. In order to maintain the fixed exchange rate, the government will need to sell foreign exchange. This would shift the supply curve to the right and maintain the exchange rate at 2P/$.

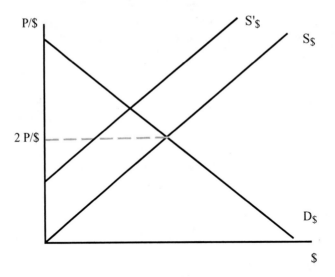

Figure 8.2 Intervention in the foreign exchange market

Maintaining a fixed exchange rate is difficult for a country that is an exporter of commodities. When commodity prices are high, the government will need to buy up the excess foreign exchange to keep the currency from appreciating. When commodity prices are low, foreign exchange will have to be supplied to the foreign exchange market to maintain the fixed exchange rate. This is just another example of the old principle that fixed prices create either shortages or surpluses. Since the exchange rate is not being allowed to change, the government at times must accumulate a surplus of foreign exchange. This accumulation will be necessary in order to supply foreign exchange whenever there is a shortage. This buying and selling of foreign exchange is known as intervention in the foreign exchange market. A country that is a commodity exporter has to be careful in managing its stock of official reserve assets. It would need to intervene in the foreign exchange markets both when there is a commodity bust and especially during a commodity boom.

Exchange controls

The previous section presented the management of a fixed exchange rate by efficiently managing the level of reserves of foreign exchange. To review, a country would accumulate reserves when the current account was in surplus. In turn, these reserves would be used during periods when a country is running a deficit. Over time, the country could maintain a fixed exchange rate by wisely managing its reserves. For most of the countries of Latin America, this was not the norm under the Bretton Woods system. During commodity booms or other favorable periods, sufficient reserves were not accumulated to cover the periodic deficits. To be fair, this was hardly a problem peculiar to Latin America. Many countries of the world were unable to do this. As we will see in the next chapter, there are a number of mechanisms that can be used for a country to cover a current account deficit. The efficient management of reserves is just a preferred option. In this section, we consider another means of managing deficits that was quite common in Latin America and other parts of the world.

To illustrate the problem, return to Figure 8.2. If the supply of foreign exchange has shifted to the left, the country has a current account deficit: the demand for foreign exchange is greater than the supply at 2P/$. With intervention, this gap is filled by the government selling foreign exchange. Now assume that the government does not have sufficient foreign exchange to shift the supply curve far enough to the right. Also, a depreciation of the currency is not an option as the country is participating in a global system of fixed exchange rates. An answer to this question is a variant of what happens when any price is being forced below equilibrium. A shortage has developed, in this case a shortage of foreign exchange. Without an increase in the price, the government may resort to rationing the available foreign exchange. The usual term for this rationing is exchange controls. Exchange controls necessarily imply discrimination in the market for foreign exchange. With floating exchange rates, the available foreign exchange goes to anyone that is willing to pay the current exchange rate. If a fixed exchange rate creates a shortage of foreign exchange, then with exchange controls the government is going to have to administer the shortage. Since this is not going to be a straightforward process, exchange controls come in a bewildering number of forms. As a result, the discussion below refers to only the more common forms they may take.

The most rigorous form of exchange controls gives the government a monopoly on dealing in foreign exchange. In this case, any holder of foreign exchange is obliged to sell it to the government at the official exchange rate. This gives the government an effective monopoly of the supply of foreign exchange. On the other side of the market, there will be more firms and individuals demanding foreign exchange than the supply owned by the government. This is not an agreeable situation. Suppose that the official exchange rate is 2P/$ and the equilibrium rate in a free market is 3P/$. If a firm in Latin America is exporting goods at the official exchange rate they are well aware of the loss of $1. On the other hand, firms and individuals that can obtain foreign exchange at the official exchange rate are well aware that this is a low price. With an excess demand for foreign exchange, the central question for the government is deciding which demands are more important than others. Some of the rationing is easy as in the case of oil, food, medicines, or imported inputs to keep the ISI industries functioning. Past these relatively easy decisions, one can imagine that the rationing process can become more difficult. One possible response to this is the existence of a system of multiple exchange rates. In this case the official exchange rate would not be uniform, but would vary depending on what the government felt were essential imports and what was less important. For example, the government could set a rate of 1P/$ for essential imports and 3P/$ for imports deemed to be less important. Such systems can lead to an extreme amount of complexity on top of the simple mechanics of managing a bureaucratic system in lieu of private sector transactions. They also form a sort of de facto industrial policy. In the context of Latin America, a multiple exchange rate system could be used to support ISI. Favored industries could obtain foreign exchange at much more favorable rates than other industries. This amounted to a subsidy to ISI industries via exchange rate policy. Part of the unwinding of ISI that led to the Lost Decade can be traced to the rapid depreciations of exchange rates that were common during this period.

8.2   Black markets in foreign exchange

If there are exchange controls in a country and the currency has become overvalued, the question becomes what the nominal exchange rate "should" be. Recall that domestic residents who possess foreign exchange are legally obliged to surrender it to the government. To a greater or lesser extent, there would be legal sanctions for failing to do this. Suppose that the penalties for illegally possessing foreign exchange are fairly small – say, a small monetary fine. If the currency becomes sufficiently overvalued, it may become logical (although illegal) to not surrender the foreign exchange to the government at the fixed price. Given that there is excess demand for foreign exchange, it is quite possible that you could find a buyer who would be willing to pay more than the fixed government rate. When the government attempts to fix any price, a *black market* will develop. If one observes that there is a black market for foreign exchange in a country, you don't even need to ask if there are exchange controls. The very existence of a black market means that the government's fixed price for foreign exchange is too low.

In this case, there are only two remaining questions. First, how overvalued is the official exchange rate? The black market rate is a reliable guide to this. Empirical estimates have shown time and again that the black market rate will closely approximate purchasing power parity. This knowledge is both a blessing and a curse. It is good in the sense that one usually does not have to conduct tedious calculations of just how overvalued the exchange rate is. One can simply go out in the street and find out. However, the answer in some cases may be disheartening. If the black market rate is 50 percent above the official rate, there is likely to be a nasty combination of an austerity program and/or a large devaluation to bring the economy back into balance. Economists will likely be able to identify countries where there is a high probability of a major devaluation. When such a currency crisis will occur is another matter.

The material above refers to exchange controls on the current account. Fortunately, such controls are a part of economic history. In most of the countries of Latin America, such controls on current account transactions no longer exist. However, there are still exchange controls on financial account transactions. Recall the material included in Table 8.1 under the financial account. To review, the private sector component of these flows are composed of FDI and movements of portfolio capital. The outflows from Latin America are not an issue as they are rather small. As we will see in the next chapter, the inflows can be substantial. To go further, the inflows of FDI are not a problem. FDI inflows may be large but they are not very volatile. Once foreign investors have made an investment in plant and equipment or purchased all or part of a domestic firm, the investment is not likely to flow out quickly. The rate of change of change of FDI may be volatile. A country might attract a large amount of FDI in one year and somewhat less the next. The point is that once the money has been invested, it is not likely to leave quickly. The same is not true of flows of portfolio capital. Portfolio capital is money that is being invested in financial assets such as stocks or bonds. This money can flow easily into a country but can just as easily leave. As portfolio capital flows in, the supply of foreign exchange can shift to the right and the exchange rate can appreciate. The reverse is true. If foreign investors remove too much portfolio capital in too short a period of time, the supply of foreign exchange can shift to the left leading to a rapid depreciation of the currency.[5] As we will see in Chapter 11, this capital flight can have disastrous macroeconomic consequences. To summarize the future discussion, capital flight can lead to a mixture of higher inflation and negative economic growth.

Capital flight is an all too real risk for developing countries and especially Latin America. As we saw in Chapter 4, it is just another part of the economic instability embedded in the history of the region. Since independence foreign investors have been periodically enamored with the economic potential of the region. The ensuing disappointment with these investments led to a number of cases of capital flight from the region. In the wake of the Asian economic crisis of the late 1990s, the term contagion has been a popular research topic among economists. Contagion refers to the tendency of investors to withdraw portfolio capital from an entire region in response to perceived economic difficulties in a single country or a subset of countries. While it may be a new topic of interest to economists, it is an old subject in Latin America. As a result, the region may be particularly susceptible to the phenomenon because of the economic history of the region. A recent example, may illustrate the point. A series of macroeconomic policy mistakes in late 1994 led to a rapid depreciation of the Mexican peso known as the *Tequila Crisis*. The crisis was country specific and not an indication of generalized economic problems in the region. At this point Latin America as a whole was beginning the process of recovery from the Lost Decade. Nonetheless, the crisis in Mexico led to a large withdrawal of portfolio capital and had adverse economic impacts on the region as a whole.[6]

These risks have led a number of countries to adopt some form of controls on movements of portfolio capital. Such restrictions can serve to limit the inflows and outflows of foreign exchange and thus help to stabilize the exchange rate. As is always the case with any policy, there are costs and benefits. The benefit is that such controls can limit the appreciation of the currency when inflows of portfolio capital are rather high. In turn, this reduces the adverse effects on the country's exports and reduces the tendency for imports to rise. In addition, such controls offer some protection against exchange rate shocks. Portfolio capital may be unable to leave the country en masse and can reduce the severity of the depreciation of the currency. In a sense, controls on the flow of portfolio capital constitute a form of insurance against large changes in the exchange rate in either direction. This form of insurance is not free. The countries of Latin America tend to be capital scarce. As shown in Chapter 2, capital is a critical input into the process of economic development. Limiting flows of capital may have the consequence of reducing the rate of economic growth. This could also diminish the growth of the K/L ratio which is an important determinant of real wages. More importantly, it is not completely clear whether or not such controls have the expected effect on the exchange rate. Different studies find varying effects depending on the country or time period studied.[7] At a minimum, assuming that capital controls work perfectly to limit movements in the exchange rate may not be a safe assumption. As a general rule, these restrictions on the free flow of capital are controversial. The traditional view of capital controls is that the growth limiting aspects of this policy are larger than the benefits of some protection against exchange rate shocks. More recent research indicates that the cost/benefit analysis may be more complex.[8] This is reflected in the implementation of such controls in Latin America. Controls on movements of portfolio capital in Chile have been extensively studied and no firm conclusions have been reached on their effectiveness. In response to an appreciation of the exchange rate, Brazil recently began taxing inflows of portfolio capital. While such policies are unlikely to become widespread, they do not appear to be quite ready for the dustbin of economic history in the region.

8.3   Capital controls in Chile

As you have no doubt noticed, in a number of places in the book Chilean economic performance and policy has been presented in a favorable light. This is not an unjustifiable bias by the authors. Chile has been something of a model of good economic policy not just for Latin America but in some cases for the world.[9] As a result, Chile would seem to be an improbable country to adopt capital controls. However, it is not quite as odd as it may seem at first glance. For more successful developing countries, rapid economic growth carries the risk of large inflows of portfolio capital. Such inflows can cause the exchange rate to appreciate to levels that may cause some of the difficulties described above. In the case of Chile there is a further problem, copper. Chile produces a third of the world's copper and it routinely accounts for 40 percent of the country's exports. Unfortunately, copper prices are extremely volatile. The result of this price volatility can be instability in the exchange rate.

From 1991 to 1998, the government of Chile imposed restrictions on capital flows as a means of limiting exchange rate volatility. These took two main forms. First, inflows of FDI were subjected to a minimum stay of one year. Controls on flows of portfolio capital were more complex. Chilean firms were limited in their ability to issue stock in foreign markets. More importantly, inflows of portfolio capital were subject to a 30 percent reserve requirement. This amounted to a tax on inflows of portfolio capital. The effects are as one would expect. Inflows of short-term portfolio capital were reduced and the maturity of capital inflows increased. The effects on the exchange rate are usually estimated to be small. Also, these controls seem to have made it marginally easier for the central bank to conduct monetary policy. The overall evaluation seems to be that in the case of Chile the controls generated small benefits and relatively small costs. However, some of the costs may be less obvious. A recent paper indicates that these controls have an interesting impact. Limiting the flows of short-run capital in a capital-scarce country should have an impact *somewhere*. One of the effects is in retrospect obvious. Larger firms were able to avoid the effects of these controls by borrowing in foreign markets. Further, since the regulations were complex they represented an extra but fixed cost of borrowing. This fixed cost naturally declined with the size of the firm. However, it was very difficult for banks to avoid the controls. The banking system in Chile, as in other countries, was a major source of capital for small and medium-sized firms. Edwards (1998) mentions these effects but in a more focused study, Forbes (2007) carefully shows the difference in borrowing costs. During this period large Chilean firms could borrow in international markets at 7–8 percent. The cost of capital for smaller firms was over 20 percent. The controls had the effect of making capital over twice as expensive for firms that naturally tend to grow faster. While the overall costs to the Chilean economy may have been small, the costs to an important part of the economy seem to be much larger. Capital controls in Chile were dropped in 1998 as overall capital flows to emerging markets dwindled. They have never re-emerged in Chile as a response to inflows of portfolio capital. Perhaps this is just another example of revealed preference.

The real exchange rate

So far in this chapter all of our analysis has focused on the exchange rate that one observes in the market. As is usual in economics we refer to this as the nominal exchange rate. The nominal exchange rate has not been adjusted for changes in inflation. From your previous economics courses you are probably familiar with the concept of real prices. Real prices are prices that have been adjusted for the effects of inflation. For example, one cannot determine whether or not a price has increased or decreased in real terms by observing the change in the nominal price. It is also necessary to know what the overall rate of inflation is. The same is true for an exchange rate. However, in this case the analysis is slightly more complicated. One has to consider not only the domestic inflation rate but the inflation rate in a foreign country. In this section, we explain the concept of the real exchange rate. The real exchange rate is the nominal exchange rate adjusted for changes in both domestic and foreign prices. As we will see, the real exchange rate is important in the context of Latin America. At times in the region, the nominal exchange rate can be quite deceptive. An understanding of the real exchange rate is crucial in understanding the economic changes that have occurred in the region over the last several decades. To borrow a thought from Paul Samuelson, the real exchange rate is an important concept, but it is not obvious. To illustrate this, let's consider a normal economic transaction. Suppose that last year you exchanged a dollar for 1,000 pesos and crossed the border and purchased a bottle of soda. Now assume that prices in the US are constant and that the rate of inflation in RCILA is 100 percent. A year later, the same transaction might look something like this. You now exchange a dollar for the 2,000 pesos and cross the border and buy a bottle of soda. Notice what has occurred. The nominal exchange rate has changed dramatically. However, a dollar still bought you a bottle of soda. Adjusted for inflation, the real exchange rate has not changed. Just a bit of consideration of this example illustrates how deceptive the nominal exchange rate can be. The example may seem extreme but as we will see in Chapter 11 situations such as this in Latin America were all too real in the late twentieth century.

To understand the real exchange rate requires a bit of logic and arithmetic. The starting point is the law of one price. The law of one price is the simple statement that identical goods sold in competitive markets should cost the same everywhere when prices are expressed in terms of the same currency. The example above was an illustration. If a bottle of soda costs a dollar in the US then it should also cost a dollar across the border. One's first reaction may be that this is ridiculous. For any number of reasons, identical goods rarely cost *exactly* the same in two countries. That is also beside the point. The law of one price and other concepts that follow should be viewed as tendencies. If the gap between the prices of goods in different countries becomes too large, then traders will start moving goods from the low-price country to the high-price country to make a profit, i.e. arbitrage. When that profit goes to zero, trading stops. Because of trade restrictions, transportation costs, and other barriers to trade arbitrage may stop before prices are equalized. The point is that prices will tend to move in the direction of equality, not away from it.

Following our earlier examples, we consider the prices in RCILA (Pr) and the US (Pus) and the peso dollar exchange rate (P/$). The relationship can be expressed as:

$$Pr = (P/\$) \times Pus$$

or

$P/\$ = Pr/Pus.$

Now let's analyze the price of soda example. In this case:

$1,000P = 1,000P/\$ \times \$1$

or

$1,000P/\$ = 1,000P/\$1$

Now put in the new price of soda in RCILA of 2,000P per dollar. The law of one price would indicate that the price of soda hasn't changed.

Another way of stating the law of one price is absolute purchasing power parity. Absolute purchasing power parity is the theory that exchange rates are related to differences in the level of prices between countries. The key difference here is the term prices. In our example of the law of one price, we were considering the price of a single good. In analyzing purchasing power parity (PPP), the focus shifts to the overall price level. This makes sense as the exchange rate applies to all transactions in the balance of payments, not the price of a single good. More specifically, we are referring to a representative market basket of goods and services that is conceptually similar to the sort of market basket used to calculate a price index such as the consumer price index.[10] To illustrate the concept, assume that a market basket of goods in RCILA costs 2P and an identical basket cost \$1 in the US. Clearly, this would indicate that the absolute PPP exchange rate should be 2P/\$. From the relationship, it becomes relatively easy to calculate changes in the exchange rate that would be necessary to satisfy the condition of absolute PPP.

The concept of absolute purchasing power parity can be carried a step further. Changes in the overall level of prices are usually presented in terms of percentage changes. Rather than stating that the market basket for a country has increased from 100 to 105, this change would usually be stated as inflation is 5 percent. This same change is what occurs when we move from absolute purchasing power parity to relative purchasing power parity. Relative purchasing power parity is the theory that a percentage change in the exchange rate (XR) is equal to the difference in the percentage change in price levels. This can be shown in more formal terms as:

$\%\Delta XR = \%\Delta Pr - \%\Delta Pus.$

Notice how easy this makes it to analyze our earlier example. If the inflation rate in RCILA is 100 percent and zero in the US, then the P/\$ exchange rate will depreciate by 100 percent.

8.4   Restaurant prices and the Mexican peso

An endless source of fascination for economists has been empirically documenting the concept of purchasing power parity. Not surprisingly, the usual finding is that PPP does not hold for every short-run period of time. However, exchange rates tend to move in the predicted direction over sufficiently long periods of time. At a more microeconomic level, if PPP seems to work in the long run then the law of one price should also be working. Studies on the workings of the law of one price are much rarer than studies of PPP. Finding identical goods where transportation costs, trade barriers, and other distortions to trade are negligible isn't easy. One famous example is the exchange rate index published by *The Economist* that is based on the price of Big Macs in different countries. In the context of Latin America, one particularly clever study examines the law of one price between Mexico and the US Fullerton and Coronado (2001) collected data on the prices of identical items in identical restaurant chains in El Paso, Texas and Ciudad Juarez, Mexico. The two cities form a large "borderplex" where for restaurants there are few barriers to trade. Citizens of either country are free to eat out wherever they can find the best value. The price ratio in this case is the price of individual menu items in Mexico and the US. Since prices change frequently, one can check to see how price changes relate to the peso/ dollar exchange rate. Much like other studies of PPP, changes in the price ratio are an unreliable guide to changes in the exchange rate. One wouldn't want to speculate in foreign exchange by eating out and checking prices on both sides of the border. A further complication is that restaurant food is hard to arbitrage. However, this study found limited evidence that in the long run, the price ratio and the exchange rate converge. Subsequent studies using longer time series tend to lend more support to this conclusion. The main point is that the different versions of PPP tend to contain a common theme. Looking for a perfect correlation between the price ratios and the exchange rate is almost accidental. However, in the long run the ratio and the exchange rate move much as theory predicts.

The discussion of purchasing power parity leads directly to the concept of the real exchange rate (RXR). The real exchange rate can be expressed as a relationship between the nominal exchange rate and prices in the two countries. The real exchange rate between the peso and the dollar can be seen as:

$$RXR = P/\$ \, (Pr/Pus).$$

Now consider the possibilities. Suppose the nominal exchange rate is 2P/\$. If prices in both RCILA and the US are equal to 100, then the real exchange rate also is 2P/\$. However, what would happen if prices doubled in RCILA and the nominal exchange rate did not change? The real exchange rate is now

4 and the nominal exchange rate is still 2. Consider what this means. Goods in the US have become very cheap relative to goods in RCILA. Anyone who can obtain pesos at 2P/$ should clearly do so. The reader is left to imagine the effect on imports into RCILA from the US. The effect on exports is grim. A dollar will only purchase 2 pesos worth of goods from RCILA. In effect, these goods have become much more expensive. The increase in prices in RCILA will not be accounted for if the exchange rate does not change.

Overvalued exchange rates have been a problem for the economies of Latin America since at least the 1950s. Until the early 1980s, the culprit was the fixed exchange rate system mandated under Bretton Woods. As this system collapsed in the early 1970s, the governments of Latin America were reluctant to allow their exchange rates to float. The example above gives a glimpse as to why. With generally overvalued exchange rates, ISI industries could purchase needed imports at artificially low prices. Others who had borrowed in dollars could likewise service debts at a reduced cost. On the other hand, exporting anything other than commodities was difficult. Exporting labor-intensive manufactured goods in a competitive world market is very difficult in the face of an overvalued exchange rate.

More recently, the problem can be either high commodity prices or large inflows of portfolio capital. Another numerical example can illustrate the point. Assume that prices in RCILA and the US are 100 and there is no inflation in either country. If the nominal exchange rate is 2P/$, then the RXR is also 2P/$. If either high commodity prices or inflows of portfolio capital increase, the nominal exchange rate will appreciate. In this case, we'll assume it moves to 1P/$. This nominal appreciation of the currency now translates into a real appreciation. Imports now become cheap and exports become expensive. Notice that there is a difference. In the case of a fixed exchange rate and high inflation, the real appreciation of the currency occurred as a result of government policy. Low inflation coupled with a floating exchange rate would have prevented an appreciation of the real exchange rate. In this case, the real appreciation has been caused by changes in the world market for commodities or changes in the demand for local financial assets by foreign investors. Notice also, that these same factors could easily cause a real depreciation of the exchange rate. Low commodity prices or capital flight could just as easily cause a real *depreciation* of the currency. It is precisely these sources of macroeconomic instability that will be addressed in Chapter 11.

Managed exchange rates

At the beginning of this chapter we covered the total inflows and outflows of money into a country by studying the components of the current account. As we saw, these flows have an effect on the exchange rate.

As a consequence, countries have to make decisions about how to manage the exchange rate. However, one has to be careful in defining the term exchange rate. Most of the time, we are referring to the nominal exchange rate posted in the market. However, the related concept of the real exchange rate is important. As shown above, the real exchange rate can change even if the nominal exchange rate does not. The real exchange rate can have important impacts on the volume of trade and on the economy overall. This makes the choice of an exchange rate regime important. The exchange rate regime is the system a country uses to manage the exchange rate and the foreign exchange market. So far in this chapter, we have considered two possibilities: a flexible or fixed exchange rate. The former is relatively rare except for a few high-income countries. The latter was common in the world economy, including Latin America prior to the early 1970s. However, since the breakup of the Bretton Woods system, it has become rare even in Latin America. However, a perfectly flexible exchange rate or a fixed exchange rate are important reference points in much the same way that perfect competition and monopoly are. Most exchange rate regimes, just like most market structures, are somewhere in between these two extremes. Officially, the IMF defines four different exchange rate regimes: a peg (fixed exchange rate), limited flexibility, managed floating, and freely floating. With a lag, the IMF classifies every member country into one of these four categories.[11] Most of the countries of Latin America have opted for managed floating. However, managed floating is a broad term that covers several possibilities ranging in the continuum between a peg and freely floating. Where a country is on this continuum depends on the degree to which it has a "fear of floating." Very few countries choose a freely floating exchange rate due to the adverse macroeconomic consequences involved with a large change in the exchange rate that occurs over a short period of time.[12] The result is that countries use a combination of capital controls, intervention in the foreign exchange market, and interest rate changes in influencing the value of the exchange rate. The possibilities go beyond the four classifications given above. The main point is that countries may not be using *exactly* the exchange rate regime that they are publicly reporting.[13]

In Latin America, Ecuador, El Salvador, and Panama use the US dollar as legal tender.[14] Bolivia, Honduras, and Venezuela have the conventional pegged exchange rate regime described above. Costa Rica and Nicaragua use what is known as a crawling peg. With a crawling peg, the nominal exchange rate is changed by a determined amount at pre-announced points in time. The main point of a crawling peg is to limit fluctuations in the real exchange.[15] Argentina, Colombia, Guatemala, Paraguay, Peru, and Uruguay use a managed float with no predetermined exchange rate target. This system eliminates the problems associated with a pegged exchange rate and leaves each country free to influence the exchange rate in response to changes in circumstances such as commodity price fluctuations. Officially, Brazil, Chile, and Mexico have exchange rates that are freely floating like the US dollar or the Euro. In practice, few if any countries in the region are unconcerned about the exchange rate. As we saw above, large changes in the nominal exchange rate can have a substantial impact on the real exchange rate. The countries of the region have learned from bitter experience that large changes in the real exchange rate can have very adverse macroeconomic consequences. Historically, many of these changes were the result of a pegged nominal exchange rate.[16] This experience has led to a reasonable compromise for managing the exchange rates of the region. The nominal exchange rate for most countries is now flexible. This frees the governments of the region from the need to constantly intervene in the foreign exchange market to peg the exchange rate. On the other hand, the real exchange rate needs to be reasonably close to purchasing power parity to avoid inappropriate changes in trade flows. The fact that large, unexpected changes in exchange rates are much less common in the region than they were in the past indicates that the lessons of past policy mistakes have been learned and that current policies are an improvement.[17] This is important as mismanagement of the exchange rate can have unfortunate consequences for the capital account which is the focus of the next chapter.

Key concepts and terms

absolute purchasing power parity – the theory that exchange rates are related to differences in the level of prices between countries.

Bretton Woods system – the global system of fixed exchange rates that functioned between 1946 and 1971.

contagion – the tendency of investors to withdraw portfolio capital from an entire region in response to perceived economic difficulties in a single country or a subset of countries.

crawling peg – an exchange rate regime where the nominal exchange rate is changed at regular intervals to stabilize the real exchange rate.

current account – an accounting of international transactions that includes goods, services, investment income, and unilateral transfers.

exchange rate regime – the system a country uses to manage the exchange rate and the foreign exchange market.

financial account – a record of the difference between the holding of foreign assets by domestic residents and domestic assets by foreign residents.

intervention – the buying and selling of foreign exchange in order to maintain a fixed exchange rate.

law of one price – the proposition that identical goods sold in competitive markets should cost the same everywhere when prices are expressed in terms of the same currency.

nominal exchange rate – the exchange rate observed in the market.

official reserve assets – government holdings of gold or foreign exchange used to acquire foreign assets.

real exchange rate – the nominal exchange rate adjusted for changes in both domestic and foreign prices.

relative purchasing power parity – the theory that a percentage change in the exchange rate is equal to the difference in the percentage change in price levels.

remittances – flows of money back to the home country from workers that are employed in another country.

unilateral transfers – grants or gifts extended to or received from other countries.

Questions for review and discussion

1 The balance on trade can give one a misleading impression of inflows and outflows into the countries of Latin America. Explain how this can happen.

2 Show what would happen to the exchange rate if there was an increase (decrease) in the demand or supply of foreign exchange.

3 If the exchange rate is fixed, then a commodity exporter would need to accumulate foreign exchange when commodity prices are high. Show why this is true.

4 Explain how exchange controls can be used to maintain a fixed exchange rate.

5 Show how capital flight could lead to a rapid depreciation of the exchange rate.

6 Describe the term contagion. How does it apply to Latin America?

7 Suppose that a RCILA adopted limits on the inflows and outflows of portfolio-capital. What might be the effect on the exchange rate? Why would a capital-scarce country in Latin America decide to do this?

8 Using the formula for relative purchasing power parity, show how high inflation in Latin America could lead to depreciation of currencies in the region.

9 Describe how a fixed nominal exchange rate could be associated with the appreciation of the real exchange rate. Why would this distinction matter for Latin America?

10 What are the four different types of exchange rate regimes? Which is the most common in Latin America? Why?

References and recommended readings

Bahmini-Oskooee, Moshen and Scott W. Hagerty. 2009. "The Effects of Exchange-Rate Volatility on Commodity Trade between the United States and Mexico." *Southern Economic Journal* 75(April): 1019–44.

Blanco-Gonzalez, Lorenzo and Thomas M. Fullerton. 2006. "Borderplex Menu Evidence for the Law of One Price." *Economics Letters* 90(January): 28–33.

Calvo, Guillermo A. and Carmen M. Reinert. 2002. "Fear of Floating." *Quarterly Journal of Economics* 117(2): 379–408.

Chanda, Areendam. 2005. "The Influence of Capital Controls on Long-Run Growth." *Journal of Development Economics* 77 (August): 441–66.

de Gregorio, Jose and Andrea Tokman. 2004. *Overcoming Fear of Floating: Exchange Rate Policies in Chile.* Central Bank of Chile Working Paper No. 302. Santiago: Central Bank of Chile.

de Gregorio, Jose and Rodrigo O. Valdes. 2001. "Crisis Transmission: Evidence from the Debt, Tequila, and Asian Flu Crisis." *The World Bank Economic Review* 15(2): 289–314.

Edwards, Sebastian. 1989. "Exchange Controls, Devaluations, and Real Exchange Rates: The Latin American Experience." *Economic Development and Cultural Change* 37(April): 457–94.

Edwards, Sebastian. 1998. "Capital Flows, Real Exchange Rates, and Capital Controls: Some Latin American Experiences." *NBER Working Paper No. 6800,* Cambridge, MA: National Bureau of Economic Research.

Edwards, Sebastian and Roberto Rigobon. 2009. "Capital Controls on Inflows, Exchange Rate Volatility and External Vulnerability." *Journal of International Economics* 78(July): 256–67.

Forbes, Kristin J. 2007. "One cost of the Chilean Capital Controls: Increased Financial Constraints for Smaller Traded Firms." *Journal of International Economics* 71(2): 294–323.

Frenkel, Roberto and Martin Rapetti. 2010. *A Concise History of Exchange Rate Regimes in Latin America.* Washington, DC: Center for Economic Policy and Research.

Fuentes, Daniel Diaz. 1998. "Latin America during the Interwar Period: The Rise and Fall of the Gold Standard in Argentina, Brazil, and Mexico," in John H. Coatsworth and Alan M. Taylor (eds), *Latin America and the World Economy Since 1800.* Cambridge, MA: Harvard University Press.

Fullerton, Thomas M. and Roberto Coronado. 2001. "Restaurant Prices and the Mexican Peso." *Southern Economic Journal* 68(July): 145–155.

Fullerton, Thomas M. and David Torres. 2005. "Milkshake Prices, International Reserves, and the Mexican Peso." 2005. *Frontera Norte* 17(Enero-Junio): 53–76.

International Monetary Fund. 2006. *De Facto Classification of Exchange Rate Regimes and Monetary Policy Framework.* Washington, DC: International Monetary Fund.

International Monetary Fund. 2007. *Annual Report on Exchange Arrangements and Exchange Restrictions 2007.* Washington, DC: International Monetary Fund.

Kamil, Herman and Benedict J. Clements. 2009. "Are Capital Controls Effective in the 21st Century? The Recent Experience of Colombia." *International Monetary*

Fund Working Paper 9/30/2009. Washington, DC: International Monetary Fund.

Quispe-Agnoli, Myriam. 2001. *Dollarization: Will the Quick Fix Pay Off in the Long Run?* Atlanta: Federal Reserve Board of Atlanta.

The Economist. 2009. "Economic and Financial Indicators," December 10.

9 Financing current account deficits

Countries don't go bust.

Walter Wriston

Yes, but their bankers do.

IMF Official

Introduction

In the previous chapter an important concept was introduced. This involves the relationship between the current account and the financial account. Over a period of time such as a year, these two accounts should be equal in magnitude and opposite in sign. Another way of putting this is that the total amount of inflows into a country should match the total amount of outflows. If a country has a current account deficit, it should have a financial account surplus. The reverse is true: a current account surplus should be matched by a financial account deficit. In the modern history of Latin America the former has been much more common than the latter. Until recently, ISI combined with overvalued exchange rates tended to create a high demand for imports coupled with difficulties in exporting goods other than commodities. This has obvious implications for the financial account. The current account deficits in the region created a relentless need for inflows into the financial account. The purpose of this chapter is to illustrate how countries at the level of economic development of Latin America usually accomplish this.

As we will see, a financial account surplus can be accomplished in a number of ways. In the previous chapter, we showed how a country could deal with current account deficits using either previously accumulated reserves or less prudently rely on a complex system of exchange controls. There are other mechanisms available. Middle-income countries frequently can manage financial account surpluses with flows of capital from capital-abundant countries. These flows can take a variety of forms. In the first several sections of the chapter, we will cover these flows in the context of Latin America. In turn, these are FDI, portfolio capital, ODA, remittances, and government borrowing from foreign financial institutions. The latter has been a source of continual problems in the region. This process has been crucial for Latin America and problems with inflows into the financial account have the capacity to create serious problems for the economic stability of a country.

Debt vs. equity

When discussing borrowing, a critical distinction must be made between debt and equity. Debt is the situation where the borrower must repay all or part of the loan plus interest at certain points in time. In this case, the ability to pay off the loan over time is critical. In the international capital markets debt occurs in one of three forms. First, firms and/or governments in Latin America could issue bonds to raise capital. Usually, selling a bond involves a promise to make periodic interest payments to the bondholder with payment of the value of the bond due at the date of maturity. Financing debt by issuing bonds in Latin America has historically been done through government borrowing as most private sector firms were not large enough to issue bonds in the global marketplace.[1] Second, governments may be able to borrow money from commercial banks in the developed countries. This form of lending is referred to as *sovereign* lending. Loans by banks to governments go back hundreds of years. As indicated in the quotations at the start of the chapter, sovereign lending may not always work out well for the lender. As indicated earlier in the book, this has been the case in a number of instances in Latin America. Finally, governments may borrow money for projects or to finance current account deficits from governments or multilateral institutions such as the World Bank or the IMF.

Capital may also flow into a country in the form of equity financing. Equity is a situation where the lender is also an owner in the company or project being financed. A common form of equity finance is FDI. The company providing all or part of the capital is to one extent or another involved in ownership and/or control of the project. A typical example would be a MNC building a production plant in Latin America. Another example would be a company purchasing all or part of an existing company in the region.[2] A second form of equity lending is the movement of portfolio capital between countries. The foreign investor owns a part of the domestic company through stock ownership but usually does not completely control the foreign firm. Equity finance is different from debt in one important respect. Debt payments have to be made no matter what the condition of the borrower is at the time the debt payment is due. Payments to the owners of equity are much more tied to current economic conditions. Owners of equity normally do not have a right to fixed payments in the form of a stream of income. Rather, they have a claim on all or part of the firm's assets. Notice that in the case of equity, property rights and the rule of law are crucial. Foreign investors need to feel that in the case of a dispute, their partial ownership of a firm will be treated impartially under the country's laws. To the extent that these systems are weak in the region, the flow of portfolio capital will be diminished.[3]

The debt versus equity distinction has been critical for Latin America. Historically, capital flowing into the region has been in the form of debt. Optimism about the future of the region has led to periodic bursts of loans to governments in the region. However, as seen above the timing of the repayment of debt is fixed. If economic conditions turn out to be less than what was expected, then governments in the region could find themselves in an uncomfortable position. If the debt cannot be repaid in full, the result could be and has been a default. Breaking this pattern of high debt and potential defaults has been a critical issue. As we move through the various means of financing current account deficits in the region, keeping the debt vs. equity distinction in mind is important.

FDI

As we saw in Chapter 2, flows of FDI into Latin America have been increasing over the last several decades. Table 2.9 showed that FDI as a percentage of GDP in the region was just 0.7 percent in 1990. For a region composed of middle-income countries, this is an exceptionally low number. By 2007, things had improved considerably. FDI as a percentage of GDP had risen to 2.9 percent. Figure 9.1 puts these flows into a longer historical framework. Beginning in 1977, flows of FDI into the region were extremely small and accounted for around 1 percent of GDP. With a small amount of variation, these numbers were typical for the late 1970s through the early 1990s. They are also not surprising. Given the economic turmoil associated with the second oil shock, low FDI in the late 1970s and early 1980s is not surprising. The low amount of FDI in the 1980s and early 1990s is not surprising as well. The poor economic performance of the region during the Lost Decade would not be consistent with large inflows of FDI. Further, the Lost Decade also coincided with major political changes in Latin America. The authoritarian governments of the past were being transformed into new democracies. While this transition certainly was positive in the long run, such transitions may make foreign firms reluctant to invest in the short run until the political situation becomes more certain.

With stronger economic performance and increased confidence in the political situation, the 1990s saw a return of foreign investors to the region. While growth in Latin America may not be as high as growth in some other regions, the data given in Table 1.1 cannot be ignored. Over 500 million consumers with rising GDP per capita is simply too big a market for MNCs to ignore for an extended period of time. By the late 1990s, FDI had risen to over $80 billion. At the peak, FDI accounted for over 4 percent of GDP in the region. These are numbers much more consistent with healthy middle-income countries. The abrupt drop in FDI in the late

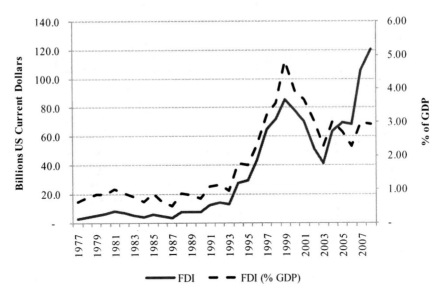

Source: World Bank (2010).

Figure 9.1 Flows of FDI into Latin America

1990s had less to do with Latin America and more to do with the state of the world economy. Financial turmoil in Asia and elsewhere followed by political violence in other parts of the world drastically reduced FDI on a global basis. Fear, uncertainty, and doubt are normally negatively correlated with FDI. Unlike many episodes in the past, the decline in FDI in the region did not originate there. This decline was followed by a rapid recovery of FDI in the region. In 2007, total FDI reached $120 billion. Now think of what has been accomplished in less than 20 years. Total FDI has risen by $100 billion in *just over a decade and a half* since the early 1990s. Since most of these investments are long run in nature, the numbers represent a very large positive bet on the future of the region. Notice also that the trend in the ratio of FDI to GDP is not nearly as positive. This is because the rate of increase in the denominator (GDP) is rising faster than was true in the recent past. Per our discussion of growth in Chapter 2, rising FDI tends to be positively correlated with increases in the rate of growth of real GDP.

These inflows of FDI also make financing current account deficits much easier. In a well-managed middle-income country, current account deficits may be normal. Such countries may be exporting inexpensive, labor-intensive goods in line with their comparative advantage. At that stage of development, imports of expensive capital goods may be essential to develop both industry and infrastructure. On the other hand, such a country should be attracting a substantial amount of FDI. Middle-income countries normally are still relatively capital scarce and the rate of return to capital should be high.

If a middle-income country is well-managed, capital should be flowing into the country from high-income countries in search of a better rate of return. The result is that if a country in Latin America has a current account deficit of 3 percent of GDP and this is matched by a similar amount of FDI, then the current account deficit should not be viewed as a problem. This allows us to further analyze Figure 9.1. In the 1970s and 1980s, something was clearly "wrong" with Latin America. For a region full of middle-income countries there was little or no FDI. Foreign investors simply are not going to invest large sums of money in an uncertain economic environment combined with an uncertain political situation. Once growth and political stability had returned to the region, foreign investors quickly responded to that change. At this point, all of the advantages of this increase in FDI are not obvious. What is obvious at this point is the positive impact on the financial account coupled with the positive effects on growth shown in Chapter 2.

Portfolio capital

As was shown in the previous chapter, the other part of the financial account is flows of portfolio capital. This represents the flow of money to purchase financial assets such as stocks and bonds. Figure 9.2 shows these flows into Latin America from 1996 to 2008. In the mid-1990s, portfolio capital flows into Latin America amounted to $50 billion per year and accounted for over 2.5 percent of GDP. The problem is that these flows are inherently more volatile. International investors in financial markets are attempting to maximize returns over a shorter period of time than is true for FDI. As returns in various countries and regions change, flows of portfolio capital change as well. Turmoil in the world financial markets in the late 1990s and early in this decade reduced portfolio capital flows into Latin America and other emerging markets. Notice that for several years, there were small portfolio capital outflows from the region. A strong recovery in these flows was followed by a collapse caused by the global financial crisis of 2008.

The data for Latin America in Figure 9.2 is not atypical. Portfolio capital can move from one country or region to another with startling speed. In part this reflects the need for investors to find the highest rate of return. Not infrequently, high returns will be found in the middle-income countries that are capital scarce. Unfortunately, high returns tend to be correlated with higher risk. As perceptions of potential returns and risk change, the flows of portfolio capital will change. As the economic environment in Latin America has improved, flows of portfolio capital are positive, but only in the long run. As shown below, in the short run capital outflows are possible. Portfolio capital flows are essential for the economic development of a country and especially for the development of modern financial markets. However, both large inflows and outflows can be destabilizing in terms of the exchange rate and possibly the economy as a whole. Controls on these flows have the benefit of insuring against such instability but at a cost of reducing the

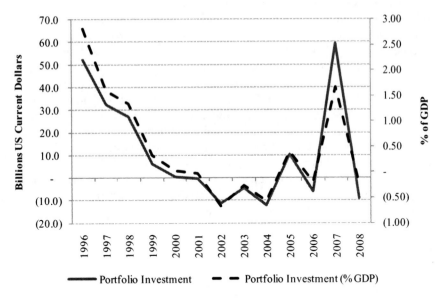

Source: World Bank (2010).

Figure 9.2 Flows of portfolio capital into Latin America

inflows in the long run. Uncontrolled flows optimize the inflows in the long run but have the potential to produce exchange rate shocks. The example given for Chile in the previous chapter is instructive. The regulation, or lack thereof, of flows of portfolio capital is an economic problem for which there is no clear-cut optimal policy.

Official development assistance

Capital may also flow into a region in the form of official development assistance (ODA). The primary purpose of these flows is to assist in the long-run economic development of the country. In many cases, the exact purpose is the development of the sort of infrastructure that is essential for economic development. A well-known example of this was the partial funding for Itaipu Dam in Brazil provided by the World Bank. ODA flows take on two general forms. First, the money can move directly from government to government. This transfer can happen in two ways. First, the transfer may be what is known as a *grant*. The money is essentially a gift from the donor country to be used for economic development or national defense. The second type of transfer is in the form of a *loan*. Loans may be used for either economic development or for supporting current account deficits. On occasion, loans end up being converted into grants. A problem with this sort of ODA is that the aid frequently is "tied" to the donor country. The donor may specify that the recipient country must use the money for a particular project. Further, there may be conditions that the money must be spent on goods and/or services produced in the donor country. The donor country has provided ODA but the transfer of the money is not quite as generous as it appears. In some cases, the developing country may end up purchasing goods and/or services that are not completely appropriate due to the restriction on how the money must be spent. In practice, for Latin America, most of this ODA was a transfer of funds from the US to the region. In most cases, these transfers may have more to do with general foreign policy objectives than economic development. Capital flowing in from multilateral institutions, such as the World Bank, are more straightforward. Loan applications are made for specific projects and capital flows in as the project is developed. Less recognized is the concomitant outflow. The money eventually has to be repaid. In this regard, the predominantly middle-income countries of the region have a respectable repayment record. However, this middle-income status has some disadvantages. Many of the multilateral institutions have focused loans and grants to low-income countries. This sort of ODA is not available to many of the countries of the region.

The data on ODA for Latin America is given in Figure 9.3 below. From the mid-1960s to the late 1970s, ODA was never more than $1 billion. During the 1980s and 1990s, ODA increased and now tends to fluctuate between $3 and $5 billion per year. As a percentage of GDP of the region, ODA has never been higher than 0.80 percent of GDP. After falling as a percentage of GDP, it rose briefly during the Lost Decade. Understandably, the amount of ODA increased during that period in response to the economic hardship

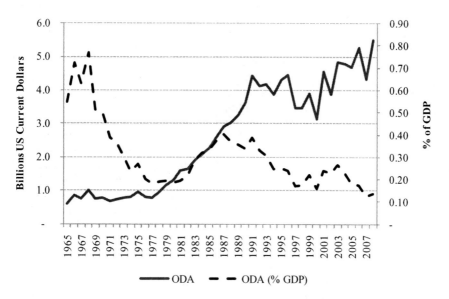

Source: World Bank (2010).

Figure 9.3 Flows of ODA into Latin America

being experienced in the region, particularly for the poor. This combination of rising ODA and stagnant GDP resulted in a temporary increase in the ODA to GDP ratio. Over the past decade, ODA received by Latin America has been relatively stable and GDP has been increasing. The result is that ODA now represents only 0.10 percent of GDP in the region. The data indicates two things about ODA in Latin America. In the first place, the flow of ODA has never been a critical factor in terms of the balance of payments in the region. Dependence on ODA as a means of supporting a deficit on goods and services generally is not sound economic policy. Second, ODA has never been a major factor in the long-run economic development of the region. The sums have simply been too small to be a critical part of the development process. At times such aid has been crucial for particular countries in the process of recovering from the frequent natural disasters outlined in Chapter 3 and for financing certain large infrastructure projects. As is shown in the data, ODA was helpful to the region in weathering the Lost Decade. However, overall ODA in Latin America has not been crucial. A far more important source of inflows is covered in the next section.

9.1   The Inter-American Development Bank

One of the ODA success stories of the region is the Inter-American Development Bank (IDB). The IDB was set up in 1959 with the aim of providing loans for economic development in Latin America and the Caribbean. The institution is headquartered in Washington, DC. It currently has 48 member countries. Of this group, 22 of the countries are nonborrowing members that have contributed capital and the remaining countries are eligible to borrow. Fifteen countries in Western Europe along with Israel and Japan have contributed capital to the institution. The IDB has a unique organization. Unlike the World Bank the developing country members control most of the decision making within the organization. Voting power is determined by its subscription to the bank's capital. This gives the countries of Latin America and the Caribbean over 50 percent of the voting power and the US controls 30 percent. Initially, this arrangement was considered risky. In effect, the borrowers control the IDB. However, the IDB has preferred creditor status which means that borrowers repay the institution before paying other creditors such as commercial banks. In this case, informal peer pressure has worked exceedingly well. In its history, only one country has ever defaulted on a loan from the IDB. This is essential as the bulk of the funds for loans are raised by selling bonds in international markets. These bonds carry a sufficiently high rating to ensure that funds can be obtained at very favorable rates. In turn, this allows for borrowers to obtain loans at rates that might not otherwise be possible.

The lending activities of the IDB are a guide to prudent practices in lending. Potential areas for loans are often identified by the institution in conjunction with governments in the region. Loan applications are reviewed for feasibility and approved projects are monitored with the disbursement of funds dependent on the execution of the project. In addition to making specific project loans,

loans are also made for sectoral adjustment and structural adjustment of the economy. Loans are evaluated for impacts on the environment and for their potential social impact. Finally, the IDB also provides funding for private sector projects in the region. The amounts involved are not inconsequential. Since its inception, The IDB has made over $85 billion in loans. It currently is able to loan approximately $10 billion per year. For a variety of reasons, ODA does not have the best of reputations. However, criticism of the activities of the IDB are few.

Remittances

A major source of inflows of money into Latin America in the twenty-first century is remittances. Remittances are flows of money back to the home country from workers that are employed in another country.[4] Remittances are hardly a new phenomenon especially in the case of Latin America. Money has been flowing from the Latin American colonies back to Portugal and Spain for hundreds of years. In more recent times, remittances from Mexico and the rest of Latin America have been increasing. What's new about remittances is the rapid increase in their absolute size. A global perspective might be useful at this point. In 1990, remittances in the world economy were approximately $30 billion. By 2005, they had ballooned to $200 billion. For Latin America the figures are no less startling. In 1980, they were less than $2 billion. By 2005, they were approximately $50 billion. From 2000 to 2005, the rate of growth of remittances was close to 20 percent. In relation to GDP, remittances have grown from 0.3 percent of GDP to 2.2 percent. For some of the lower-income countries of Central America, remittances are between 10 and 20 percent of GDP. Flows of remittances to the region are now on a par with total FDI and far larger than ODA.[5] Despite the expected decline in remittances attributable to the recent global economic disturbances, they will remain an important economic factor in the region.

The sheer size of remittances now makes them important in terms of the balance of payments. Since they are accounted for under unilateral transfers, they work to offset outflows in other parts of the current account. By definition, their contribution to this balance affects the financial account. To the extent that they reduce current account deficits, they reduce the size of the financial account surplus. A logical extension of this is that remittances can lead to an appreciation of the domestic currency. An extension of this is that remittances lead to greater use of financial institutions and fosters growth in that sector. Overall, there is limited evidence that remittances enhance economic growth.[6] However, the growth of remittances has been so fast that research on the subject is still relatively new. Remittances are having obvious impacts on the region, but the exact extent of these impacts is still under study. However, their effect on the balance of payments is clear.

Debt

The dismantling of the Bretton Woods system of fixed exchange rates had profound effects on Latin America. While the US abandoned fixed exchange rates, there were several attempts in the early 1970s to resurrect the system. Even outside of Latin America, there was widespread reluctance to move to a global system of floating exchange rates. The first oil shock of 1973 ended any thoughts of returning to fixed exchange rates. For countries that were major oil importers, the demand for foreign exchange increased along with the price of oil. In this situation, countries could either devalue their currencies or borrow a sufficient amount of foreign exchange to continue to finance current account deficits. This was precisely the choice faced by most of the countries of Latin America. Given the structure of the economies of the region, major depreciations of the exchange rate would have been devastating. It has already been mentioned that such an event can create a painful mix of inflation, low growth, and high unemployment. Major depreciations also would make it much more difficult to sustain ISI industries if necessary imports suddenly became more expensive. The decisions made by the governments of the region were not uniform. However, the region as a whole was slow to adopt floating exchange rates. Many countries continued on a system of fixed exchange rates. Others pursued more complicated systems of depreciating their currencies more slowly. While the specific details differ by country the result was invariably the same. The current account deficit could not be covered with inflows of ODA, FDI, and portfolio capital. For most countries, accumulated reserves had long since vanished. By the mid-1970s, this meant borrowing from international capital markets. For better or worse the funds were available. The flow of money into the OPEC countries found its way into international financial institutions such as large commercial banks. With the world economy in recession, the need for borrowing for business investment was reduced. In turn, these institutions became willing to loan large amounts of money to developing countries to finance current account deficits. The result was that many of these recycled "petrodollars" were loaned to countries in Latin America. The first surge of borrowing in the early to mid-1970s was moderate in the sense that the countries of the region overall were able to manage the burden of debt. Unfortunately, the region's luck did not hold. The second oil shock produced another unprecedented surge of borrowing. Initially, the region was able to manage this debt and some of the worst effects of this event. By the early 1980s, the burden of debt had become unsustainable. At this point, increasing numbers of countries in the region were forced into major depreciations of their exchange rates as capital inflows decreased dramatically.

The data on debt in Latin America is shown in Figure 9.4 below. From 1970 to the late 1980s the long-term debt of the region increased from a small amount to nearly $400 billion. As a percentage of GDP the statistics are even more striking. Long-term debt rose from only 15 percent of GDP

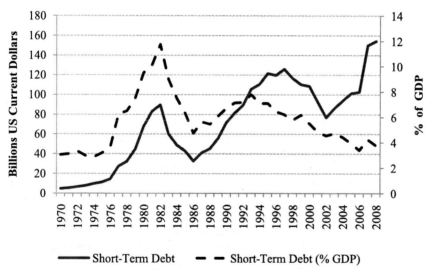

Source: World Bank (2010).

Figure 9.4 Latin American debt

to nearly 50 percent. The difference with the last 20 years is instructive. Long-term debt has continued to rise to $700 billion. However, the ratio of debt to GDP has fallen back to under 20 percent. A similar story emerges from the data on short-term debt. For the region, it rose from a negligible amount in the early 1970s to over $80 billion in the early 1980s. As financial conditions became more difficult, short-term debt was cut to less than half that amount by the late 1980s. With an interruption early in this decade, short term debt has climbed to $150 billion in 2008. As a percentage of GDP, short-term debt peaked at 12 percent of GDP in the early 1980s. Like long-term debt, the ratio is now back to where it began in the 1970s at 3 to 4 percent of GDP. Putting long-term and short-term debt together gives an overall picture of debt in Latin America. At the start of the 1970s, total debt was comfortably less than 20 percent of GDP. At the peak in the 1980s, debt was over 50 percent of GDP. In approximately a decade, the region had taken on debt equivalent to 30 percent of GDP.

As the data above indicates, over the 1970s and early 1980s the external debt of Latin America increased substantially. This is not necessarily a bad thing. If the borrowed money by the governments of the region had been invested in productive assets that enhance economic growth then a rising level of debt could be a positive thing. On the other hand, if the debt is being used to intervene in the foreign exchange market to support an overvalued exchange rate, that is not quite so positive. In this case a rising level of debt is buying faster economic growth in the short run at the risk of a default on the debt and/or lower economic growth in the future caused by a major depreciation. Like all debt, money owed by citizens, firms, or the government has to be repaid. In this case, there is one important difference. For most countries, foreign debt cannot be repaid in domestic currency. Repayment of foreign debt must be made in an acceptable foreign currency. When debt payments come due, foreign exchange must be available. In order to make timely payments on foreign debt, two factors become critical.

As was covered in the previous chapter, countries have official reserve assets. These represent the stock of foreign exchange a country possesses at a point in time. In some time periods, inflows of foreign exchange will exceed outflows. In this circumstance, the stock of official reserve assets will rise. At other times, outflows may exceed inflows and the stock will fall. Official reserve assets are important in that they represent a cushion of foreign exchange. If inflows of foreign exchange temporarily decrease or outflows increase, the country can still pay for imports or debt repayments if the level of official reserve assets is sufficiently high. However, if this level is extremely low then a country may face the uncomfortable choice of imports versus debt repayments. There may not be enough foreign exchange for both.

The other critical factor is the debt service/export ratio. This ratio expresses the amount of debt repayment a country must make in relation to its earnings from exports. Since foreign debt must be paid in foreign exchange, the ability to make these payments is critical. The lower this ratio is, the easier it will be for a country to make debt repayments. However, if this ratio is high, the country may experience difficulties in repaying foreign debt. Putting these concepts together, one can get a picture of a country that can afford to take on more debt. A country with a high level of international reserves coupled with a low debt/export ratio should be able to comfortably repay foreign borrowing. On the other hand, a country with a low level of reserves and a high debt/export ratio may have difficulty handling more borrowing. Neither factor is a perfect predictor of a country's ability to repay debt. However, the level of both factors influences the probability that a country will be able to handle different levels of foreign borrowing.

The data in Figure 9.5 clearly shows the strain the region was under in servicing its debts. Debt service payments peaked in the early 1980s at

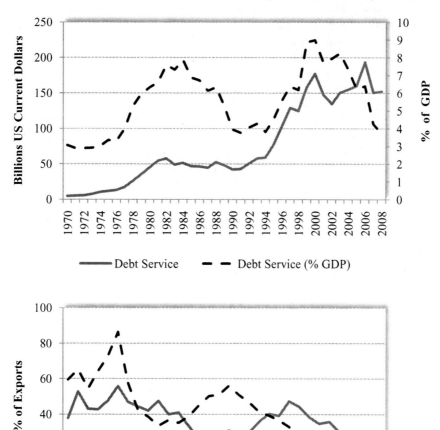

Source: World Bank (2010).

Figure 9.5 Debt service in Latin America

80 percent of exports. Aside from servicing debt the region had little money left for necessary imports. At the same peak, debt service payments amounted to 8 percent of GDP. In effect, the region was transferring nearly 10 percent of GDP to creditors.

These concepts should give one a clearer picture of the situation of Latin America in the 1970s. The first oil shock increased the demand for foreign exchange in the region. This increase occurred so quickly that any stocks of official reserve assets soon went to very low levels. Without major currency depreciations, a substantial amount of debt was acquired to support exchange rates that were not being adjusted fast enough. The result was a large increase in the numerator of the debt/export ratio. On the other hand, a combination of slow growth in the world economy, overvalued exchange rates, and reliance on commodity exports meant that the rate of growth of exports was slow. The denominator of the debt/export ratio could not keep up with increases in the numerator. A steadily rising debt/export ratio coupled with low levels of official reserve assets makes further borrowing difficult. If these numbers become increasingly problematic, then both domestic and foreign investors eventually may conclude that a major depreciation of the exchange rate is inevitable. The result may be capital flight that simply hastens the inevitable depreciation. In the 1970s and early 1980s, such situations became depressingly common in the region. For the countries affected by this process, the only recourse usually was borrowing from the lender of last resort, the IMF.

The role of the IMF

In the previous chapter, we described the role of the IMF under the Bretton Woods system of fixed exchange rates. In this section, we will go into more detail about the role of the IMF in that system and how this has evolved over time. Originally, the IMF was set up to assist countries that had temporary current account deficits and lacked a sufficient quantity of official reserve assets to support a fixed exchange rate. A graph of this situation is shown in Figure 9.6. The supply and demand for foreign exchange are at an equilibrium that is higher than the fixed exchange rate. In this circumstance, the quantity demanded of foreign exchange (Q_m) is higher than the quantity supplied (Q_x). If the country cannot borrow the requisite amount of foreign exchange from other lenders, then the country could borrow it from the IMF. This would allow the country to shift the supply of foreign exchange to the right and maintain the official exchange rate. When the IMF was created in the 1940s each member country was required to contribute a quota determined by the relative size of the country in the world economy. The total contributed created a pool of official reserve assets that could be loaned to countries with current account deficits. Initially, countries could

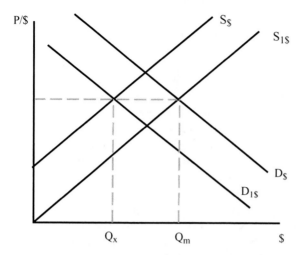

Figure 9.6 The effects of IMF austerity programs

borrow up to 125 percent of their quota. The total was divided into five tranches. Borrowing in the first tranche carried no conditions. Borrowing in the higher tranches required that the country sign an agreement with the IMF to take policy steps that would correct the current account deficit. The purpose of this *conditionality* was to correct the imbalance by reducing the demand for foreign exchange. Recall from the previous chapter that the demand for foreign exchange was influenced by domestic income and relative prices. To reduce the demand for foreign exchange, the IMF would request changes in domestic policy that decreased the rate of growth of GDP and reduced inflation. A commonly required change was a tightening of fiscal policy. The IMF would request some combination of lower government spending and higher taxes to reduce GDP and reduce the demand for foreign exchange. A tightening of monetary policy in the form of a reduction in the rate of growth of the money supply and higher interest rates also was usually a part of conditionality. Collectively, these IMF mandated conditions were usually referred to as an *austerity program*. In one sense, the programs would normally work. Declines in GDP and inflation would push the demand for foreign exchange to the left in Figure 9.6. External balance would be restored. However, the price of success frequently was a domestic recession purposefully engineered by the government but designed by a foreign entity. In a high-income country this might be considered a distasteful, but temporary, loss of sovereignty necessary to maintain a fixed exchange rate in a world where this was the norm.[7] The effects on developing countries such as those in Latin America were much more serious.

In a low- or middle-income country without social safety nets an austerity program could cause significant economic hardship. In most of the developing parts of the world, the IMF was not a popular institution. This was especially true in Latin America. During the 1960s and early 1970s, there was very little private capital flowing into the region. Countries in the region became regular "customers" of the IMF, the World Bank, and the IDB. The result was that for the average resident of the region the phrases IMF and austerity program were all too well understood. Borrowing from the IMF became associated with potential economic hardship. Austerity programs engendered by borrowing in the higher tranches of a country's quota meant that the demand for foreign exchange would have to be reduced by a large amount. Such borrowing also meant even more stringent austerity programs.

The slow motion collapse of the fixed exchange rate system in the 1970s created an odd situation for the IMF. The system it was supposed to support was disappearing. At about the same time as the attempts to reconstruct the global system of fixed exchange rates was becoming futile, oil prices soared. Countries in Latin America and elsewhere increased their borrowing from the IMF. Conveniently, the IMF created a number of new "facilities" that allowed countries to borrow far more than 125 percent of their quota.[8] However, the countries of the region were well aware of the costs of borrowing from the IMF. At the same time, capital became available from large international banks, particularly in the US. The acquisition of debt from this source allowed the region to maintain fixed exchange rates or depreciate at a slower rate. Borrowing from the IMF continued during the decade but at a slower pace because of the ability to borrow elsewhere. The second oil shock in 1979 dramatically increased the level of borrowing to finance the associated increase in current account deficits. By the early 1980s, it was becoming clear that borrowing on this scale was not sustainable. Mexico's default in 1982 began a chain reaction in the region as lending from financial institutions was withdrawn. At this point, the only source of finance was the IMF. The second oil shock was accompanied by slow growth in the world economy, low commodity prices, rising payments on previously accumulated debts, and IMF austerity programs. The predictable result was little or no growth in many of the countries of the region.

While the IMF was created to finance temporary current account deficits in a fixed exchange rate system, it increasingly was lending large amounts of money to countries in the region that were already heavily indebted. It was also attempting to get other creditors to reschedule the existing debt to make the situation more manageable for the countries involved. By the late 1980s, it was clear the institution could not continually support current account deficits on this scale. At this time, it was also clear that the region could not support the transfer of real economic resources necessary to fully pay off all accumulated debts. A series of negotiations among the most indebted countries of the region, the creditors, the IMF, and the US government resulted in a reduction of the total amount of debt to a level consistent with a resumption of economic growth.[9] By the late 1990s, many of the countries had been able to repay the reduced level of debt. The role of the IMF in this period is controversial. Its lending to countries of the region was a necessary cushion but it came at the price of painful austerity programs. Its participation in the negotiations with commercial banks and the US government led to charges that it was overly concerned about the financial health of private sector banks in high-income countries. Perhaps this is a reflection of the more general problem of the role of the IMF in a world of floating exchange rates.

By the late 1980s, it was becoming increasingly clear that many of the countries of the region would not be able to repay the accumulated debt in total. While the IMF had provided needed foreign exchange in the early and mid-1980s, growth in the region had stagnated. With a large burden of accumulated debt and little growth, it was becoming increasingly unlikely that the total amount of debt could be repaid. Servicing this debt was still taking nearly half of export earnings. More importantly, servicing debt was requiring 5 to 6 percent of GDP in a region of middle-income countries. This situation could not continue. Further IMF lending was not economically feasible. There had been little growth in the region for ten years and GDP per capita was falling. In the end, a solution was brokered by the US government. The debt of most of the countries of the region was replaced by 30-year bonds. These new bonds had an interesting characteristic. They had a face value that was 65 percent of the value of the original bonds. In the end there were no winners. The governments of the region borrowed far too much in the late 1970s and early 1980s. The commercial banks providing the loans were insufficiently attentive to the ability of the borrowers to repay their debts. Given the size of the debt, whether or not IMF austerity programs would work was questionable. The history of the Lost Decade provides the answer to that question. In Latin America as elsewhere, a mix of imprudent governments and financial institutions is detrimental to the economic health of both the citizens of the borrowing countries and owners of the financial institutions.

Key concepts and terms

debt/export ratio – the ratio of a country's debt payments to its exports.
default – the inability of a country to repay all or part of its foreign debt when it is due.
equity – inflows of foreign exchange in the form of FDI or portfolio capital.

Questions for review and discussion

1   Describe the difference between financing a current account deficit using debt versus equity.
2   Describe the importance of flows of FDI and portfolio capital to Latin America.
3   What is ODA? Why is it important in the context of Latin America?
4   What are the effects of remittances on the economic development of Latin America?
5   Describe the evolution of debt in Latin America since the 1970s.
6   How has the composition of debt changed in Latin America from the 1960s to the present?
7   What contributes to a default on a country's debt? How does this apply to Latin America?
8   Why is the debt/export ratio important? Why did this ratio rise in Latin America in the 1970s and 1980s?
9   Describe the role of the IMF in a global system of fixed exchange rates.
10   What was the role of commercial banks in the debt crisis of the 1980s?

References and recommended readings

Acosta, Pablo, Pablo Fajnzylber, and J. Humberto Lopez. 2008. "How Important Are Remittances in Latin America?" pp. 21–49 in Pablo Fajnzylber and J. Humberto Lopez (eds), *Remittances and Development: Lessons from Latin America*. Washington, DC: World Bank.

Blustein, Paul. 2003. *The Chastening*. New York: Public Affairs Press.

Borensztein, Eduardo, Kevin Cowan, Barry Eichengreen, and Ugo Panizza. 2008. *Bond Markets in Latin America: On the Verge of a Big Bang?* Cambridge, MA: MIT Press.

Edwards, Sebastian. 1998. *Capital Inflows into Latin America: A Stop-Go Story?*. NBER Working Paper No. 6800. Cambridge, MA: National Bureau of Economic Research.

Edwards, Sebastian (ed.). 2007. *Capital Controls and Capital Flows in Emerging Economies*. Chicago: University of Chicago Press.

Fajnzylber, Pablo, J. Luis Guasch, and J. Humberto Lopez (eds). 2009. *Does the Investment Climate Matter? Microeconomic Foundations of Growth in Latin America*. Washington, DC: World Bank.

Fajnzylber, Pablo and J. Humberto Lopez. 2008. "The Development Impact of Remittances in Latin America," pp. 1–19 in Pablo Fajnzylber and J. Humberto Lopez (eds), *Remittances and Development: Lessons from Latin America*. Washington, DC: World Bank.

Meyer, Carrie. 2000. *The Economics and Politics of NGOs in Latin America*. Santa Barbara, CA: Praeger.

Vizcarra, Catalina. 2009. "Guano, Credible Commitments, and Sovereign Debt Repayment in Nineteenth-Century Peru." *Journal of Economic History* 2 (June): 358–87.

World Bank. 2008. *Migration and Remittances Factbook 2008.* Washington, DC: World Bank.

World Bank. 2010. *World Development Indicators*, Washington, DC: World Bank.

10 Macroeconomic policy in Latin America

> ... what shouldn't be done is to ideologize economic policy. What matters is what works and what doesn't. A fiscal deficit is neither of the right nor the left, it's a problem of management.
>
> Leonel Fernandez

Introduction

In several parts of the book, we have alluded to the effects of fiscal and monetary policy on the economies of Latin America. In addition, we have mentioned that some of the chronic economic instability in the region can be linked to inappropriate macroeconomic policies. In this chapter, we begin to explore these problems in more depth. However, one needs to be aware that with respect to macroeconomic policy, it is not possible to take the long historical view that was used in some previous chapters. Macroeconomic data is very incomplete prior to 1945. The result is that our discussion of macroeconomics for the region refers to the post-war world. In this case, this is less of a problem for Latin America. Macroeconomic imbalances developed in the region from the 1950s to 1970s which culminated in serious economic difficulties in the 1980s. These effects linger in the region in the twenty-first century. The result is that a more truncated history of macroeconomics is not as inappropriate as it would be for another subject, such as commodities. Not accidentally, the time period under consideration is the same as was used for ISI. The two issues are not quite inseparable, but they are definitely related to one another.

The key to understanding macroeconomic policy in Latin America starts with a discussion of fiscal policy. In the first part of the chapter, we present the basic data on fiscal policy in the region over the last several decades. The combination of low tax revenues and high government spending resulted in large government budget deficits. The following section explains what these deficits would tend to do to GDP and the price level. Further, these deficits had to be financed. In most cases, this involved the creation of money and an increase in the money supply. As we will show, this process can produce serious macroeconomic consequences. Again, the effects of large changes in the money supply will be explained. The final section of the chapter outlines some of the factors that contributed to large fiscal deficits and large changes in the money supply that came to be typical for the region in the second half of the twentieth century.

Fiscal policy in Latin America

In some of the previous chapters, we indicated that fiscal policy had been a persistently weak aspect of economic management in Latin America. In a well-managed economy, the government budget is essentially balanced when the economy is operating at potential real GDP. Potential real GDP (Y_p) is the amount of final goods and services an economy is producing at full employment.[1] To go further, such an economy may pursue countercyclical fiscal policy. At Y_p, the economy is not in any need of stimulus from the government budget. If the economy is in danger of slipping into a recession, some combination of increased government spending and/or lower taxes may be appropriate. If there is a danger of the economy producing a level of output greater than Y_p, then lower government spending or higher taxes may contribute to economic stability. Another way of putting this is that a balanced government budget is prudent if the economy is at full employment. A government budget deficit is a reasonable response to a recession. Economic growth that is too fast may call for a fiscal policy that intentionally produces a surplus in the government's budget.

The situation described above is an ideal scenario that assumes that fiscal policy in the country is being used in a prudent way to offset the effects of the business cycle in a free-market economy. If you look back to Chapter 1, this was the first item in the list describing the Washington Consensus. Any government should at least make the attempt to align fiscal policy with macroeconomic conditions. To be honest, very few governments in the world are able to accomplish this. Even in OECD countries, democratically elected governments tend to produce perpetual government budget deficits. However, as we will see below, a government budget deficit will not create serious macroeconomic difficulties as long as it is relatively small. What is typical in these countries is a relatively small deficit if the economy is at Y_p and a larger deficit in recessions. Relatively small is an important term in this context. The size of the government budget deficit has to be measured relative to the size of GDP. In practice, this is the sum of government spending on goods and services (G) minus government revenues (T) divided by GDP. In most circumstances a deficit of 1 or 2 percent of GDP would not be a cause for concern.

Until the 1990s, the problem with fiscal policy in Latin America was twofold. First, governments in the region ran perpetual deficits. Government budget surpluses are rare under the best of circumstances. However, governments in well-managed countries understand that a surplus is a desirable policy goal under certain circumstances. As we will show below, in the context of Latin America even a relatively small fiscal deficit may be a problem. A more serious problem in Latin America has been the size of the deficits. If the deficit becomes a large percentage of GDP, then any prospect for macroeconomic stability has been lost. The situation for Latin America is shown in Table 10.1 below. In the 1970s, budget deficits in the region averaged a bit over 2 percent of GDP. For the 1980s, the situation deteriorated and deficits averaged nearly 4 percent of GDP. However, the two columns for 1982 and 1987 are instructive. In 1982, deficits averaged an alarming 7 percent of GDP. By 1987, the deficits were back down to 4 percent of GDP. However, notice that some of the deficits during the decade for particular countries were astonishingly large. For the 1990s, deficits in the region were again below 2 percent. In the last decade, they are approaching 1 percent.

An intriguing question comes out of the data presented above. Why were fiscal deficits so large and persistent in Latin America during the latter part of the twentieth century? While there is no firm answer to that question, there are some factors that contributed to the problem. The first factor has been alluded to before. The raising of tax revenue in the region has been historically problematic. During the colonial period, avoidance of paying taxes to the Spanish government made perfect sense. Much of the revenue would revert to Portugal or Spain as opposed to being spent in the region.

Table 10.1 Fiscal deficits in Latin America (percentage of GDP)

	1970s[1]	1980s[1]	1982[2]	1987[2]	1990s[3]	2000s[3]
Argentina	−3.86	−0.71	−7	−4	−0.81	0.11
Bolivia	−4.20	−3.65	−16	1	−2.76	−3.60
Brazil	−0.64	−14.61	−3	−12	−5.50	−3.89
Chile	0.00	0.00	−1	0	1.46	2.55
Colombia	0.00	0.00	−5	−1	−1.03	−1.83
Costa Rica	−3.89	−1.76	−1	−3	−2.96	−2.11
Ecuador	−1.40	−1.10	−4	−2	−1.72	1.53
El Salvador	−0.88	−11.03	−8	1	−1.98	−1.88
Guatemala	−1.34	−2.96	−5	−1	−0.96	−1.71
Honduras	−1.05	−5.34			−3.03	−3.11
Mexico		−7.92	−15	−14	−0.40	−0.45
Nicaragua	−5.56	−2.32	−20	−17	−1.73	−2.43
Panama	−7.29	−5.02	−11	−4	−0.61	−1.01
Paraguay	0.00	0.00	0	0	−0.65	−0.84
Peru	−3.07	−5.29	−3	−6	−2.97	−0.74
Uruguay	−0.95	−2.07	−9	−1	−3.30	−2.19
Venezuela	−0.44	−1.19	−4	−4	−1.90	0.09
Latin America	−2.16	−3.82	−7	−4	−1.82	−1.27

[1] Computed by authors using IMF GFSM database (1986).
[2] Edwards (1995).
[3] Inter-American Development Bank, Latin America and Caribbean Macro Watch Tool.

Under these circumstances, tax evasion was understandable. One of the legacies of colonial rule was relatively weak government institutions, including the ability to levy taxes. Along with this problem was the concentration of income and assets that was partially a legacy of colonialism and partially the result of post-independence commodity booms. This concentration puts the higher-income groups in a good position to resist direct taxation of either income or assets. Thus, governments in the region traditionally have been in a poor position to raise revenue from the source with the highest ability to pay. Inequality also plays a part on the expenditure side. An unequal distribution of income increases the propensity of government to attempt to redress this problem through public expenditures. This may involve relatively high spending on social programs that are difficult for the government of a middle-income country to afford. While this sort of spending is understandable, in an environment where tax revenue is low, the result may be relatively large fiscal deficits. Financing these deficits may be difficult. This process, and its consequences, are the subject of the next section.

Financing deficits and the money supply

In the previous section it was shown that fiscal deficits historically have been a problem in Latin America. In this section we will first assume that a fiscal deficit has become an intractable problem for a representative country in Latin America (RCILA). Given a deficit, the country now has two options. The preferred option would be to borrow the money to cover the deficit. In developed countries this is a routine transaction. The government would simply sell bonds to the public and use the proceeds of the sale to fund government expenditures. There is a critical assumption in this process. The sale of new government bonds assumes that there are willing buyers.[2] The only remaining question is how many. If the government has an excellent credit rating, then the bonds are perceived as being virtually risk free. In this case the government can raise the necessary funds at a low interest rate. Government debt that is perceived as being somewhat more risky can still be sold, but the interest rate will be higher. On the other end of the spectrum is a government that cannot sell bonds. If a country has a history of defaulting on its debts then understandably there may be no demand for its bonds. Latin America has been unfortunate in this regard. Since independence, defaults on debt by the governments of the region have been commonplace. The result was that through much of the latter part of the twentieth century it was difficult for the governments of the region to finance deficit spending by borrowing.

In the frequent event of a government budget deficit in RCILA, the government was left in the position of financing the deficit via the creation of new money. Our task at this point is to demonstrate why this can cause significant economic problems. To do this, we will need to explain some of the relationships involved in determining the supply of money. First, consider the following relationship.

$$B = Cp + R$$

where B is equal to the monetary base; Cp is cash in the hands of the public; and R is the reserves of the banking system. Cp is practically self-explanatory: it is the coins and paper money held by the public. The reserves of the banking system may need further explanation. If a deposit is made to a bank, the bank is legally obligated to hold a portion of this deposit in reserve (i.e. it cannot loan it out). The total of these reserves for all banks in a country is R.[3] From the monetary base, we can now proceed to the money supply.

$$Ms = B * 1/r$$

or

$$Ms = Cp + D$$

Where Ms is the money supply; r is the percentage of deposits banks must keep in reserve; and D is the total amount of demand deposits in RCILA. To keep things simple, assume that r is equal to 0.10. This would mean that if someone made a 100 peso deposit in a bank in RCILA, the bank would have to keep 10 pesos on deposit. The other 90 pesos could be loaned out. What happens next is interesting. The 90 pesos is new money. Whenever a bank makes a loan, new money is created. In a free banking market with fractional reserve banking, banks create money when they make loans. To see this more clearly, consider the balance sheet of a bank in RCILA.

Assets	Liabilities
R = 10	Deposit = 100
Loans = 90	

Notice what has occurred here. The bank is holding 10 pesos in reserve. It has made a loan of 90 pesos. Both the reserves and the loan are assets. The liability is that the depositor can still spend 100 pesos. The supply of money is now 190 pesos. The process does not stop here. The 90 pesos will eventually end up as a deposit. From here a bank would have to hold 9 pesos and could make a loan of 81 pesos. The 81 pesos is also new money. One could continue to do the calculations from here but fortunately there is a simpler way of accomplishing the same thing. This is the meaning of 1/r or the banking money multiplier. The banking money multiplier is the multiple by which a change in B translates into a change in the money supply. If we assume that r is equal to 0.1, then the money multiplier is 10. This may seem like innocuous arithmetic, but this relationship is crucial. If B changes by 1 peso, then the money supply of RCILA increases by 10 pesos. This is why the monetary base is sometimes referred to as *high powered money*. Any change in B will have a large effect on the money supply.

We are now in a position to examine how a fiscal deficit can affect the money supply. Again assume that the government cannot borrow the necessary funds. If it could, the effect of the deficit on the money supply would be neutral. The government would be borrowing the money instead of another entity (firms or individuals). This might push up interest rates, but there is no effect on the money supply.[4] However, if the government has to print money to cover the deficit, the effect on the money supply can be dramatic. To illustrate this, let's assume some data for RCILA which is shown in Table 10.2.

First, notice that GDP is equal to 1 trillion pesos. Now suppose that government spending is 200 billion pesos or 20 percent of GDP. Next assume that tax revenues are 150 billion pesos or 15 percent of GDP. The resulting fiscal deficit is 50 billion pesos or 5 percent of GDP. In a 1 trillion peso economy, this wouldn't seem to be a problem. If the government has to print the money in order to cover the deficit, then the monetary base increases by 50 billion pesos. The next step is crucial. If B increases by 50 billion, then the money supply increases by *500 billion*. As we will see in the next section, such a dramatic increase in the money supply will have large impacts on the economy of RCILA.

A reasonable question at this point is the role of the central bank. In any economy, the central bank is in charge of managing the supply of money. It does this by having the right to loan money to the government. In a high-income country this would be rare. If the government runs a fiscal deficit, it would normally be covered by borrowing from the financial markets. It would not usually borrow from the central bank as the effects on the monetary base and the money supply would be too dramatic. In most cases, the central bank is under no obligation to loan money to the government. It can if it chooses to but this would normally be imprudent. Institutional arrangements have been set up to insure that the central bank is independent of the government. With this independence, the central bank can manage the supply of money without regard for the finances of the government. Unfortunately, until recently central banks in Latin America were not independent. If the government ran a fiscal deficit, the central bank was obliged to loan the government

Table 10.2 Change in the money supply in RCILA

GDP	B	Ms	Deficit	ΔB	ΔMs
1 trillion	10 billion	100 billion	50 billion	50 billion	500 billion

money. Technically, the books of the central bank balance. It has acquired an asset, a loan to the government. The corresponding liability is the new money created to finance the deficit. This new money increases the monetary base by an identical amount. Eventually, the money supply will increase by a multiple of that amount. Under these circumstances, the central bank is not really managing the money supply. In reality, the supply of money is being determined by whoever is running the government. In a sense, fiscal policy is determining monetary policy. The experience of most countries has been that allowing the government to determine the money supply does not work very well. The nonindependent central banks of Latin America were classic examples of this. In the latter half of the twentieth century, fiscal deficits in the region were the norm. What was also the norm was the central bank loaning the money to the government to cover the deficit. In the next section, the effects of this will become more clear.

The money supply, prices, and GDP

> Inflation is always and everywhere a monetary phenomenon.
>
> Milton Friedman

In the previous section we showed how a relatively small fiscal deficit can lead to an extremely large change in the money supply. In this section, the effects of this change in the money supply will be examined more closely. A change in the money supply is one of the most powerful influences on the state of the economy. Both real GDP and the price level are influenced by changes in the supply of money. In the first part of this section, some basic relationships between the money supply, the price level, and real GDP will be developed. In the second part of this section, we will examine how the money supply affects these variables using a basic macroeconomic model.

The equation of exchange

The simplest way to look at how the money supply affects the economy is by examining the equation of exchange. The equation of exchange is a basic framework for analyzing the interactions among the money supply, the price level, and real GDP. More formally the equation is:

$$M V = P Q$$

where M is the money supply; V is the velocity of money; P is the price level; and Q is real GDP. All of the terms in the equation of exchange should be familiar with the exception of the velocity of money. The velocity of money simply is an expression of the fact that the money supply, if spent only once in a year, would not buy nominal GDP. On average, money is spent more than once in a year. For example, consider the data in Table 10.2.

The nominal GDP of RCILA is 1 trillion pesos and the money supply is 100 billion pesos. The velocity of money in this case is 10. This can be determined by dividing nominal GDP (P Q) by the money supply (M). On average each peso is being spent 10 times during a year. To summarize, the money supply multiplied by the velocity has to be identically equal to the price level multiplied by real GDP.

The relationship given above is an identity. Now let's make some assumptions about the movements of these variables over time. First, let's assume that the velocity of money is constant. In the short run this is not an unrealistic assumption. From one year to the next, the V is not likely to change by a large amount.[5] Second, assume that Q grows by a certain amount every year. In effect, this is the growth rate of potential real GDP. In the case of RCILA, this might amount to 6 percent per year under good circumstances.[6] Now assume that the government desires price stability. The goal is to limit increases in P. In order for this to occur, then changes in M need to be roughly equivalent to changes in Q. In other words, price stability requires that money supply growth would be similar to the rate of growth of potential real GDP.[7] In practice, for the middle-income countries, maintaining this equality is not easy. If there is no local bond market, then the central bank has to use changes in the discount rate or changes in the reserve requirement to influence the monetary base. When the central bank makes a loan to a private sector bank, the monetary base expands. When the loan is paid off, it contracts. By lowering or raising the discount rate, the central bank can increase or decrease the monetary base and the money supply. Likewise, changes in the legal reserve requirement (r) change both the monetary base and the money multiplier. An increase in r reduces the money supply and a decrease in r increases it. Under the best of circumstances, obtaining a growth rate of the money supply that will insure price stability requires very talented people at the central bank. For most middle-income countries this isn't possible. What is possible is keeping inflation at a low enough level to prevent the disruption of normal economic activity. In this context, a rate of inflation of 5 percent or less is sufficient. Given the institutional difficulties of controlling the money supply in a developing country, this is no mean feat. The equation of exchange is a very useful device for thinking about these issues. Keeping inflation at acceptably low levels ultimately means keeping the rate of growth of the money supply at levels consistent with something like price stability.

One should now be able to see more clearly what the data presented in the previous section mean. Suppose that a country is running a fiscal deficit and is unable to borrow to cover the deficit. If the central bank is obliged to loan the government money, the monetary base will expand. This expansion of the monetary base leads to a multiple expansion of the supply of money. A deficit that is even a small percentage of GDP can quickly lead to an enormous increase in the monetary base and the supply of money. This expansion can quickly outstrip the increase in potential real GDP. Once the economy is at full employment, the logic of the equation of exchange becomes inexorable. A large increase in the money supply leads to a large increase in the price level. In effect, fiscal policy becomes monetary policy. The deficits in the region in the 1970s and 1980s turned into large increases in the money supply. This can be seen in Table 10.3.

The data shown in Table 10.3 is consistent with Table 10.2. As fiscal deficits in the region increased, the growth rates of the money supply increased. In the 1960s, money supply growth in the region was under 20 percent. This is high, but not potentially ruinous. By the 1970s, money supply growth had more than doubled as budget deficits became larger. The fiscal deficits of the 1980s shown above set the stage for enormously rapid growth in the money supply. Even ignoring some of the larger numbers in the column, money supply growth in the region was rapid. By the 1990s, the situation had improved dramatically. Money supply growth was still too high, but the rate of growth had been noticeably reduced. In the last decade, the rate of growth of the money supply for the region now looks "normal" for a collection of middle-income countries. A sure sign of progress is that the highest number by far in the column would have looked like a "good" number in the 1980s.

Per the equation of exchange, the changes in the money supply in Latin America translated into changes in inflation. These changes are shown in Table 10.4 below. Again, starting in the 1960s, rates of inflation in Latin America were fairly typical of middle-income countries. The average rate of inflation in the region was less than 10 percent. As fiscal deficits and money

Table 10.3 Changes in the money supply in Latin America (average annual percentage change)

	1960s	1970s	1980s	1990s	2000s
Argentina	27.3	136.2	477.0	143.7	14.1
Bolivia	16.4	26.1	786.0	27.9	12.4
Brazil	54.5	48.7	624.1	739.8	17.1
Chile	43.0	193.0	32.7	20.9	12.2
Colombia	18.2	29.2	28.9	28.1	9.5
Costa Rica	9.2	29.2	29.4	18.0	22.0
Ecuador	10.9	20.9	−3.1	10.8	22.5
El Salvador	8.4	16.1	7.1	14.6	4.5
Guatemala	10.0	17.6	14.6	17.6	18.1
Honduras	11.4	15.7	12.3	27.2	15.6
Mexico	13.4	24.9	61.3	34.5	8.5
Nicaragua	11.0	21.6	1638.2	950.0	11.2
Panama	12.6	19.8	4.4	18.2	9.8
Paraguay	15.9	24.0	26.5	22.9	11.9
Peru	15.6	34.2	331.0	694.2	9.1
Uruguay	44.9	72.8	65.1	46.7	11.7
Venezuela	8.6	22.5	18.5	41.5	38.2
Latin America	19.5	44.3	244.4	168.0	14.6

Source: World Bank (2010).

Table 10.4 Changes in the rate of inflation in Latin America

	1960s	1970s	1980s	1990s	2000s
Argentina	22.4	132.9	565.7	252.9	8.9
Bolivia	5.7	15.9	1383.2	10.4	5.3
Brazil	-	-	354.5	843.3	7.1
Chile	26.6	174.6	21.4	11.8	3.7
Colombia	11.5	19.7	23.5	22.2	6.5
Costa Rica	2.1	9.8	27.1	16.9	11.2
Ecuador	4.4	11.9	34.0	39.0	19.2
El Salvador	0.4	9.4	18.5	10.6	3.8
Guatemala	0.7	8.9	12.1	14.8	7.6
Honduras	2.3	6.6	7.4	19.7	8.5
Mexico	2.5	14.7	69.0	20.4	5.2
Nicaragua	-	-	-	-	8.9
Panama	1.1	6.0	3.2	1.1	2.4
Paraguay	3.8	11.1	20.2	16.4	8.9
Peru	9.9	26.5	481.3	807.9	2.6
Uruguay	51.4	59.3	57.6	48.9	8.7
Venezuela	1.0	6.6	23.0	47.4	20.4
Latin America	9.7	34.3	193.9	136.5	8.2

Source: World Bank (2010).

supply growth accelerated during the 1970s, the rate of inflation increased dramatically. While a regional average of 34.3 percent isn't good, the situation grew far worse during the 1980s. The *average* rate of inflation in the region was nearly 200 percent. This is such a devastating rate of inflation that normal economic activity becomes difficult. Also, the effects of this on the welfare of the poor are hard to imagine. As one might have guessed from Tables 10.1 and 10.3, the situation improved in the 1990s. Inflation moderated to a regional average of 136.5 percent. This is still far too high but represented a dramatic improvement from the Lost Decade. The fiscal restraint of the last decade has worked in the usual way. As governments in the region have learned to achieve a better balance in the government finances, the rate of growth of the money supply has moderated. In turn, this has accomplished far lower rates of inflation. The progress that has been made in the region is remarkable, but technically predictable. In a middle-income country it is essential for fiscal policy to be prudent in order to keep inflation from devastating the economy. As we will see in the next section, these gains in lowering inflation came at a heavy cost in the short run.

The inflationary process

The equation of exchange is an exceptionally useful framework for thinking about how changes in the money supply affect the price level. However, it has some important limitations. First, it is a long-run concept. In the context of macroeconomics, the long run is usually a time period of more than two years.

Second, since the equation of exchange is a long-run concept, changes in the money supply have no influence on either real GDP or the level of employment. In this section, the process of inflation will be covered using a more flexible model. This will allow us to show how changes in the money supply affect the economy over shorter periods of time. The model also can be linked to the previous analysis shown with the equation of exchange.

Analyzing changes in the economy, caused by changes in the money supply, can be shown most easily using a macroeconomic model that incorporates both changes in aggregate demand and aggregate supply. To begin our analysis we will consider the model for the long run as it is just a different way of reaching the same conclusions that were obtained in the previous section. In Figure 10.1 the price level (P) is shown on the vertical axis.[8] The horizontal axis is real GDP. Also, notice already that we have graphed the two variables that form the right-hand side of the equation of exchange in the previous section. Also notice that in Figure 10.1, the aggregate demand curve slopes downwards and to the right. As the overall price level increases, the overall demand for goods and services declines and vice versa. If the only thing that changes is the price level, then there are only movements from one point to another along an existing aggregate demand curve (AD). Recalling the components of GDP, if any of these components changes, then the AD curve will shift. If consumption, investment, government spending, or the trade balance increases or decreases, then the AD curve will increase or decrease, respectively. A change in the money supply can cause a change in AD. An increase in the money supply could increase consumption by the public. Such an increase could cause an increase in nominal income and an increase in consumption. Second, an increase in the money supply could reduce interest rates and stimulate both business investment and residential investment.

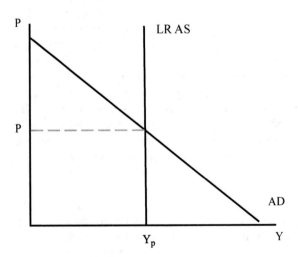

Figure 10.1 The equilibrium price level and real GDP

In order to find a macroeconomic equilibrium, Figure 10.1 includes a long-run aggregate supply curve (LRAS). This supply curve has two important characteristics. First, in the long run aggregate supply is perfectly inelastic (i.e. a vertical line). This is because in the long run there is no relationship between the price level and real GDP. An example may illustrate the point. Suppose that in RCILA the price level doubled over the next five years. What else would occur? As the price level doubled, all other prices in the economy such as wages, interest rates, asset prices, etc. would also roughly double. The result is that in the long run the price level has no effect on the level of economic output. Second, the point at which the LRAS curve crosses the horizontal axis has meaning. This point coincides with potential real GDP (Y_p). This is the point where in the long run the economy is producing, assuming normal utilization of capital and labor. In Figure 10.1 the long-run equilibrium for RCILA occurs at Y_p and P.

We are now in a position to link Figure 10.1 with the earlier material on the equation of exchange. Assume that the supply of money increased dramatically as shown in Table 10.3 above. As was previously explained such an increase would cause a large increase in AD. This is shown as an increase from AD to AD_1. Over several years this would not change the output of the economy overall. It would still be producing an output consistent with Y_p. Consumption, investment, and government spending would all be increasing. Over a period of several years this increase in aggregate demand would only influence the price level as wages and other prices adjusted to the higher price level. What is occurring in the long run is a bit more complicated but is worth going over in the context of Latin America. This is shown in Figure 10.2 below. As was shown in Chapter 2, the central problem of Latin America has been slow economic growth. Economic growth can be shown in the figure as a movement of the LRAS curve to the right over time. As the LRAS curve shifts, Y_p also shifts along with it. However, if economic growth is slow then the movement of both LRAS and Y_p will likewise be slow. Now think of this and the macroeconomic policy goal of having a stable price level. In order to accomplish this then the AD curve must be shifting to the right at approximately the same rate as the LRAS curve or the rate of growth of Y_p. This situation is shown in Figure 10.2 with the new equilibrium of AD_1 and $LRAS_1$. In this case real GDP has grown over time but the price level is stabilized. For this outcome to occur the central bank must be very careful. If the LRAS curve is not shifting to the right quickly then the central bank cannot let the money supply grow too rapidly. In a well-managed country, an independent central bank that is technically competent can accomplish this. The problem in Latin America is that a combination of a nonindependent central bank and a large fiscal deficit would push the growth of the money supply far higher than the growth of Y_p. In this case the AD curve might increase to AD_2. Since the growth of AD far exceeds the growth of Y_p, the price level can rise substantially. This result may at first seem puzzling. Why would a government engage in policies that

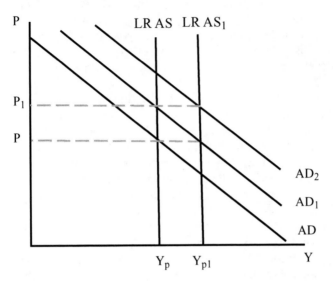

Figure 10.2 The price level and changes in aggregate demand

would lead to substantial inflation that damages almost everyone's economic welfare? In the next section, at least a partial answer to that question will be provided.

Economic populism

In order to answer the question posed at the end of the previous section, we need to go a bit further in our analysis of how the money supply affects the economy. Both the equation of exchange and the aggregate demand and aggregate supply model shown in the previous section give valid results for the long run. In this case the long run means something like three to five years. At this point our attention is turning to the more usual time frame for macroeconomic analysis which is less than two years. This is convenient in a discussion of economic populism. The term refers to the tendency of governments to pursue policies that will produce the most favorable economic outcomes in the short run.[9] As we will see, such policies can have extremely unfortunate macroeconomic consequences in the long run.[10]

To begin our discussion, consider Figure 10.3 below. As before the figure contains both the LRAS curve and the AD curve that we used above to analyze changes in the price level and real GDP. The critical difference here is that the figure includes the short-run aggregate supply curve (SRAS). The SRAS curve slopes upwards and to the right indicating that in the short run there is a positive relationship between the price level and real GDP. The optimal point for the economy is labeled point A in the figure. This is where LRAS, AD, and SRAS all intersect. Any points to the left of point A

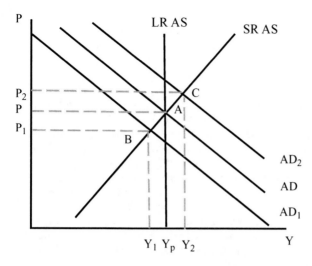

Figure 10.3 Changes in aggregate demand and changes in the price level and real GDP

are undesirable. Suppose that AD fell from AD to AD_1. Real GDP would fall from Y_p to Y_1 and the price level would fall from P to P_1. This is a classic recession where GDP is below potential, unemployment rises, and inflation is not a problem. In the context of Latin America, a more common problem is illustrated by Point C. In this case AD has shifted from AD to AD_2. This increase in AD produces a higher price level. However, it also produces output greater than Y_p and low unemployment. As one can imagine, the mix of a government budget deficit mixed with an expansion of the money supply can produce this sort of outcome.

10.1 Inflation and structuralist economics

The material in the preceding section implies that inflation always is caused by increases in the money supply that are larger than changes in long-run aggregate supply (LRAS). This simple explanation of inflation has roots running back hundreds of years. In the context of Latin America, this excessive creation of money is easily traced to fiscal deficits. A reasonable question is why governments in the region unleashed massive inflation when its causes are not exactly an economic mystery. Part of the answer can be attributed to the concept of structuralist economics that was mentioned in the first chapter. To briefly summarize, structuralist economics is the idea that the structure of an economy can have important effects on economic outcomes, in this case inflation. The basic idea is undeniably true. Even in Latin America the structure of the economy of Guatemala is quite different than that of Mexico or Brazil. It is unlikely that an identical set of policies would have exactly the same effects in all countries of the region.

In the structuralist view of the economy, the story that inflation occurs as a result of the money supply increasing aggregate demand to too high a level is only a part of the story and perhaps not the most important part. Rather than focusing on aggregate demand, the structuralist approach to inflation emphasizes problems with *aggregate supply*. In their vision, the economies of Latin America were more prone to inflation because they tended to have supply problems that tended to push up SRAS. Such an increase in the price level caused by a decrease in SRAS is usually referred to as cost-push inflation. Some of the factors that could cause such decreases in the short run included exchange rate depreciations and during the 1970s, oil shocks. As we will see in the next chapter, these factors can push the SRAS curve to the left. The structuralists also emphasized other factors that tended to make inflation more prevalent in the region. As a result of ISI many product markets in the region were less than perfectly competitive which makes it more difficult for prices to adjust. On the production side of the market, trade restrictions and rigid labor markets make controlling costs of production more difficult. Further, if inflation becomes an economic fact of life, producers and consumers adjust their actions accordingly and inflationary expectations become deeply embedded in the system.

It is a short step from emphasizing supply constraints as a cause of inflation to downplaying the role of the money supply in creating the problem. What this meant was that there was a tendency in the middle decades of the twentieth century to emphasize these supply factors as a cause of inflation which conveniently shifted the focus from excessive money supply growth driven by lax fiscal policy. This was enhanced by the academic debate raging in the developed countries over the importance of the money supply in macroeconomic activity.[11] In terms of macroeconomic policy, for a time it was possible to blame inflation in the region on structural rigidities in the economies of the region as a primary cause of inflation. As the inflation problem worsened in the 1970s and 1980s and the economic debate over the cause of high inflation became more settled, the structuralist approach to inflation has faded in importance. This is perhaps unfortunate. In most cases, excessive money supply growth is the cause of inflation. However, structural problems in the economy can exacerbate the problem. To this extent, some of the problems the structuralists identified may not be the cause of inflation but they can make it more difficult to control. If these factors are prevalent in an economy, then the government will need to be exceptionally vigilant concerning the deficit and the central bank may need to be even more wary of inflation. In this sense, the recent tendency to dismiss the structuralist approach to inflation as irrelevant economic history is on a par with the earlier view that the money supply is not very important.

If this were the end of the macroeconomic story, then the effects of a fiscal deficit and the expansion of the money supply could seem rather benign. Point C involves more GDP and lower unemployment. The cost is a higher price level. In the context of the developing countries of Latin America, this may not be a suboptimal outcome. Unfortunately, point C is not a stable equilibrium. As the price level increases, workers, consumers, and businesses will start expecting higher prices. As their *inflationary expectations* change the SRAS curve will begin to shift to the left.[12] This movement is shown in Figure 10.4 below. As inflationary expectations adjust, a new stable equilibrium will be established at point C or the intersection of LRAS, SRAS, and AD occurs. The level of real GDP returns to Y_p and the unemployment will rise as the economy moves from point B to point C. The expansionary fiscal and monetary policies have created the following scenario. For a period of time the expansionary policies raised real GDP and lowered unemployment. The cost was a moderate increase in the price level. As inflationary expectations increase, the SRAS curve eventually shifts to the left and the price level rises further. The increase in real GDP and the decline in unemployment were temporary. Unfortunately the increase in the price level was *permanent*. The policy bought temporary growth and employment at the cost of permanently higher prices. The graph illustrates the logic of economic populism. Policies can be pursued that render short-run economic benefits that may be politically popular. It is frequently the case that such policies produce undesirable economic outcomes in the long run. If such a scenario were an occasional random event, the damage to an individual economy in the region might be tolerable.

Unfortunately, the situation described above frequently is not an idiosyncratic event but rather the beginning of an unfortunate pattern shown in Figure 10.5 below. As before, the initial expansionary fiscal and monetary policies led the economy from point A to point B and eventually to point C. For any number of reasons, policy makers may want to again increase real GDP to a level higher than Y_p. In Figure 10.5 below, this is shown as a movement along SRAS$_1$ from point C to point D. Real GDP increases again and the level of unemployment decreases. The price level again and begins to increase. However, with some lag the SRAS will begin to shift upwards

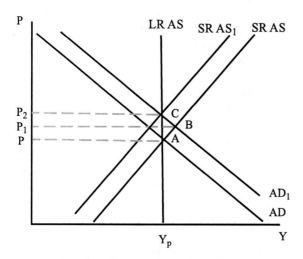

Figure 10.4 The effects of changes in inflationary expectations

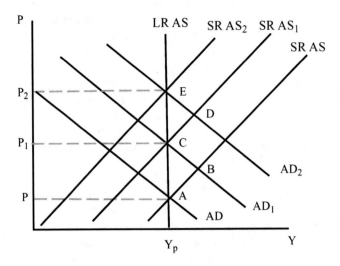

Figure 10.5 Long-run increases in the price level

once more to SRAS₂. A new long-run equilibrium is established at point E. Real GDP and the unemployment rate have returned to their initial levels with a new permanently higher price level.

This can be an understandably easy pattern for economic policy to slip into. Let's go back to a previous section of the chapter and consider the genesis of this problem. For Latin America, the difficulty begins with fiscal policy. Gathering tax revenue in the region has long historical roots. It has never been easy for governments in the region to collect substantial amounts of tax revenue. Moving into the twentieth century, spending on education, infrastructure, other forms of social spending, and spending associated with ISI increased dramatically in many countries of the region. In many cases, financing these deficits required increases in the money supply described earlier. The initial effects of these deficits were benign. GDP growth increased, unemployment fell, and the cost in terms of higher prices was modest. The continual application of these expansionary policies did not work nearly as well. As the public becomes increasingly accustomed to higher prices, the effects of the expansionary policies become ever more short lived. The movements of the SRAS curve become increasingly rapid and the stimulative effects on real GDP and unemployment become shorter. As a result the movements of the economy become more like the long-run situation described earlier in the chapter where the economy is practically moving straight up the LRAS curve with shorter and briefer deviations to the right of Y_p. In effect, the expansionary policies are imposing ever larger costs in terms of the price level coupled with ever smaller benefits. In the end the price level may have reached levels where normal economic activity becomes difficult. Such situations require a different set of macroeconomic policies designed to reduce the price level to tolerable levels and maintaining real GDP at a level close to potential real GDP. As we will see this can be a very painful process that is described in the next chapter.

10.2 Economic populism in the twenty-first century

The main feature of populism is the institutional underdevelopment it provokes. Populism hates limits to the ruler's power that sound institutions would otherwise bring about. As a consequence, the countries that experience populism do not have strong institutions, like an independent Central Bank, an active Supreme Court, or a democratically elected Congress.

Paulo Rabello de Castro and Marcio Ronci

As has been shown in this chapter, most countries in Latin America have managed to obtain either small fiscal deficits or surpluses. In turn, this has allowed countries to more easily moderate money supply growth and rates of inflation. This is not universally the case. The data below is for a country in the region that is having increasing difficulties maintaining a balanced budget. Not surprisingly, the rate of inflation is increasing. Since inflation is high, the nominal exchange rate is depreciating.

Table 10.5 Fiscal deficits, inflation, and the exchange rate

	Budget deficit (% GDP)	Inflation rate (annual)	Nominal exchange rate
1999	0.7	20	0.6

For some countries, the learning curve is flatter than it is for others.

Key concepts and terms

aggregate demand – the relationship between the total quantity of goods and services demanded by all sectors of the economy and the price level.

aggregate supply – the relationship between the total quantity of goods and services that an economy produces and the price level.

central bank – the financial institution in a country which is in charge of managing the supply of money.

discount rate – the interest rate charged by the central bank on loans to private sector banks.

economic populism – the tendency of governments to pursue policies that will produce the most favorable economic outcomes in the short run.

equation of exchange – a basic framework for analyzing the interactions among the money supply, velocity, the price level, and real GDP.

monetary base – the sum of cash in the hands of the public and the reserves of the banking system.

money multiplier – the multiple by which a change in the monetary base (B) translates into a change in the money supply.

money supply – the sum of cash in the hands of the public (Cp) and demand deposits (D) in an economy.

potential real GDP – the amount of final goods and services an economy is producing at full employment.

Questions for review and discussion

1   Relate the concept of potential real GDP to economic growth in Latin America.
2   Describe the evolution of government budget deficits in Latin America from the 1970s to the current decade.
3   If a government runs a budget deficit and cannot borrow, the deficit translates into an increase in the monetary base. Explain why this is true.
4   Show how a budget deficit of 5 percent of GDP could produce a large expansion in the supply of money.
5   Describe why having an independent central bank is important in maintaining a low rate of inflation.
6   Using the equation of exchange, show how the data in Tables 10.3 and 10.4 are related.
7   Draw a graph showing the inflationary process in the long run.
8   What is economic populism? How can it be related to aggregate demand (AD)?
9   Show how short-run policies that reduce unemployment can lead to inflation in the long run.
10 Using the data in Table 10.4, describe the likely evolution of inflationary expectations in Latin America from 1970 to the current decade.

References and recommended readings

Baer, Werner. 2008. *The Brazilian Economy*. 6th ed. Boulder, CO: Lynne Rienner.

Cardoso, Eliana and Ann Helwege. 1992. *Latin America's Economy: Diversity, Trends, and Conflicts*. Cambridge, MA: MIT Press.

Chong, Alberto and Carmen Pages. 2010. "Taxes and Productivity: A Game of Hide and Seek," pp. 153–180 in Carmen Pages (ed.), *The Age of Productivity: Transforming Economies from the Bottom Up*. New York: Palgrave Macmillan.

Dornbusch, Rudiger and Sebastian Edwards (eds). 1991. *The Macroeconomics of Populism in Latin America*. Chicago: University of Chicago Press.

Edwards, Sebastian. 1995. *Crisis and Reform in Latin America: From Despair to Hope.* Washington, DC: World Bank.

Rabello de Castro, Paulo and Marcio Ronce. 1991. "Sixty Years of Populism in Brazil," pp. 151–69 in Rudiger Dornbusch and Sebastian Edwards (eds), *The Macroeconomics of Populism in Latin America.* Chicago: University of Chicago Press.

Tanzi, Vito. 2007. *Argentina: An Economic Chronicle. How One of the Richest Countries in the World Lost Its Wealth.* New York: Jorge Pinto.

Wiesner, Eduardo. 2008. *The Political Economy of Macroeconomic Policy Reform in Latin America: The Distributive and Institutional Context.* Northampton, MA: Edward Elgar.

World Bank. 2010. *World Development Indicators,* Washington, DC: World Bank.

11 Macroeconomic stability

That which does not kill us makes us stronger.

Friederich Nietzsche

Introduction

In the previous chapter the effects of fiscal and monetary policy in the context of the economies of Latin America were explained. In general, the goal of macroeconomic policy is to obtain a level of real GDP consistent with potential real GDP and a stable price level. Even for a developed country this is not an easy task. Until recently, macroeconomic outcomes in Latin America were rarely even close to this ideal outcome. In the region, unemployment and underemployment have been persistent problems. As we saw in the previous chapter, controlling inflation has been particularly difficult. In the main, these problems are the result of the structure of the economies of the region and poor policy choices. By the late 1970s, a combination of factors made the continuation of the policies of the post-war era increasingly unsustainable. This led to a painful and protracted period of macroeconomic stabilization. By this we mean the process of introducing macroeconomic policies that would reduce inflation and other economic imbalances, and provide the basis for more sustainable growth in the region.

Unfortunately, these imbalances were so numerous that it will be necessary to consider them in stages. The first section of this chapter more fully covers a problem that was briefly covered in Chapter 5. Exporting commodities can complicate macroeconomic policy for any country. For Latin America as a region, this is especially true. In this section, we consider these problems in isolation from any other macroeconomic difficulties. The same is true for large changes in the price of oil. Most of the countries of Latin America are oil importers. The oil shocks of the 1970s created problems for much of the world economy. Countries can react to these shocks in different ways and the reaction of the region to the two oil shocks tended to exacerbate existing macroeconomic problems. More specifically, the oil shocks of the 1970s contributed to inflation. As we saw in Chapter 8, high inflation is inconsistent with fixed exchange rates. The movement from fixed to flexible exchange rates frequently is not a smooth process and created yet another source of macroeconomic instability. In addition, the debt taken on by many countries of the region in the 1970s and 1980s eventually led to problems necessitating the assistance of the IMF. The austerity programs that came with borrowing from this source tended to make a poor macroeconomic environment even worse. The culmination of the above factors goes a long way towards explaining the "Lost Decade" of the 1980s. Sometimes the whole is even worse than the sum of the parts. The final section of the chapter details the substantial progress the countries of the region have made towards macroeconomic stability.

Commodity price shocks

In Chapter 5, we covered the impact of commodities on the economies of Latin America. The initial focus of the chapter was on how commodities had influenced the historical evolution of the economies of the region. The chapter went on to cover the sometimes problematic relationship between commodities and economic development in the long run. In Chapters 8 and 9, it was mentioned that changes in commodity prices can have an influence on the exchange rate, the current account, and the economy at large. However, these influences are more short-run in nature and we require a different sort of model to analyze these effects. From the basic model that was developed in the previous chapter, we can now examine more carefully the effects of changes in commodity prices on the rate of growth of GDP, unemployment, and inflation. From this analysis, the response of macroeconomic policy to these changes will be easier to analyze. As before, the analysis of these changes will be made with respect to a representative country in Latin America (RCILA). While this is convenient, the importance of commodities to the economies of the region is not uniform. Before beginning, it might be a good idea to go back to Table 5.3 and review the information in the table on the ratio of commodity exports to total exports and the ratio of exports to GDP. This would give one a better sense of the relative importance of commodities to the overall economy of various countries in the region. This section begins with a brief review of the microeconomics of commodity prices and their effects on exchange rates. This is followed by the analysis of how these changes in prices and exchange rates can affect the overall economy. The section concludes with a discussion of the difficulties that these changes can cause for macroeconomic policy in a country.

At this point, let's briefly review the fundamental problem with commodities. Recall that the demand for commodities is typically inelastic. This means that changes in price have very little influence on the quantity demanded. For example, very large changes in the price of oil do not affect the consumption of oil by very much in the short run. The same is true for the supply curve. Relatively large changes in the price do not influence the quantity supplied in the short run by a large amount. Under these conditions, small changes in either the demand curve or supply curve can produce substantial changes in the price of a commodity. As was shown in Figure 5.2, changes in demand can be the source of these price changes. Likewise, price instability can be caused by changes in supply shown in Figure 5.3. Price changes can be truly extreme under the right set of circumstances. Increases in demand coupled with decreases in supply can create rapidly rising prices for a commodity much as will be covered in the next section on oil. Conversely, decreases in demand accompanied by increases in supply can cause a collapse in prices. It is not uncommon for these exaggerated changes in price to occur over a relatively short period of time, such as six months.

For Latin America, these large changes in commodity prices can affect the macroeconomic performance of the economies in the short run. To consider this more carefully, we can combine the information contained in the expenditure approach to GDP and the model of aggregate demand and aggregate supply developed in the previous chapter. Recall that the expenditure approach to GDP can be represented by:

$$Y = C + I + G + (X - M)$$

where C is consumption by the public; I is investment; G is government spending on goods and services; and (X – M) is the balance on goods and services. Now if the ratio of exports to GDP (X/Y) is high then rapid changes in exports can have a substantial effect on macroeconomic performance in the short run. Commodities now come into the picture. If X/Y is relatively high and commodities are a high percentage of total exports, then changes in commodity prices have the potential to influence the overall economy.

Now consider what can occur if there is a large change in commodity prices that occurs in very short period of time. Assuming that commodities are a large percentage of exports and the ratio of X/Y is high then large changes in the price of commodities can have a substantial impact on the aggregate demand curve for a country. This is what we mean by a commodity price shock. The effects of a commodity price shock can be outlined in Figure 11.1 below. In the figure the economy is initially in equilibrium at point A. Now assume that there is a large increase in the price of one or more of a country's commodities that occurs in a short period of time, such as six months. Further assuming that commodity exports are a nontrivial percentage of GDP, the effect would be to increase aggregate demand from AD to AD_1. In the short run, the economy would end up at a new equilibrium at point B. Real GDP is now past Y_p and the price level has risen. Neither of these undesirable outcomes was the result of policy decisions and may easily have been unanticipated. The problem is now with the evolution of fiscal and monetary policy. Both policies had been set for a level of aggregate demand consistent with AD and point A. With the unanticipated upward pressure

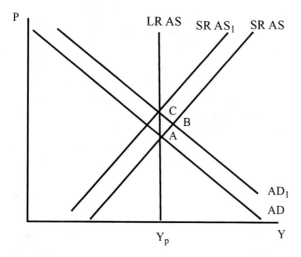

Figure 11.1 Macroeconomic effects of a commodity price shock

on aggregate demand, macroeconomic policy effectively is now too loose. With no change in fiscal or monetary policy, the rise in the price level will begin to increase inflationary expectations. Rising inflationary expectations eventually would start shifting the SRAS curve to the left. With no change in macroeconomic policy, the economy could end up at point C. This would be consistent with potential real GDP but with a higher price level. With no change in policy, the commodity price shock has left its mark on the economy, a higher price level. To prevent this outcome, policy makers will need to move rather quickly in response to a movement of aggregate demand from AD to AD_1. A combination of somewhat tighter fiscal and monetary policy would tend to reduce the movement of the economy from point A to point B. At a minimum, such a move would diminish the possibility of the even more undesirable movement of the economy from point B to point C.

While easy to do in theory, in practice it would be much harder for two reasons. First, forecasting large changes in commodity prices is difficult. By their nature such changes normally are unpredictable. Second, the initial stages of a commodity boom can seem rather benign in a macroeconomic sense. Real GDP is rising which increases employment, profits, and government tax revenues. The price level is increasing but initially this increase may seem to be a small price to pay for the initial burst of prosperity. It is up to the policy makers to adjust fiscal and monetary policy to prevent the later effects of the boom that are not so benign from setting in. With regard to fiscal policy this involves some combination of cuts in government spending and/or increases in taxes to restrain the increase in aggregate demand. If done quickly the necessity of these changes may not be apparent to the public at large and may well not be popular. An appropriate monetary policy would involve decreasing the rate of growth of the money supply. Normally, this would involve increases in interest rates. Again, the necessity of these changes may not be fully apparent. The timing and magnitude of these changes may be excruciatingly difficult to get right. Effectively, the policy makers are trying to calibrate the timing and magnitude of changes in fiscal and monetary policy to offset changes in aggregate demand caused by volatile commodity prices that are difficult to forecast. A response that is too small and late runs the risk of failing to stop an inflationary boom. A response that is premature or too severe would run the risk of triggering an unnecessary recession. If the economy is well managed the policy makers may prefer the latter mistake to the former. Acting too aggressively may trigger a recession but such a mistake can be reversed more easily as the SRAS curve will remain stable. Changing policy by an insufficient amount is a harder mistake to compensate for once inflationary expectations begin to rise.

11.1   Copper prices and the Chilean economy

Being very conservative, Chile is considered to be one of the best managed economies in Latin America. A substantial part of this opinion is Chilean macroeconomic policy, in particular fiscal policy. As indicated in the section above, macroeconomic policy is crucial for a country where commodities are an important part of exports and GDP. Over the period 1996 to 2003, mining accounted for 46 percent of the country's exports. Copper alone accounted for 39 percent of exports.[1] The effect of exports on GDP is potentially high. From 2003 to 2008, mining accounted for 18 percent of GDP on average. Copper mining is dominated by COLDECO (Corporacion Nacional del Cobre de Chile) supplemented by the production of a number of foreign-owned firms. All profits from COLDECO are returned to the government and foreign companies pay taxes on their operations in Chile. Copper prices are extremely volatile and the percentages above indicate that the entire economy can be influenced by changes in these prices. Further, it is anticipated that commodity prices will continue to be an important factor for the economy in the long run as copper continues to be important and other minerals, especially lithium, become more important.

The primary device Chile has developed for dealing with commodity-related macroeconomic instability has been a "rule" for fiscal policy. The goal of fiscal policy is to generate a structural surplus of 0.5 percent of GDP annually.[2] In this context, "structural" refers to government spending and tax revenue that would occur if the economy were at full employment. For a country without significant commodity exports this is equivalent to government spending and tax revenue at potential real GDP (Y_p). For a commodity exporter such as Chile, the calculation is a bit more complicated. One now has to factor in the price of one or more commodities and the changes in revenues coming from the mining companies. All of these estimates are subject to political manipulation. Chile avoids this by using independent panels of experts to estimate the trend rate of growth of the economy and the long-run price of copper. The structural surplus has been used to recapitalize the central bank, to finance contingent liabilities for the social security system, and to create a buffer for changes in the exchange rate and capital flows. Surpluses in excess of the target have been placed in various sovereign wealth funds. These assets have grown to more than 13 percent of GDP. While the fiscal rule has not been completely successful in insulating the economy from effects of changes in commodity prices, it has clearly made the economy more stable than would otherwise be the case. Moreover, the economy is now more stable in this decade than it was in the 1990s. The fiscal rule was designed for macroeconomic stability and to provide revenues from commodities for future generations. However, in a disaster-prone region the existence of sovereign wealth funds may provide a buffer against unexpected events such as the recent earthquake in Chile.

Oil shocks

A fundamental reality of the world economy until the 1970s was that oil was a relatively cheap commodity. As the box in Chapter 5 indicated, OPEC was formed in 1960 to mitigate relatively low oil prices. Again, the material in that chapter indicated that low commodity prices contain the seeds of their own destruction. Low prices engender insufficient development of new sources of supply. If demand for the commodity is increasing over time, then eventually prices will rise, sometimes dramatically. This turned out to be the case with oil. Although a political event triggered a spectacular rise in the price of oil in late 1973, the combination of low supply coupled with high global demand had set the stage for rising prices. The large increase in the price of oil over a short period of time defines the term oil shock. The stabilization of oil prices after the first oil shock was short-lived. The world economy suffered a second oil shock in 1979 that drove prices to unprecedented levels in real terms.[3] In a sense, an oil shock is just a special case of a commodity price shock. For Ecuador, Mexico, and Venezuela this rise in oil prices produced the effects on aggregate demand that were described in the preceding section. For the rest of the region, the price increases created macroeconomic difficulties.

11.2   The price of oil: a brief history

Figure 11.2 below shows changes in the price of oil from the early 1970s to 2009. In 1973, oil prices rose dramatically in response to an oil embargo by Saudi Arabia. Oil prices had been extremely low for decades and a price of $10 per barrel was a shock to the world economy. Recall from Chapter 5 that OPEC was formed in the 1960s as an attempt to increase oil prices. It took a war in the Middle East and an embargo to accomplish what OPEC was unable to do. The slowing of the world economy in the 1970s led to moderate oil prices until 1979. A political crisis in Iran led to the suspension of oil exports and a rapid increase in prices. This price increase was so large that demand growth was dampened for many years. Prices fell back into the

$10 to $20 per barrel range for much of the remainder of the century. The low prices caused low investment in new oil supplies. As is frequently the case, strong world demand coupled with low supply led to a surge in prices late in this decade. Prices have fallen from their peaks, but are still high by modern standards.

For the oil-producing countries of Latin America, surges in prices can lead to destabilizing changes in aggregate demand. On the other hand, prolonged periods of low prices may lead to extended periods of slow economic growth. For the majority of the countries of the region that import oil, the long period of relatively low prices enhanced growth. The price spikes of the 1970s contributed to macroeconomic policies that led to the Lost Decade. While the most recent price increase lowered growth in the region, it was not nearly as devastating as the increases of the 1970s. The majority of the oil importers now have economies much better structured than the ISI-dominated economies of the 1970s. Also, most countries of the region now have much more prudent macroeconomic policy which makes it easier for them to weather oil shocks.

For many of the countries of the region, macroeconomic conditions in 1973 left them ill-prepared to deal with rising oil prices. While Latin America is a commodity-rich region in general, most of the countries of the region are oil importers. ISI coupled with loose fiscal and monetary policies meant that the economies of the region began the decade of the 1970s at or close to potential real GDP. This policy mix described in the preceding chapter was already causing difficulties with respect to price stability. An oil shock simply compounds that problem. In order to see this more clearly, the effects of an oil shock are shown in Figure 11.3. In the figure, the economy of RCILA is

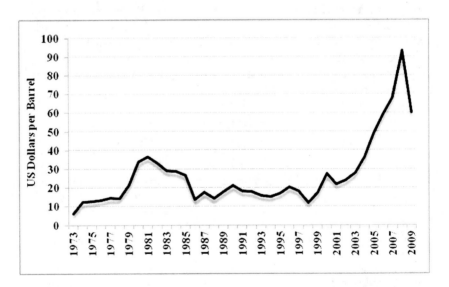

Figure 11.2 The price of oil (per barrel)

shown in equilibrium at point A where the economy is also at Y_p. The effect
of an oil shock is to shift the SRAS curve backwards and to the left. An oil
shock tends to increase the costs of production for most goods and services.
This is particularly true for an economy that must import virtually all of its
oil. This pervasive increase in the cost of production is what gives rise to the
leftward shift of the SRAS curve. Given AD, the new short-run equilibrium
for the economy is now at point B. This point illustrates the twin macroeconomic difficulties of an oil shock. First, real GDP has fallen from Y_p to Y_1. The
economy is now in a recession, and unemployment and underemployment
will rise. To make matters even worse, the price level is rising. In the context
of Latin America this upward pressure on prices was occurring at the same
time the countries of the region were struggling with reductions in real GDP.

Point B presents policy makers with three unpalatable choices. Since
point B is not at Y_p, this is a short-run equilibrium. A more stable long-run
equilibrium eventually will be established somewhere along the LRAS curve.
There are three possible outcomes. The first possibility is in some senses the
most difficult. Over time consumers and firms in the economies of the region
would learn to adjust to higher oil prices by using the now expensive resource
more efficiently. The countless small and large adjustments will allow the
SRAS curve to move back to its original position at point A. Inflationary
pressures will eventually subside and real GDP will return to its previous
level (Y_p). Unfortunately, this process could take years and involves tolerating
higher prices and lower real GDP. In the context of a middle-income country,
choosing this option could mean an extended period of both higher prices
and higher unemployment among a population that was not affluent to begin
with. Such patience by the public might be possible in a high-income country
but might be understandably in shorter supply in different circumstances.

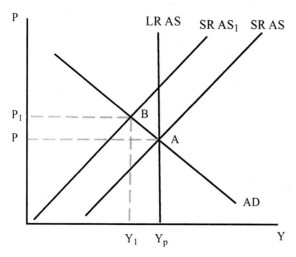

Figure 11.3 Macroeconomic effects of an oil shock

Much the same can be said of another option. If social preferences for low inflation are strong, then the optimal policy response might be reducing AD to keep the price level constant. This would be accomplished by some combination of tighter fiscal and/or monetary policy. In the case of the former, this would mean either higher taxes and/or lower government spending. Raising tax revenue in Latin America has always been problematic. Cutting government spending in this situation might well mean cutting social services during a recession in a poor country. Tighter monetary policy would involve reducing the rate of growth of the money supply with the attendant higher interest rates. The reduction in business activity would mean both lower profits and higher unemployment. In a high-income country with an aversion to inflation such a policy response was not uncommon. In Latin America, the recession induced by the oil shock made this response unlikely.

As in many parts of the world, the policy response in much of Latin America to the two major oil shocks was to attempt to stabilize real GDP and unemployment. A policy mix that would accomplish this involves an expansionary fiscal policy composed of lower taxes and higher government spending. This fiscal policy in Latin America had the usual effect of producing an expansion of the money supply outlined in the previous chapter. As before the effects of these policies combined with an oil shock are shown in Figure 11.4. Again the oil shock has the effect of shifting the SRAS curve to the left. The economy of RCILA moves from point A to point B. Real GDP falls and the price level increases. This time the policy response is different. Expansionary fiscal and monetary policies serve to shift the AD curve to the right. The economy establishes a new equilibrium at point C. Real GDP and employment have been stabilized but at a cost of a higher price level. In the context of Latin America this policy choice makes some sense as higher unemployment in a middle-income country with limited social safety nets would be difficult to tolerate. On the other hand, the price level has risen.

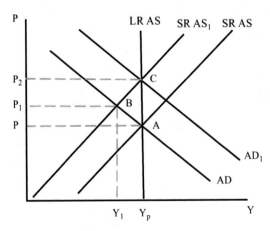

Figure 11.4 Policy responses to an oil shock

Inflation is a particular burden for the poor so the benefits of the stabilization of real GDP and unemployment has to be tempered by the costs imposed by inflation. Since this policy mix was common in the region in response to the oil shocks one must presume that policy makers considered the lower GDP and higher unemployment to be more costly to the population than the higher price level. However, the cost in terms of inflation were quite high.

Debt and exchange rate shocks

The oil shocks of the 1970s left Latin America in an uncomfortable position. As was covered in Chapter 8, the countries of the region preferred to maintain fixed exchange rates. Fixed exchange rates were essential to continue ISI as a development policy in the region. Unfortunately, the rising price of oil imports was putting a serious strain on the economic systems of the countries of the region. As we saw in the previous section, rising oil prices tended to reduce real GDP and raise the price level. Stimulative fiscal and monetary policies were adding to inflationary pressures. Severe balance of payments problems compounded these difficulties. In the first part of this section, we will review some previous material to set the stage for what occurred later in the decade and in the early part of the 1980s.

First, let's go back and consider the effects of rising oil prices on the economies of the region. By the 1970s, current account deficits in the region were already common. The supply of foreign exchange earned from commodity exports was frequently insufficient to meet the demand for foreign exchange at the fixed exchange rate. This situation is shown in Figure 11.5. At the fixed exchange rate, the quantity demanded of foreign exchange is higher than the quantity supplied. As was shown earlier, this shortage of foreign exchange could be covered by measures such as exchange controls and restrictive trade policies that reduced the demand for foreign exchange. While this perpetual

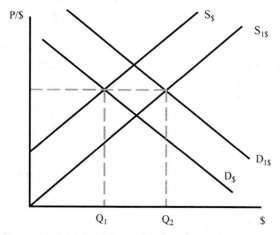

Figure 11.5 Maintaining a fixed exchange rate

shortage of foreign exchange was not an optimal situation, it was in some sense manageable at the time. With the first oil shock of 1973, the situation became much more difficult. Rising oil prices had the effect of shifting the demand for foreign exchange from D to D_1. With the exchange rate still fixed, the current account deficit increases dramatically. The usual mixture of exchange controls and restrictive trade policies could not close this gap. The solution was to borrow foreign exchange from banks in developed countries and use the proceeds of the loans to intervene in the foreign exchange market and stabilize the exchange rate. In the figure this is shown by the shift of the supply curve from S to S_1. In the aftermath of the first oil shock the borrowing seemed to be on a reasonable scale in the sense that most of the countries were able to service the debt. The process was aided by a decline in oil prices during the mid- and late-1970s. The subsequent macroeconomic equilibrium was not optimal as inflation was high in much of the region. Further, current account deficits were putting downward pressure on real GDP. However, some of the harsher consequences of higher oil prices had been averted. Unfortunately, the situation was worse than it appeared on the surface. As inflation increased with a fixed exchange rate, the real exchange rates in the region began appreciating. This appreciation tended to increase imports and make a problematic situation with respect to exports even worse. Current account deficits during the 1970s tended to widen even with a moderation in oil prices.

The second oil shock made the policy responses of the 1970s unsustainable. Expansionary fiscal and monetary policies were driving inflation to crippling levels. Again the higher oil prices necessitated borrowing which drove the total amounts of sovereign debt to unsustainable levels. The ratios of debt to GDP and the debt payments to exports eventually could not support further borrowing. Without the foreign exchange to intervene in the foreign exchange markets, exchange rate shocks now became a common occurrence. To review, this situation can be seen from Figures 11.4 above and 11.6 below. Because exchange rates in the region were frequently overvalued, the size of the depreciations were sometimes large. Such large exchange rate shocks can have traumatic macroeconomic consequences. The situation is shown in Figure 11.6. Like an oil shock, the large depreciation of the exchange rate increases the price of all imported goods. This includes commodities, imported inputs, and finished products. The effect of this is an enormous shift of the SRAS curve to the left. If the economy started out in equilibrium at point A, the exchange rate shock quickly moves it to point B. Real GDP falls dramatically and the price level rises. This creates an unfortunate increase in both the level of unemployment and rising inflation. In this case, inflation was already a problem in the region and the depreciations made this situation even worse. The main thing at this point is that the economies of the region were now to the left of Y_p. Eventually some sort of long-run equilibrium was going to be established along the LRAS curve. However, in this case the policy responses were limited and not always determined by the

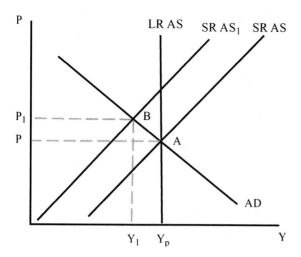

Figure 11.6 Macroeconomic effects of an exchange rate shock

governments of the region. This painful readjustment to a stable, long-run equilibrium is described in the next section.

The Lost Decade

Much of the point of the earlier material in this chapter was to prepare for a discussion of the Lost Decade of the 1980s in Latin America. The exceedingly bad economic conditions in the region had their roots in the previous decades. As the oil shocks affected the region, governments responded by pursuing expansionary fiscal and monetary policies in an attempt to stabilize GDP and employment. In order to maintain some exchange rate stability, increasing amounts of debt were accumulated. By the early 1980s, the region was burdened with high inflation, slow economic growth, and an increasing burden of debt. This situation can be summarized in Figure 11.7 below. The oil shocks and increases in inflationary expectations were putting continual pressure on the SRAS curve. Unfortunately, this pressure was all to the left. The result of this pressure was slower growth, higher unemployment, and an ever-higher price level. Macroeconomic policy in the region was geared toward offsetting the effects on real GDP and unemployment. This created some upward pressure on aggregate demand. However, counteracting this was the downward pressure being exerted by the current account balance. Overvalued exchange rates coupled with the export of little more than commodities suppressed exports. On the other hand, imports other than oil became increasingly cheap. The ability to purchase imports was being supported by the intervention in the foreign exchange market that prevented the usual adjustment of exchange rates to this situation, i.e. depreciation. The result was that rising trade deficits were exerting downward pressure

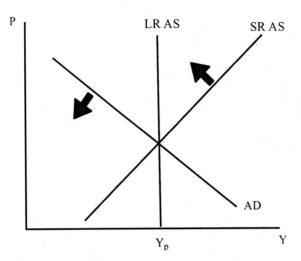

Figure 11.7 Macroeconomic effects of oil shocks, inflationary expectations and current account deficits

on aggregate demand. The situation created something akin to a macroeconomic treadmill where increasingly stimulative macroeconomic policies could barely keep pace with external factors limiting growth. Both were exerting upward pressure on prices and increasingly overvalued currencies.

As described in a previous chapter, the build-up of debt during the 1970s proved to be unsustainable. Ratios of debt to GDP and the ratio of debt payments to exports could not be maintained. In many countries the sudden cessation of borrowing forced the withdrawal of intervention in the foreign exchange markets. Without intervention, the supply of foreign exchange shifted quickly to the right and the depreciation of currencies was rapid. This set the stage for classic exchange rate shocks. The rising price of imports inexorably fed its way into the prices for commodities, intermediate goods, and final goods. The effect on domestic price levels was pronounced. Adding exchange rate shocks to the preexisting oil shocks and rising inflationary expectations put extreme leftward pressure on the SRAS curve of the economies of the region. Everything else equal, the predictable effects were lower output and a rising price level. In this environment, stimulative fiscal and monetary policy was something like adding gasoline to a fire.

One would be tempted to think that the depreciations of the currency would have reduced the pressure on the current account by increasing exports and sharply reducing imports. Somewhat counterintuitively, depreciations have a tendency to worsen the current account in the short run. The *volume* of exports does not increase immediately due to the depreciation, and foreign exchange earnings may not increase. On the other hand, the volume of imports may not decrease quickly and the amount of foreign exchange needed to purchase imports increases immediately. This phenomenon is commonly known as the J-curve, shown in Figure 11.8. After a depreciation, the current account has a tendency to become more negative initially and then improve.[4] For a country that has had to depreciate the currency as a result of the loss of the ability to borrow, the situation can become desperate. The depreciation initially is causing a deterioration in the current account. A steady flow of imports may be essential for the functioning of the economy even if GDP is below Y_p. Finding a short-term source of foreign exchange in this situation may be critical to prevent even further losses of real GDP.

In the 1970s and 1980s, this source of funding was the IMF. It was virtually the only institution in the world economy that was set up to loan foreign exchange to countries in need of short-run financing of current account deficits. As described earlier, the IMF imposes conditions for this lending. This is not so much a preference by the institution as a legacy of Bretton Woods. Initially, the IMF was set up to provide short-run loans under a fixed exchange rate system. In this situation a brief period of austerity would produce a sufficient drop in the demand for foreign exchange to balance the current account. The institution had even developed models that would produce an "answer" in terms of the amount of austerity required for a country to obtain a current account balance and repay the lending. The term "short-run" becomes important at this point. The drop in the demand for foreign exchange necessary to obtain this result could only be accomplished with a concomitant drop in aggregate demand. The magnitude of the austerity programs needed to obtain this drop in aggregate demand was large. To do this over a period of several years meant extremely contractionary fiscal and monetary policies were mandated by the IMF in exchange for short-run loans of foreign exchange. While the austerity programs that accompanied these

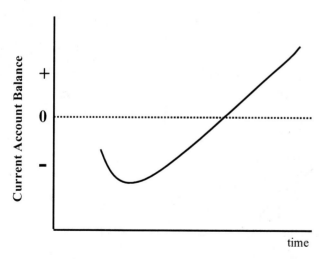

Figure 11.8 The J-curve

loans were associated with serious recessions, the alternative for the countries was even worse. Without adequate supplies of foreign exchange much of the industry that had been developed over the preceding several decades could not function. The short-run macroeconomic equilibrium combining the exchange rate shocks with reductions in AD necessary to obtain IMF loans is shown in Figure 11.9. The exchange rate shock has shifted the SRAS supply curve to the left by a large amount. This moves the economy from point A to point B. Since the shift was so large, point B represents both a recession and a higher price level. While point B is an uncomfortable macroeconomic equilibrium, the IMF was requiring reductions in AD in this situation. Putting the austerity programs on top of the exchange rate shock is shown by a fall in aggregate demand from AD to AD_1. This drop in aggregate demand produces a new equilibrium at point C. While the pressure on the price level has been reduced the drop in real GDP becomes even more severe.[5]

To a greater or lesser extent, point C is reflective of the 1980s in Latin America. It is useful to think about what was occurring in terms of the expenditure approach to GDP. Inevitably, a large drop in aggregate demand is accompanied by a large drop in consumption by the public. In a high-income country such a drop is troublesome. Consumers may buy fewer houses, cars, and durable goods, and social safety nets protect the incomes of those at the bottom of the income distribution. In the middle-income countries of Latin America drops in consumption are much more likely to entail drops in expenditures for basic necessities such as food, housing, and health care. In addition, both residential and nonresidential investment usually fall dramatically in such circumstances. Residential consumption slows as even the upper reaches of the income distribution are going to be adversely affected by a serious recession. Nonresidential investment will typically fall dramatically

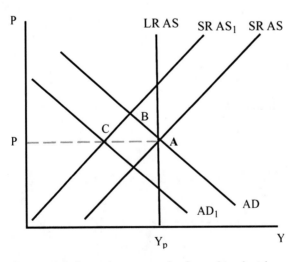

Figure 11.9 An exchange rate shock combined with an austerity program

with a large decline in GDP.[6] A classic Keynesian policy response to decreases in consumption and investment would be an increase in government spending. In this case the imposed austerity programs prevented this response. Indeed, government spending in many cases was being cut in order to obtain fiscal balance. The same logic was applied to the reduction of taxes to increase consumption.[7] Despite the economic hardships, the focus of policy was the reduction of imports and an increase in exports necessary to produce a current account surplus. This surplus was necessary for the countries of the region to continue to repay previously accumulated debt. In effect, intertemporal consumption had hit the region with a vengeance. Borrowing in the 1970s had allowed the region to avoid some of the painful drops in real GDP that would have occurred because of the oil shocks. Unfortunately, the accumulated debts of that decade meant the painful adjustments of the Lost Decade.

These problems were compounded by the decline of ISI in the region. During the preceding decades, the support of SOEs had made fiscal policy difficult. SOEs made it extremely difficult for governments in many countries to achieve a fiscal balance. The imposition of fiscal austerity meant the end of government subsidies to many SOEs. The withdrawal of subsidies led to a wave of privatizations of firms in the region. Changes in trade policy such as the elimination of quotas as a means of protection left industries in a much more competitive environment than was previously the case. The same is true for the exchange controls that came with the switch from untenable fixed exchange rate to more flexible exchange rates. These changes in industrial policy would have been difficult for many industries in the region in a period of normal economic growth. Adding negative economic growth to these policy changes meant that many of the newly privatized firms had little chance of survival. Effectively, this meant the demise of much of the industrial base of the region. In theory, the resources being released from the ISI industries would be briskly reallocated to more efficient sectors of the economy. Again, without the reductions in real GDP more of this would have occurred. Under the circumstances, labor and capital formerly employed in these industries languished in the short run due to the poor economic climate. The effects of this restructuring on the rate of growth of real GDP is unclear. It clearly did not enhance economic growth in the decade but the magnitude of the effect is uncertain.

11.3 Macroeconomic instability in Brazil

Almost no other country in Latin America has had to work as hard to achieve macroeconomic stability as Brazil. In a sense this is odd as Brazil is the largest and most diverse economy in the region. A large internal market frequently makes it easier to achieve stability as the economy may be less susceptible to external shocks. Further, macroeconomic stability in Brazil is important not only for the country but for the region. Stability in Latin America overall coupled with instability in Brazil is hard to imagine. For Brazil, serious problems began with the oil shocks of the 1970s, particularly the second. Brazil was a textbook case of the situation shown in Figure 11.4. By 1980, the rate of inflation was over 100 percent. By 1983, the country had defaulted on its debt, producing a serious exchange rate shock. Figure 11.5 shows the results. A new policy, the Cruzado Plan, involved issuing a new currency. Such a move may create the illusion of stability but unless the underlying policies change, inflation will return. Despite two other "plans" aimed at reducing inflation, by 1990 prices were rising by 70 percent *per month*. The response was the Collor Plan which froze wages and bank deposits, and taxed financial transactions. It failed. All of these plans had a common thread. They were attempts to reduce inflation without resorting to fiscal and monetary policies that are consistent with price stability. Dealing with the effects of inflation, rather than the causes, is likely to be ineffective. By the mid-1990s, policy had changed. Inflation was subsiding but the government was still reluctant to allow the exchange rate to float. So reluctant, that in the aftermath of the Tequila Crisis of 1994 and the Asian Crisis of 1997, the central bank was willing to risk recession to prevent a depreciation of the currency. The macroeconomic problems of the late 1990s finally forced the government to allow the exchange rate to float. Fast forward to 2008 and consider the response of the Brazilian government to the global economic crisis. Government spending was raised, monetary policy was loosened, and the exchange rate was not much of an issue. A far cry from the ill-founded "plans" of the 1980s and virtually identical to the reaction of any high-income country.

The recovery from the Lost Decade

The recovery from the Lost Decade of the 1980s involved a protracted period of poor economic conditions shown in Figure 11.7 above. The process of recovery has been long and is still a work in progress. The necessary, but hardly sufficient, condition for recovery was restoring some balance to fiscal policy. As we described in an earlier chapter, persistent fiscal deficits were one of the main drivers of excessive money supply growth. In turn, this was making it virtually impossible to control inflation. During the 1980s and 1990s, the majority of governments in the region were able to reduce or eliminate fiscal deficits. In hindsight, this is a rather incredible accomplishment. It was not always a smooth or continuous process, but with exceptions Latin America has become a region where balanced government budgets have become the norm. This has allowed central banks in the region to pursue monetary policies more in line with price stability. As inflation subsided, inflationary expectations in the region began to fall. Once this process sets in, macroeconomic outcomes begin to improve dramatically. This can be seen in Figure 11.10 below. Point C in the graph corresponds to point C in Figure 11.9. As inflationary expectations begin to fall, the SRAS curve begins to shift to the right. This shift produces two positive effects. First, real GDP begins moving back towards potential real GDP (Y_p). As Y increases, a positive feedback loop begins to occur. With increased output, the level of unemployment falls. As both increase, the government finances improve. Tax revenues increase and the level of spending on some social programs decreases. Less pressure is put on the government budget which in turn makes the conduct of monetary policy less difficult. Second, the price level begins to fall. As the population experiences a reduction in inflation, inflationary expectations continue to fall. Unfortunately, since inflation had been so high for so long, this was not a short process. As economic conditions improved, consumption and investment began increasing AD. A combination of rightward shifts in both AD and SRAS eventually produces an equilibrium at point A. It took years of real GDP below Y_p to obtain a new stable equilibrium at this point. With variations by country, most of the countries of the region were at this point by the start of the twenty-first century. The importance of this achievement is hard to describe. If one had made the statement in 1985 that by 2010 the majority of the countries of Latin America would have balanced budgets, low inflation, and real GDP close to potential real GDP, the statement would have been met with some degree of skepticism. What was once difficult to imagine has now become the "norm."

However, it is a bit too easy to overemphasize the accomplishment of macroeconomic stability. Recall the problem that we outlined in Chapter 2. The problem with Latin America historically has been that it has not grown as fast as was possible. Much of Chapter 2 was devoted to an analysis of this problem. However, one of the neglected factors in that analysis was macroeconomic instability as an impediment to growth. If inappropriate fiscal and monetary policies are creating high inflation, then this becomes a drag on economic growth.[8] With inflation as a problem, producers and consumers waste resources dealing with inflation rather than producing more goods and services. With a return to sound fiscal and monetary policies and the accompanying low levels of inflation, potential real GDP can grow more quickly. Economic growth in Latin America over the last 20 years is

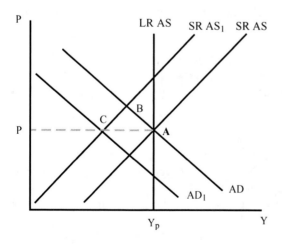

Figure 11.10 The effects of falling inflationary expectations

a case in point. Unfortunately, macroeconomic stability is a necessary, but hardly sufficient, condition for achieving a rate of growth in line with the best case scenario. The host of institutional factors outlined in that chapter still exist. Progress on these issues is being made but it is hard to say that for the region this sort of progress is occurring quickly. As a result, optimism over the economic future of the region has to be tempered. The hard-won macroeconomic stability will only increase growth so much. Faster growth in the future is more dependent on stronger institutions, better infrastructure, and increasing the stock of human capital. At this point, rapid improvements in these areas seem implausible. Perhaps, but one would have had similar reservations in 1985 about macroeconomic stability.

Key concepts and terms

commodity price shock – a large change in commodity prices that affects the overall performance of the economy.
J-curve – the tendency for the trade balance to deteriorate in the short run following a depreciation of the exchange rate.
oil shock – a large increase in the price of oil over a short period of time.

Questions for review and discussion

1   Using the expenditure approach to GDP, show how a change in commodity prices can influence real GDP.
2   Graphically show the effects of a commodity boom and bust on real GDP and the price level. Explain the appropriate macroeconomic policies needed to offset these effects.
3   Describe the macroeconomic effects of an oil shock on an oil-importing country.
4   In response to an oil shock, the countries of Latin America tended to respond with expansionary fiscal and monetary policies. What factors led to this policy choice?
5   For an oil-exporting country, an oil shock is just a special case of a commodity price shock. Explain why this statement is true.
6   Describe how the oil shocks of the 1970s led to a build-up of debt by the countries of the region.
7   How is the existence of a substantial amount of debt related to the probability of an exchange rate shock?
8   Compare the macroeconomic effects of a commodity price shock and an exchange rate shock. What are the differences in the factors influencing the probability of the two events?
9   List and describe the factors that accounted for large drops in real GDP in Latin America during the 1980s.
10 Describe the recovery of Latin America from the economic problems of the 1980s.

References and recommended readings

Edwards, Sebastian. 1989. "The Debt Crisis and Macroeconomic Adjustment in Latin America," *Latin American Research Review* 24: 172–86.

Edwards, Sebastian. 1995. *Crisis and Reform in Latin America: From Despair to Hope*. Washington, DC: World Bank.

Edwards, Sebastian. 2010. *Left Behind: Latin America and the False Promise of Populism*. Chicago: University of Chicago Press.

Fajnzylber, Fernando. 1990. *Unavoidable Industrial Restructuring in Latin America*. Durham, NC: Duke University Press.

Organization for Economic Co-operation and Development. 2010. *OECD Economic Surveys: Chile*. Paris: OECD.

The Economist. 2007. "Adios to Poverty, Hola to Consumption." pp. 21–23. August 18.

The Economist. 2007. "Dreaming of Glory: A Special Report on Brazil." pp. 1–16. April 14.

12 Poverty and inequality

To whom much is given, much is expected.

Luke 12:48

Introduction

At a number of points in the book, we have mentioned or briefly discussed the issues of poverty and inequality in Latin America. Poverty has an obvious connection to the region. Only a small group of countries in the region has any realistic hope of joining the ranks of the high-income countries in the near future. On the other side, most of the countries of the region are middle-income countries. While Latin America is relatively well off by global standards, poverty for hundreds of millions of people is still a daily fact of life. The average income data for the region masks the reality that among the world's regions income in Latin America is the most unevenly distributed. In the first two sections of the chapter, we consider the data and consequences of poverty and inequality in the region. In the third part of the chapter, the more commonly understood causes of poverty and inequality in Latin America are covered. A final section covers the list of public policy changes that have been used and are evolving to address these issues in the region.

Poverty in Latin America

We begin this chapter by reviewing some information that was reported in Chapter 1. As was indicated in that chapter, by global standards Latin America is solidly middle class. The less encouraging side of the data is that only a few countries in the region could possibly be thought of as high-income. Table 12.1 reviews this data. GDP per capita in the region is $7,735. While this is lower than the world average, it is more than double the average for middle-income countries. However, the differences within the region are wide. Three of the poorest countries have GDP per capita under $2,000. On the other side, there are three countries with GDP per

Table 12.1 Population, GDP, and GDP per capita for Latin America, low-,
middle-, and high-income countries

	Population (millions)	GDP[1] (billions)	GDP per capita[1]
Argentina	39.9	328.5	8,236
Bolivia	9.7	16.7	1,720
Brazil	192.0	1,575.2	8,205
Chile	16.8	169.5	10,084
Colombia	45.0	243.8	5,416
Costa Rica	4.5	29.7	6,564
Ecuador	13.5	54.7	4,056
El Salvador	6.1	22.1	3,605
Guatemala	13.7	39.0	2,848
Honduras	7.3	13.3	1,823
Mexico	106.4	1,088.1	10,232
Nicaragua	5.7	6.6	1,163
Panama	3.4	23.1	6,793
Paraguay	6.2	16.0	2,561
Peru	28.8	129.1	4,477
Uruguay	3.3	32.2	9,654
Venezuela	27.9	314.2	11,246
Latin America	530.3	4,101.5	7,735
HIC	1,068.7	43,309.6	40,525
MIC	4,652.3	16,722.1	3,594
LIC	976.2	564.6	578
World	6,697.3	60,557.0	9,042

Source: World Bank (2010).
[1] Data in current US dollars

capita above $10,000. While adequate by global standards, the region is far
away from the affluence of the developed countries where GDP per capita
averages over $40,000. On the surface, Latin America seems relatively well
off by global standards.

As is frequently the case with Latin America, only looking superficially
at the overall data can be quite misleading. By global standards, extreme
poverty is defined as income a bit above $1 per day. Similarly, absolute
poverty is defined as just over $2 per day. Table 12.2 presents the data for
Latin America relative to the other developing regions of the world. The data
presents a mixed picture of poverty in Latin America. By global standards
less than 10 percent of the population of the region is living in extreme
poverty. Further, some progress has been made in reducing extreme poverty.
A less promising picture emerges when considering less extreme poverty. In
2004, over 20 percent of the population of the region is living on a bit more
than $2 per day. In this year nearly a third of the people of the region are
poor to extremely poor by global standards. Notice that from the next row
for the developing countries overall, the poverty rates in Latin America seem
much better than average. The comparison is a bit deceiving as it includes

Table 12.2 Poverty in Latin America and the world, 1981–2004

Region	Extreme Poverty Rates (US $1.08 per day)		Poverty Rates (US $2.15 per day)	
	1981	2004	1981	2004
Latin America	10.77	8.64	28.45	22.17
Sub-Saharan Africa	42.26	41.10	74.52	71.97
East Asia and the Pacific	57.73	9.05	84.80	36.58
Eastern Europe and Central Asia	0.70	0.94	4.60	9.79
Middle East and North Africa	5.08	1.47	29.16	19.70
South Asia	51.75	34.33	88.53	77.12
Total	40.14	18.09	66.96	47.55

Source: Chen and Ravallion (2007).

the poverty-racked areas of Africa and South Asia. The comparison is even more troubling if one looks at the data for 1981 versus 2004. The extreme poverty rate has fallen by a grand total of 2 percentage points in the last several decades and by approximately 6 percentage points for the higher standard of $2.15 per day. Compared to the dramatic declines in poverty rates in Asia, progress against poverty in the region has been lagging. In this regard, progress in Latin America has been troublingly similar to Africa.

While instructive, Table 12.2 is masking some useful information. As with other issues, poverty in Latin America is hardly homogeneous. Further, the data given in the table is based on global standards of poverty. These standards are based on a sense of absolute poverty. Absolute poverty is defined as the amount of money necessary to meet certain basic thresholds of human existence. Outside of the definition of absolute poverty, what constitutes "poor" becomes more specific to individual countries. For example, poverty in a high-income country is a standard of living that most people in the world would aspire to. The same is true even within Latin America. Someone considered poor in Chile might well be considered to be relatively well off in some of the lower-income parts of the region. These differences give rise to the concept of relative poverty. Relative poverty is a standard of living that an individual country constructs to measure the number of citizens it wishes to define as poor. Table 12.3 is designed to illustrate this point.

First, notice that by the global standard of extreme poverty, there is still a significant problem in the region. For the higher-income countries of the region, extreme poverty is less than 10 percent. More troublingly, extreme poverty still afflicts between 10 and 20 percent of the population in six countries. In two of these countries, nearly 1 in 5 fall into the category of

Table 12.3 Relative poverty in Latin America

	$1.25 per day (2000–2007)	$2 per day (2000–2006)	Poverty percentage
Argentina	4.5	11.3	
Bolivia	19.6	30.3	65.2
Brazil	5.2	12.7	21.5
Chile	<2	<2	17.3
Colombia	16.0	27.9	64.0
Costa Rica	2.4	8.6	23.9
Ecuador	4.7	12.8	46.0
El Salvador	11.0	20.5	37.2
Guatemala	11.7	24.3	56.2
Honduras	18.2	29.7	50.7
Mexico	<2	4.8	17.6
Nicaragua	15.8	31.8	47.9
Panama	9.5	17.8	37.3
Paraguay	6.5	14.2	
Peru	7.9	18.5	53.1
Uruguay	<2	4.2	
Venezuela	3.5	10.2	
Latin America	8.4[1]	16.6	41.4[2]

Source: United Nations Development Programme (2009).

Notes
[1] <2 was counted as 2 percent in calculating the average for Latin America.
[2] average of the 13 countries calculating this statistic.

extreme poverty. Likewise, the percentages still are depressingly high for the higher global standard of around $2 per day. There are only four countries in the region where this is less than 10 percent of the population. The average for the region from 2000 to 2006 is 16.6 percent. Taken together, approximately 25 percent of the population of Latin America is either extremely poor or poor by global standards. Again, the comparisons to the poorer regions of the world are not encouraging. A substantial portion of the population of the region is existing on incomes more typical of East Asia or Africa, than a region of the world normally considered to be middle-income. Further, the problem is not wholly confined to the poorer countries of Central America. The percentages are only low for Chile, Mexico, and Uruguay. A surprising amount of absolute poverty exists even in some of the more affluent countries of the region.

As mentioned above, relative poverty is something that each society must decide how to define on its own. Since much of the region is neither high-income or low-income, the standard of poverty set by individual countries will vary. However, in a rough sense, each country-specific definition is important. The third column of Table 12.3 provides a window into how each country measures itself in terms of the percentage of the population that it defines to be "poor." Defining such measures is never easy and four of the countries of the region essentially have declined to do so. For the 14 countries that have a working definition of relative poverty, the statistics tell a lot about how the countries of the region see themselves with respect to poverty. Of this group, only two countries have less than 20 percent of the population defined as poor in relative terms. Of the rest, virtually all of them consider over a third of the population to be poor. Five of these countries are reporting poverty rates of over *50 percent*. The average for this set of countries is 41.4 percent. In virtually any country, poverty rates of this magnitude would be considered a social catastrophe. In Latin America high poverty rates are the *norm*. What is also normal is a substantial amount of income inequality. This is a natural consequence of a region with relatively high incomes by global standards coupled with a substantial amount of both absolute and relative poverty. In the next section, we consider the measurement and extent of income inequality in Latin America.

Income inequality

The data in the previous two sections form the basis for a discussion of income inequality in Latin America. In terms of GDP per capita, by global standards much of Latin America is solidly middle class. By just superficially looking at the overall data the region seems relatively well off. The second section of the chapter showed that the overall data on GDP per capita for the region is deceiving. Latin America contains a shockingly high percentage of the population that is poor by global standards. By the standards each country sets for itself, the picture is even bleaker. Under the best of circumstances, countries of the region are reporting poverty rates of 20 to 50 percent or even higher. Combining relatively high average incomes with high rates of poverty leads to an inescapable conclusion: the distribution of income is highly unequal. To anyone with a passing familiarity with the region this is hardly surprising. The problem has been noted for centuries. While impressions and anecdotal information are not to be dismissed off-hand, economists like to put things in a more numerical way. This is the purpose of this section. First, we need to define how economists measure income inequality. With this measurement in mind, we can then see more precisely just how unequal the distribution of income is in the region.

To measure income inequality, one needs some benchmark against which to measure inequality. To begin, imagine a world where the total available income was perfectly distributed. In this case each 10 percent of the population would receive exactly 10 percent of the income. Now imagine the world as it is. In this case, the top ten percent of the population receives more than 10 percent of the income. At some point, one of the deciles would start receiving less than 10 percent of the income. The process would continue until one observed the percentage of income being received by the bottom decile. To make this process less tedious, economists use a single statistic which expresses the extent to which the actual distribution of income deviates from perfect equality. This statistic is known as the Gini coefficient. The Gini coefficient is a measure of the deviation of the actual income distribution from perfect equality. The statistic varies from 0 to 1. Perfect equality corresponds to a Gini of 0. On the other side of the spectrum, perfect inequality is 1. In the world economy, no economy conforms to either extreme. For the purpose of reference, a Gini coefficient below 0.3 would be considered a low level of inequality. On the other side, a value of 0.70 or above would be considered high. For many of the world's countries, the Gini coefficient tends to be in the 0.30 to 0.40 range. With the concept of the Gini coefficient in mind and some sense of what constitutes low, high, and average it now becomes easier to analyze the relative position of Latin America with respect to income inequality.

As one can see in Table 12.4 below, the position of Latin America with respect to income inequality is not favorable. The Gini coefficients given in the table confirm the conventional wisdom that the distribution of income for the region is the most unequal among the world's major regions. The average for Latin America is 0.524. For comparison purposes, the US has one of the most unequal distributions of income among high-income countries. The Gini coefficient for the US is 0.408. Canada, Portugal, and Spain are more typical of high-income countries with Gini coefficients of 0.326, 0.385, and 0.347, respectively.[1] As in virtually all of the regional economic data that we have studied in this book, the degree of income inequality for Latin America is not homogeneous. However, in this case the degree of variance is less than is usually the case. The lowest Gini coefficient is 0.462 for Uruguay and the highest is 0.585 for Colombia. The range for the region is only a bit over 0.12. Even the lowest coefficients are high by global standards. On the other hand, even the highest coefficients are less than a very high coefficient of 0.70. For Latin America, the striking thing about the data is its relative *uniformity*. Every country in the region has a high Gini coefficient, just some a bit more so than others. This commonality is more striking than the differences. The data simply reflects what seemed to be the case from the previous section. The coexistence of high levels of poverty in middle-income

Table 12.4 Income inequality in Latin America, 2007

Country	Gini Coefficient
Argentina	0.50
Bolivia	0.582
Brazil	0.550
Chile	0.520
Colombia	0.585
Costa Rica	0.472
Ecuador	0.544
El Salvador	0.497

(continued)

Table 12.4 Income inequality in Latin America, 2007
(continued)

Country	Gini Coefficient
El Salvador	0.497
Guatemala	0.537
Honduras	0.553
Mexico	0.481
Nicaragua	0.523
Panama	0.549
Paraguay	0.532
Peru	0.496
Uruguay	0.462
Venezuela	
Latin America	0.524
Portugal	0.385
Spain	0.347
Canada	0.326
US	0.408

Source: United Nations Development Programme (2009).

12.1   The Human Opportunity Index

The results shown above for the Gini coefficient for Latin America represent an outcome. It reveals a snapshot of the distribution of income for a particular year. However, this outcome is the result of the opportunities the population had at earlier points in time to make economic progress. In order to lower the Gini coefficient in the future, it is important to provide more opportunities for a larger part of the population to improve their standard of living. As a result, it would be desirable to have some measure of the availability of economic opportunities now so that poverty and inequality could be reduced in the future.

Paes de Barros, *et al.* (2009) have made an attempt at quantifying equality of opportunity in Latin America by constructing the Human Opportunity Index. It is a measure of the average access and inequities in access to basic services for children. Education is measured by the number of children completing sixth grade on time and school attendance from ages 10 to 14. Housing is measured by access to clean water, sanitation, and electricity. The overall index is a composite of the education and housing indicators. The focus on children is sensible as increasing their opportunities increases their chances for success later in life with the potential to reduce poverty and inequality in the future.

The results of this exercise are shown in Table 12.5 below. As is usual, the range in the region is large in all cases. The averages for education, housing, and overall are 76.4, 65.8, and 71.1. These averages are masking ranges from 51 to 90 for education; 34 to 94 for housing; and 46 to 91 overall. The best results are for education but the range for access to clean water, sanitation, and electricity seems to be considerably worse. Obviously, this data is not a perfect

Table 12.5 Human Opportunity Index, 2005

	Education	Housing	Overall
Argentina	89	88	88
Bolivia	83	41	62
Brazil	67	77	72
Chile	90	93	91
Colombia	78	69	74
Costa Rica	79	94	86
Ecuador	80	69	74
El Salvador	65	46	55
Guatemala	51	50	50
Honduras	62	44	53
Mexico	88	75	82
Nicaragua	59	34	46
Panama	81	57	69
Paraguay	74	59	67
Peru	83	49	66
Uruguay	85	85	85
Venezuela	84	89	86
Latin America	76.4	65.8	71.1

Source: Paes de Barros, *et al.* (2009).

exercise in measuring the degree of opportunity for children. However, it is obviously a useful start for policy purposes. All of the measures used in the index are based on the average access (supply) and inequalities in that access. It is quite possible for average access to improve over time which may reduce poverty but if inequalities in access persist the effects on the distribution of income may be muted. Further, the gaps between education and housing vary enormously across countries. For example, Costa Rica has the highest degree of opportunity in housing but is only above average in education. For Bolivia, the situation is reversed. Education and housing are general problems in the region but to varying degrees. The implication is that policies designed to increase economic opportunity will vary considerably by country.

countries strongly implies a high level of income inequality. As this high degree of inequality is pervasive for the region, perhaps the roots of this problem can be traced to similarities in the economic history of the region and more recently similarities in economic policies.

Causes of poverty and inequality

At a number of points in the book, we have pointed out that a certain characteristic or economic policy has had an adverse impact on either poverty or inequality or both in Latin America. In this section, we will review a number of these points and expand on some of them. Be aware that the topic is fraught with difficulties. Poverty and inequality in Latin America, or anywhere else for that matter, is not a simple thing to explain. As was seen above, both poverty and inequality are relative concepts. Further, the normal workings of a society operating under democratic capitalism are naturally going to produce some degree of inequality. There is no single, simple explanation such as capitalism, historical factors, or government policy. Rather there are a number of factors that to a greater or lesser extent *contribute* to the existence of poverty and high levels of inequality. What follows is a listing of factors that tend to worsen these problems in Latin America.

Historical roots

It is not too much of an exaggeration to say that modern Latin America was born with poverty and inequality figuratively baked into the economic system. The initial conditions in the late fifteenth and early sixteenth centuries involved the wresting of land and assets from the indigenous people of the region. The initial mineral wealth of the region and the later development of commodities for export created incentives for particular institutions to develop. More specifically, the rents generated from the production of commodities were to the greatest extent possible transferred to the governments of Portugal and Spain. These transfers were aided by concentrating land and resource holdings into a small part of the population. While convenient for the transfer of resources to the colonial powers, the institutional environment led to serious inequality. There was little or no incentive to provide land, education, or political power to the large mass of the people of the region. The indigenous population and later the African slaves benefited little from the abundance of resources. The result was a highly stratified economy with extremely high levels of income inequality.[2]

The independence movements of the early nineteenth century had the potential for reducing the level of inequality. Fewer resources were being transferred to the colonial powers which held the potential for the new governments of the region to improve the incomes of the poor. Instead, independence in many cases was followed by decades of political violence. Such internal instability will reduce economic growth in any country and Latin America was no exception. Under such circumstances, the poorer members of society not only do not progress but are the most vulnerable to the economic hardships produced by political instability. The end of this instability in the mid-nineteenth century ushered in an era of relative prosperity. This "Golden Age" improved the average income of the population of the region. Unfortunately, the progress was not evenly spread. The end of political instability did not lead to widespread participation in the political system, i.e. democracy. Rather, political power in the region became concentrated in the hands of the owners of land and other resources. Such a situation is not conducive to either concerns about poverty or inequality. To a greater or lesser extent, this situation persisted until the late nineteenth century. Growth was being fostered by the exports of commodities as Latin America became more integrated into the world economy. However, if the earnings from these exports are very concentrated in a small part of the population then growth, in and of itself, may not reduce inequality.[3] From the forgoing discussion, notice that the initial inequality created by colonial rule persisted for nearly *500 years*. Such long-entrenched inequality is not going to be easily reduced in a short period of time even under the best of circumstances.

ISI

> Yes, there are oligarchies in Latin America. They are no longer oligarchies of landowners and ranchers; instead they are industrial oligarchies and business groups that have prospered under protectionist power. To eliminate these oligarchies one doesn't have to eradicate their external manifestations – their money – but rather the system that made them possible.
>
> Plinio A. Mendoza,
> Carlos A. Montaner, and Alvaro V. Llosa

From the section above, the export of commodities tended to make the distribution of income in Latin America more unequal. The concentrated holdings of land and other resources became a primary driver of inequality. In the late nineteenth and early twentieth centuries, the region began to develop a small manufacturing sector. As noted before, the advent of the Great Depression and the subsequent global trade war made exporting from this small base difficult. Latin America already had high tariffs at this point and the global trade war exacerbated this trend. The existing level of protectionism also found a justification in popular policy prescriptions of the time. It was argued that due to declining terms of trade for Latin America that it would be advantageous to reduce imports by replacing them with domestic production, i.e. ISI. The ultimately catastrophic effects of the collection of policies associated with ISI contributed to income inequality in the region in several ways.

First, the system encouraged the development of either private sector firms or SOEs to produce products to replace imports. Most of these firms were operating with explicit or implicit government subsidies. These subsidies came in the form of loans on attractive terms, various forms of protectionism, and an overvalued exchange rate. In addition, many of these firms were operating in markets where the degree of competition was low. This mix of policies has the potential to increase inequality. The owners of such firms could reasonably be expected to make relatively high profits. On the other hand, consumers are likely to be paying relatively high prices for lower-quality goods. The vast majority are being made worse off while the gains from this arrangement are concentrated.

Secondly, the trade policy associated with ISI had the potential to increase inequality. Free trade has a tendency to increase the price of the abundant factor of production. In the case of Latin America this would have meant the development of industry that intensively used cheap semi-skilled labor. However, it would have reduced the returns to capital in the region. This sort of development has the potential to reduce the level of inequality. Wages might have risen for a large number of workers and the returns to the owners of capital would have been smaller.[4] The protectionism associated with ISI worked in the opposite direction. High tariffs and quotas artificially encouraged the development of capital-intensive industries. The subsidies mentioned above added to this tendency. The result was the development of a profitable capital-intensive industrial base. Perversely, trade policy was increasing the return to the *scarce* factor of production as opposed to the abundant factor, labor. The policy favored the relatively well off at the expense of the larger group of semi-skilled workers. Further, workers in ISI industries benefited indirectly from the profitability of the sector. The existence of these profits and the ability to form unions helped a minority of workers in ISI industries to earn wages in excess of what were available in the rest of the economy. The benefits of ISI were spread a bit more widely, but much of the population lost income as a result. Wages were lower outside of the protected sector and the prices paid by most consumers for domestically produced products were high. International trade has the potential to reduce income inequality in a labor-abundant country. This outcome can be negated if a country persists in developing industry based on comparative disadvantage. The adverse implications on the distribution of income are just another in a long list of problems associated with ISI.

Business and labor market regulation

For any country, excessive regulation of markets can create adverse consequences. While there is no perfect set of business or labor market regulations, there are tradeoffs that if ignored can cause significant problems. In Latin America, a combination of a difficult business environment coupled with the extensive regulation of labor markets is both slowing economic growth and contributing to inequality. While there is some debate over the effects of economic growth on the distribution of income, it is rarely argued that slower growth makes the poor better off in absolute terms. A thriving private sector is normally seen as a prerequisite for the reduction of poverty and perhaps eventually lowering the degree of inequality. As was mentioned earlier in the book, Latin America is not an easy place to do business. Business is always more difficult in a developing country. Inadequate infrastructure and other inherent difficulties make running a firm in Mexico City somewhat different than operating in a large city in a high-income country. In a well-managed developing country, the government is careful not to make these disadvantages even more onerous through thoughtless taxation and regulation. Unfortunately, for Latin America, this situation is common. The general perception of the region, now backed up by a growing amount of research, is that the tax and regulatory environment is a significant drag on growth. Further, this sort of environment favors the development of large enterprises that have the resources to deal with complicated and at times overlapping levels of regulation. This tends to drive smaller firms into the informal sector and reduces the chances of these firms to grow to an optimal size. A business environment favoring large firms over small and medium-sized enterprises (SMEs) is not likely to contribute to the reduction of income inequality.

This problem is reinforced by labor market regulation. In labor markets, there is always a tradeoff between the security of existing workers and the creation of new jobs. For example, making it more difficult for firms to shed workers makes firms more reluctant to create new jobs. Among the world's regions, Latin America has among the most generous levels of support for existing workers. This is so much the case that many SMEs could not profitably operate and comply with all relevant labor market regulations. Again, the result is a large number of SMEs operating outside of the formal sector of the economy. Frequently, SMEs must be able to adjust their use of labor quickly in order to survive in the long run. Firms that are unable to do this face the choice of not doing business or operating outside of the legal framework of business in the informal sector. In turn, this has created a dual labor market in much of Latin America. Workers in the formal sector receive higher wages and other protections from the normal operation of the labor market. Workers who are not so fortunate typically find work in the informal sector operating with lower wages and no or little job security. The effects on the distribution of income are obvious.

Educational inequality

One of the most common relationships in economics is between productivity and wages. In real terms, wages can only increase to the extent that productivity increases. The productivity of labor can be influenced by a number of factors such as the institutional quality of the society that workers are functioning in. Productivity also is heavily tied to the amount of human capital that workers possess. In turn, the amount of human capital embodied in a worker is partially a function of education. First, a higher level of education directly increases human capital. Secondly, education levels influence the ability of workers to continue to acquire human capital during the course of their careers.[5] As a result of these relationships, the distribution of income in a country can be influenced by the returns to and the distribution of human capital. In turn, the distribution of human capital is influenced by the distribution of educational opportunities. Not surprisingly, educational inequality in Latin America is high.

The data on educational inequality is shown in Table 12.6 below. At first glance, the data seems to be reasonable. Expressed as Gini coefficients, education is not as unequally distributed in the region as income. While this is the case, this also is true for the world. The global average is 0.428.

Table 12.6 Educational inequality in Latin
America, Gini coefficients

Argentina	.273
Bolivia	.537
Brazil	.393
Chile	.313
Colombia	.486
Costa Rica	.426
Ecuador	.449
El Salvador	
Guatemala	.626
Honduras	.468
Mexico	.384
Nicaragua	.587
Panama	.339
Paraguay	.398
Peru	.431
Uruguay	.342
Venezuela	.472
Latin America	.433

Source: de Ferranti, *et al.* (2004).

Still, this is encouraging as education in Latin America is not as unequally distributed as in the world as a whole. Educational inequality is far worse in Africa and Asia with Gini coefficients for these regions of 0.618 and 0.479, respectively. This is encouraging until one considers that the Gini coefficient for the high-income countries is 0.275. Relative to some of the other data on inequality for the region, in terms of education the situation is better. Moreover, educational inequality has been falling since the 1960s.[6] However, this data is based on the distribution of the number of *years* of education obtained. Thus the data is based on the quantity of schooling but says little about the quality of education. An educational system may well be successful at increasing the amount of time students spend in formal schooling but somewhat less successful at providing the basic human capital needed to succeed in a modern economy.

Unfortunately, limited data on the quality of education overall in Latin America indicates that the quality of schooling is a problem. The measurement of educational outcomes on an international basis is relatively recent. The OECD has created the Program for International Student Assessment (PISA) to try to gain a better understanding of educational outcomes around the world. Data is available for all OECD countries and a limited number of developing countries.[7] At this point, only six countries in the region are participating in the project. The data for these countries and Canada, Portugal, Spain, and the US is given in Table 12.7. To better understand the data, scores over 500 in the table put a country in a very high position. For example Canada is ranked fourth, seventh, and third in

Table 12.7 Educational outcomes in Latin America, PISA scores for 2006

	Reading	Mathematics	Science
Argentina	374	381	391
Brazil	393	370	390
Chile	442	411	438
Colombia	385	370	388
Mexico	410	406	410
Uruguay	413	427	428
Latin America	403	394	408
Portugal	472	466	474
Spain	461	480	488
Canada	527	527	534
US	474	489	

Source: OECD (2007).

the world in reading, mathematics, and science, respectively. On the other hand, Portugal, Spain, and the US have PISA scores in the middle of the distribution for the sample of countries available. For Latin America, data is only available for six countries. From this limited sample, students in Latin America are well behind students in Portugal, Spain, and the US and far behind a highly-rated country such as Canada. Notice also that this sample is skewed. The countries of Latin America included in the sample are among the higher-income countries of the region. If the results for these countries are relatively poor, then it is difficult to imagine that the scores for some of the poorer countries of the region would be better. Unfortunately, these data makes sense put together with the data on educational inequality. Inequality in educational opportunity will tend to lead to lower student performance. Large numbers of students in Latin America have some schooling, but the percentage attending is lower with each level of education. The situation also contributes to poverty as real wages are negatively influenced by a lack of educational achievement.

Reducing poverty and inequality

Given the long history of poverty and inequality in the region, reducing either one of these problems is not going to be an easy task. Given the troubling amount of absolute poverty that still lingers in the region, the reduction of poverty is a priority. Inequality in the distribution of income is obviously still a problem. Fortunately, policies to reduce poverty will usually also work to reduce inequality. In this section, we cover some of the more general themes involved in both reducing poverty and inequality. In doing so we recover some of the material from the previous section and add some other material on addressing these issues. These general themes are economic growth, the regulation of business and labor, educational inequality, and the role of the state.

Economic growth

The reduction of poverty in Latin America is dependent on maintaining or improving economic growth. As we saw in Chapter 2, the central economic problem of the region is that growth has been relatively slow. Over time, relatively slow growth makes it much more difficult to improve the welfare of those at the bottom of the income distribution. The dramatic reduction of the number of people living in absolute poverty in Asia over the last 50 years is a dramatic example of what economic growth can accomplish. As was also outlined in that chapter, increasing economic growth is not a simple formula but the broad outlines of increasing growth in Latin America are understood. The easiest factor to address is increasing the stock of capital by increasing the historically low savings rates in the region and through more effective use of this capital. Further, the reduction of barriers to FDI accomplishes much the same thing. In any country, an increase in the K/L ratio increases productivity and real wages, and works to reduce the level of poverty. In addition, FDI normally increases the level of total factor productivity which further increases growth and incomes. A more difficult factor for Latin America is the improvement of institutional quality. Modern research on economic growth has identified institutional quality as one of the most important factors for economic growth. While Latin America does not suffer from the deficiencies in institutional quality prevalent in low-income countries, there is substantial room for improvement that would enhance growth. Unfortunately, institutional quality is a multifaceted term and knowing precisely how to proceed on this front is still difficult to determine with any degree of precision. To the extent that poor institutional quality is hindering growth, it is also hindering the reduction of poverty and just perhaps contributing to greater inequality in the distribution of income.

Regulation of business and labor

Every country needs a framework to regulate the activities of business and the relationship between employers and employees. However, it is also important to construct regulation that will accomplish the goals of regulation without reducing economic growth. The general consensus, recently backed up with data, is that Latin America hasn't been able to accomplish this. Doing business in the region usually involves a large amount of time and cost that does not seem to be contributing much in the way of improving social welfare. Such a poor regulatory climate reduces growth and increases poverty. There are similar problems with the taxation of business. Taxes on businesses are a fact of life in any country. It serves no useful purpose for taxes to be so high that they are widely evaded or to be so complex that compliance costs reduce the ability of firms to grow. Likewise this constraint also reduces overall economic growth and hinders the reduction of poverty.

This degree of regulation may also exacerbate inequality. Needlessly complex business regulations and tax compliance costs contribute to the development of a large informal business sector in the region. Small firms that cannot deal with compliance costs are resigned to the informal sector and may not grow to an optimal size. Such constraints on a significant portion of a country's business community reduce growth and inhibit the reduction of both poverty and inequality.

Much the same can be said of excessive regulation on conditions of employment. There is always a tradeoff between protecting the conditions of employment for existing workers and the creation of new jobs. For example, making it difficult or expensive to reduce the workforce of a firm makes the firm more reluctant to hire new workers. In the case of Latin America, such regulations increase the unit cost of labor in the region for semi-skilled and skilled workers. In turn, this reduces the ability of the region to trade on one of its sources of comparative advantage, an abundance of semi-skilled labor. The effects on economic growth are not positive as slower growth once again reduces the ability to mitigate poverty. This sort of labor market regulation contributes to inequality. For workers in the formal sector of the economy, wages may be high by local standards and job security may be high. For those workers who are less productive, jobs are still available. However, these jobs may only be plentiful in the informal sector where wages are lower and labor market regulations are not observed. Such a dualistic labor market cannot be expected to contribute to the reduction of income inequality.

Educational reform

In a modern economy, the accumulation of human capital is a critical component of economic growth. Everything else equal, the rapid accumulation of human capital increases the rate of economic growth. The accumulation of human capital is critically dependent on the quality of a country's educational system. The productivity of the labor force and the real wages that they can earn are positively correlated with the possession of human capital. The human capital a worker possesses and their ability to acquire more over the course of a working life determines both initial wages and the ability to increase income in the future. In this regard, the educational system of Latin America is considered to be deficient. In the first place, overall spending on education is not high. The region spends about 4 percent of GDP on all levels of education. This level of spending has been sufficient to reduce illiteracy rates in most countries to relatively low levels. Unfortunately, this level of spending has not changed significantly for decades.[8] In such a case, improvements in education become dependent on increasing the productivity of the educational system. The limited data on educational attainment given in a previous section indicates that students in the region lag behind the level of education obtained in OECD countries as well as other middle-income countries. Also, as shown above, part of the problem is the degree of inequality in educational opportunities. Education is very unequally distributed in the region. The result is that human capital accumulation is lower than it could be and the distribution of human capital becomes unequal. Such a situation contributes to both poverty and the perpetuation of high levels of income inequality. Despite what has been accomplished in the twentieth century, reform of the educational system in much of Latin America to make it more effective and equitable is a pressing need.

The role of the state

The changes outlined above that would reduce poverty and inequality in Latin America would be desirable but would not work quickly. Improving institutional quality, reforming business and labor regulation, and reforming educational systems are the work of years, at best. The time lag between reforms and positive effects on poverty and income inequality would involve similar time lags. For such reasons, governments wishing to reduce poverty or income inequality frequently pursue more short-run measures to mitigate these problems. To a greater or lesser extent, most high- and middle-income countries pursue a variety of policies designed to reduce poverty and income inequality. In general, these involve progressive tax systems, direct transfers of resources, or other programs designed to more directly address such problems in the short run. The countries of Latin America are no different in this regard. Each country has its own set of policies that are at least superficially aimed at the improving the welfare of the poor and addressing income inequality. It is beyond the scope of the discussion to study such systems for even one country, let alone the entire region. However, there is one way to capture the workings of the state with regard to poverty and the distribution of income. To do this we will refer back to the concept of the Gini coefficient.

The Gini coefficients reported in Table 12.4 above refer to the distribution of disposable income. This refers to income after taxes and transfer payments. To get an idea of the role of the state in reducing inequality, it would be useful to compare this measure of income inequality with a Gini coefficient based solely on *market* incomes. Fortunately, recent research makes this comparison possible.[9] The results show that the role of the state in changing the distribution of income in Latin America is modest at best. The Gini coefficient for market income is only 0.02 above disposable income. What this means is that the operation of taxes and transfer payments in the region has very little impact on the distribution of disposable income. Theoretically, progressive taxation should be working to reduce income inequality. This is true in Latin America. However, taxes change the Gini coefficient by approximately 0.01. The effects of transfer payments is a bit larger but still in the 0.01 to 0.02 range. The latter is important as transfer payments tend to have the most dramatic effects on lowering the level of poverty and inequality. A comparison with Europe is useful to illustrate the point.

The market Gini coefficient for Europe is 0.46. However, in Europe transfer payments change the Gini coefficient by 0.10. The lowest level of transfers in Europe, Portugal, changes the Gini coefficient by 0.06. The role of taxes is smaller. In Europe it changes the Gini coefficient by 0.05. In Latin America, market incomes are more unevenly distributed than in Europe. A key difference for Latin America is that the role of government in reducing inequality is modest.

12.2 Bolsa Familia

It is unusual for a program that distributes cash to the poor to be widely hailed as a model for reducing poverty and inequality. If not carefully designed, direct transfers of income can work to reduce poverty in the present but create negative incentives which may perpetuate poverty and inequality in the future. The Bolsa Familia program in Brazil is seen as a model program in the sense that it simultaneously reduces current levels of poverty while at the same time creating incentives to reduce poverty and inequality in the future. The basic benefit of the program is a cash transfer to families living in extreme poverty with no conditions for receiving the money. The interesting part of the program is the cash transfers to higher-income families who fall below the poverty line. This program provides a cash transfer per child *conditional* on the children receiving vaccinations and school attendance. As a result, the program attacks poverty immediately by transferring cash to the poorest Brazilians. Family income increases immediately and income inequality is reduced. The interesting effects will occur in the future. Vaccinations are a cost-effective means of improving the health of children now and in the future. Regular school attendance increases human capital and the ability to accumulate human capital over the course of a working life. Giving immediate incentives to improve school attendance has potentially large benefits for the children of the poor by increasing productivity and real wages in the future. The overall Brazilian economy may benefit going forward if this enhances economic growth. The effects of the program are potentially large as it covers over 11 million families or 44 million individuals. The overall cost of the program is also interesting. It currently accounts for 0.5 percent of Brazil's GDP. It is only 2.5 percent of total government spending. At this cost, the program would not have to produce enormous benefits in order to cover the cost of the program. Because the program was only initiated in 2003, rigorous assessment of the benefits precludes any firm conclusions of the benefits. However, the modest cost coupled with large potential benefits makes the program an unusually promising policy.

Overall, the government's role in reducing poverty and reducing inequality could be improved. The endless complications of doing business in the region lower growth and impede the reduction of poverty. Likewise, the effects of labor market regulation reduce growth and contribute to poverty. Further, they may work to increase inequality by encouraging the growth of the informal sector where wages are lower. For the most part, education in Latin America is produced by the state. Low educational quality reduces the accumulation of human capital and depresses wages for the vast majority of the workers of the region. High levels of inequality in education tend to perpetuate already high levels of inequality. Governments have the ability to mitigate high levels of income inequality produced by the market through taxes and transfer payments. As shown above, these effects in Latin America are small. In the end, we will leave it to the reader to decide whether Latin America's primary economic problem is due to the poor quality of firms and workers in the region or the poor quality of government. One would now hope that the spread of democracy in Latin America will give the people of the region the chance to obtain policies that are more likely to improve the welfare of the average citizen.

Key concepts and terms

absolute poverty – the amount of money necessary to meet certain basic thresholds of human existence.

Gini coefficient – a measure of the deviation of the actual income distribution from perfect equality.

productivity – the amount of output produced in a given period of time by a unit of labor.

relative poverty – a standard of living that an individual country constructs to measure the number of citizens it wishes to define as poor.

Questions for review and discussion

1   "By global standards, Latin America is neither desperately poor nor rich." Using the data in Table 12.1, explain this statement.
2   Describe the percentage of the population of Latin America living on less than $2 per day. Relate this to the data on per capita GDP in Table 12.1.
3   Define the terms absolute and relative poverty. How do these terms apply to Latin America?
4   What is the Gini coefficient? How does it apply to Latin America?
5   Describe how commodities and colonial rule interacted to increase income inequality in Latin America.
6   What is the relationship between ISI and poverty and inequality in Latin America?
7   Describe the relationship between wages and productivity and put this relationship into the context of Latin America.
8   How does inequality in education contribute to income inequality in Latin America?
9   Describe the difference between income inequality based on market incomes and overall income inequality.

10 To what extent have government actions changed income inequality in
the region?

References and recommended readings

Arroyo Abad, A. Leiticia. 2009. "Inequality in Republican Latin America: Assessing
the Effects of Factor Endowments and Trade." *Global Prices and Income History
Group Working Papers, 12.*

Breceda, Karla, Jamele Rigolini, and Jaime Saavedra. 2009. "Latin America and
the Social Contract: Patterns of Social Spending and Taxation." *Population and
Development Review.* 35(December): 721–48.

Chen, Shaohua and Martin Ravallion. 2007. "Absolute Poverty Measures for the
Developing World, 1981–2004." *World Bank Policy Research Working Paper
4211.* Washington, DC: World Bank.

Damon, Amy and Paul Glewwe. 2009. "Three Proposals to Improve Education
in the LAC Region: Estimates of the Costs and Benefits of Each Strategy," pp.
45–91 in Bjorn Lomberg (ed.), *Latin American Development Priorities: Costs
and Benefits.* New York: Cambridge University Press.

de Ferranti, David, Guillermo E. Perry, and Francisco Ferreira. 2004. *Inequality in
Latin America: Breaking with History?* Washington, DC: World Bank.

Galiani, Sebastian. 2009. "Reducing Poverty in the LAC Region," in Bjorn Lomberg
(ed.), *Latin American Development Priorities: Costs and Benefits.* New York:
Cambridge University Press.

Goni, Edwin, J. Humberto Lopez, and Luis Serven. 2008. "Fiscal Redistribution
and Income Inequality in Latin America." *World Bank Policy Research Working
Paper No. 4487.* Washington, DC: World Bank.

Lopez, J. Humberto and Guillermo Perry. 2008. "Inequality in Latin America:
Determinants and Consequences." *World Bank Policy Research Working Paper
No. 4504.* Washington, DC: World Bank.

McEwan, Patrick J., Miguel Urquiola, and Emiliana Vegas. 2007. "School Choice,
Stratification, and Information on School Performance: Evidence from Chile."
Economia. 8(Spring): 1–27.

OECD. 2007. *PISA, 2006: Science Competencies for Tomorrow's World.* Paris:
OECD.

Paes de Barros, Ricardo, Francisco H. G. Ferreira, Jose R. Molinas Vega, and Jaime
Aaavedra Chanduvi. 2009. *Measuring Inequality of Opportunities in Latin
America and the Caribbean.* Washington, DC: World Bank.

Thorbecke, Erik and Machiko Nissanke. 2008. "The Impact of Globalization on the
Poor in Latin America." *Economia.* 9(Fall): 153–86.

United Nations Development Programme. 2009. *Human Development Report,
2009.* New York: United Nations.

Willamson, Jeffrey G. 2009. *History without Evidence: Latin American Inequality
since 1491.* NBER Working Paper 14766. Cambridge, MA: National Bureau of
Economic Research.

Glossary

Absolute advantage – the ability of a country to produce a good using fewer resources than another country.

Absolute poverty – the amount of money necessary to meet certain basic thresholds of human existence.

Absolute purchasing power parity – the theory that exchange rates are related to differences in the level of prices between countries.

Ad valorem **equivalent (AVE)** – the level of protection provided by a quota expressed as the percentage difference between the world market price and the domestic quota-constrained price.

Ad valorem **tariff** – a tariff that is measured as a percentage of the value of the imported good.

Aggregate demand – the relationship between the total quantity of goods and services demanded by all sectors of the economy and the price level.

Aggregate supply – the relationship between the total quantity of goods and services that an economy produces and the price level.

Autarky – a situation where a country does not engage in economic relations with the rest of the world.

Balance of payments – a summary of all the international transactions of a country's residents with the rest of the world during a year.

Bretton Woods system – the global system of fixed exchange rates that functioned between 1946 and 1971.

Capital flight – the movement of money out of a country in response to adverse political or economic events.

Capital-intensive – the condition that the production of a good requires a high K/L ratio.

Capital-to-labor ratio (K/L) – the amount of capital per unit of labor used in the production of goods and services.

Cartel – an organization of producers that attempts to stabilize the price of a commodity by changing market conditions.

Central bank – the financial institution in a country which is in charge of managing the supply of money.

Command and control (CAC) – a policy to control pollution that sets an allowable level of pollution for producers.

Commodity – products where one unit of the product is indistinguishable from another unit.

Commodity price shock – a large change in commodity prices that affects the overall performance of the economy.

Comparative advantage – the ability of a country to produce a good at a lower opportunity cost than another country.

Comparative disadvantage – the situation where a country can produce a good only at a relatively high opportunity cost.

Contagion – the tendency of investors to withdraw portfolio capital from an entire region in response to perceived economic difficulties in a single country or a subset of countries.

Cost/benefit analysis – an analysis using all relevant costs and benefits to determine the appropriate level of economic activity.

Crawling peg – an exchange rate regime where the nominal exchange rate is changed at regular intervals to stabilize the real exchange rate.

Currency substitution – the holding of financial assets in foreign currency as a protection against losses.

Current account – an accounting of international transactions that includes goods, services, investment income, and unilateral transfers.

Debt – borrowing by countries in the form of bonds or bank loans.

Debt/export ratio – the ratio of a country's debt payments to its exports.

Default – the inability of a country to repay all or part of its foreign debt when it is due.

Dependency theory – the idea that the world economy is a system controlled by the developed countries (the center) to the detriment of the developing countries (the periphery).

Discount rate – the interest rate charged by the central bank on loans to private sector banks.

Dutch disease – a term used to describe the effects of commodity exports on other parts of the economy.

Econometrics – the use of statistical techniques to analyze economic data.

Economic populism – the tendency of governments to pursue policies that will produce the most favorable economic outcomes in the short run.

Effective rate of protection – a measure of the amount of protection provided to an industry by a country's tariff schedule.

Encomienda – the granting of land in the colonies for use by a Spanish citizen during the colonial period in Latin America.

Environmental Kuznets curve – a curve showing the relationship between GDP per capita and the level of pollution.

Equation of exchange – a basic framework for analyzing the interactions between the money supply, velocity, the price level, and real GDP.

Equity – inflows of foreign exchange in the form of FDI or portfolio capital.

Exchange controls – various forms of government controls on the buying and selling of foreign exchange.

Exchange rate – the price of one currency in terms of another currency.

Exchange rate regime – the system a country uses to manage the exchange rate and the foreign exchange market.

Exchange rate shock – a large depreciation of a country's currency that occurs in a short period of time.

Factor-price equalization – the premise that international trade will reduce differences or equalize factor prices between countries.

Financial account – a record of the difference between the holding of foreign assets by domestic residents and domestic assets by foreign residents.

Financial repression – government policies that influence the savings and investment decisions of individuals and financial institutions.

Fiscal policy – a macroeconomic policy that uses government spending and/ or taxation to affect a country's GDP.

Foreign direct investment (FDI) – the purchase of real assets, such as production facilities, in a foreign country.

Foreign exchange – currency or deposits in financial institutions of another country.

General Agreement on Tariffs on Trade (GATT) – a trade agreement reached after World War II designed to reduce the level of protectionism in the world economy.

Geography hypothesis – the idea that geographic, climatic, and ecological factors can affect economic growth.

Gini coefficient – a measure of the deviation of the actual income distribution from perfect equality.

Gross Domestic Product (GDP) – the market value of all final goods and services produced in an economy in a year.

Growth accounting – an examination of the factors that explain economic growth in a country or region.

Harris–Todaro model – the theory that rural to urban migration is caused by differences in the relative expected incomes obtainable in the two areas.

Heckscher–Ohlin model – the theory that a country's comparative advantage is based on its endowment of the factors of production.

Heterodox economics – a term describing the collection of schools of thought in economics that are currently outside of the mainstream of the economics profession.

Human capital – the education, training, and job skills embodied in labor which increase its productivity.

Import Substitution Industrialization (ISI) – a set of policies designed to replace imports of industrial products with domestic production.

Industrial policy – a policy or set of policies designed to stimulate the growth of an industry or affect the industrial structure of a country.

Industrial structure – the percentage of output that is accounted for by each industry within a country.

Inelastic – the property of a demand or supply curve so that changes in price have only a small impact on the quantity demanded or supplied.

Institutions hypothesis – the idea that the quality of a country's institutions is a major determinant of its economic growth.

International Monetary Fund (IMF) – a multilateral agency created in 1946 to promote international monetary stability and cooperation.

Intervention – the buying and selling of foreign exchange in order to maintain a fixed exchange rate.

J-curve – the tendency for the trade balance to deteriorate in the short run following a depreciation of the exchange rate.

Labor-intensive – the condition that the production of a good requires a low K/L ratio.

Latifundia – large tracts of land held by individuals in Latin America for farming or mining.

Law of one price – the proposition that identical goods sold in competitive markets should cost the same everywhere when prices are expressed in terms of the same currency.

Lost Decade – a period of low growth in Latin America during the 1980s.

Market-based initiatives (MBI) – the use of market signals to influence producer behavior with regard to pollution.

Market failure – a situation where the production or use of a good or service does not occur where the marginal costs equals marginal benefits for society as a whole.

Mercantilism – a policy imposed on colonies requiring that all international trade be done through the colonial power.

Minifundia – small landholdings owned by individuals in Latin America for subsistence farming.

Monetary base – the sum of cash in the hands of the public and the reserves of the banking system.

Monetary policy – the policy of the central bank with respect to the growth rate of the money supply and interest rates.

Money multiplier – the multiple by which a change in the monetary base (B) translates into a change in the money supply.

Money supply – the sum of cash in the hands of the public (Cp) and demand deposits (D) in an economy.

Multilateral trade negotiations (MTNs) – a process of reducing tariff and nontariff barriers to trade among member countries of GATT or the WTO.

Multinational corporations (MNCs) – corporations with operations in more than one country.

National treatment – the situation where a country's laws are blind with respect to nationality.

Negative externality – a cost to society of producing a product that has not been included in the market price.

Neoliberalism – in a Latin American context, the tendency to shift government economic policy from a heavy reliance on government intervention in the economy to more market-based economic policies.

Nominal exchange rate – the exchange rate observed in the market.

North American Free Trade Agreement (NAFTA) – an agreement to establish a free trade area consisting of Canada, Mexico, and the US.

Official development assistance (ODA) – the transfer of resources from developed countries to developing countries to assist in the process of economic development.

Official reserve assets – government holdings of gold or foreign exchange used to acquire foreign assets.

Oil shock – a large increase in the price of oil over a short period of time.

Opportunity cost – the cost of a good is the amount of another good that must be given up to release enough resources to produce the first good.

Organization of Petroleum Exporting Countries (OPEC) – a cartel that attempts to stabilize the price of petroleum in the world economy.

Pollution haven – the idea that a country with lower levels of environmental regulations may be able to produce and export pollution-intensive products more cheaply than countries with stricter regulations.

Portfolio capital – the purchase of financial assets, such as stocks and bonds, in a foreign country.

Positive externality – a benefit to society of a good or service that is not included in the market price.

Potential real GDP – the amount of final goods and services an economy is producing at full employment.

Production function – a graph showing the relationship between real GDP and the factors of production.

Productivity – the amount of output produced in a given period of time by a unit of labor.

Protective tariff – a tariff designed to protect domestic industry from foreign competition.

Quota – a government policy that limits imports of a product to a certain number of units.

Real exchange rate – the nominal exchange rate adjusted for changes in both domestic and foreign prices.

Real interest rate – the nominal interest rate minus the expected rate of inflation.

Regional trade agreements (RTAs) – a trade agreement between two or more countries that provides tariff reductions for only those countries that are members of the agreement.

Relative poverty – a standard of living that an individual country constructs to measure the number of citizens it wishes to define as poor.

Relative purchasing power parity – the theory that a percentage change in the exchange rate is equal to the difference in the percentage change in price levels.

Remittances – flows of money back to the home country from workers that are employed in another country.

Repartida – the portion of the output earned by owners of encomiendas that was owed to the Spanish government in Latin America.

Resource curse – the empirical regularity that countries rich in commodities frequently experience low economic growth.

Revenue tariff – a tariff imposed by government whose primary purpose is raising revenue for the government.

Sovereign debt – a debt instrument guaranteed by a government.

Specific tariff – a tariff that is measured as a fixed amount of money per unit imported.

State-owned enterprises (SOEs) – an enterprise owned and operated by a national government.

Stolper–Samuelson theorem – the premise that international trade will reduce the income of the scarce factor of production and increase the income of the abundant factor of production in a country.

Structural unemployment – unemployment that occurs as labor moves from one part of the economy to another.

Structuralist economics – the idea that the structure of an economy can have important effects on economic outcomes.

Structure of protection – an analysis of the variation in tariffs in a country.

Tariff – a tax on imported goods.

Terms of trade – the price of exports divided by the price of imports.

Total factor productivity – an increase in GDP not accounted for by changes in the labor force or the stock of capital.

Trade creation – the efficiency gain that results from an RTA because more efficient member countries displace less efficient member countries.

Trade diversion – an efficiency loss that results from an RTA because less efficient member countries displace more efficient nonmember countries.

Trade policy – government actions that influence the flow of goods and services to and from a country.

Tragedy of the commons – a situation where individuals acting solely in their self interest may end up depleting a limited natural resource.

Unilateral transfers – grants or gifts extended to or received from other countries.

Washington Consensus – a term referring to a loose collection of primarily market-based economic policies.

World Bank – a multilateral institution that makes loans to developing countries to enhance economic development.

World Trade Organization (WTO) – the organization created in 1995 to replace GATT. The WTO administers multilateral trade agreements and settles trade disputes.

Notes

1 Latin America and the world economy

1 The acronyms HIC, MIC, and LIC will be used in some tables to stand for high-, middle-, and low-income economies, respectively.
2 For the classic reference on trade and growth see Edwards (1993).
3 Why this is true will be shown in the next chapter.
4 For a similar exercise, see Duade and Fernandez-Arias (2010).
5 For example, the country with the most Neoliberal economic policies in Latin America is Chile. However, the country has been governed by a left-of-center coalition (Concertacion) for the past two decades. Either the coalition is deeply confused or Neoliberal economic policies are not as out of the mainstream as they are sometimes portrayed.
6 For a description of how this occurred, see Williamson (2004).

2 Economic growth and Latin America

1 Field (2007) has made an extremely interesting connection between squatting, the supply of labor, and child labor in Peru. She finds that squatting entails leaving at least one adult home at all times to protect the "property." This leads to a lower labor supply by adults and a higher tendency to put children in the workforce.
2 See World Bank (2008a) and World Bank (2008b).
3 On this point see Henisz (2000) or Staats, et al. (2005).
4 The material in this box is adapted from Interamerican Development Bank (2006).
5 For more details see Maddison (2001).
6 For far more details on these issues see Interamerican Development Bank (2004).
7 For more information on this issue see Djankov, et al. (2003).
8 This data is from World Bank (2009).
9 See Maloney (2004) for more details.
10 See Maloney, et al. (2001).
11 For a more complete discussion of this point see Reinhart and Talvi (1998).
12 This problem is extensively analyzed in de la Torre, et al. (2006).
13 The data ignores outflows of FDI in the region. With the exception of Chile, these outflows are insignificant.
14 For a review of human capital in Latin America see Gimenez (2005).
15 For more on this point see Chapter 12.
16 On this point see Barro and Lee (2001a and 2001b).
17 For more details see Navarro, et al. (2010).

18 See Blyde (2004).
19 As explained above, R&D should be a negligible factor in Latin American economic growth and is generally excluded from consideration.
20 Economic data for Latin America prior to World War II is still being developed. The causes of economic growth in the region prior to that time is a field of study still in its infancy.
21 Similar results may be found in Cole, *et al.* (2005).
22 These results are in line with research by Bils and Klenow (2000) on human capital accumulation and growth. Their results include data on a number of countries in Latin America.
23 Restrictions on FDI will be covered in Chapter 9.
24 For a more complete discussion of Latin American versus the rest of the world see Fernandez-Arias, *et al.* (2005).
25 An early example of this work is North and Thomas (1973).
26 Chapter 5 of de Soto's book, *The Other Path*, is an excellent case study of business regulation in Latin America.
27 For a more extensive discussion see Acemoglu, *et al.* (2001, 2002).
28 For a more complete discussion see Acemoglu and Robinson (2008).
29 For examples see Tommasi (2006) or Interamerican Development Bank (2006).

3 Growth and the environment in Latin America

1 However, it is not appropriate to try to correct small negative externalities if the cost of dealing with them is larger than the externality.
2 In this section only the two most common examples of MBIs are presented. However, there are a much larger number of these instruments available. For examples in a Latin America context, see Huber, *et al.* (1998).
3 See Seroa da Matta (2003).
4 This section drew heavily from the outstanding case study by Garcia-Johnson (2000).
5 See Gallagher (2004) for evidence on Mexico.
6 A further mitigation is the privatization of many firms in Latin America over the last three decades. Huber, *et al.* (1998) have found that public sector firms tend to have less incentive to control pollution than private sector firms.
7 See Huber, *et al.* (1998).
8 For example, see Foster, *et al.* (2009).
9 The discussion is deliberately ignoring the negative externality of degradation of the land that may occur because of deforestation. This externality exists but it is harder to quantify and does not occur in all cases.
10 Even this figure is uncertain as many private titles to land may not be legally valid.
11 This section draws heavily on Gallagher (2004).
12 Because the literature on these issues for Latin America is quite limited, the best overall reference in this area is Copeland and Taylor (2003).
13 The correlation between increasing openness (more trade) and economic growth is not something about which there is a lot of doubt. See Edwards (1993) on this point.
14 This highly simplified explanation of trade will be covered in more detail in Chapters 6 and 7.
15 For an early empirical test see Birdsall and Wheeler (1993). Most subsequent research simply confirms their findings.
16 For a thorough discussion of these issues see Copeland and Taylor (2003).

4 Latin American economic history

1 Haciendas were sometimes also engaged in mining or light manufacturing activities.
2 Although the UK did not formally exist until 1707, we will use the term UK throughout the book for consistency.
3 All of this was rather imprecise as the concept of longitude was not well defined until the late eighteenth century.
4 For an excellent history of this topic see Klein and Vinson (2007).
5 The Portuguese royal family fled to Brazil during the Napoleonic Wars. After returning to Portugal, the King's son declared the country independent, saving the country the trauma of a civil war.
6 This period is sometimes referred to as the "*belle époque.*"
7 See Williamson (1999) for more on the lowering of transportation costs in the late nineteenth century.
8 The current boom in demand for commodities emanating from the growth of China, India and other large developing countries is a similar story.
9 A more extensive discussion of commodities is contained in the next chapter.
10 Most immigrants from the Middle East came from Lebanon and Syria.
11 The contribution of these groups to the already rich diversity of the region covered in Chapter 1 is a significant positive externality that is difficult to quantify. Imagining modern Latin America without these groups as a part of the economy and culture is difficult.
12 For a more complete discussion of this topic see Reynolds (1983).
13 In a modern Latin American context, the example of Cuba is instructive in this regard.
14 A specific tariff is levied as a certain amount of money per unit imported. An *ad valorem* tariff is levied as a certain percentage of the value of imports.
15 This is not a universal choice. One could just as easily begin the period in 1930. For an example see Cardoso and Helwege (1992).
16 A note of caution is in order on this point. There is a counterfactual question: How fast would GDP per capita have grown under another set of policy choices? That is an interesting question for which there is no precise answer.
17 The development and eventual demise of most of these SOEs will be covered in Chapter 6.
18 During the first wave, things got to the point that investors literally loaned to fictitious countries in the region.

5 Latin America and primary commodities

1 Some of these issues will be covered in more detail in Chapters 8 and 11.
2 The term "black gold" was coined in this period.
3 In many cases, the production of nonagricultural commodities is capital intensive.
4 Many of these areas left a legacy of spectacular architecture that allows one a glimpse of the wealth commodity booms can confer.
5 This should be easy to imagine. Suppose that in the twenty-first century a new, large supply of gold was discovered. This extra supply might depress the price of gold for a time but the effects are not likely to last long as world demand is continually increasing.
6 More technically, the income elasticity of demand for nonagricultural commodities is usually higher than for agricultural commodities.
7 A more detailed explanation of macroeconomic management with commodity exports will be given in Chapter 11.

8 For an alternative view of the resource curse, see Lederman and Maloney (2008).
9 This issue is a problem that rarely vanishes completely. The recent tension between exporters of agricultural commodities in Argentina and the government is just the most recent example of a longstanding problem.
10 The outcome is not always final. See Manzano and Monaldi (2008) for examples for the oil industry in Latin America.
11 Perhaps the most famous of these nationalizations was the takeover of American oil interests in Mexico in 1938.
12 These effects will be covered in more detail in Chapter 8.

6 Import substitution in Latin America

1 A more detailed description of Latin American trade policy is given in the next chapter.
2 We will encounter structuralist economics again in a discussion of inflation in Latin America. It has reappeared more recently in the more rigorous work of Lance Taylor.
3 In a Latin American context, the Brazilian economist Celso Furtado was the most well-known proponent of this approach.
4 See the UN's *Relative Prices of Exports and Imports of Underdeveloped Countries* (1949).
5 For anyone with an interest in either the man or the times, the biography by Dosman (2008) is required reading.
6 The flaws will become more obvious as we move through the material.
7 An old joke among economists is that if government officials could actually do this, they would be much better off working for an investment company.
8 More information on Latin America and GATT will be presented in the next chapter.
9 This is part of the problem of the generally low rate of savings in the region that hinders economic growth.
10 This situation would be unlikely to occur if the rate paid on savings was not being controlled. In defense of the countries of Latin America, such controls were not unknown in the developed countries before the 1980s.
11 For more details on this, see Edwards (1995).
12 In defense of Brazil, some high-income countries in Europe attempted the same approach with similar results. Even the World Bank partially funded the efforts of the Brazilian government.
13 Petrobras is currently in talks with Pemex concerning using their technology to develop oil offshore in Mexico. A comparison of the relative success of the two companies is interesting.
14 Many countries used multiple exchange rates where the price of foreign exchange depended on the proposed use.
15 For an excellent description of this process in Mexico City, see Ross (2009).
16 This point will be more clear in Chapter 12 on poverty and income distribution.
17 At this point we are omitting some details that will be covered in Chapter 9. These details do not alter what follows in any important way.

7 Latin American trade policy

1 All of our examples are based on the labor theory of value. In this context, this assumption makes the analysis easier but no less valid. In a subsequent section, we will consider trade with many factors of production.
2 For an excellent discussion of this issue see Cypher and Dietz (2009).
3 The discussion is based on data given in Clemons and Williamson (2002).

4 Recall that the supply curve contains a normal profit as a cost of production. A normal profit is defined as the opportunity cost for the producer.

5 At this point we will consider transportation costs to be zero. At a later point in the chapter, we will show the effects of these costs.

6 There is the somewhat more complicated case of the large country whose imports can affect the world market. As shown in Chapter 1, Latin America as a region would not qualify as a large country, much less any of its constituent countries.

7 What we have shown graphically is the basis for the quote at the beginning of the chapter.

8 For more details see Mesquita Moreira *et al.*, (2008).

9 Vote maximizing behavior is a standard feature of the branch of economics known as public choice. The insight is that politicians attempt to maximize votes much like consumers and producers attempt to maximize welfare and profits, respectively.

10 For a more complete discussion of this problem see Coatsworth and Williamson (2002).

11 For a more thorough discussion of these problems see Williamson (2003).

12 There is also the possibility of a compound tariff which is where imports are subject to both a specific tariff and an *ad valorem* tariff.

13 For more on the tariff history of Latin America, see Coatsworth and Williamson (2002).

14 See Clemens and Williamson (2002) for more information on this.

15 For another set of estimates of tariffs in the region see Franko (2007).

16 For specific examples see Cardoso and Helwege (1992).

17 Specifically, this was the Reciprocal Trade Agreements Act, which moved the overall conduct of US trade policy from the legislative to the executive branch of government.

18 Because GATT was not technically an organization, it did not have members but contracting parties.

19 This includes antidumping duties, countervailing duties, and escape clause cases. For more details, see Sawyer and Sprinkle (2009).

20 A single market entails the harmonization of regulations and taxes that tend to distort trade. Progress within MERCOSUR on this front has been limited. However, as the EU has discovered, this process is exceedingly difficult.

21 Empirically this is almost always the case.

8 Exchange rate policy

1 It is normal for high-income countries to have a surplus in trade in services and for middle-income countries to have deficits in services.

2 For convenience, we are not including transactions in the capital account. These transactions include changes in the holdings of nonfinancial assets such as the purchase of a condominium in Miami by a resident of the region. However, the capital account does include debt forgiveness which can be a significant factor in some cases.

3 In reality, they frequently do not exactly match due to the difficulties of recording every transaction. The result is that balance of payments statements have another line for statistical discrepancy.

4 For a sense of this period, see Fuentes (1998).

5 Thomas Friedman has dubbed the community of international investors involved in the movements of portfolio capital "the electronic herd."

6 For a more detailed account of the Tequila crisis and its aftermath, see de Gregorio and Valdes (2001). The debt crisis of the early 1980s is a less clear

case of contagion as debt problems were affecting many of the countries in the region.

7 For a sense of this debate in the context of Latin America see the results for Chile in Edwards and Rigobon (2009) versus the results for Colombia in Kamil and Clements (2009).

8 For a survey of the literature and a sense of the conflicting results see Chanda (2005).

9 As an example, in late 2009 Chile was the second country in Latin America to be invited to join the Organization for Economic Cooperation and Development (OECD).

10 In the case of PPP calculations, the Producer Price Index is normally used as it contains fewer items that cannot be traded in international markets.

11 For the latest data, see IMF (2007).

12 See Calvo and Reinert (2002) for more on this point.

13 For a short discussion and classification system see IMF (2006).

14 This is also known as dollarization. For more on this see Quispe-Agnoli (2001).

15 As one might guess, crawling pegs were much more common in Latin America during the high inflation years of the lost decade.

16 For an excellent history on this issue see Frenkel and Rapetti (2010).

17 For an interesting description of the evolution of exchange rate policy in Chile see de Gregorio and Tokman (2004).

9 Financing current account deficits

1 One of the more encouraging signs in the region is the development of local bond markets and the ability of some firms in the region to raise capital in international markets. For more detail, see Borensztein, *et al.* (2008).

2 The former type of FDI is known as greenfield investment. The latter is known as mergers and acquisitions (M&A).

3 For more on these issues see Fajnzylber, *et al.* (2009).

4 Remittances generally are derived from balance of payments statistics. However, there is no universally accepted definition of remittances and the data is not quite as reliable as other statistics such as imports of goods.

5 See Acosta, *et al.* (2008) for more detail.

6 For more details see Fajnzylber and Lopez (2008).

7 Under the Bretton Woods system, borrowing by high-income countries from the IMF was rare.

8 A list of the currently available facilities is available at www.imf.org.

9 This arrangement is frequently referred to as the Brady Plan.

10 Macroeconomic policy in Latin America

1 Potential real GDP is a constructed number assuming a normal level of unemployment of the labor force. As a result, it should be considered more of a constructed policy target than a precise number.

2 What is being described is known as a primary market for government bonds.

3 Coins and paper money held by the banks are counted as part of reserves.

4 This process is frequently referred to as crowding out. If the economy is at full employment, government borrowing may increase interest rates and reduce borrowing by the private sector. If the economy is at less than full employment, this is less of a problem.

5 In the long run, V will usually slowly increase as the financial system of a country becomes more developed. The knowledge about financial development in

Latin America is not large as the study of this aspect of economic development is rather new.

6 Notice that the change in Y_p was the subject of Chapter 2.

7 In this discussion we are avoiding the problem of the relevant money supply. In practice, the money supply may be defined in different ways depending on which assets are included.

8 In this case, the price level is a price index and not the single price of a good or service.

9 This is but one definition of populism. Its virtue is brevity but there are more complete definitions available. For more on this see Dornbusch and Edwards (1991).

10 Our definition of economic populism follows the more recent tendency to use the term with respect to macroeconomic policies. However, this has not always been the case. For an outstanding discussion of these changes see Cardoso and Helwege (1992).

11 This is a reference to the old Keynesian vs. Monetarist debate in macroeconomics that was common in the 1960s and 1970s.

12 We are implicitly assuming either adaptive expectations or rational expectations with institutional rigidities. The assumption is that the movement of the SRAS curve would not occur quickly.

11 Macroeconomic stability

1 Other mining exports are molybdenum and more recently lithium.

2 The original target was 1 percent of GDP but was reduced in 2008.

3 See the box in this section for more data on real oil prices.

4 If the initial condition was a surplus, the same effect would occur.

5 Notice the different context from the Bretton Woods system of fixed exchange rates. In that system austerity programs did not occur along with exchange rate shocks. Unfortunately, IMF policy never really accounted for that change.

6 Nonresidential investment responds to changes in the *rate of growth* of real GDP, i.e. the accelerator. Thus, a dramatic drop in real GDP can induce a very large drop in nonresidential investment.

7 However, the reduction of taxes was a less viable option in Latin America due to the historically low percentage of taxes collected in relation to GDP.

8 We are intentionally neglecting the effects of political instability on growth.

12 Poverty and inequality

1 For more on Latin American income inequality versus the rest of the world, see Lopez and Perry (2008).

2 For a dissenting view of this description, see Williamson (2009).

3 For a more detailed treatment of this period see Arroyo Abad (2009).

4 This is just the usual comparison of economic development in Latin America versus East Asia.

5 As was pointed out in Chapter 2, the amount of human capital in an economy also is an important determinant of economic growth.

6 See de Ferranti, *et al.* (2004) for details.

7 See OECD (2007) for further details.

8 For more on this see Damon and Glewwe (2009).

9 See Goni, *et al.* (2008) and Lopez and Perry (2008).

Index

Aavedra, Jaime 309
absolute advantage 171–2; definition 202
absolute poverty 290–3; definition 308
absolute purchasing power parity 223; definition 227
accelerator 322
Acemoglu, Daron 61, 62, 317
Acosta, Pablo 248, 321
ad valorem equivalent 187; definition 202
ad valorem tariff 190, 318; definition 202
Africa: educational inequality 302; poverty 292; slavery 106
aggregate demand: austerity programs 284; changes 260–1; commodity price shocks 271–5; debt 279–81; definition 267; economic populism 262–7; exchange rate shocks 279–81; inflation 261–7; Lost Decade 281–5; money supply 260; price level 261–6
aggregate supply: changes 261–6; definition 267; inflation 261–6; inflationary expectations 264–6; Lost Decade 281–5; long run 260–2; oil shocks 275–9; potential real GDP 261–2; price level 261–6; real GDP 261–6; short run 262–6
agriculture: colonial period 100–1; commodities 124–41; ISI 160; MTNs 195–6
air pollution 81–2
Aizenman, Joshua 169
Aldemaro, Romero 95
American Economic Review 61, 62, 95, 169, 204
Andean Pact 198

Argentina: air pollution 82; balance on trade 210; CAN 199; commodity exports 135; competitiveness 59; corruption 59; current account balance 210; deforestation 84; doing business 59; educational attainment 49; educational inequality 302; educational outcomes 303; FDI 47; fiscal deficit 252; forest resources 84; GATT/WTO 196; GDP 4, 291; GDP per capita 4, 291; government effectiveness 59; human development index 6; human opportunity index 297; income inequality 295; inflation 259; intellectual property rights 27; judicial independence 31; K/L ratio 43–4, 177; labor force 37; labor market flexibility 42; MERCOSUR 199; money supply 258; natural disasters 70; plantation forests 84; population 4, 291; poverty 293; property rights 25; rule of law 29; saving 47; social security 40; RTAs 199; unions 41; urbanization 83; water pollution 79–80; water supply 80
Arroyo Abad, A. Leticia 309, 322
Asia: economic growth 11–12; educational inequality 302; poverty 292
austerity programs 283–5
Australia: commodities 11; RTAs 199
autarky: definition 121; effects of 180–1
automobile industry 166–7

Baer, Werner 122, 268
Bahmani-Oskooee, Moshen 228

CPSIA information can be obtained at www.ICGtesting.com
Printed in the USA
BVOW01s1158220114

342677BV00003B/33/P

9 780415 497336